D0323339

Compass of the World

THE MACMILLAN COMPANY
NEW YORK · BOSTON · CHICAGO · DALLAS
ATLANTA · SAN FRANCISCO

MACMILLAN & CO., LIMITED
LONDON · BOMBAY · CALCUTTA
MELBOURNE

THE MACMILLAN CO. OF CANADA, LIMITED
TORONTO

Compass of the World

A Symposium on Political Geography

Edited by
HANS W. WEIGERT
and
VILHJALMUR STEFANSSON

Maps by RICHARD E. HARRISON

NEW YORK
THE MACMILLAN COMPANY
1944

First printing.

PRINTED IN THE UNITED STATES OF AMERICA

And he said also to the people, When ye see a cloud rise out of the west, straightway ye say, There cometh a shower; and so it is.

And when ye see the south wind blow, ye say, There will be heat; and it cometh to pass.

Ye hypocrites, ye can discern the face of the sky and of the earth; but how is it that ye do not discern this time?

Luke 12:54–56

The earth is the Lord's, and all that therein is; the compass of the world, and they that dwell therein.

Psalm 24:1

The Sword versus the Spirit

The statesman who conducts foreign policy can concern himself with values of justice, fairness, and tolerance only to the extent that they contribute to or do not interfere with the power objective. They can be used instrumentally as moral justification for the power quest, but they must be discarded the moment their application brings weakness. The search for power is not made for the achievement of moral values; moral values are used to facilitate the attainment of power.

NICHOLAS JOHN SPYKMAN

Force is powerless to organize anything. There are only two powers in the world: the sword and the spirit. In the long run, the sword is always defeated by the spirit.

NAPOLEON I

Contents

CHAPTER IV · THE NORTHWARD COURSE

Introduction

This book aims at filling, so far as possible, a wide gap which the politico-geographical thinking and planning in the United States must try to bridge. The American public has become increasingly aware that the shrinking of the world brought about by the rapid advance of industry and technology necessitates a new vision. That vision requires, in particular, certain vital applications of today's geography to the politics and strategy of the United States as a leading partner in the rebuilding of a shaken and suffering world.

Most Americans realize the importance of this task. However, on the whole, their understanding has remained foggy. The appraisal of America's relation to other countries, based on geographical factors, is only too frequently limited to more or less glittering generalities. Historical thinking here and elsewhere has been molded for many years by a geographical view that is no longer true. Since Pearl Harbor the nation has become conscious of this fateful lag, and of its mortal danger. Yet perplexity still exists as to how to draw the inevitable conclusions from the fact that today's geography and its impacts on foreign politics and strategy are basically different from yesterday's. It was only yesterday that we watched the rest of the globe from isolation behind seemingly secure ramparts. History is geography set in motion. Never in man's history has the movement been so rapid and turbulent as in our day.

This book is intended to correct some of the basic misconceptions of political geography which threaten to confuse the minds and the plans of statesmen, soldiers, and the general public alike. The time has not yet come to attempt a complete appraisal of geography's impact on world politics in our day. Instead we are trying to call attention to a few, but vital, aspects of human geography which need understanding and readjustment in the task of winning the war and a lasting peace.

One of the issues to be clarified is the ideological approach to a new geography. Convinced of the enemy's superior understanding of geography as a determining factor in world history, many of us have swallowed not only the tangibles of German geopolitics, but also the intangibles of a materialistic power politics as an ultimate end. Thus we have seen the dangerous beginnings of an American geopolitics, with blueprints for American imperialism riding the waves of the future. It favors a disillusioned balance-of-power solution on the basis of regional groupings, in preparation for what the sponsors of such "realistic" plans consider inevitable: the Third World War.

The editors and writers of this book, widely as they may differ regarding details, agree that acceptance of the ideology and creed of geopolitics would be a dangerous step towards international Fascism. They refuse to accept the ethics of a geopolitics "made in Germany" and imported to this country. This kind of geopolitics is a poison in our system the more dangerous because it is often not immediately recognizable as alien to our political ideals and to the war and peace aims of the United Nations. Therefore, the opening articles deal with the ideological aspects of geography in international politics; they have in common the warning against the acceptance of the power-political scheme which has found expression in the pseudo science of geopolitics. Beyond that, other papers included in the first chapter on "The New World: Geography and Geopolitics" deal with problems of a more general character; they touch upon fundamental issues in the border regions of geography and geopolitics. A paper concerned with the balance-of-power idea has been included in this chapter; for the balance-of-power concept represents a strong ideological root of geopolitics. "The Peaceful Solution of Boundary Problems" is the subject of a further article.

The second chapter bears the title "New Directions and Skyways." Its articles continue the attempt to express and define the fundamentals of a new geography in a shrinking world whose sea lanes and highways are paralleled by skyways. The articles of this chapter are entitled "World View and Strategy," "The Myth of the Continents," "World Airways," "The Logic of the Air," and "American Air Transport Faces North."

Sir Halford Mackinder's concept of the "Heartland" and its fateful role in the history of our time has experienced a renaissance in our day. Land power and land-based air power have made old prophecies come true and have sharpened our eyes for the understanding of the secular role certain pivotal areas play in our time. This is the underlying idea which links the articles in a chapter entitled "Reflections on the Heartland"; two come from outstanding British geographers, Sir Halford Mackinder and James Fairgrieve. The other three are by American geographers.

Eight essays are included in the chapter "The Northward Course." While stressing particularly the role which the territories, air paths, and sea lanes of the American North and its neighboring zones are called upon to play in the destinies of this country, the editors have considered the roles of other regions in a global picture. As pointed out before, this book does not aim to cover the entire field of political geography in an encyclopedic manner. Yet the emphasis on the North is more than incidental. The majority of us, brought up in an Atlantic orientation towards Europe, had too long neglected our northern spheres and the links which connect the North of America with the other great land powers—the U.S.S.R. and China.

The articles included in the chapter "The Northward Course" are regional studies; but they are also illustrations of a more general concept of political geography—a concept based on the fact that the changes which characterize the political geography of our age are globe-embracing and revolutionary. Therefore the lessons which the North, as a pivotal zone in our time, can teach us, apply equally to other regions and have far-reaching repercussions in them. It is not always easy to see these interrelationships and to draw from them the necessary conclusions affecting the course of American politics and strategy in the future. The

North is only one case of the general principle that man finds it easier to change the face of nature than to change his own mind.

"Reflections on Asia" is the title of another chapter, composed of two essays. Within the scope of the present book, it would be impossible to cover even a small part of the geopolitical problems with which Asia confronts us. Yet the editors felt that the book would remain a torso if it avoided entirely the appraising of politico-geographical and ideological problems of Asia in relation to the rest of the world.

The last chapter ("The Shifting Balance of Man Power") tries to shed light on regional and demographic factors which are truly of a world-revolutionary nature. Here again, the contributions are not meant to cover a global field. Instead, attention is called to certain population trends and their impact on international relations, neglected by statesmen and students of foreign politics alike. These essays should help bring about a better understanding of the fact that certain regions—particularly in the U.S.S.R.—have achieved a pivotal importance in our age partly because of their geographical advantages, but equally because of their demographic developments. The fateful repercussions of the shifting balance of man power will be evident a few decades from now. We do well to sharpen our eyes, as early as possible, for these things to come.

The essays here presented are but pieces in a mosaic which only the future will reveal in its entirety. Although they must remain sketchy, they are meant to show the outlines of a new geography set in motion. They attempt to deepen our understanding of the fateful forces which blaze the trails of a new period of history. May that understanding not be too little, and may it not come too late!

As a symposium, this book has many defects which are self-evident. On the other hand it has, we feel, definite advantages. The subject dealt with is so great and so complex that a single author can hardly present more than a textbook discussion without flavoring his book strongly with personal opinions. Both, we want to avoid. All our contributors have limited their discussions to subjects they have particularly studied. Yet there is something more than the common interest in the study of political geography that makes them a team. They all subscribe, whether or not their subjects give them the opportunity to express this view explicitly, to the belief that our interrelated world cannot be governed by the power-political schemes of yesterday's geopolitics. They realize that the future of this country depends on its readiness and ability to find ways of peaceful cooperation with all the nations of our small world.

The editors want to stress, however, that the opinions expressed in the various contributions are those of the authors, not of any government agencies or other institutions with which they may be connected; and the viewpoints of individual contributors do not necessarily reflect those of the editors or of the other authors.

HANS W. WEIGERT AND VILHJALMUR STEFANSSON

West Hartford, Conn., and Bethel, Vt.

Acknowledgments

Part of the material used in this volume (sixteen of twenty-eight articles) was published in articles and books. For the inclusion in this symposium, the material previously published has been revised and brought up to date by the authors. Some of these papers have been completely rewritten.

Grateful acknowledgment is made to the publishers who have granted permission to reprint from articles or books:

Atlantic Monthly: A. MacLeish, "The Image of Victory," July, 1942.

Geographical Review: I. Bowman, "Geography *vs.* Geopolitics," 1942, No. 4.

American Journal of International Law: Q. Wright, "The Balance of Power," 1943, No. 2.

Columbia University Press: chapter "The Peaceful Solution of Boundary Problems" in S. W. Boggs, *International Boundaries*, 1940.

Foreign Affairs: E. Staley, "The Myth of the Continents," April, 1941; Sir Halford Mackinder, "The Round World and the Winning of the Peace," July, 1943; V. Stefansson, "The North American Arctic" (there entitled "The American Far North"), April, 1939; H. W. Weigert, "Asia Through Haushofer's Glasses" (there entitled "Haushofer and the Pacific"), July, 1942.

Newsweek: "World Airways."

Fortune: "The Logic of the Air," April, 1943; V. Stefansson, "Arctic Supply Line," July, 1942.

Houghton Mifflin Co.: chapter "The Influence of Geography and Climate upon History" in E. Huntington, *The Pulse of Asia*, 1907.

University of London Press, Ltd.: chapter "Geography and World Power" in J. Fairgrieve, *Geography and World Power*, 8th ed., 1941.

Ryerson Press, Toronto, Canada: G. Taylor, *Canada's Role in Geopolitics*, 1943.

University of Chicago Press: Q. Wright, chapter "Population Trends and International Relations" in *A Study of War*, 1943.

New York Times Magazine: A. J. Dimond, "The Aleutians," Nov. 18, 1942.

Journal of Geography: G. B. Cressey, "Siberia's Role in Soviet Strategy," 1942, pp. 81–88.

Compass of the World

CHAPTER I

The New World: Geography and Geopolitics

I

The Image of Victory

By ARCHIBALD MACLEISH

ARCHIBALD MACLEISH, born in Glencoe, Ill., A.B., Yale, 1915, Litt.D., 1939; LL.B., Harvard, 1919. Librarian of Congress.

"The Image of Victory" has appeared in slightly different form, in the *Atlantic Monthly,* July, 1942.

This war presents a curious paradox: a curious division of minds precisely at the point at which the minds of men engaged in war are commonly united. Men engaged in war are commonly agreed on one thing at least—the victory they mean to win. We are not altogether agreed on that point. We are determined that we shall win a victory. But what victory, we do not altogether know. We have the will to victory. But the idea of victory, the conception of victory, eludes us.

I do not wish to be misunderstood. I am not discussing the morale of the American people. What I have in mind is the honest apprehension, the loyal doubt, the understandable anxiety of those who are determined we shall win this war; who are willing, if need be, to die to help their people win it; but who are nevertheless unable to understand clearly, or to imagine precisely, what our victory in this war will be. Specifically, what I have in mind is the understandable confusion of a generation of young men who were brought up to believe that the last war, though won, was lost, and that the war in which we are now engaged is nothing but the last war fought again; who therefore and most reasonably ask each other and ask us what victory this war can truly win—what victory other than the negative, defensive victory we won before, or won and lost before, or only lost.

Those who ask this question understand very well what *defeat* in this war would mean. Indeed it would be impossible for them not to understand. The evidence is before them everywhere they look: in the starvation and misery and death of Poland; in the death and starvation and slavery of Greece; in the French prisons at the first light when the volley rattles and the hostages chosen by lot, picked out of their cells by lot, and by lot lined up in the half-light, and by lot shot down, are murdered. What they do not understand is victory. Victory as the mere absence of defeat is something they do not wish to think about. They know that kind of victory, and how it tastes. But victory as victory—victory as an affirmative thing—they cannot easily imagine. Victory as an affirmative thing means something won. A disarmed enemy is not something won: a disarmed enemy is merely something prevented. And so too of a world order to assure peace in the future: a world order to assure peace is also something prevented—in the future. These things are desirable. They are valuable. We should have secured them twenty years ago. But are they victory? Are they the sum and substance of the victory we mean to win?

It is an understandable question, and those who ask it have every reason to ask. They will not be answered by words which tell them that Nazism and all its works are evil. They know Nazism and all its works are evil and they mean to destroy both it and them. Neither will they be answered by talk about our cause—talk which says our cause is freedom and freedom is a cause worth fighting for in any country. They know very well that freedom is our cause. They know that freedom was never more clearly the cause of any people than it is ours: that despotism and tyranny were never more cynically avowed by any enemy than by the enemy which threatens us. They believe also that freedom is worth fighting for. They mean to fight for it. They mean to win also. But nevertheless they are not satisfied.

And they are right not to be satisfied.

They have proposed to themselves an end and they mean to attain that end, but they cannot conceive it. They feel themselves moving at an uncontrollable speed and by their own will, their own effort, toward an end, a goal, they cannot in any way imagine. They intend to gain a victory—but what victory? What will it mean to them? What will it mean to any man? The misery, the economic dislocation, the inane prosperity followed by the meaningless hunger of the victory we won before? Or something else? And, if so, what else? Land? Islands? They cannot imagine the usefulness of land or islands. Empire? It is difficult to talk these days of empires. They think of victory in the future: they think of empires in the past. They have no patience with those who talk of empires or of islands now. They wish to know how they are to imagine their victory in terms they can believe in and understand.

It is this that people mean when they ask their leaders to tell them what we are fighting for. They do not mean that they wish to be told *why* we are fighting. They know very well why we are fighting. They always knew the why of this fighting even when the appeasers and the isolationists and the opportunists and the plain moral cowards were telling them they need never fight—that the fighting was no concern of theirs. Neither do they mean that they wish to be told what we are fighting *against*. They have had no doubt what we were fighting against from the first shot of the first gun in Poland. Some of them knew before that, in Spain and in other countries. What they mean is precisely what they say: they wish to know what we are fighting *for*—what we propose to bring to pass by our fighting. Now that we are engaged in this war; now that we are engaged against enemies we know and for reasons we understand; now that we are engaged in this war and intend to fight this war—what do we propose to win *from* it and *by* it?

It is an understandable question but it is, nevertheless, a curious question—a question which reflects the doubtful and still confusing experiences of the last twenty-five years and particularly of the years which followed the last war. Even the young men who ask this question most, and who most have right to ask it, speak out of the confusion and bewilderment of that experience. They have the sense of change in their bones and in their blood, but they have in their heads the shadows and the disappointments of their fathers' years. They trust themselves but not their time, and therefore they question their time. They are right, I think, to question it. But I doubt that the answer they are looking for is as far off as they sometimes think.

Certainly it is not as far off as the answers they are sometimes given would lead them to believe. And for this reason: that the answers they are given are, for the most part, answers not as to the meaning of their victory but as to the structure of the world their victory will make possible. The answers, in other words, are answers about that far-off unreal country called the "post-war world"—the world the economists and the statesmen and the technicians will construct out of the rubble of the pre-war world when the victory is won. But it is not this, I think, the young men wish to know. They are not concerned, most of them,—they are not concerned yet,—with the economy or the international organization of the world which will follow their victory. They wish to know—certainly they wish to know—whether they will return to tramp the streets for jobs as their fathers did. They wish to know whether they will have to fight their war a second time in their forties and their fifties as their fathers, they believe, are now obliged to fight a second time the war they won. But before they come to these things—before they come to the economic order or the international controls—they wish to understand what their victory itself will be. They wish to see the shape of their victory as the Greeks, who made shapes of victory out of stone, once saw it. They wish to believe in their victory as itself a creative and accomplishing thing.

I do not think it is impossible for them to see this or believe in it. On the contrary, it would seem to me that the answer they require is already in their mouths. If they will trust themselves, if they will trust their own sense of the changing time, if they will look ahead and not back, they will give themselves their answer. For if anything about this war is certain, it is this: that those who win this war will win the future of the world.

They will win it not in some metaphorical or poetic sense, but in the most precise and practical meaning of the term. They will win the future of the world to such an extent that they will be able to change not its governments only, but its geography, its actual shape and meaning in men's minds. And they will win it not for now, not for a generation, but, if they have the courage and the will, for all the future men can now foresee. Whatever the Nazis may say about *Lebensraum*, whatever their Far Eastern accomplices may say about Greater-Asia Coprosperity Spheres, whatever our own imperialists may say about a new imperium, it is not for continents or islands or for seas between them that this war is fought. This war is fought on the one side to dominate, on the other side to liberate, an age—a new age, an age which every man who lets his eyes look forward can now see.

The sense of the new age, the new world, has troubled men for generations. They have had the sense of the future in them a long time. Change after change in the machinery of their lives has thrown their minds forward. For the most part they have been deceived. The changes have proved, for the most part, to be changes on the surface only; changes of convenience or of habit; water out of a tap instead of water out of a well; power out of a steam kettle instead of power out of a mule; light from a wire instead of light from wax. But the sense of the future has haunted them nevertheless. And now the sense of the future has come true. They see before them—those who have eyes to see—a world so different, different in so clear a sense, that they have no choice but to accept its difference.

Most of us thought of the airplane in the years between the wars as a new gadget—an automobile which flew. We had been confused by a long list of inventions, each more spectacular than the last, of which the airplane was the latest. Even when this war began, we did not understand its meaning. We told each other that after the war there would be thousands of planes as there were millions of cars after the last war, and everyone would have his own. The plane was simply another gadget in a gadget universe, a new convenience. We do not think that now. We know

now that the plane is capable of altering the geography of our world—and therefore the history of our world. We know that the world which the airplane dominates will be a different world from the world which went before. We see before us, in other words,—or we can see it if we look,—an age new in its essential possibilities and therefore a new age.

The ages of human history are not created by mechanical inventiveness, but there have been, in the history of our race, mechanical inventions which have changed the possibilities, and thus the minds, and thus, for better or for worse, the men. Landlocked men thought of the earth as a huge island surrounded by an unknown, undiscoverable sea. Seafaring men, as they extended their laborious mastery of the water, attempted to think of the earth as a globe, but succeeded only in imagining it as a belt of traversable water and inhabitable land fenced off between the two impenetrable polar caps of ice and fog and cold—a globe in theory, but in fact a globe-encircling river with temperate or tropic shores. That the mastery of the air will fix a different image in men's minds, an image which will father a new age, no one who knows the meaning of that mastery can doubt—no one who knows what voyages men and planes have made already in this war: the long flights of the ferrying command, the bombing thrusts at unbelievable objectives, the regular runs from continent to continent.

Indeed the image is already forming. To men of my generation, born in a seafaring world, the port of Murmansk lies east across the Atlantic and on east around the Scandinavian peninsula, thousands of sea miles. But Murmansk, to the flyers, is a bare eleven hundred miles north across the polar sea from Greenland. To us Greenland is farther east than New York City and therefore farther than New York from Tokyo. To the airmen, New York to Tokyo is seven thousand miles; Greenland to Tokyo around the pole five thousand. To us the straight line from La Guardia Field to Foynes in Ireland is north of east, straight out across the Atlantic. To them the shortest line, but not the straightest,—for no distances along the globe are straight,—

curves north along the edge of Newfoundland, along the curving of the earth, and on around.

No one can doubt that the world which mastery of the air creates will be a different world. But the nature of that world—its human character—is still uncertain. And it is that nature which the outcome of this war will fix. One or the other, the Nazi image of the airmen's earth or ours, will be imposed upon the world that follows. We know them both: the Nazi image because the Nazis have spelled it out for us a hundred times; our own because already we begin to see its outlines. We can guess even now what the image of the airmen's earth will be if free men make it. If those who have the mastery of the air are free men and imagine for themselves as free men what their world could be, their world will be the full completed globe—the final image men have moved toward for so long and never reached.

Never in all their history have men been able truly to conceive the world as one: a single sphere, a globe having the qualities of a globe, a round earth in which all the directions eventually meet, in which there is no center because every point, or none, is center—an equal earth which all men occupy as equals. The airmen's earth, if free men make it, will be truly round: a globe in practice, not in theory. Already, under the compulsions of the war, a generation of young men has come to think in terms of globes. It is with strings on globes, not rulers on navigating charts, that the officers of the ferrying command plot out their distances, and it is always with the curving of the earth in mind that the young pilots of the bombing commands imagine to themselves their flights. The obstacles which limited the earth to men in ships are not obstacles to men in planes. Cold to the airmen is no barrier: they find it everywhere and occupy it in all climates. Ice to the airmen is no wall: they cross it easily as land or water. Distance is no hindrance. The limited voyages of even the greatest ships were voyages across a seeming-level sea. The great flights of the bomber planes and the ferry planes of this war are flights *around* the earth, not across it. The famous clipper which was caught by the war in Australian waters and made its way *west* to New York: the two ships which flew into Moscow with the Hopkins mission and returned, one east and one west, to meet on an American airfield—the men who flew these ships were men who had the sense of the roundness of the of the earth as no men could have had it before the air was mastered.

If we win this war—if we and the free peoples united with us win this war—the image of the age which now is opening will be this image of a global earth, a completed sphere. But if the Nazis win, the image will be very different. The air-earth as the Nazis see it is not the earth swept forward to the final and completed sphere, but the earth thrown backward to the ancient landlocked island of the centuries before the seas were opened. The official Nazi architects of this official Nazi air-earth are the Nazi geopoliticians—the professors and the generals of the Haushofer school of generals and geographers. To the Nazi geopoliticians, the true picture of the world is not the picture of a globe, but of a "world island" with a "heart land" at its center. The "heart land" is Germany. The "world island" is the vast land-linked mass of Europe, Africa, and Asia. Around this island are the seven seas. And anchored off the island shores in tributary dependence to the iron Main are all the other continents and islands of the earth—the Americas, Australia, Greenland, all the rest. From the Nazi "heart land," air power will dominate the "world island." From the shores of the "world island," air power will dominate the seas—as air power dominated the seas off Malaya and the Pacific archipelagos. Across the seas the threat of air power will hold the tributary continents and islands in subjection. It is not, I assure you, a dream. It is a geography. It is a geography which has worked in the Eastern Mediterranean and the Southwest Pacific, and which the Nazis mean shall work for the whole earth.

If the Nazis win, in other words, the new age of air power will be the old landlocked age of mythological men, and the image of the airmen's earth will be the image of the central island and the encircling sea. It is curious to recall, in this context, that there was some talk and more writing a year or two ago about the Nazi New Order as an order new not in name only but in truth—an order so new, so revolutionary, that it had the future in it like a wave. It is curious to remember that some who loved the air and knew the air accepted for themselves and even taught this theory. For surely, whatever else the Nazi New Order may be,—and there are millions of living and half-living and no longer living Frenchmen, Dutchmen, Poles, Norwegians who could tell us what it is,—whatever else the Nazi New Order may be, it is not the new order of the airmen's age. It is indeed the precise opposite of that order: the denial and suppression and destruction of that order—a denial and suppression so complete and so brutal that a man might wonder whether the Nazis had not fought this war precisely for that purpose, precisely to use the mastery of the air as an instrument to abort the promise of that mastery; promise that to them was threat.

It is against this Nazi New Order of death, and new revelation of old ignorance, that this war is fought. But not *against* them only. Those who think it is—those who think of this war as a negative, defensive war, those who question what our victory in this war can be—have not considered very carefully the nature of the time we live in: the opening, eventful nature of this time. They have not considered that there lies ahead of us, by every certainty, an opening age, and that that age belongs by right of its own logic to the free—to us and to all free men. They have not realized that in preventing our enemies from conquering that age and distorting that age we must conquer it ourselves; that in driving out and forever forbidding those who would have seized the future, we will seize it; that in destroying by force of arms the suppressive and tyrannical image the Nazis would have stamped upon it, we must inevitably stamp an image of our own. So far indeed is it from being true that the nature of our victory is difficult to name, that no man who considers what the struggle truly is can fail to name it. We who win this war will win the right and power to impose upon the opening age the free man's image of the earth we live in. We who win this war will win the future. The future which will follow from this war belongs to us.

Neither mastery of the air nor power in the air nor the airmen's global image of the earth can make, alone, the world we hope to live in. There are no panaceas and no cures, and the future of any people is a continuation of its past—a hope shackled by history. Nevertheless we know, all of us, the power of images in our lives and in the lives of nations. We know that those who think their world a free place of free movement, of free commerce both in men and words, are already free men, whatever limitations are put upon their freedom by brutality or force. We know also that those who do not think of their world in this way, who accept another image of their world, are slaves however they hold themselves, or however they move in apparent freedom from one place to another. We know therefore what it means to win this war.

For hundreds of years, thousands of years, the sea was the great symbol of freedom, and men struggled in many wars over many centuries to keep it so. To be free was to go on the sea waters. There was no man, said the ancient Saxon poet, but "longing comes upon him to fare forth on the water." It was the same with the Greeks and with all ancient peoples. The sea was freedom. The sea was the great symbol of freedom. Men, once they had built ships and learned the winds, would fare forth on the water. They would go and come freely; trade back and forth; exchange cloth and grain and iron; exchange words; exchange beliefs; discover new continents. For two thousand, three thousand years it was the opening endless sea which men followed for their freedom.

Now there is a new element upon which men can fare forth. Men have mastered the air. And the question now—the question, whether we so intend or not, on which this terrible war is fought—is whether the air will be a new symbol and a new practice of an even greater freedom, or whether it will not; whether the air will be to the sea what the sea was to the locked land, or whether it will not; whether the air will be an instrument of freedom such as men have never dared to dream of or an instrument of slavery such as men had never thought to feel—an instrument of slavery by which a single nation can enslave the earth and hold the earth in slavery without the hope or possibility of rebellion and revolt.

To win this war for freedom is not to win a doubtful victory. To win this war for freedom is to win the greatest triumph any nation, any people, ever won.

2

Geopolitics and International Morals

By Edmund A. Walsh

Rev. Edmund A. Walsh, S.J., born in Boston, Mass. Ph.D., Georgetown; LL.D., University of Delaware and University of Detroit; D.Litt., Georgetown. Regent, School of Foreign Service, Georgetown University, and Vice President of the University.

Author: *The Fall of the Russian Empire* (1928), *The Last Stand: An Interpretation of the Soviet Five-Year Plan* (1931), *Ships and National Safety* (1934), *Les Principes Fondamentaux de la Vie Internationale* (Paris, 1936), and numerous pamphlets and articles on international politics.

Geopolitics, by which is meant a combined study of human geography and applied political science, descends from a very ancient and mixed ancestry. Hence it was not exactly news for students of geography and international politics to be informed from Munich and Berlin that there is a definite relationship between the geographic environment and the political evolution of states as well as of peoples; or that space, size, location, economic resources, physical aptitudes, and moral qualities must be harnessed to the needs of national policy—or that climate and geography preceded history, economics, and political institutions in influencing the evolution of the race. *Ab assuetis nulla fit passio.* We are not excited by the familiar. Aristotle (384–322 B.C.) often pointed out the dependence of political science on geography; Strabo the Greek geographer (born 63 B.C., died A.D. 21) wrote for statesmen and politicians; in the Middle Age, Albertus Magnus (1206–1280) was preeminent for his geopolitical knowledge, even predicting the Suez Canal; Montesquieu (1689–1755) devoted much of Book XIV of his *Esprit des Lois* to the influence of geography on political variations and human conduct; Karl Ritter (1779–1859) made geography the *causa causans,* the prime influence, in determining the course of civilization; Immanuel Kant in the eighteenth century philosophized voluminously on geography as a basic influence on history; at the beginning of the nineteenth century Baron Dietrich Heinrich von Bülow was called "the mad baron" because of his geopolitics, and so alarmed the monarchs of Europe that the Russian Tsar clapped him into a dungeon at Riga, where he conveniently expired. Anticipating Professor Renner of Columbia Univeristy, von Bülow had divided continental Europe into twelve viable states.

Thomas Jefferson's acquisition of Louisiana in 1803 was geopolitics in its very definition. To secure one key city and an open port he purchased an empire and suggested to Congress that it overlook "metaphysical subtleties." The celebrated Russian historian V. O. Kluchevsky wrote his monumental *Course of Russian History* from a geopolitical point of view, as he declares in his opening chapter without specifically mentioning the word. Seward's purchase of Alaska in 1867 gave far more evidence of politico-geographic acumen than is commonly attributed to that tempestuous member of Lincoln's cabinet. Frederick Jackson Turner's "The Significance of the Frontier in American History" was a striking geopolitical monograph. Theodore Roosevelt had a very practical understanding of geopolitics as applied to the Isthmus of Panama. And surely Homer Lea—that amazing adventurer from California who became American military adviser to the Chinese government and who, as early as 1909, prophesied in minute detail the strategic stages in the Japanese attack on the Philippines in 1941—had as keen a sense of "political torsions in the monsoon lands" as Haushofer ever had. All these precursors of the Munich specialists lacked only classification; they were geopoliticians without portfolio.

In more recent times geopolitics as a systematic discipline descended from two Germans, a Swede, an American, an Englishman, and numerous Japanese expansionists. The Swede and the Germans acknowledged paternity and rejoiced in it. The Englishman, Sir Halford J. Mackinder, though never classifying himself as a geopolitician, nevertheless gave decided impetus to the subject by his celebrated theory of "the Heartland." Admiral Mahan did not live long enough to know how profoundly his writings on sea power influenced the geopolitikers of Munich and Berlin. They accepted him as authentic and regarded his conclusions as valuable source material. Japan has been persistently and without deviation practising a geopolitik of her own since the annexation of Korea in 1910. Her geopoliticians have not emphasized organization but rather minimized and rationalized their creeping imperialism in soft terms—emigration policies, as Count Komura described it in his "Continental Program" of 1909 or the "Greater East Asia Coprosperity Sphere" as explained to the Chinese in recent years.

General Haushofer, the final and best known Germanic exponent of the euphemism, was resident in Japan long enough to conceive a deep respect for the planned imperialistic program of Japanese statesmen. As an eyewitness he studied and savored each progressive advance with a connoisseur's discrimination. He acknowledged their geopolitical wisdom and instinct for lebensraum—"a gift which the Japanese enjoy to an almost unrivalled degree." He speaks of them as "this noble race" which recognized "the political dynamics" of the East, and he frequently points to them as models for imitation by Germany. He professes particular admiration for their subtle technique of spatial evolution—the "step back" of jujitsu and *sûmo* (wrestling) in which a seeming retreat encourages an overrash opponent to expose himself to a swift and devastating assault. "This is the school," he warns his own countrymen, "through which Japan went and through which Germany must go" (*Das japanische Reich in seiner geographischen Entwicklung*, Vienna, 1921).

Friedrich Ratzel, who died in 1904, was professor of geography at Leipzig and Munich, and a voluminous producer of important studies and miscellaneous pamphlets,—some twenty-four volumes and one hundred monographs. The necessity of a space-conception is always emphasized in his teachings and he warned his German followers that the decline of every state may be traced to complacency and satisfaction with a small space.

Space, he insists, is not merely a vehicle for political forces, it is itself a political force of prime importance. This spatial instinct

(*Raumsinn*) is developed principally in his *Ueber die Gesetze des raümlichen Wachstums der Staaten* (Laws of the Territorial Growth of States, Leipzig, 1896); also in expanded form in his *Political Geography* (1897). In that treatise, Ratzel formulated seven so-called laws of imperial expansion, all tending to rationalize his political conclusions that this planet is too small for more than one great, amalgamated state. And, though not directly mentioned by name, the ultimate conqueror in this cosmic battle for survival of the fittest clearly should be the German state. Hitler frankly adopted the same principle, at least with Europe as a beginning: "The political Testament of the German nation regarding its foreign policy," he writes in the fourteenth chapter of *Mein Kampf,* "shall and must always contain the following idea: Never allow the formation of two continental powers in Europe. Regard as an attack against Germany every attempt to organize a second military power on the German borders, even if it be only in shape of the formation of a state with potential military powers, and consider it not only a right, but also a duty to prevent with all means, even to the extent of using arms, the formation of such a state or to destroy it, should it have already come into existence."

Because of his earlier investigations in the realm of plant morphology and animal life, Ratzel adopted the biologic viewpoint respecting the state as well. The state for Ratzel is a quasi-organism evolving in a Darwinian process to higher forms or else devolving into decadence. To remain static means loss of character and vitality. Ratzel's foremost disciple in the United States was Ellen Churchill Semple, whose lectures on the new concept of geography at the University of Chicago and at Clark University inaugurated a distinct school of geographic thought in this country whose tendencies, like those of Ritter and Buckle, are to overstress environment in the formation of cultures and civilizations. Miss Semple died in 1932, leaving an enthusiastic following of American geographers as devoutly prone to the sociology of geography as Vilfredo Pareto was to the mathematics of sociology. She did much to add another single-answer school to those other oversimplifiers of complex human relations who crowded the eighteenth and nineteenth centuries. As Henry Adams put it: "Forty years ago our friends always explained things and had the cosmos down to a point."

Ratzel answered the Sphinx with the confident pronouncement that it was geography and space which solved the world riddle. Life is movement, he argued; since, then, the surface of the earth is static and unchanging, obviously it is humanity which must supply the dynamic force. The state is humanity organized; hence states must respond as states, i.e., they must expand. That, he contended, is the great law of their being, both physical and intellectual. It is a categoric imperative which cannot be obeyed if they remain ignobly resigned to the confines of a specific area. They must obey the "space-conquering forces" (*raumüberwindende Mächte*). Ratzel's successors, Kjellén and Haushofer, embraced the argument with gusto—and bettered the instruction.

Rudolf Kjellén, professor of government at Göteborg University in Sweden, enthusiastically followed and expanded Ratzel's leadership. It is claimed for Kjellén that he christened the subject, Geopolitics. The term first appears in his *Der Staat als Lebensform* (The State As a Form of Life, Stockholm, 1917, Berlin, 1918). In this work the author considers the state as an organism whose principal attribute is power. First things should be studied first, he maintained. Since political science, in his opinion, had too long been in the hands of legalists who regarded the state primarily as a creation of law, Kjellén set out to emancipate sociology from the lawyers and endow the legal skeleton with socio-geographic flesh and blood. Five aspects are proposed for study and analysis—but in the natural and logical order of their importance. What previously had been considered in last place, he would put first; what had been first, he would put last:

Geopolitik—geography and the state,
Demopolitik—population and the state,
Oekopolitik—economic resources of the state,
Sociopolitik—social structure of the state,
Kratopolitik—governmental organization.

Kjellén not only retained Ratzel's view of the state as a biological unit possessing the characteristics and vitality of a living organism but added an important development of his own. He enlarged the concept by including the idea of folk. Nationality, he argued, gives expression to the "folk individuality" of the state. Territory and space, consequently, are fortified by mysticism, by inclusion of the folk-concept, which, because of its migrant connotation, can be made to cover vast and new territories. Wherever the folk is found, there the parent state may and should follow. Expansion is thus blessed as a sacred duty of a state conscious of its obligations to blood-brothers in other areas. Obviously National Socialism welcomed such scientific benediction of racial imperialism and invoked the dogma in order to "rescue" Germans and alleged German interests, first in Austria, then in the Sudetenland and throughout Central Europe. The paradoxical inclusion of Western Slavs in Czechoslovakia and Poland, of Scandinavians in Denmark and Norway, Hellenes in Greece, Southern Slavs in Yugoslavia, Eastern Slavs in White Russia and the Ukraine, and Latins in France, Belgium, and Rumania was either ignored or submerged in prepared justifications, such as intolerable "incidents" and "military necessity." Geopolitics, like American architecture of the nineties, is *capable de tout.*

Professor Karl Haushofer succeeded to the heritage of Kjellén, whom he greatly admired, on the latter's death in 1922. Haushofer's personal qualifications, matured by military and diplomatic experience, fitted him to a nicety for the task of drafting geographic and historical arguments to the service of the rising Nazi power. Born in 1869, he became an officer in World War I and led his weary troops back to a humiliated Germany; as military observer, attached to the Japanese Army, he studied the Far Eastern situation from the vantage point of Tokyo; finally, as professor of geography in the University of Munich, he was enabled to organize and mobilize an encyclopedic amount of factual information against the day when Germany would be prepared to strike. An accomplished linguist, he spoke six foreign languages, including Chinese, Japanese, Korean, and Russian. With Haushofer geopolitics became a sheathed sword for achieving the German dream of revenge and domination. It was Hitler who unsheathed the blade and threw away the scabbard.

We know from his own writings the time and place where geopolitics became Haushofer's chosen lifework. Although he was a geographer and a Pan-Germanist, the determination to begin the organized and scientific education of postwar Germany was born in the hours when he was leading his troops homewards in the bitter defeat of 1918. The route lay through the remnants of Germany's border provinces. He observed the "keen frontier instinct" of other peoples and lamented the apathy of his own respecting lebensraum and the role of frontiers. The "inner need" which he felt himself, and which he believed his people would soon experience, "created the impulse and the plan for this work" (*Grenzen in ihrer geographischen und politischen Bedeutung* [The Geographic and Political Significance of Frontiers], Berlin, 1927, 1939). His residence in Japan laid the foundation for his constant hope that this "geopolitical giant of the monsoon lands" would become, with Germany, a revolutionary nemesis against the Versailles powers and Western plutocracies. Ignoring the non-Aryan origin of the Japanese, he visualized their cooperation with a vengeful Germany as "a symbiosis of cultural politics."

Haushofer early sensed the importance of the work accomplished by the English geographers Sir Halford J. Mackinder and James Fairgrieve. He thought so highly of Fairgrieve's *Geography and World Power* [1] that he had it translated into German (by his wife) and wrote a preface to it himself. From Mackinder he borrowed the root idea which was to energize German geopolitical thought. It first appeared in a paper, "The Geographical Pivot of History," read before the Royal Geographical Society, London, on January 25, 1904, by Sir Halford, then Reader in

[1] Cf. James Fairgrieve's contribution to this volume, p. 190.

Geography at Oxford and later Director of the London School of Economics and Political Science. On that occasion he presented a remarkable analysis of the interrelation of geography and politics not only on the continent of Europe, but elsewhere throughout the world and in history. Russia, he pointed out, is the pivot state in the balance of power in modern times; the United States, by advancing into the Pacific, has become an eastern power, making the real divide between east and west the Atlantic Ocean; Latin America, he observed, may have a decisive influence in any future conflict involving Germany:

> As we consider this rapid review of the broader currents of history, does not a certain persistence of geographical relationship become evident? Is not the pivot region of the world's politics that vast area of Euro-Asia which is inaccessible to ships, but in antiquity lay open to the horse-riding nomads, and is today to be covered with a network of railways? . . . Outside the pivot area, in a great inner crescent, are Germany, Austria, Turkey, India and China, and in an outer crescent, Britain, South Africa, Australia, the United States, Canada and Japan. In the present condition of the balance of power, the pivot state, Russia, is not equivalent to the peripheral states, and there is room for an equipoise in France. The United States has recently become an eastern power, affecting the European balance not directly, but through Russia, and she will construct the Panama Canal to make her Mississippi and Atlantic resources available in the Pacific. From this point of view the real divide between east and west is to be found in the Atlantic Ocean.

The address was followed by a discussion from the floor. Mr. Spenser Wilkinson, a prominent writer on naval strategy, before embarking on a specific comment, observed with some asperity: "As I was listening to the paper I looked with regret on some of the space that is unoccupied here and I much regret that a portion of it was not occupied by members of the cabinet." Again, in 1919, as warning to the victorious Allies gathered at the peace conference, Mackinder published *Democratic Ideals and Reality,* in which he saw a future peril to world peace in Germany's potential domination of Russia and the east. "When our statesmen are in conversation with the defeated enemy," he warned, "some airy cherub should whisper to them, from time to time, this saying: 'Who rules east Europe commands the Heartland; who rules the Heartland commands the World-Island; who rules the World-Island commands the World.'"[2]

This reference to "Heartland" and "World-Island" is Mackinder's graphic method of restating his basic thesis that the three continents, Europe, Asia, and Africa, constitute, as it were, one great cultural, political, and economic island set in the 75 per cent water-content of the globe; around it the lesser land areas are grouped in relatively minor importance. They are appendages to that main land mass situated in the eastern hemisphere. The heart of the island he conceives as stretching from the Volga to the Yangtze and from the Himalayas to the Arctic Ocean, a wholly continental area not open to the control of sea power. Organized domination of that immense sweep of territory by a virile people would shift the balance of power for the entire world. Such was the vision of this true pioneer of modern geopolitics, Sir Halford Mackinder. Haushofer himself frankly acknowledged the preeminent wisdom of Mackinder, referred to him frequently, often reproduced his map of the heartland, and frankly built his system on the Englishman's premises. Control of the heartland of Europe by Germany became Haushofer's pivot thereafter. A strong, self-contained, inland power with impregnable interior lines of communication and defense, with a self-sufficient economy and a powerful military organization would form the nucleus of continental supremacy. Around it and subordinated both politically and economically, Germany's minor satellite states would then be organized as reservoirs of supplies and services for the Master Race. From this integrated fortress would next radiate the Germanic program for that ultimate world domination which Friedrich List had outlined for Ger-

[2] The spectacular emergence of air power and its demonstrated function in modern warfare, while it seriously modifies, does not wholly destroy, Mackinder's argument. He reaffirms it in his contribution to this volume, "The Round World and the Winning of the Peace," p. 161.

many as early as 1841 in *The National System of Political Economy.*

In Adolf Hitler, imprisoned in the Landsberg fortress after the abortive Munich putsch of 1923, Haushofer found a ready instrument of propaganda and a transmission belt for the pseudo science of geopolitics. Visiting both Hess and Hitler in their prison, the Herr Doktor began his indoctrination.

On Hitler's release Haushofer functioned in the field of history, economics, and geographic strategy exactly as Fritz Thyssen and other financial interests did in the initial stages of Hitler's career, for which they furnished the finances and business brains. Thyssen, with melancholy hindsight, records their contributions and final elimination in that tragic confession of disillusionment, *I Paid Hitler.* Whether Haushofer used Hitler or Hitler used Haushofer, and to what extent, is of academic interest. The fruits of their team-play soon became manifest and serious for the world. That is what counted. Some informed observers have denied that Haushofer directly controlled or even seriously influenced Hitler's foreign policy. Such intimacy is even ridiculed by many as sensationalism—and smiled at by Nazi officials. The degree of contact is irrelevant. Haushofer is not alone a person; he became a school, a movement, a symbol, and a driving force. His subsidized Institute, as a fact of record, created a definite geopolitical atmosphere in modern Germany which enveloped both the makers of policy and the masses of the people to an extent which is undeniable. The half-educated Hitler was a mosaic of influences: the amoral statecraft of Machiavelli, the mystic nationalism and romanticism of Wagner, the organic evolution of Darwin, the grossly exaggerated racialism of Gobineau and Houston Stewart Chamberlain, the messianic complex of Fichte and Hegel, the military braggadocio of Treitschke and Bernhardi, and the financial conspiracy of the Prussian Junker caste. It was Haushofer who served as channel of unification between theory and action. The German General Staff doubtless were sympathetic to Haushofer's broad thesis and certainly Chapter XIV of *Mein Kampf* has much of Haushofer in it. The basic, incontestable truth is that Haushofer, directly in some instances, indirectly in others, coordinated, integrated, and rationalized the whole field of comparative geography for the uses of the Führer—and in a manner particularly attractive to a mentality such as Hitler's, which in 1923 must have been conscious of wide gaps in its historical and scientific information. As General Ludendorff in *Der totale Krieg* (Total War) outlined the new military tactics of total warfare, so Haushofer most skillfully and methodically expounded global geographic strategy.

As Hitler rose to power, the prestige and function of geopolitics ascended with him. It became a dynamic driving rod in the mechanics of statecraft. A huge personnel was mobilized by Haushofer to comb the earth for significant facts and geographic information. His "Strategic Index" became a filing system which embraced the entire world and placed at the disposal of the German General Staff what was probably the most complete and classified body of knowledge ever assembled for eventual military operations. It was created by reports from five sources:

(1) The German diplomatic service, which forwarded general information;
(2) The Foreign Institute at Stuttgart of Germans Abroad, which enrolled German nationals domiciled abroad in a network of detailed espionage;
(3) Section UA-1, the Gestapo Foreign Division, which supervised difficult espionage assignments;
(4) Dr. Goebbels' agents located in German tourist agencies and steamship lines, to whom was assigned the analysis of the foreign press for the purpose of determining the most effective forms of propaganda;
(5) Geopolitical specialists—the miscellaneous scientists, historians, naturalists, sociologists, economists, educators, geographers, cartographers, agronomists, oceanographers, statisticians, camouflaged tourists, and other scouts of lebensraum who, in one guise or another, penetrated to every corner of the globe and reported on their significant features.

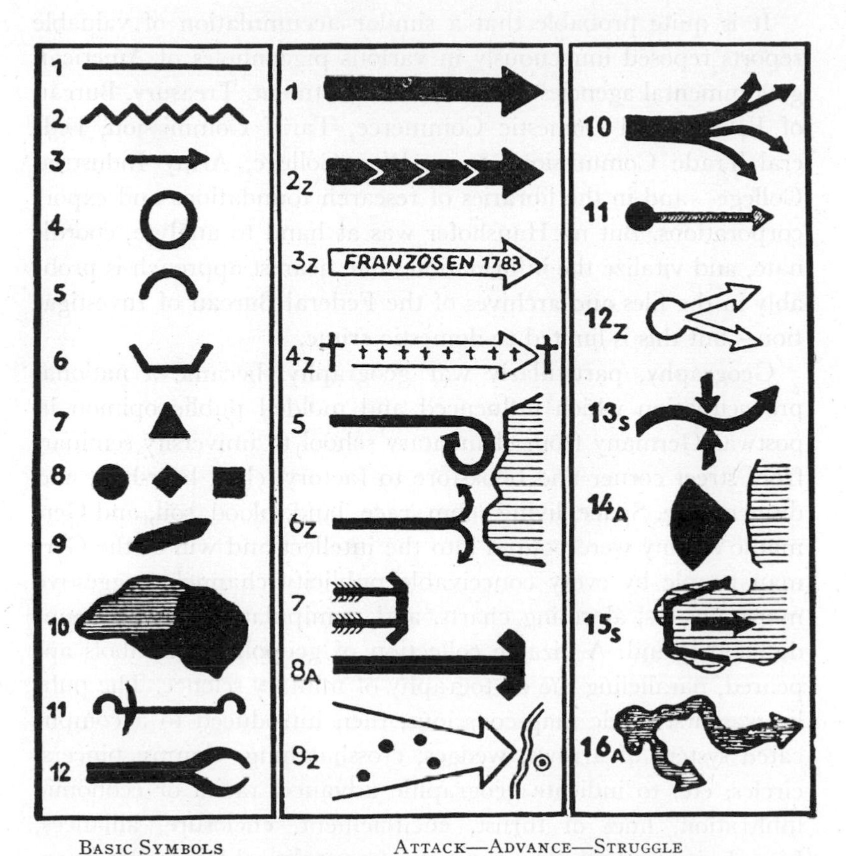

Basic Symbols

1. The line
2. The zigzag line
3. The arrow
4. The circle
5. The half-circle
6. The demipolygon
7. The wedge
8. The target
9. The peg
10. Crosshatching
11. The clamp
12. The pincers

Attack—Advance—Struggle

1. Direct attack
2. Phases of attack
3. Hollow arrow with explanation
4. Symbolic arrow—advance of Christianity
5. Frustrated attack
6. Frustrated attack
7. Frontal attack
8. Frontal attack
9. Attack from several points—from a league of cities
10. Radiating attack from one source
11. Planning arrow — center of the movement
12. Split attack from a particular region
13. Attack intercepted and strangled
14. Mass attack on limited area
15. Natural approach to a given area
16. Routes of attack through channels predetermined by nature

Zeitschrift für Geopolitik, Vol. XII, No. 4 (Apr., 1935).

It is quite probable that a similar accumulation of valuable reports reposed innocuously in various pigeonholes of American governmental agencies—the State Department, Treasury, Bureau of Foreign and Domestic Commerce, Tariff Commission, Federal Trade Commission, Army War College, Army Industrial College—and in the libraries of research foundations and export corporations. But no Haushofer was at hand to analyze, coordinate, and vitalize the information. The nearest approach is probably in the files and archives of the Federal Bureau of Investigation—but this is limited to domestic crime.

Geography, particularly war geography, became a national preoccupation which influenced and molded public opinion in postwar Germany from elementary school to university seminar, from street corner and bookstore to factory, club, beer-hall, and dinner table. Space, living room, race, land, blood, soil, and Germanic destiny were poured into the intellect and will of the German people by every conceivable publicity channel. Suggestive maps, posters, alarming charts, and manipulated statistics inundated the land. A bizarre collection of geopolitical symbols appeared, paralleling the cartography of military science. The public was first made map-conscious, then introduced to a complicated system of arrows, wedges, crosshatching, clamps, pincers, circles, etc. to indicate geographic advance, racial or economic infiltration, lines of thrust, encirclement, enclosure, alliances, boundaries, and other movements of geopolitical forces. See p. 23.

For the literati, appropriate publications were catalogued to the number of three thousand titles. Even novels were composed to stimulate the sense of lebensraum, through recital of harrowing adventures of Germanic heroes in search of space and opportunity.[3] Learned periodicals such as the *Zeitschrift für Geopolitik* cultivated the intellectuals and furnished a periodical survey of the entire world focused always to Germany as central point of reference.

[3] *Volk ohne Raum* (A People Without Space), by H. Grimm, 1926; *Alle Wasser Böhmens fliessen nach Deutschland* (All the Waters of Bohemia Flow Towards Germany), by F. Bodenreuth, 1939.

The June, 1937, issue of that journal was devoted almost exclusively to Czechoslovakia. The deployment of grievances, maps, charts, statistics, and tendentious history constituted sure and ominous warning that attack and absorption were in the making. The same preliminary education and careful preparation can be detected in the progressive arguments respecting Austria—from the November issue of 1934 straight up to the invasion of 1938. Systematic reading of the *Zeitschrift* could have warned any small nation contiguous to Germany as to its probable fate. Frequent and angry attention to their country should have caused the uneasiness experienced when an undertaker measures certain of his neighbors with a calculating eye.

A new jargon flourished and became current even in non-geopolitical circles: *Raumenge,* confined space; *entwehrter Raum,* disarmed space; *Grossraum denkend*, thinking in terms of vast space; *Raumsinn,* instinct for space; *anthropogeographische Dynamik,* dynamics of racial geography; *Blut und Boden,* race and land; *Grenzgefühl,* sensitivity to frontiers; *Bewusstsein des Lagewerts,* sense of the value of location; *Wachstumsspitzen,* marginal growths, e.g., Gibraltar, Hong Kong, and Singapore; *räumliche und zeitliche Selbstbestimmungstreben*, striving for self-determination in terms of space and time. These and similar cabalistic catchwords were directed to the German intellect as justification for war. But the marching song of German troops advancing to battle dispensed with all academic pretense, came down to cases, and inflamed the will: "Heute gehört uns Deutschland, Morgen die ganze Welt" (Today Germany belongs to us, tomorrow the whole world). The latest and most fearsome etymological hybrids to arrive on the scene are *Geomedizin,* some sort of geopolitical medicine; *Geopsyche,* the influence of weather and climate on the soul; and *Geojurisprudenz,* a brand of geopolitical legality to displace international law.[4]

What did Haushofer add to previous exponents of human

[4] Much of the language used by German geopoliticians is evidently based on the assumption that depth and intelligibility are contradictory terms. The ensemble constitutes a collection of gigantic nebulosities equalled only by Spengler but often surpassed by Hegel.

geography? Universality, practicality, and definite political objectives. He went far beyond the regional and limited scope of his classic predecessors in that field and became global; he discarded objectivity for subjective prejudices and interpreted geographic phenomena mainly in their relationship to the interests of Germany, thereby committing treason against that very scientific credo which Germany has so noisily worshiped as her outstanding creation. He committed intellectual suicide on the altar of a vulgar and unscientific superstition.

What did Hitler add to Haushofer's geopolitical trickery? Action, striking power, the will to end the long symposium and begin the indicated conquest. Conviction of the Germanic destiny had been planted in his consciousness from long brooding over the writings of Fichte, Hegel, Treitschke, Nietzsche, Houston Stewart Chamberlain, Rosenberg, and similar messianic preachers of Teutonic superiority. That fixed idea exhausted the capacity of his brain and his soul, there not being much else there to dispute its presence. He simply condensed all previous arguments into *Mein Kampf,* made that explosive synthesis an obligatory textbook for postwar Germany, invoked the Treaty of Versailles as a collateral and immensely popular polemical motive, and then prepared his World Revolution over some seven years of feverish armament. When ready, he exploded the prepared dynamite into the face of an astounded, a demoralized, and a shocked continent. Europe, to be sure, was demoralized and shocked. But it should not have been astounded.

II

No informed European or thoughtful American should fail to recognize that the German geopolitik is precisely what its name signifies—the politics of a wholly earthy conception of life and human destiny. It was the logical culmination of a process of secularization both of the mind and of cultural institutions which had been in progress since the Renaissance and the Industrial Revolution. Both these historic discoveries turned men's gaze earthward. The former corrupted the soul of Europe and squandered the supernatural heritage of Christendom by its ecstatic worship of material beauty and artistic brilliancy. The joy of scintillating wit and the silkiness of hedonistic living cultivated by the men of the Renaissance resulted in a worship of the form, the color and delicacy of things, to the detriment of the basic meaning of man and the primacy of his spirit. Even the Madonna was frequently secularized into a thinly disguised copy of Venus.

This one-sided, distorted Humanism introduced a paganism of taste, charm, and refinement, which, coupled with personal depravity in high places, cancerous morals, simony, and nepotism, weakened respect for ecclesiastical authority and hastened the religious revolt of the northern nations in the sixteenth century. In statecraft it produced Machiavelli and justified the Haushofers. Its economic counterpart of the eighteenth century introduced a new solvent in the shape of prodigious commercial productivity and increased pleasure in the manufacture, distribution, and exchange of marketable commodities. The Renaissance of Catholic Italy worshiped the contour of man's body, his raiment, his art, his rediscovered classics, ornaments, and food; the Industrial Revolution of Protestant England shifted the idolatry to his mass production of anything capable of being priced and marketed. Both missed the value of man *per se*. Both set fashions of thought and norms of judgment the momentum of which dominated the modern mind for the next several centuries. Both conspired to hasten the second Fall of Man. Both prepared the soil for the emergence of Prussia, whose historic tendency has been to minimize law and exalt force.

The scientific trend ran in the direction of emancipating research from moral obligation and spiritual control. Men cynically insisted that science had nothing to do with values or moral considerations, but only with the discovery of unsuspected relationships, uncatalogued substances, and unknown forces. The use to which these revelations would be put did not enter into the account. Science, it was claimed, had no conscience. From that postulate it was an easy step to the assertion that scientists had none either—and needed none. This overemphasis on material factors soon became a fascination. Growing by what it fed on, the fascination next became virtual deification of matter and force and form, to the further detriment and neglect of spirit and ideals. The blight spread from the economic sphere to metaphysics, education, sociology, and statecraft. Naturalism became the hallmark of intellectual acceptability, science having handed down a verdict against the soul on the ground that the existence of such a substance—or accident, or force—had not been verified in any test tube, nor registered on any spectrum or measured on any voltmeter.

This autonomy and primacy of matter was joyfully accepted by the geopoliticians at the eleventh hour and interpreted realistically in terms of geography. The dignity of human personality, the natural rights of men inhabiting other desirable territory, the restraints of International Law, and the intangible elements of racial differentiation were all subordinated to the mechanistic and impersonalized philosophy cultivated with increasing intensity in Europe and elsewhere for a hundred years before the Nazi Revolution. Darwinism—essentially a theory of plant and animal evolution—was transferred bodily by Haushofer and Hitler to geographic, social, and political phenomena. Conquest was justified as a biological necessity for the "quasi organism" of the State. Only the fittest nations would survive. The state that lacked territory should simply seize it if conquest was feasible, or absorb it if that process proved more practical. That was the evident law of nature, and hence survival became the prerogative of master races. Geopolitics was appointed to be the "geographical conscience of the state."

The evil effect of this wholesale worship of naturalism had already seeped down to the very firesides of domestic tranquillity and softened the moral fiber of western man. Nazi Germany attacked at precisely the moment when spiritual resistance was at its lowest ebb. Geopolitics, like Technocracy and the libido complex of Freud, was another single-answer device, but with a difference. When geography was finally invoked by the geopoliticians in their turn, it was invested with miraculous potency by a powerful government already predisposed to political amoralism in international relations. From Johann Gottlieb Fichte (1762–1814) Prussia inherited the special type of gross chauvinism expounded in his *Addresses to the German People* published in 1808. It was in his fourteenth Address that Fichte reached the zenith of racial egotism: "All ages, all wise and good men who have ever breathed upon this earth, all their thoughts and intuitions of something loftier, mingle with these voices and surround you and lift up imploring hands to you; even, if one may say so, Providence and the Divine plan in creating a race of men . . . the Divine plan, I say, solemnly appeals to you to save its honor and its existence . . . Thus are you of all modern peoples the one in whom the seed of human perfection most unmistakably lies, and to whom the lead in its development is committed. If you perish in this your essential nature, then there perishes together with you every hope of the whole human race for salvation from the depth of its miseries . . . There is, therefore, no way out; if you go under, all humanity goes under with you, without hope of any restoration."

It will not mitigate the historical and poisonous significance of these outbursts to maintain that they were only the isolated exaggerations of a heated imagination smarting under the humiliation of Napoleon's victory over Prussia at Jena, or indignant at the French dragoons then patrolling the streets of Berlin. Fichte was first rector of the University of Berlin, which became the center of nationalism and spokesman of the Prussian government from 1809 onwards. Fitche's pronouncements became the bible of Prussian chauvinism and the sacred book of German foreign policy.

In 1818 he was succeeded in the chair of Philosophy by Georg Wilhelm Friedrich Hegel, who continued and enlarged the concept of the totalitarian state. Hegel resurrected Machiavelli by maintaining that the state is the final expression, the most complete embodiment of social and ethical ideals, the nearest approach to divinity—it is divinity on earth, the conscious spirit

(*Geist*) of man participating in the process of ascertaining the Divine will. Hegel's influence in this investiture of a given state apparatus with total and suprahuman authority was perpetuated throughout Germany by his works, which became, with those of Fichte, the political curriculum imposed on German youth. This deification of the state made Prussia infallible in its own estimation, above international law and sole judge of interstatal morality. Only the best organized states should survive, the weaker political organisms being destined to give way to the more masterful powers.

It was Friedrich Nietzsche who supplied for the Prussian state the next ingredients of totalitarian thought. He furnished a technique and a procedure. Born in 1844, Nietzsche died a victim of syphilis in 1900, in an insane asylum. What did he teach? What has Nazi Germany incorporated into its policies from this incarnation of sheer brutality and animality? A gross egotism, worship of one's own individual thought, a lifelong crusade to deify the superman who shall rule the earth—and the concept of leadership (*Führerprinzip*). "My destiny," writes Nietzsche in *Ecce Homo,* "ordains that I shall be the first decent human being. . . . I was the first to discover truth." In the light of that comforting discovery, he then reconstructs European history in his celebrated vision of the superman. Nietzsche's hero would be a reincarnation of the Teutonic tribesmen who once overran Europe. Not burdened by morals, they were free from every social restraint. They were, he records, "a herd of blond beasts of prey" exulting in their conquests.

And how is their paganism to be restored? By the Will to Power and the Transvaluation of all Values. This ethical metamorphosis is to be achieved by redefining the concepts of good and evil. It is power, the will to power, and the feeling of power which constitute the essence of good. "Evil" is only another name for weakness. Happiness will derive from the consciousness that power is increasing and resistance overcome. There should be no truce in the quest for power; contentment will be found only in the acquisition of power through war and more war. Efficiency, not virtue, shall be the measure of greatness, and the moral aspects are simply to be ignored. Inefficient or weak individuals and nations must disappear—and they should be helped on their way to extinction. Such is the Nietzschean vision of progress as recorded in the *Antichrist*.[5]

National Socialism, including geopolitics, used Nietzsche copiously and admitted him to the Nazi Pantheon. The most recent biography is from the pen of Professor Crane Brinton of Harvard and appears in the biographical series Makers of Modern Europe (Harvard University Press, 1941). If Nietzsche was one of the architects of modern Europe, should the world have been surprised when the house collapsed?

Later, from his vantage point as professor of History in the University of Berlin, Heinrich von Treitschke continued the tradition of arrogance and amoral statecraft. For twenty years, until 1896, he poured into the souls of German youth his glorification of Prussia and his canonization of war, as "an institution ordained of God." Germany's vital interests, he proclaimed, extend to "the Slav, the Scandinavian and Romance countries." His formula for "inferior peoples" was simple and laconic: "Each dragoon who knocks a Croat on the head does far more for the German cause than the finest political brain that ever wielded a trenchant pen." In international politics he taught: "The sin of weakness is the sin against the Holy Ghost." The omnipotent Prussian state would be the savior of Europe if only strong-minded man would learn how to sacrifice culture for force. Such titans were Treitschke's ideal of humanity. "How high they tower above those detestable mediocrities [people clinging to right and virtue] who are becoming so terribly numerous at the present day."

By careful selection of such material, by repetition, flattery, denunciation, and by mass-indoctrination under a resolute leadership which made Nazi propaganda a classic demonstration of the art of preparing a revolution, the orators of National Social-

[5] Haushofer adopted the same thesis in *Weltpolitik von heute,* pp. 115 ff. Small states, he maintains, have no right to exist.

ism convinced sufficient numbers of the German people that the Nietzschean ideal of superman was incarnate in them. The cult of Nietzsche's "magnificent blond brute" (*The Genealogy of Morals*, Essay 1, Section 11) became a political force which created a will to power unexampled in modern history. The transvaluation of all values was prudently limited at first to the Treaty of Versailles and the rectification of specified geographic frontiers. That was a revolutionary discipline necessary during the initial stages of psychological preparation. Hitler devoted fifteen years to the prelude of propaganda. But underneath the technique lurked always the full Nietzschean rage for apocalyptical destruction of Democracy and Christianity. Understanding of this duality should not be interpreted as wholesale indictment of the entire German people, among whom are to be found Nature's quota of reasonable men, charitable spirits, and much Christian conscience. But these elements are ruthlessly suppressed, or dead, or in concentration camps or in exile. The dominant Teutonic mentality is Nietzschean, Hegelian, and Fichtean. Haushofer and his geopoliticians simply clothed the permanent quality of Prussia in a new vocabulary and called this synthetic science "geopolitics." That is the imperious actuality, that is the armed menace of the hour with which the world must deal. It is the final paroxysm of a culture in transition—one age dying, another struggling to be born. The extent and intensity of the present world convulsion indicates either a great death or a great birth. Probably both.[6]

Geopolitics, then, may be viewed in several ways. Many American scholars are inclined to dismiss it as so exaggerated and overdrawn as to forfeit all claims for serious refutation. Some commentators describe it as one of the greatest hoaxes of history. Others, however, regard it as an extremely dangerous weapon which should be met by a vigorous counterattack in kind. The

[6] The stubborn, rationalized insistence on Germanic destiny may be further illustrated by reference to the works of Wagner, Clausewitz, Bernhardi, Schelling, La Garde, Gobineau, and Langbehn. Taken together, the Pan-German school is a complete demonstration of the wisdom expressed by A. Clutton-Brock in his *The Ultimate Belief*: "Nothing is so dangerous to the mind as a false absolute, and the false absolute of the Germans is Germany."

truth would seem to lie somewhere between these extremes—probably nearer to the cautious than to the contemptuous. That it is exaggerated has, the author hopes, been demonstrated in the preceding pages. Respecting the arrogance involved, there should be neither compromise nor condonation. The extent to which serious German scholars have gone in demonstrating the inferiority—even subhumanity—of other respectable peoples, such as Poles and Czechs, is amazing and incredible. But the incredible must not be allowed to obscure the reality of the danger involved. The Germanic claim to world supremacy ceased to be an academic theory on September 1, 1939. It became a military fact which can be met and resolved only by superior military force—if Western civilization is to be preserved, albeit chastened and purged of unwholesome accretions. Christianity and Democracy are at one respecting the fundamental impasse. The abhorrent doctrine of racism, which substitutes blood, race, and land for the salvific life and death of Christ, makes National Socialism as direct a denial and positive menace to Christianity as was the Mohammedan invasion of Europe and the militant atheism of Marxian Communism. Many students of Communism are even prepared to admit that Nazism soon became the more formidable enemy of religion. No group in Europe has been more fearless in denouncing the grave menace of racism than the German Catholic Hierarchy and the more courageous leaders of Protestant belief in Germany. If the neo-paganism inherent in the theological content of the Nazi creed should prevail by force of arms, Christianity would be driven back into the catacombs, not only in Germany but wherever such conquest is consummated. If the political, economic, and social organization which has been imposed so callously on the conquered territories of Central Europe should ever become permanent by Axis victory throughout the entire Old World, then Democracy must retreat to the Atlantic world and prepare itself for the final, titanic conflict of the hemispheres. The concept of Law would then make its last stand in the two Americas.

So much for the geopolitics of the past and present. The pattern of a future geopolitics, born of sanity and law and equity, is even now beginning to grow discernible in broad outlines as the tremendous problems of postwar reconstruction come nearer and nearer. Whatever geographic, ethnic, and economic validity may remain, after heavy discount, in the claims of German geopoliticians must be faced with objectivity and remedied with frankness and courage. They do not concern Germany alone but all Christendom. The errors, weaknesses, and crimes of the past can best furnish the starting point of reference for the reform of international conduct in the future. Already there are well over a hundred serious projects in formation to rehabilitate the postwar world. The projects range from the Union Now of Clarence Streit to the regional groupings of the late Nicholas Spykman.

But all these devices will prove ropes of sand against recurrent violence unless the spirit of man be purged of the gross materialism and worship of speed, motion, and external form which have characterized the modern mind since the Renaissance and the Industrial Revolution. The Four Freedoms, Atlantic Charters, Bills of Rights, Freedom of the Seas, and International Law have never yet and never will be secured by economists, statesmen, or financial wizards. Such instruments are but externalities and legal symbols responding to something that lies deep and invisible within the human soul. International Law is only a control; it is not a cure of human passion.

The statesmen, economists, and miscellaneous specialists who will gather at the peace conference will doubtless propose many admirable remedies in the sphere of political technology, international trade, finance, boundaries, and social security. But they will be pouring water into a sieve unless the superstructure of the world's social organization rests on something more universal than international economics, which are invariably colored by national interest. The axe must be laid to the roots. If the makers of the new world-peace fail in their most important function, they will not have another chance for an unpredictable period of worse interstatal anarchy. And they will fail if they cling to the ancient heresy that the human will can be trained and controlled by penalties alone, unaided by motivation and spiritual perception. If they do fail, a glacial cap will settle over the soul of an exhausted humanity newly disillusioned, and the ice age of international relations will return. They will simply create another plague of spurious geopolitics.

The best prophylaxis in the field of external strategy will be an American geopolitics based on international justice, international honor, the sanctity of the given word, and mutuality of international respect. Since such motives have failed to influence the Axis mentality, America must continue to mobilize her striking power and falter not in using it fearlessly and without scruple in the service of freedom and the inalienable rights of human personality. Such an objective does not imply new imperialism nor surrender to the worst features of power politics, but fulfillment of the heavy moral obligations attaching to great power and economic affluence. Political and military power can be an instrument of justice as well as of injustice and arrogant aggression. "It is excellent to have a giant's strength," wrote Shakespeare, but "tyrannous to use it like a giant." Geopolitics can ennoble as readily as corrupt. It can choose between two alternatives—the value of power and the power of values. That is the challenge confronting America at this threshold of a new epoch in the history of the race. But in the meantime resistance to evil should be prolonged without compromise, and force applied with inflexibility of will and at any sacrifice until all governments understand that he who wantonly takes the sword shall perish by it. But, victory once achieved, a new challenge will stand knocking at the door of the Peace Conference.

During the years of Hitler's campaign to capture the organs of government in Germany, a historic race was in progress on the continent of Europe, a race between two ideologies and two grandiose concepts of power. The spectacular Five Year Plan of Joseph Stalin was being sold—and successfully sold—to the Russian Revolution, as a thousand-year vision was being unfolded to Germans in revolt. Teuton and Slav, historic rivals, were on the march again while England slept and France disintegrated.

Lenin's internationalism and Stalin's industrialized soviets became familiar public facts in the postwar period. The Teutonic claims were finally climaxed in 1939 by Hitler's order of the day affirming that the destiny of Germany was about to be determined for the next thousand years.

These two concepts, Communism and Nazism, included an identical objective—World Revolution. They jointly expressed the two most dynamic principles in the European balance of power, and by their content and universalism were inexorably destined for eventual collision. Two such claimants for universal hegemony could not co-exist and simultaneously activate their programs for long on the same continent—a fact which was basically clear to both long before the German attack on Russia in June, 1941. Both, in their own way, accepted the belief of Hitler formulated in *Mein Kampf* (Chapter V, page 440): "Political parties are inclined to compromise; world-concepts never. Political parties count on adversaries; world-concepts proclaim their infallibility." Both secretly understood the nature of the breathing space afforded by the Russo-German nonaggression pact of August, 1939. For Germany that truce provided welcome relief from the haunting spectre of Soviet divisions on its eastern borders and thereby enabled Hitler to launch World War II with confidence and undivided mind. For Russia it supplied a precious time-element to prepare for the inevitable struggle between the two titans most concerned with domination of Mackinder's Heartland.

Hitler's decision to attack his Muscovite rival abruptly restored the true *status quaestionis* of Central Europe. The amazing Russian resistance simply threw her, not so much into the camp of the Allies, as back into her original domestic defensive position respecting Hitlerite Germany. In step with the logic of events and under pressure of new circumstances the Kremlin wisely shifted to a less intransigent position respecting World Revolution and the status of religion in the U.S.S.R. By first dissolving the Third International, then welcoming the election of a Patriarch to preside over the Orthodox Church, and finally by scrapping the offensive "Internationale" and substituting a new national anthem in praise of the motherland, the Soviet Union has scored three distinct psychological triumphs over Nazi Germany. But it would be premature to conclude that her basic external policy has been altered to a corresponding degree. Realistic understanding of the Soviet achievement in repelling Nazi Germany must rest on one frank premise: she is fighting a common enemy, not guaranteeing nor underwriting the common objectives of other United Nations. The appearance in Moscow of a Free Polish Committee, a Free German Committee and a Free Austrian Committee, all formed and operating under Soviet auspices, served fair notice that Europe is not to be reconstructed solely from Casablanca, Cairo, and Quebec. If the unhappy appeasement policy pursued prior to 1939 in favor of the Nazis resulted only in blood, sweat, and tears, miscalculation of the Soviet Union's special geopolitics can easily lead to disunity, friction, and acute danger in the hour of Allied victory.

Certain events of January and early February, 1944, emphasized the necessity of tempering optimism with political realism. Soviet Russia's attitude on the Polish frontier revealed that Moscow considered that problem as an exclusively domestic issue not open to debate or requiring consultation with the United Nations. The British Cabinet promptly announced that His Majesty's government would not recognize any transfer of territory effected later than September, 1939—unless such a re-allocation of sovereignty was approved by the included population. The government of the United States offered to serve as mediator in the dispute, but the tender of good offices was refused by Moscow. The British press and government joined in vigorous denunciation of a report circulated by the Moscow *Pravda* to the effect that British agents had been detected in secret peace negotiations with Nazi Germany.

Hard on the heels of these disturbing incidents came the official Soviet decree that each of the sixteen constituent Republics of the Union shall henceforth exercise direct control over its foreign relations, with the right to appoint its own diplomatic representatives in foreign lands. This move was interpreted in some quarters as legitimate constitutional reform, in line with the times, and intended to decentralize the previous exclusive control exercised in that field by Moscow over the diverse nationalities found in the Soviet Union. Elsewhere it was considered as a bold *coup d'état* of power politics designed to confront Western Europe with fifteen new international entities pledged to support Soviet policies in Eastern and Central Europe.

All these unilateral decisions resulted in a new wave of skepticism respecting the fate of the Atlantic Charter and the solidarity proclaimed in the Conferences at Moscow and Teheran.

It would likewise be infantile complacency to maintain that the United Nations were 100 per cent right and Germany 100 per cent wrong in the premises leading to the present world tragedy. Wisdom and folly, virtue and iniquity are not so neatly distributed among mortals, particularly when men are angered to the extent of shedding blood. The record of both contestants will show a chastening admixture of human weaknesses, errors of judgment and frequent failures to achieve the full purity of motive claimed by extremists and chauvinists in both camps. Social justice and inspired treatment of minorities have not been an exclusive monopoly of the British Empire, else there would have been no Black and Tans in Ireland or Gandhi in India; wisdom and consistency have not been shining ornaments in American foreign policy since 1898, though princely generosity has always characterized our dealings with nations in distress; the preservation of order, security, and tranquillity has not been the genius of government in China since the fall of the Manchu dynasty despite the sincere efforts of her more enlightened statesmen; democracy, religious freedom, and equal justice under law have not entered into the common estimate held of Soviet Russia in the family of nations.

By the same measure of honesty, not all the sicknesses of postwar Europe since 1918 can be traced to Germany. Her colossal crime against humanity consists not in her bill of grievances against the Treaty of Versailles nor in her obstinate refusal to accept indefinitely an inferior position on the continent, but in the hypocritical and brutal methods adopted to redress the stated inequality and in the license accorded pathological leaders to conspire against the peace of the world in the name of the German people. However wrong we may have been, or however troubled in conscience, the Nazi government put itself so completely and violently in the wrong that only one course was left in common decency to the United Nations. Berlin demanded judgment by fire and sword, and on that hazard she freely elected to stand or fall. But nature abhors a vacuum even in the sphere of political control of a people. The compelling problem, then, will soon arise: what substitute will rush in to occupy her vacated space in Europe? A vacuum in nature must be promptly filled, or else the pressure of circumambient forces may crush the hollow framework.

If the airy cherub whom Mackinder summoned to breathe warnings (unheeded) into the ears of statesmen gathered at Versailles is still in office, may he keep plucking at the ears of the new negotiators with a similar warning:

Do not imagine that the Anglo-American program for a reconstructed world has descended direct from Sinai.

Do not lay the flattering unction to your souls that it will be universally accepted by those most intimately concerned, impoverished and exhausted though they be.

Do not ignore the social revolution that has taken place in the thinking of the masses since 1918.

Above all, do not forget that Moscow lies much nearer to the pulse of Eurasia, India, and China than do London and Washington.

3

Geography *vs.* Geopolitics

By Isaiah Bowman

Isaiah Bowman, born Waterloo, Ontario. Ph.D., Yale, 1908. Sc.D., Bowdoin, 1935, Arequipa and Cuzco, Peru, 1941. LL.D., Dartmouth, Charleston, Dickinson, University of Pennsylvania (1935), Harvard and University of Wisconsin (1936), University of Western Ontario and Queens University (Ontario) (1937). President, The Johns Hopkins University. Director American Geographical Society, 1915–1935. President of the American Association for the Advancement of Science (1943).
Author: *South America,* 1915; *The New World: Problems in Political Geography,* 1921; *International Relations,* 1930; *The Pioneer Fringe,* 1931; numerous other books and articles on geography and land settlement.
"Geography *vs.* Geopolitics" is a condensed version of a paper published in the *Geographical Review,* 1942, pp. 646–658.

> Yielding to some untoward bias, they entangle themselves
> in words, and confound themselves in subtleties.
> —Alexander Hamilton, *The Federalist.*

The current discussion of German geopolitical writings involves the names, outlook, and reputation of certain American geographers. What was their position respecting geopolitics before general condemnation of Hitler and the Nazi program began? Did they foresee the evil consequences of German perversion of truth in the alleged new science of geopolitics which made use of the overlapping data of history, political science, and geography? It has recently been declared that American geopolitics was developed before it was taken up in Germany. The bad effect of this assertion touches more than personal or professional repute. It has given the question a national context.

Geopolitics presents a distorted view of the historical, political, and geographical relations of the world and its parts. It identifies no universal forces or process like gravity. It is relative to the state to which it is applied. At least so say its advocates. Its arguments as developed in Germany are only made up to suit the case for German aggression. It contains, therefore, a poisonous self-destroying principle: when international interests conflict or overlap, *might* alone shall decide the issue. Against "geopolitical needs" democracy opposes moral rights. Let us look first at the way in which this opposition arises.

American democracy strives to achieve certain explicit purposes stated in a body of doctrine expressed in the first instance in our Declaration of Independence and subsequently in the Constitution with its amendments. It is at bottom the union of two principles: (1) promotion of the general welfare through the consent of the governed, and (2) respect for individual human rights. Doing evil things in the name of an alleged good cause is not the cornerstone of its philosophy. Democracy is an agreement upon purposes and a selection of means that a people's sense of justice approves. When the Reichstag in 1914 unanimously approved the German government's program, which had involved the violation of Belgian neutrality, it was expressing its sense of justice and giving its moral approval. By such approval it hoped to hasten the day of victory and peace. There you have also agreed purposes, a sense of justice, and moral approval! What was wrong with them?

Democracy starts with the individual. It believes in his general freedom to speak and act as he chooses, provided he speaks the truth and acts so as not to harm the other members of his society: the natural and multiform "conflict of interests," greatly expanded in our complex modern societies, is resolved by laws passed by popular legislatures. There is no such thing in democracy as the worship of the state as an organism governed by "scientific" laws and rules applied by a dictator. On the contrary, it alleges that "the best society is that which increases spontaneity and life and variety," and that the state cannot itself produce an acceptable social life, it can only foster the forces which produce it. We hold, with Lord Acton, that liberty is possible only where there are other centers of organization than political. The state needs the voluntary support of its many-sided people, and "its business is to safeguard by harmonious regulation the rich various life of voluntary associations in the state." [1] Non-

[1] A. D. Lindsay, *The Essentials of Democracy.* Philadelphia, 1929.

political centers of organization in a democracy keep the public reminded of common purposes within a wide circle of diverse action and freedom. They promote lively and local discussion, independent thinking, and a richer context for majority decisions.

Having force behind it, a state is or should be the engrossing object of every citizen's concern. For nonpolitical associations do not have such force. One can resign from them. The good citizen can never resign his citizenship—that is, his participation in and his responsibility for the use of state power.

The resulting democratic "culture" is not a thing imposed by government upon the individual or imposed upon other states by violence in the name of progress, or peace, or superiority, or the so-called "inevitabilities of geopolitics." It is one of many cultures possible in a world at peace, each suited to the genius of its people and the limitations of its total environment, geographical, political, economic, and social. Each distinctive culture has grown up within a given environmental framework that has left an indelible mark upon it. Both the richness and the peril of the modern world spring in part out of these circumstances.

It is the antithesis of voluntary cultural diversity, spontaneity, and respect for human rights and welfare that we find in the Nazi philosophy. The point of beginning with the German citizen today is the state; the line of his progress is violence to the individual; the goal of his policy is the enslavement of his neighbor. His is the bad-neighbor policy. We misrepresent German political thought if we suppose that the present war is merely a result of German reaction to the Treaty of Versailles. It is a result of German political and philosophical thinking and ambition for two hundred years. The Treaty of Versailles became a plausible pretext for reasserting an old philosophy. The record discloses that most republican leaders of postwar Germany gave only lip service to the principles of democracy and international cooperation. The solemn assurances given in October, 1918, when the defeat of Germany and her request for an armistice raised the question of democratic responsibility, lasted for fifteen years only. After that the government was no longer "free from arbitrary and irresponsible influence," and the promised responsibility of the Chancellor to the people came to an end.[2]

Versailles gave German leaders new examples of the frustration of German aims to conquer the world. The Nazi political program has its roots in something very deep in German life and history: a way of rationalizing greed and violence. Nothing has so clearly revealed the essential primitiveness of the German theories of government as the history of political thought in Germany for the past hundred years. Its "laws" of nation growth, its recent "science" of geopolitics which assumes that "political events depend upon the soil," its assertion that "determining forces which dictate the course of states" carry over into a mystical state of mind where "science ceases and belief begins" (Kjellén)—these are among the doctrines that are separated from democracy by an abyss so wide that today only war can bridge it.

Can any informed person now suppose that German leaders had a tenderer philosophy? The power makers, the architects of the German state, expressed themselves clearly and often on this theme. Hear the testimony of Bismarck on Alsace and Lorraine. He is not speaking in 1871 but in 1895:

> Their annexation was a geographical necessity. It is quite presumptuous to ask us to worry whether the Alsatians and Lorrainers want or do not want to be German. That is none of our business.[3]

If "the fatherland stands for war," as Treitschke concluded, the doctrines upon which Nazism are founded follow naturally. One cannot understand either the present-day Germany or the historical Germany who does not take the trouble to get at the root of the irreconcilable differences between them and us. No one can see the depravity of Nazi geopolitics who thinks that it is merely another way of reading political history and the political map.

We fight today a crooked and evil philosophy armed, in the

[2] Solf to Wilson, October 20, 1918. In *The German Delegation at the Paris Peace Conference,* by Alma Luckau (New York, 1941), p. 144.
[3] Address at Friedrichsruhe, April 24, 1895.

case of Germany, with continental power. A whole nation has been deceived and reduced to intellectual servitude by hokum. In our future plans and dealings we must take this fact into account. It has taken war, the concentration camp, the hostage killings, plundered Dutch, Belgian, Greek, and Polish peoples (among many), fifth-column technique, and all the rest to convince America how implacable and far-reaching are the means which the exponents of that evil philosophy are willing to employ.

Nine years ago I prepared a paper for the Washington meeting of the Pan American Institute of Geography and History entitled "A New Chapter in Pan-American Cartography." In it I proposed a program of cooperation that should reflect American political philosophy and the policy of the good neighbor in the field of scholarship. For urgent reasons I wish to put that philosophy, through quotation and otherwise, in contrast with the marauding spirit of German geopolitics that purports to be based on "laws" and that attempts to apply reason and so-called "scientific deduction" to the Nazi program of conquest and enslavement.

In this paper of 1935 I proposed a Pan-American Atlas on a cooperative basis. The exact text and the fate of the proposal are of some importance now because of subsequent events in Europe. It was not a proposal to learn how to use science to "conquer" Latin America after the fashion of the German geopolitikers, but how to work together for common ends, and specifically how to do so through cultural exchange, trade, and general economic improvement. The date of the paper is also important. At the time of its publication there was no new hemisphere policy of defense, Munich lay three years ahead, and the American public had no fear and little thought of war.

The joint research proposal begun in 1920 (the Millionth Map of Hispanic America) has grown steadily into a still wider cooperative project, embracing all the countries of the Western Hemisphere. Supported by source material from practically every government and private scientific association in Hispanic America and even by government appropriations from a few, used in the settlement of successive boundary disputes between sovereign states, the map with its many attendant publications has become a great international undertaking in *mutual* welfare.

In the very period in which this cooperative enterprise was being pushed forward vigorously, another set of social and political values was in process of formulation in Europe. By 1933 when Hitler took over control of Germany these values were fully deployed and exploited and became the basis of his program previously set out in detail in *Mein Kampf*. The background of the related discussion within Germany is of vital importance to us, both now and in our future dealings with the German people.

Slowly and almost against their will the American people became aroused to Nazi dangers. At first we thought of security in terms of the mollusk. The hemisphere was our shell. When danger became obvious, the public search began for the meaning of Nazi designs in terms of German political philosophy and historiography. When successive treacherous blows fell within the Western Hemisphere we could not fight back in Europe only or Japan only. We had to fight wherever there was fighting: our commitments suddenly became planetary. We and our sons began to sail great-circle courses of thought and action. The whole "wide improbable atlas" was opened daily as our military situation tied every neighborhood, large and small, to the rim of the world. Hitler's design was world dominion. We finally saw that our resistance must be as bold and far-flung as his design.

Thus all of us began to think geographically and to regard the map in terms of political ideas and systems. Port Moresby, Mayotte Island, and Dutch Harbor were regarded in terms that include all the lands and seas, the peoples and resources, the governments and ideologies that lie between. Suddenly we realized that even the remoter solitudes will not have their solitude restored after the war, and that victory this time means for America no resumption of something called "normal." We are obliged this time to think our way out as well as fight our way out of our international difficulties.

In the daily excitements that follow these realizations we are all strategists, statesmen, critics, and devisers. The boldness and imaginative quality that we urge upon our leaders find their counterpart in the rising flood of public comment on all international problems. This reflects commendable interest and enthusiasm in a free-speaking democracy. There is danger in it only when, under the guise of "science" or institutional name or academic rank, wholly unsound and uncritical conclusions are set forth that purport to be based on "law," or reason, or trained judgment, or "the lessons of history." Geopolitics has migrated from Germany to America, not from America to Germany, and even the most ignorant and fantastic misconceptions and political immoralities have been widely disseminated in its name, and truth has been given spurious labels.

There were forewarnings, even before Hitler came to power. We were then riding on a high tide of prosperity, and Hitler, by newspaper report, was a street fighter, house painter, and shrill demagogue. Hindenburg controlled Germany, we thought. The League of Nations was the focus of international interests. German philosophy and geopolitical ideas were remote and academic so far as popular interest was concerned.

In 1922 a German scholar, the late Alexander Supan, published the second edition of his political geography (first edition, 1918). In earlier years he had published a great work on the population of the earth based on a comprehensive assemblage of statistical material. Some of his later publications in physiography and colonial geography are also marked by scholarly qualities. His political geography, published after World War I, is colored by defeat. He gives his imagination full play and puts no restraint upon his prejudices. He searches for "system," for "laws" akin to those governing the physical world. My review of 1924 [4] referred to his work as follows:

It is characteristic of the German school of political geography that its logic so often rests upon mere classification, and the descent is not far from this to *obiter dicta* and the worship of ritual and

[4] *Geographical Review,* Vol. XIV (1924), pp. 665–666 (Alexander Supan, *Leitlinien der allgemeinen politischen Geographie: Naturlehre des Staates,* 2nd ed., edited by Erich Obst, Berlin and Leipzig, 1922).

mummery. There is much that is excellent in Supan's book, and to this we shall presently give full credit. Here, the point of emphasis is the spirit and logic of the work as a whole. The worst example of the illogical is in the first paragraph of the first page: institutions are the means of achieving civilization; the state furnishes the means of existence of such institutions; the state is the foundation of civilization or culture; one cannot think highly enough of the state.

I remarked further, with respect to his critique on boundaries:

Even if by some process of necromancy boundaries were adjusted on all frontiers to national needs and if proper economic advantages and political scope were given to every nation, the equilibrium would last but for a moment, just as in the case of an equal distribution of wealth among a whole population. Birth rates differ, industries and natural resources differ, vital energy and initiative differ. Inequalities arise from these and other causes, and strife and shifting boundaries once more occur. There is virtue in the argument of "organic boundaries" and the philosophy of *Lebensraum*, but they are open to abuse like the arguments based on history and military necessity of which much use was sought to be made at the Paris Conference of 1919. Curzon's argument regarding the protection of the Indian frontiers is the inevitable one employed in advocating "natural frontiers" and in following a purely territorial policy.

Supan's book ends on a bitter note that refers particularly to the loss of the German colonies as a violation of any possible economic system. He inquires meaningly, "Cannot Slavs and Germans unite as a counterpoise to Anglo-Saxons, Latins, and Japanese?"

In 1934 there was published the third volume of a trilogy of books entitled "Macht und Erde" ("Power and Earth"), prepared by the Work Group for the *Zeitschrift für Geopolitik*, founded by Karl Haushofer in 1924. Haushofer was a contributing editor. The first edition of my book on problems in political geography, entitled *The New World,* had appeared in 1921, and Maull, one of the authors of "Macht und Erde," states that the trilogy was prepared as the German answer to *The New World.*

The method of my book was to deal realistically with the

political problems of the postwar world. Its philosophy was one of gradualness of change by rational means. It interposed no ideological preconceived "system" between a problem and its solution in a practical world in which historical accident, not design only, had played so large a part. It sought to analyze real situations rather than justify any one of several conflicting nationalistic policies. Its morality was a responsive and responsible world association based on justice as given fully in the first chapter of the fourth edition (1928). Looking at the competitive world, deeply shaken by the colossal losses of the war, it emphasized the need for "experimentation in the field of cooperative [planning]."

It was this point of view that was the object of attack by the advocates of geopolitics in Germany. The word "rational" means one thing to us and the opposite to the German geopolitical school. For gradualness they would substitute violence. By cooperation they mean that the cooperator eats the cooperee, on the theory of racial superiority. If there is to be a world association, a "new order," Germany must set its terms and impose its unique interpretation. If there is competition for resources and markets, the theory of *Lebensraum* gives Germany priority and justifies seizure. The only political experiment that has united Germany is war.

Deeply disturbed by the rapid growth in Germany of the pseudo science of geopolitics and alarmed by its territorial theories and implications as displayed in widest panorama in the *Zeitschrift für Geopolitik,* I attacked the school and its work in a group review in 1927.[5] The review opens with the sentence, "Political geography is still merely a term, not a science." Regional description and statistical and cartographic techniques are recognized as the special tools of the geographer in setting out the intimate life of communities. The review continues: "Some of the most important elements of culture seem not to get into the political geographies of continental Europe, namely, ethics, good manners, the elevation of fairness into a fine art, *cultured* living!"

[5] *Geogr. Rev.,* Vol. XVII (1927), pp. 511–513.

Maull's "Politische Geographie" was specially selected for condemnation in my review because, as I then stated, "to put facts into a series, to invent mnemonic schemes is to achieve neither learning nor science." Such a mnemonic scheme is his table of nations classified by area and population, which puts Liberia and Norway in the same group, likewise Afghanistan and Chile. Colonial quotients, so called, represent the same kind of error: England 8.4, Germany 0.2, only gives a historical fact a scientifically sounding name! As if all colonial quotients should be equal to be "scientific" and just, as between colonial powers.

Downright dishonesty naturally follows the use of such terms and arguments. The July, 1942, issue of *Foreign Affairs* has an article by H. W. Weigert on "Haushofer and the Pacific" (pp. 732–742).[6] Haushofer is quoted as criticizing the United States because its "extensive colonial space structure" makes it unable to understand the population pressure of Central Europe and Eastern Asia. The article continues: " 'It is an exceptional case,' writes Haushofer, 'when an American, Isaiah Bowman, becomes impressed by the population density of Japan and admits that "it must overflow its boundaries." ' Haushofer forgets to say, however," adds Weigert, "that Bowman added, 'if not by people then by exports.' This instance of Haushofer's utter disregard of all attempts to solve such problems by international economic coöperation is characteristic," he concludes.

The phrase "utter disregard" is much too weak. It is utterly dishonest, unless we believe in constant war, to talk in terms of "population pressure" as a thing to be relieved by theft of territory from a neighbor. Modern transport, credit facilities, technologic equipment and skill, expanding demands of human societies with a rising standard of living have given every nation access to relief from such pressure through industry and trade. It is not strictly true that when Japan exports a bale of silk to America she exports a man, but there is a large measure of truth in it. Japan had access and relief as a result of World War I and took full advantage of it.

[6] Cf. chap. V, article 25, p. 395.

But a rapidly growing share in world trade was not enough. Japanese imperialism came into full flower when industrial expansion and trade success put into the hands of Japanese militarists the tools of territorial conquest. Whether we take territories won in the fateful year of 1931 (Manuchuria) or those earlier conquests of Formosa and Korea, the subsequent relief of population pressure in Japan has not been through emigration but through trade. Japanese migration and settlement have been negligible.

In 1934 I said of doctrinaire writings in the international field in which geographical facts are marshaled to support political claims and philosophies:

> If the economics of Poland collides head-on with the economics of Germany we cannot merely turn to the map and rearrange its parts as if we were free to plant supine peoples upon vacant territory. The historical commitment is there and we cannot ignore it.[7]

Why can we not rearrange the map at will if we are strong enough to enforce our will? We can if we accept Treitschke's doctrine: "The triumph of the strong over the weak is the inexorable law of life." If we believe that there is an inescapable compulsion in strength to assert itself to the advantage of its owner, then we move ahead remorselessly to do what greed suggests and power makes possible.

In my view the "geographical-basis-of-power" idea of Ratzel, as set forth in the first edition of his political geography (1897), is completely unsound. In Germany it has become a ritual, something that one believes, something useful because it fits the national ambition to conquer and govern in the name of *Lebensraum,* a concept that has been expanded from its earlier purely descriptive economic meaning to one that gives territorial expansion a pseudoscientific justification. Thus expanded it has become one more catchword in the jargon of Hitler's National Socialism. The relations of land and society are not capable of

[7] Isaiah Bowman, *Geography in Relation to the Social Sciences* (*Report of the Commission on the Social Studies, Amer. Hist. Assn.,* Part 5). New York, Chicago, etc., 1934, p. 212.

such isolated "scientific" expression. Society is a growing complex. "We deal with rapidly developing and diverse human societies in relation to an earth of which we have an ever-expanding knowledge." [8]

In the face of this perversion of fact to philosophy I advocated the study of real groups of *men* rather than easy book generalization about *mankind*. Whether we are dealing with geographic relations, demographic data, or economic statistics, we are only in the fact-and-tool stage of investigation so far as national states and national policies are concerned. Scholarship alone supplies certain definite imperatives in policy making, notably in the fields of conservation, law, and public health, to mention but three examples; but the policies that are adopted represent the people's lethargy or will, foresight or the lack of it, justice or injustice, and the power or powerlessness of leaders in shaping public opinion. A national policy is the "diagonal of contending varieties" of the people's thought and action. It cannot be otherwise under the rule of "consent of the governed." The concept of justice did not come out of a library, however important libraries are in conserving the concept and disseminating and expanding knowledge about it. The several fields of scholarship furnish in and of themselves no end philosophy of politics, no guaranteed political design. They can, however, suggest possibilities and dangers in the realm of political relations, choices, moralities, purposes, and powers, beginning with the record of human experimentation.

Today we are compelled to draw a wide circle around our national problems, now inextricably commingled with the problems of sixty other nations. English experience supplies a useful moral. Gladstone said in 1869 that England should have no joint interpreters:

> England should keep entire in her own hands the means of estimating her own obligations upon the various states of facts as they arise; she should not foreclose and narrow her own liberty of choice by declarations made to other Powers. . . .

[8] *Ibid.*, p. xi.

England thought otherwise on the morning of September 3, 1939, when Neville Chamberlain reported that Germany had begun the invasion of Poland and announced: "We are at war." Intervention and withdrawal had marked the traditional policy of England in continental Europe. Thus we, too, occasionally emerge from our Western Hemisphere shell on the principle of limited liability only. This time we say that our emergence is permanent, that we must now make sure of our future, that we are only as imperishable as our resolution. These are polemical assertions, however. They are not inspired by divine revelations. Shall we be forever secure against "the resistless forces of re-birth," or escape the weakening effect of blind reliance upon "democracy" as a magical doctrine?

The tremulous balance of international forces will vex us at the end of the war. We shall be confused and fatigued by the complexities and responsibilities in which war has involved us. We shall want things certain and simple again: we once called it "normalcy." There is no sure "science" to bring us out of these new deeps of international difficulty. Geopolitics is simple and sure, but, as disclosed in German writings and policy, it is also illusion, mummery, an apology for theft. Scientific geography deepens the understanding. But, like history or chemistry, it has no ready-made formulas for national salvation through scientifically "demonstrated" laws. There are only two "laws" that will guarantee permanent peace in a world in which the choice lies between freedom and slavery: justice based on the doctrine of human rights, and the cooperative exercise of power to enforce justice.

4

The Balance of Power

By QUINCY WRIGHT

QUINCY WRIGHT, born in Medford, Mass. A.M., University of Illinois, 1913, Ph.D., 1915. Professor of International Law, University of Chicago. Author: *Control of American Foreign Relations,* 1922; *Mandates Under the League of Nations,* 1930; *The Causes of War and the Conditions of Peace,* 1935; *A Study of War,* 1942, and many other studies on international law and relations.

"The Balance of Power" is a revised version of an essay published in the *American Journal of International Law,* Vol. XXXVII (1943), pp. 97–103, under the title "International Law and the Balance of Power."

The work of the Congress of Vienna has recently been described as "a remarkable achievement in the art and technique of peace making." [1] There may be some dissent from this judgment among liberals who recall the suppression of democratic and nationality movements during the generation which followed, and among internationalists who recall that this suppression led to violent explosions after 1848, and a generation of international and civil wars during which, as Count Beust remarked, Europe ceased to exist as a unity.[2]

Nevertheless, this judgment can find much historical support. The century from Waterloo to the Marne witnessed the most rapid increase in population and welfare in European history, and the least war in Europe of any century since the Renaissance and possibly since the *Pax Romana.*[3] The underlying structure of the Peace of Vienna was the balance of power. The States were so bounded and organized that aggression could not suc-

[1] Joachim von Elbe, *American Journal of International Law,* Vol. XXXVI (1942), p. 474. See also Guglielmo Ferrero, *Peace and War* (London, 1933), p. 128; Ferrero, *The Reconstruction of Europe: Talleyrand and the Congress of Vienna, 1814–1815* (New York, 1941), pp. 338, 345.

[2] The Austrian Minister's *bon mot,* "Je ne vois plus d'Europe," was actually made in 1870 in answer to a Russian suggestion that Europe should intervene in the Franco-Prussian crisis. Friedrich Ferdinand, Count von Beust, *Memoirs,* transl. Henry de Worms, London, 1887, Vol. II, p. 205.

[3] Q. Wright, *A Study of War* (Chicago, 1942), pp. 237, 256, 271, 639: on population changes, see *Ibid.,* pp. 210, 466, 644–646.

ceed unless it was so moderated and so directed that the prevailing opinion of the Powers approved it. Such approval was generally given to the Balkan revolts which gradually disintegrated the Ottoman Empire, to the Belgian revolt which separated that country from the Netherlands, to Prussian and Sardinian aggressions which united modern Germany and Italy, and to numerous aggressions in Africa, Asia, and the Pacific which increased European empires, and extended European civilization to these areas.

Among the wars of this century, the Chinese Taiping rebellion (1850–1864), the American Civil War (1861–1865) and the Lopez War in Paraguay (1865–1870) were the most costly in human life. There was more war and conquest, more loss of life and property through war, in North America, in South America, and in Asia than in Europe.[4] Under the balance of power system, Europe was relatively tranquil and prosperous. The remainder of the world was more restless and belligerent, though, with the exception of Africa, it shared in the increases in population and prosperity which characterized the world as a whole during this period.

Many feel a nostalgic desire to return to the conditions of that fortunate century. Many point out that the principles of national self-determination and international organization, upon which the Treaty of Versailles was based, proved less enduring than the principles of legitimacy and balance of power which underlay the Vienna settlement. Recent books and articles have set forth

[4] In addition to the Taiping, American Civil, and Lopez wars, in each of which the war deaths were over 600,000, there were six wars during the period in which such losses were from 100,000 to 200,000 (Crimean, 1854–1856; Italian, 1859; Franco-Prussian, 1870–1871; Russo-Turkish, 1878–1879; Russo-Japanese, 1904–1905; and Balkan, 1912–1913), and three wars in which such losses were from 30,000 to 60,000 (Russo-Turkish, 1828–1829; Austro-Prussian, 1866; and South African, 1899–1901). Of these 12 most serious wars, 2 were fought in the Americas, 1 in Africa, 2 in the Far East, 4 in the Near East, and 3 in Western and Central Europe. Of a total of 87 wars during this period, 17 were fought in North and Middle America, 10 in South America, 7 in South and Central Africa, 8 in the Far East, 8 in the Middle East, 20 in the Near East, and 17 in Western and Central Europe. See Q. Wright, *Op. cit.*, pp. 644–646; Samuel Dumas and K. O. Vedel-Petersen, *Losses of Life Caused by War* (London, 1923), pp. 40–59.

with skill the geographic, economic, and strategic conditions which statesmen should keep in mind under the assumption that the balance of power will be the political basis of the settlement after World War II.[5]

For these reasons it is important to consider whether the conditions which made the balance of power a successful system of world politics in the nineteenth century still prevail. Has there been adequate reason for the widespread revolt against that system which has developed in the twentieth century?

In the writer's opinion the balance of power can no longer function effectively. The alternatives which the world faces are an imperial organization of the world by conquest, or a federalistic organization of the world by general consent. These alternatives constitute the issue about which the war is being fought.

It is important that the citizen adjust his thinking both to the kind of world which is likely to emerge and to the possible world which he would prefer. If absolute rights of territorial sovereignty and self-help, if national policies of intervention and neutrality, and if a world political structure of balanced military power no longer accord with practice, with conditions, or with human interests, if a new political structure of the world is imminent, important modifications in the principles both of international law and of international politics are to be anticipated.

Political and legal systems influence each other, and both are influenced, though sometimes rather slowly, by economic, social, and technical changes. We may be sure that the political system after World War II will be influenced by the traditional concepts of international law, though we may hope that it will be influenced in greater measure by the requirements of new economic, social, and technical conditions. We may, however, expect that the direction of change in international law will be influenced primarily by the system of world politics which pre-

[5] Nicholas J. Spykman, *America's Strategy in World Politics* (New York, 1942); Arnold Wolfers, "Anglo-American Postwar Co-operation and the Interests of Europe," *American Political Science Review,* Vol. XXXVI, p. 36 (Aug., 1942); Guglielmo Ferrero, *The Principles of Power: The Great Political Crises of History* (New York, 1942).

vails. By world politics is meant the interrelationships of the actual centers of political power.

The most significant changes in the nineteenth century were the inventions in communication and transportation, the systematic application of industrial and geographic division of labor, the tremendous increases in production and in population, the rise of ideas of democracy and of nationality, and finally the industrialization and totalitarianization of war.[6] These changes were not entirely independent of one another. The increase in communication and transportation resulting from inventions influenced the division of labor, the increases in population, production, and trade, and the character of war. The progress of democracy and the increase of wealth stimulated inventiveness. The rise of nationalism influenced and was influenced by changes in the character of economy, of war, and of communication.

It is not, however, to be inferred that these movements were all consistent with one another. Nationalism at times supported, and at times opposed, democracy and liberty. Both democracy and international trade found their progress halted by the totalitarianization of war and the exaggerations of nationalism. Whatever may have been the causes and the interrelationships of these changes, their reality is susceptible of statistical demonstration, and their combined influence has been hostile to the successful functioning of the balance of power system.

That system worked well during the nineteenth century because one Power, Great Britain, was in a peculiarly favorable position to act as a balancer and did so act; because governments in general were free to direct policy rapidly and intelligently according to balance of power principles; because trade, industry, and agriculture were relatively unaffected by diplomacy and war; and because wars could usually be localized and neutrality was frequently practicable. The great changes of the twentieth century affected all these conditions adversely. Britain's island base has been made vulnerable by the airplane and the subma-

[6] These tendencies can be traced back to the Renaissance period, but they became much more important during the nineteenth century.

rine; its navy has been made less effective for blockade because of these inventions and various changes in naval architecture; its capacity to operate the balance of power efficiently has been weakened by the increasing influence of democracy in the conduct of foreign policy; its free commercial system and its wealth have been impaired by the governmentalizing tendency of nationalism and of total war; its relative power position has been diminished by the rise of extra-European Great Powers (the United States and Japan). Britain is no longer in a position to throw a determining influence one way or the other in order to maintain the balance while it, itself, remains invulnerable.

It has been suggested that the United States might step into the role of balancer.[7] While less vulnerable than Britain to either military or economic attack, the United States is politically even less able to make the rapid and secret maneuvers upon which a successful balancing of power depends. Elihu Root pointed out in 1917:[8]

> Because democracies are not fitted to conduct foreign affairs as they were conducted in de Tocqueville's day, the prevalence of democracy throughout the world makes inevitable a change in the conduct of foreign affairs. Such affairs when conducted by democratic governments must necessarily be marked by the absence of those undertakings and designs, and those measures combined with secrecy, prosecuted with perseverance for which he declares democracy to be unfit.

"Democracies," according to Root, "are absolutely dependent for their existence upon the preservation of law." American foreign policy has in fact developed upon the assumption that the government, limited by the check and balance system of the Constitution, neither could nor ought to play the game of power politics. In the past, policies of isolation and neutrality, combined with reliance upon law and arbitration, were in the main satisfactory; but they failed under the new conditions of the twentieth century world. These policies were in considerable measure

[7] Spykman, *Op. cit.*, pp. 468–472.

[8] Elihu Root, "The Effect of Democracy on International Law," *Proceedings Am. Soc. Int. Law, 1917*, pp. 7, 9.

abandoned after the Spanish War, and the effort to return to "normalcy" during the 1920's led to both economic and political disaster.

The history of the 1930's demonstrated the vast superiority of despotisms over democracies in the game of power politics. Hitler, Mussolini, and Japan were able to hold together and to divide and confuse the democracies, while they augmented their armaments and took one strategic position after another. In an age in which democracy insists on extending the influence of public opinion to the control of foreign as well as domestic affairs, democracies cannot compete successfully in a world governed by balance of power principles. They may eventually fight successfully, but they can neither frighten nor appease the despotisms, they can neither prevent nor localize war, and to win war they must sacrifice much of their democracy. Under conditions of total war and the balance of power system, democracy can function successfully neither in time of peace nor in time of war. If democracy and human liberty are to survive, the nations that espouse these principles must find some device other than the balance of power to give them political security.

The balance of power system, under contemporary conditions, is even more hostile to international trade and free economy than it is to democracy and liberty. In the nineteenth century wars seldom involved over 10 per cent of the economy and man power of the nation. Internal trade ordinarily went on as usual, and even international trade was in large measure protected by rules of maritime law. Belligerents found it in their interest to distinguish the armed forces and the government of the enemy from its merchants, workers, and farmers, since the latter contributed little to the military effort. Exemptions of the latter from the rigors of war, though never pushed as far as Franklin would have liked, were important, and on the whole observed. Modern war, however, absorbs over half the economy and population of the State. The nation is mobilized for war, and the government directs economy and trade. Under these conditions no class of the enemy can be exempt from the rigors of war, and the neutrals must be prevented from even indirect trade with the enemy. Economic life is transformed during war, and military preparation for total war requires that even in time of peace nations make themselves as self-sufficient as possible. Governments must intervene in the productive process to assure that war materials and factories will be available. In short, the balance of power system requires under modern conditions of war that every nation governmentalize its economy, devote its economy to increasing its power, forgo the benefits of geographical division of labor, lower its general standard of living; and it increases the strain between have and have-not nations, thereby adding to the economic causes of war.

With such compulsions, neutrals may find peace worse than war, and all Powers with sufficient military potentiality to influence the result may find it in their interests or be forced to enter the combat. Under a balance of power system, wars involving great Powers have always tended to spread. There have been very few during the last three centuries which did not eventually involve all of the Great Powers of the time. The rate of spread, however, has markedly increased during the last generation with the shrinking of the world, the development of interdependence, and the industrialization of war.

From these considerations, it seems clear that the balance of power as the structure of world politics is incompatible with democracy, with free enterprise, with welfare economy, and with peace. It has even come to be incompatible with the international law which, during most of the nineteenth century, supported it. These are the conditions which citizens and governments face. Nostalgic sentiments, ancient customs, and artful dialectics will not modify the influence of modern inventions in communications, transportation, and war. Nor will they eliminate the existence of a world population dependent for its living upon an extensive international trade and demanding more freedom, more political influence, and more prosperity.

It was not utopianism which led Wilson and Smuts in 1918, and has led Churchill and Roosevelt in 1941, to encourage the public to believe that the balance of power was to be superseded. These men understood that the conditions of the world made that system no longer adequate. We have witnessed during the twentieth century the familiar lag of political and legal adjustment behind economic, social, and technical changes. The insight of Wilson and Smuts was not appreciated, and efforts were made to rehabilitate the balance of power, with the results which were to be anticipated. It is to be hoped that the insight of the present leaders of democracy will be more widely understood.

5

The Peaceful Solution of Boundary Problems

By S. Whittemore Boggs

S. Whittemore Boggs, born in Coolidge, Kansas. B.L., Berea, 1909; A.M., Columbia, 1924. Geographer U.S. Department of State since 1924. Technical Adviser U.S. delegation, Conference for Codification of International Law, The Hague, 1930. Official delegate, international geographical congresses, Cambridge, Paris, Warsaw, Lima.

Author, *International Boundaries: A Study of Boundary Functions and Problems* (Columbia University Press, 1940), and of articles in professional periodicals.

"The Peaceful Solution of Boundary Problems" is Chapter XI of the author's *International Boundaries,* with minor revisions.

A glare as of klieg lights is playing upon international boundaries, and the attention of peoples is being focused upon boundary problems. Many of the problems are very complicated and not generally understood, and are therefore easily misrepresented by slogans and catchwords which may have little bearing on the fundamental issues involved. Boundaries have been subjected to extraordinary pressures and stresses, and anxious millions lived for years in dread of what might happen. The need for peaceful solutions of all boundary problems is manifest.

If a stranger to our planet were to have explained to him how great are the boundary problems that harass mankind, and if he were to visit a typical boundary and to observe how inconspicuous it is (almost imperceptible in many cases), he would probably be dumbfounded. He would doubtless inquire how such an artificial, man-made line could prevent men from visiting their friends and neighbors and from buying and selling goods to their obviously mutual advantage across these unfenced frontiers. He would miss the things that really divide—differences of language, traditions, and social organization, and an insufficiency of human understanding that transcends the narrow limitations of present international boundaries.

The disturbing influence of frontier questions is usually persistent, as recorded, for example, in the treaty of 1881 between Colombia and Venezuela in these words: ". . . being desirous to put an end to the question of territorial boundaries which, for the space of fifty years, has unsettled their relations of sincere friendship, and natural, ancient, and indispensable fraternity. . . ."[1] The "sincere friendship" of many nations has been clouded for years by boundary controversies.

The boundary problems that disturb relations between contiguous states have many origins. In the newer countries, where boundaries have not yet been precisely determined and where too little geography was known when the line was first defined, problems issue from unavoidably vague definition of the boundary, or from delays in surveying and marking upon the ground astronomic boundaries that mean nothing until they are so marked.[2] Problems likewise arise in desires for access to the sea, to means of communication, or to source materials. Elsewhere boundary problems spring from local incidents which may expand into national issues unless promptly and effectually handled.

Where a territorial claim is definitely involved, there is most likely to be an appeal to history. In general, there is recourse to historical antecedents in relation to boundaries where friction has already developed, whereas history is forgotten where the boundary operates smoothly and satisfactorily. In other words, the past is recalled chiefly when difficulties arise in the present functioning of the boundary and when dissatisfaction breeds trouble and leads to rationalization of the desire for some sort of relief and change.

That seemingly intolerable boundary situations are frequently not the offshoot of local conditions should not be overlooked. They may be the result of policies adopted at the capital of one state or at the capitals of both states, perhaps with little appreciation of the human factors of the frontier populations.

[1] Treaty between Colombia and Venezuela, Sept. 14, 1881; English transl. *British and Foreign State Papers,* Vol. LXXIII, p. 1107.

[2] See Israel C. Russell, "Geography and International Boundaries," *Bulletin of American Geographical Soc. of N.Y.,* Vol. XXXV, pp. 150–151 (Apr., 1903); Sir Thomas H. Holdich, *Boundaries in Europe and the Near East* (London, 1918), p. x.

Whatever the origin of a boundary problem, peaceful settlement is more necessary now than ever before. The solution of international boundary questions by peaceful means may be treated in three categories:

(1) Peaceful settlement of disputes concerning boundaries which have not hitherto been precisely defined and demarcated;
(2) Peaceful modification of boundaries already definitely established, concerning the location of which there is no dispute, the shift in the boundaries being made to the mutual advantage of both countries;
(3) Peaceful solution of problems relating to established boundaries, by modification or simplification of their functions, but without shifting the boundaries themselves.

BOUNDARIES THAT HAVE NOT BEEN DEFINITELY ESTABLISHED

The definition of a boundary in words in a treaty or other agreement is little assurance that disputes will not arise regarding its application to the surface of the earth. Until a boundary commission has made a survey, erected monuments, and made a report (which may perhaps be accepted formally by the governments, by treaty or protocol), disagreement may occur regarding a surprising number of questions. If the boundary is described as following a river, questions may arise concerning the sovereignty of islands, or the course of the river at the time the treaty was negotiated, and whether or not the changes in course have occurred by avulsion or accretion; and in the absence of accurate maps or aerial photographs (as of the date of the treaty) there may be no sure means of ascertaining the earlier course of the river.

If the boundary follows a line in the mountains, disputes may arise concerning the location of the watershed line (perhaps in an area of interior drainage) or concerning the crest of the main range. Even a geometric or astronomic line may give rise to dispute, if an extended network of precise geodetic surveying, to which the boundary survey may be tied, is not already available.

Boundaries which have not been fixed upon the ground may,

therefore, be the source of problems that may assume large proportions. The peaceful solution of such problems often requires treatment quite different from that of questions relating to boundaries definitely and indisputably established.

The procedures to which recourse may be had in boundary problems are the same as in other international difficulties. Direct negotiations between the two governments concerned are almost always tried first. If the gulf of misunderstanding is too great to be spanned by direct negotiations and if good relations are strained or interrupted, one or more third countries, through their respective departments of foreign affairs, may tender their good offices or may consent to mediate between the two countries directly concerned. Lastly, the disputant countries may resort to arbitration, and undertake to find an arbitrator who is mutually acceptable and who will assume the responsibility.

For a third country to assume the obligations involved in exercising good offices, mediating, or arbitrating in a boundary dispute is sometimes a more thankless task than would be imagined. The feelings of people in both countries may have been aroused or may later be incited until the general conviction in each country is that a decision awarding less than that country's total claim is a denial of historic justice. The mediator or arbitrator consequently runs the risk of becoming unpopular in one or both countries which he has consented to serve. The refinement of detail involved, the infinite patience, tact, and skill required in keeping the disputant parties in a mood to continue negotiations, or to accept decisions or concessions which are made in their own best interests, are quite beyond the comprehension of the proverbial "man in the street." The task is easier and less hazardous if mediation or arbitration is undertaken by international action instead of by a single country, and is rendered still simpler if the disputants agree to a minimum area or to a very restricted problem to be subject to mediation or arbitration. The importance of maintaining or restoring peace, however, in so far as it affects the general interests of the mediating or arbitrating power and of many other nations as well, may make it worth while to assume the risks entailed in tendering good offices or in accepting the role of mediator or arbitrator.

The almost infinite variety of boundary problems, the mass of topographic and human factors to be mastered in all their geographic complexity, and the legacy of historic associations corroborate the observation of Lord Curzon:

> It would be futile to assert that an exact Science of Frontiers has been or is ever likely to be evolved: for no one law can possibly apply to all nations or peoples, to all Governments, all territories, or all climates. The evolution of Frontiers is perhaps an art rather than a science, so plastic and malleable are its forms and manifestations. . . .[3]

The question may well be asked, "What sort of man is qualified to settle a major boundary controversy?" This was asked of an eminent European statesman who had wide experience on boundary commissions in Europe and the Near East. "The clever man," he replied, recalling his experience in dealing with politicians, military men, economists, geographers, and others in proposing and making boundary settlements; he observed that any specialist is likely to have a narrow point of view and to overemphasize certain factors instead of considering all the pertinent aspects of the problem.

For a peaceful solution of a difficult problem relating to an unsettled boundary, the wisdom of Solomon is often needed. With all the technical assistance that is available, to let the major decisions be made by one who tempers the legal and tangible factors with shrewd and human wisdom is very desirable. The acceptance of a decision relating to so vital a matter as a national boundary may depend upon confidence in the impartiality and integrity of character of an arbitrator or of commission members even more than upon competence in all of the relevant fields of technical knowledge.

[3] George Nathaniel, Lord Curzon of Kedleston, *Frontiers* (Romanes Lecture, 1907—2d ed., Oxford, 1908), p. 53.

Whoever finds himself called upon to settle a boundary dispute will experience difficulty in tapping the best literature for enlightenment and assistance. Much could be done to make available the best boundary literature. Something in the English language, covering the entire field, is greatly to be desired.[4]

PEACEFUL MODIFICATION OF ESTABLISHED BOUNDARIES

Many serious problems concern definitely established and monumented boundaries the *location* of which arouses no dispute whatever. Some of those problems could be solved, or the situations could be ameliorated, if the boundary were shifted to another position. It is generally assumed that such boundary changes can not be made except by means of war. However, occasional modifications of established boundaries are made without the use or the threat of force but solely for the mutual advantage of the nations directly interested. A few instances are noted to point the way to other peaceful improvements in established boundaries.

We should pass over the numerous instances of minor rectifications of established boundaries, as they do not sufficiently involve the principle to which we refer. That such minor modifications be made, however, is important. France and Germany, for

[4] Lapradelle, *La Frontière,* is probably the best general text and the best organized (except for the lack of an index): it treats systematically the various stages of delimitation, has a chapter on the frontier regime, and appendices such as one of instructions to a boundary commission; it also contains a table of boundary arbitrations, 1714–1923. Adami, *National Frontiers,* likewise contains a wealth of material of practical importance in settling a boundary dispute: the footnotes in this volume and Lapradelle are unusually good. Moore, *Digest of International Law,* Vol. I, pp. 615–766, is useful. For an excellent series of brief notes on international arbitrations, including a number of boundary arbitrations, see the section entitled "Instances of International Settlement Involving the Application of the Principle of International Arbitration," pp. 769–917 (covering the period 1783–1903) in Darby, *International Tribunals;* in the same volume see also (pp. 520–44) "Rules for International Arbitration," by Marquis Corsi. (A handbook on boundary-making, by Stephen B. Jones will probably be published by the Carnegie Endowment for International Peace, in 1944. This manual deals with the practical stages in boundary-making, as a handbook for statesmen, treaty editors, and demarcators.)

example, made certain rectifications in their boundary in 1925 and 1937.[5]

A notable example of a peaceful boundary change is one made by Belgium and Portugal in their territories in Africa in 1927.[6] As a part of a comprehensive adjustment of colonial questions, Portugal ceded to Belgium about one square mile of territory near the mouth of the Congo River adjacent to the port of Matadi in the Belgian Congo; this was to enable Belgium to enlarge its port facilities and to make feasible the construction of a railroad from Matadi to Léopoldville on the Congo. In exchange for that small but very important territory, Belgium ceded about 1,350 square miles of the Congo to enlarge the territory of Portuguese Angola, with certain understandings regarding Portuguese railroad building through that territory, on the line from Benguela, on the coast, to the Katanga region. In spite of the exceptional inequality of the areas, they were regarded as approximately of equal value, and both countries believed that they profited by this exchange of territory. This African territory, it is true, involved no complicating historical factors such as there are in Europe.

Another example taken from Africa is the modification of the eastern end of the boundary between Egypt and the Anglo-Egyptian Sudan. By the treaty of 1899,[7] the boundary followed the 22d parallel of north latitude eastward to the Red Sea. The astronomic line was found to cut across tribal territories; a zigzag line traversing the treaty boundary and known as the "administrative boundary," was therefore adopted, without treaty formality. This line is more commonly represented on maps, although some maps and atlases show the treaty line; occasionally a map shows both lines.

[5] Treaty between France and Germany, signed Aug. 14, 1925, ratifications of which were exchanged May 15, 1928 (*Journal officiel de la République française,* May 19, 1928, pp. 5555–81); Treaty between France and Germany signed Dec. 16, 1937 (*Reichsgesetzblatt,* Teil II, 1938, No. 33, Aug. 25, 1938, pp. 393–414, with sketch maps).

[6] Convention of July 22, 1927.

[7] Agreement between the British government and the government of the Khedive of Egypt, relative to the future administration of the Sudan, signed at Cairo, Jan. 19, 1899, Hertslet, *Map of Africa by Treaty,* Vol. II, p. 620.

Modifications of their common boundary made by Turkey and Iran (Persia) afford another example of changes in a definitely fixed frontier. Here several villages have been exchanged to the mutual advantage of both countries.[8]

The exchange of territories effected by Bolivia and Peru in 1909 deserves special note.[9] The arbitral award, which by the treaty between Bolivia and Peru, December 30, 1902, was to be without appeal, was rendered by President Figueroa Alcorta of Argentina, July 9, 1909. The area previously in dispute between the two countries was large, and the arbitral award fixed a compromise boundary which could have been demarcated as the definitive boundary of Bolivia and Peru. Desiring a different line, however, Bolivia and Peru followed a course worthy of emulation. They first accepted the award, by the Polo-Bustamante protocol of September 15, 1909, in which they stated "their entire satisfaction with the award." The line thereby became, in a real sense, an "established boundary." Two days later, by a protocol for the exchange of territories and the rectification of the frontier, they modified the boundary to their mutual satisfaction.[10] That boundary, with minor adjustments, has since been demarcated.

The difficulties in making boundary modifications of appreciable magnitude in populated areas usually seem so great as to preclude serious consideration. When the advantages in shifting the lines are manifest, the obstacles should come to be regarded

[8] The boundary was definitely established in 1913–14. The changes were made in 1932 and relate to villages in three areas along the frontier. See "The Turkish-Iranian Boundary," *Geographical Journal,* Vol. XCI, pp. 57–59 (Jan., 1938), with map.

[9] See *International Boundaries,* by the author, p. 84, and map, p. 83.

[10] The problem of establishing the Bolivia-Peru boundary in the period 1902–9 was complicated by contemporary developments relating to the Bolivia-Brazil and Brazil-Peru boundaries, with which we are not concerned here. For an account of the Bolivia-Peru arbitration and the 1909 protocols, with brief descriptions of the several boundaries and citations to documentary sources, see Ireland, *Boundaries, Possessions and Conflicts in South America,* pp. 103–7. For a convenient English translation of the arbitration treaty, the award, and the two 1909 protocols, see *British and Foreign State Papers,* Vol. C, pp. 803–4, and Vol. CV, pp. 572–81. For a map showing the 1909 protocol line and the differences of the 1909 award line see Boggs, *International Boundaries,* Figure 12, p. 83.

as less formidable than they now appear; it is fortunate when there is a minimum of grandiose talk and a maximum of common sense and good will. If such changes are made when animosities have not been aroused, as they are by war, the people living adjacent to the line can usually adjust themselves without great difficulty to the new frontier, especially if the modification is in their interest.

THE SOLUTION OF BOUNDARY PROBLEMS WITHOUT BOUNDARY CHANGE

The insistent demand for modification of the boundary is, in some areas, based on the uncritical assumption that, merely because the boundary is working unsatisfactorily, it could be made to function more smoothly if it were shifted to another position. The functions of the boundary have been taken for granted as normal and unchangeable, and change of locus of the frontier is therefore imagined to be the only solution of the problem.

In broad perspective, however, we have observed [11] that the functions of boundaries vary greatly the world over, and that they have passed through a long evolution and have, in fact, greatly changed within the last two or three decades, particularly in Europe. Change of boundary functions, chiefly by progressive simplification, offers the surest relief from many of the burdens associated with present boundaries the world over.

The steps taken in the direction of simplification of boundary functions were wholly inadequate, especially in the interwar period in Europe. The existence of the need was recognized, and sincere attempts were made in the direction of simplification of customs procedures, passport practices, communications and transit regulation, transmission of hydroelectric power, and so forth. The retrospective view shows how futile were these efforts to stem the tide that had strongly set in toward proliferation of regulatory and restrictive practices.

[11] See Boggs, *International Boundaries,* especially chap. I, "The Changing Role of Boundaries in a Changing World," and chap. VI, "European Boundaries and Their Functions."

Solution of boundary problems without shifting the boundaries themselves may be effected in several ways, chiefly:

(1) By simplifying the regulations applying to a *single boundary*, through bilateral action—including the reduction of tariffs and the simplification of customs and passport formalities.

(2) By *regional* simplification of boundary functions, as for Europe or a large portion of the Continent, or for the Western Hemisphere as a whole.

(3) By formation of economic and other practical associations, which may override one or more international boundaries and embrace parts of two or more nations, or entire continents, based upon whatever sort of regionalism is pertinent, according to the problem or interest involved. Wholehearted action in the direction of such integrations is needed in many parts of the world.

ADAPTING THE ROLE OF BOUNDARIES TO MODERN REQUIREMENTS

In common with economic and political problems of all sorts, questions relating to international boundaries are today of almost infinite complexity. The recurrence of war intensifies and perpetuates the boundary problems.

There are no boundaries so "good" that they cannot become the occasion of serious, even dangerous, misunderstandings; and there are no boundaries so "bad" that they cannot be made to work, given the mutual intent to make them work. Problems may arise relating to any boundary, which hereafter must be solved by peaceful means.

Boundaries will be changed by force as long as nations resort to war or the threat of war. A "war to end war" will not succeed. If there is ever to be a peace to end war it must be based upon local autonomy and world economy. These two objectives may seem unrelated, but they are as apposite as thumb and fingers and must be employed together if peace is to be grasped and held. Their achievement may be gradual and progressive, but their acceptance as objectives might be widespread when peace is restored.

The need of local autonomy creates demands for "self-determination" and makes enforced assimilation of linguistic and religious minorities almost futile. If regard for the separate capacities, feelings, and traditions of homogeneous communities and states is lacking, effective cooperation in the production and distribution of goods commensurate with present requirements is impossible. On the other hand, until the necessity of working toward a world economy is recognized (to be initiated and promoted only by the voluntary cooperation of nations with a will to peace), power politics with periodic recourse to war may continue.

In suiting the role of boundaries to the requirements of a rapidly changing world, different adaptations are required to reconcile the interests of local autonomy and world economy. The first necessitates respect for homogeneous communities, several of which may be included within a single customs union and may employ a common monetary system. The second requires general simplification of boundary functions, the lowering of many trade barriers, the production of goods where they can be produced most economically, and their exchange for goods which can be obtained advantageously elsewhere. In whatever way society may seek to establish local autonomy and world economy, it is unwise to transplant rigid concepts regarding such matters as boundaries, and to attempt as if with a cookie-cutter to pattern the ideas of one continent upon those of another continent. Americans are likely to assume that their own simple type of federation could be applied without essential variation to any other part of the world. But the solution of world problems is not so easy. In the conduct of war, the closest adaptation to topography and other geographic factors has long been recognized as necessary. Organization for viable peace requires equally intelligent adaptation to geographic factors—to the great differences in climate, soil productivity, and the distribution of mineral resources, as well as to human associations and traditions. As a corollary to such adaptation, the functions of boundaries should be regarded not as being uniform and static but as varying normally from place to place.

The number of active and incipient boundary disputes in various parts of the world in times of peace is greater than might be supposed.[12] The problems involved in solving these controversies are complex and varied. In areas where there is friction on boundaries already established, the situation may be greatly eased, in perhaps all instances, either by peacefully shifting the boundary for mutual advantage, or by appreciably simplifying the functions which the boundaries are made to serve.[13]

One of the means of effecting peaceful solution of boundary problems is to nip in the bud each incipient dispute. Referring to the International Joint Commission, United States and Canada, Elihu Root characterized its work as "a signal illustration of the true way to preserve peace—by disposing of controversies at the beginning, before they have ceased to be personal and nations have become excited and resentful about them." [14] The state of Massachusetts has long had, for each city or town, two or more "fence viewers" [15] whose duties relate to the mainte-

[12] Europe, the most highly industrialized continent, whose parts are inherently the most interdependent, is divided into national compartments much smaller than those of any other continent. This is shown by comparing the number of miles of boundary per 1,000 square miles of area (in the second column below); the total length in statute miles of all boundaries (conservative measurement) in the different continents is given in the first column.

Europe	17,357	4.0
Europe west of the U.S.S.R.	14,846	7.3
Asia	26,113	1.6
Asia except the U.S.S.R.	17,505	1.7
Africa	28,670	2.5
Africa, omitting boundaries of the Union of South Africa with other British territories	26,887	2.4
North America	11,433	1.3
North America, omitting the Canada-Labrador boundary	9,957	1.1
South America	18,961	2.7

For further details see Boggs, *International Boundaries*, p. 13 and Appendix A.

[13] The literature on boundaries needs to be supplemented to be of most use to those undertaking to solve boundary problems along the lines suggested above. There is little in the available literature regarding the functions of boundaries and their evolution, and little concerning the influence of boundaries upon the lives of people and the affairs of nations. An important contribution could be made through comprehensive studies embracing the social history of boundaries, the correlation of the workings of boundaries with pertinent geographic factors, and the peaceful solution of boundary problems.

[14] Lawrence J. Burpee, "From Sea to Sea" (an article on the International Joint Commission), *Canadian Geographical Journal*, Vol. XVI, p. 27 (Jan., 1938).

[15] *Massachusetts General Laws (1932).*

nance of fences between private property; they act in cases of disputes relating to refusal or neglect to repair or rebuild partition fences, and the like. Officials or commissions with somewhat analogous duties might, perhaps, be appointed to pass upon boundary controversies between nations.

The peaceful solution of international boundary problems requires that the problems themselves be played down and that public emotions be not aroused. The men who act upon international boundary controversies need to shun publicity. Many people love almost any kind of struggle, even a dog fight—at least as spectators. Scarcely any kind of controversy needs to be kept at low temperature, way below the boiling point, so much as an international boundary dispute.

In order that boundary problems may be amicably solved, every conceivable factor should be taken into consideration when new frontiers are to be established, and the best human wisdom should be applied in placing the boundary where it promises to function with least friction and to occasion a minimum of expense. Once the boundary has been established, the functions which it serves should be kept as simple and nonirritating as possible. Progressive simplification of boundary functions is needed in nearly all parts of the world in which boundary friction has developed. Finally, provision should be made for prompt, impartial, and wise handling of incidents and disputes that do arise.

CHAPTER II

New Directions and Skyways

6

World View and Strategy

By RICHARD E. HARRISON *and* HANS W. WEIGERT

RICHARD E. HARRISON, born in Baltimore, Md.; B.A., Yale, 1923; B.F.A., Yale School of Architecture, 1930. Independent cartographer whose maps have been published in *Fortune* and in numerous books. Author of articles on cartographical subjects; in preparation, "Look at the World, the Fortune Atlas for World Strategy."

HANS W. WEIGERT, born in Berlin, Germany. Dr. juris utriusque, University of Freiburg. Professor of Area Studies and Political Science at the University of Pittsburgh and Professor of International Relations at Trinity College, Hartford (on leave of absence).

Author: *German Geopolitics,* 1941; *Generals and Geographers: The Twilight of Geopolitics,* 1942; and articles on political geography and international relations.

It is only in recent years that we have come to realize that the psychological isolationism of the United States was largely due to an antiquated "vision" of the world. This world view, which many of us thought was the only possible and correct one, saw the "Western Hemisphere" in happy and secure insular isolation. The surrounding oceans formed in our imagination a gigantic and impenetrable Maginot Line. Such a view, and equally the political and strategical vision of American statesmen and military men, was based on certain elementary and basic concepts of geography and cartography.

Germany, under William II, had tried desperately to break down the barriers of this geography, which was essentially the geography of the Sea Power age—a predominantly British Sea Power age. Victory bred complacency, and the Allies forgot quickly that they had narrowly escaped disaster. As to geography, this complacency produced downright ignorance and almost fatal misknowledge. The vast majority of Americans and—let us emphasize this right at the beginning—of educated people *all over the world* has learned in the little red schoolhouse an outmoded and utterly antiquated geography, whenever this geography was not limited to the local scene or to clearly discernible regional aspects, but tried to revolve around continents and oceans, and the world itself. The main trouble with our geographical education as a tool for the understanding of world politics and economics was that we, like our fathers and grandfathers, literally did not realize what it meant if we said that the world is round. Today we pride ourselves on possessing what especially the armchair strategists love to call the "global" view. But few realize its implications. We cannot avoid depriving the new catchword of its glamour if we really mean business by stating that it is a round world and a small one at that, surrounded by a navigable ocean of air several miles deep. An extremely elementary axiom demands that he who wants to acquire a global view must turn to the globe. It is only blushingly that we repeat that *all* maps lie and distort, while the globe does not; for to express this simple truth means saying something that is known today by every high-school student. Yet our generation has definitely not grasped this truism and acted upon it when understanding and action was of vital importance to the destinies of the nation. Only recently have we begun to perceive the iron lessons of the war which make us see the world through new glasses.

The realization that we have not looked at the world directly, which was responsible for our shortsighted world view of yesterday, is one of the most fascinating experiences of this war. Until yesterday, the world map which dominated the imagination of men was the Mercator map. We are now beginning to understand that this world map which the ingenious Flemish map maker drew four hundred years ago was destined to make history. What makes the misconceptions resulting from the Mercator projection so fascinating and important, is the fact that it had for a long time an iron grip on the naval, military, and teaching professions in all nations. Since this is a global war, understanding of our own strategy, and of the strategy of the enemy as well, necessitates an understanding of the world view which produced such strategy.

We have seen the world *not* globally. We have accepted Mercator's blueprint. This blueprint indeed served admirably as long as we were mainly concerned with the equatorial zones

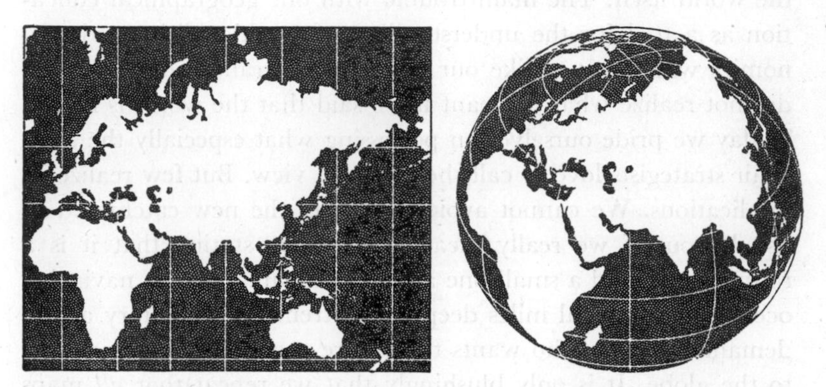

FIG. 2. Mackinder's World Island shown on the Mercator and orthographic projections. The Mercator, a better map in some respects, fails to reveal the crucial position of North America across the Polar Sea and does not even suggest the roundness of the earth.

and their sea lanes. Our blunder began when we granted Mercator a monopoly, and came to use his world map almost exclusively. We continued using it when land power and land-based air power became pivotal in the greatest of all world conflicts. In a world war that is mainly being fought in the northern hemisphere this proved to be an almost fatal misjudgment; for the Mercator projection whose center of accuracy is along the equator cannot possibly show the relationship between the power spheres of the contending great Powers.

This is one part of the story. Since the American people and American military leadership have in time realized their mistakes, the story of geographic ignorance in the United States as a determining factor in the strategy of the war is, fortunately, beginning with "Once upon a time" (which means the day before yesterday).

What we have not learned so far, is to adopt a constant flexibility in the process of forming a world view. A world view is one in our time that measures distances not merely by miles, but also by flying-time hours and minutes; it is not static but extremely dynamic. The dynamism that must be applied to geographic vision necessitates a constant mobility of imagination, in order to enable one to view the world, not only from a firmly fixed point (for instance, Washington, D.C., or somewhere else in the States), but from wherever the power centers of vital military decisions lie at a given moment. Only the globe permits such constant change of bird's-eye views. But this kind of "global" view is fading only too easily from our memories. Therefore, we need maps which, for instance, make us see the Pacific world in the direction of Japan, as seen from Munda, or the Australian continent as it appears to a Japanese naval commander off the Truk islands. This is the kind of "vision" which we really need if we are to achieve the mobility of imagination which gives us the right compass for action and makes us, at the same time, anticipate and understand the enemy's action. Yet, it is even difficult for an American to visualize the enemy's world through the glasses of our closest allies, to "see" the *Festung* Europe (or the *Festung* Germania) as it appears before the eyes of a Britisher in England, or of a Soviet general in the Caucasus or on the Leningrad front. We do not use our imagination to view the enemy's world (or our own world, at that) through the glasses of our Chinese allies. This Maginot Line barring our imagination rises to almost insurmountable heights if we try to "see" the world or parts of it from the enemy's position, as in the case of the Japanese off Truk, or of a Japanese commander on the Manchurian front facing the vast continent of the Soviet Union behind the Amur River. And why don't we perch secretly on top of Hitler's ivory tower of imagination and dwindling inspiration, in the Bavarian mountains? How does his evil spirit picture the continent of North America in all its power getting ready for action across the seas?

If we are to believe one of the most sacred fables peddled by our armchair strategists, we must see in the dreamer of Berchtesgaden and his general staff a bunch of profound military planners who, until very recently, had a unique monopoly of "the global view." One of these widely quoted "experts" on strategy used to travel with a Cassandra speech on geopolitics in which he revealed the secret that Hitler would map his strategy by

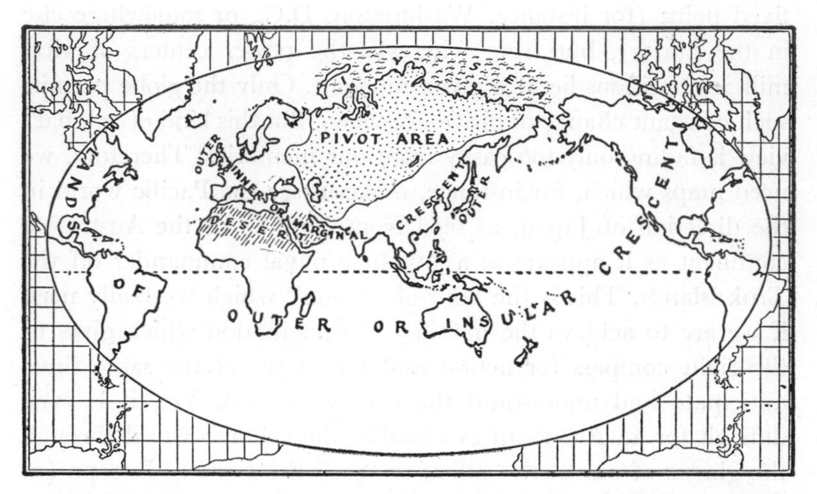

FIG. 3. The oval encloses Mackinder's famous map, model for Haushofer's thinking, as it originally appeared in the *Geographical Journal,* London, 1904. Since the oval obscures the fact that it is on the Mercator projection, the map here has been extended into the corners of the rectangle.

using the globe, or a pole-centered azimuthal map, while Roosevelt and Churchill would be photographed inevitably bent over flat maps. Their inability to visualize a round world, he warned, might cost us the victory. That was said in the winter of 1942–1943. Even more recently, the story that Hitler has a secret weapon in his new geography was repeated by Professor G. T. Renner who made this statement: "The airplane has created a new geography of the world. Axis leaders knew this several years ago and have been taking advantage of it, but few Americans are yet really aware of it." [1] A newsreel on "Geopolitics" showed

[1] *Harper's,* June, 1943, pp. 38–41.

General Haushofer spinning a sinister web of strategy on the Polar equidistant projection.

These tales sound exicting, but, fortunately, they are fairy tales. The truth is important: the Axis ringleaders, remarkable as their inborn understanding of *tactics* is, have never acquired what Napoleon described as the main prerequisite of *strategy,*

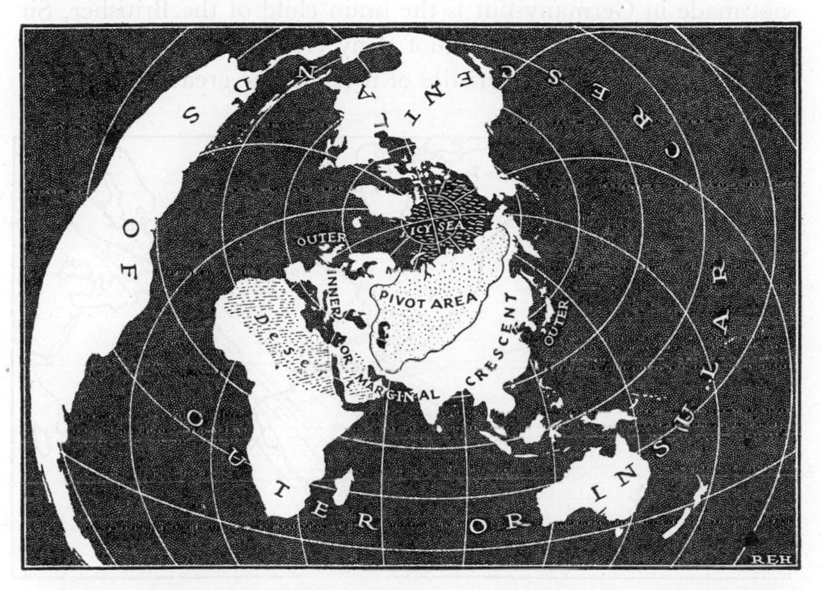

FIG. 4. Mackinder's designations are here transposed to an azimuthal equidistant map centered in the Pivot Area or Heartland. This gives a more revealing picture of the relationship of the Heartland to the other continents.

the geographical sense. If they by now have learned some of the basic lessons of a global geography, they have done so considerably later than the leaders of the United Nations. This time the sigh, "Too little and too late," comes from the other corner of the ring! By following the road of geography and geopolitics in Germany as it reveals itself clearly in their maps (Fig. 2), we can prove that the Germans of today, far from being geographic wizards, have been caught napping when Destiny added a new chapter to its book of geography. And that, we think, is important to know. Not because the awareness of the enemy's blunders should lull us into false optimism, but because an understanding of the flaws in his strategy adds one more weapon to our arsenal. Of course, we do not mean to voice a verdict against geography in Germany. In fact, German geographers before the advent of Hitlerism ranked among the first in the world. As to General Haushofer's geopolitics, which in its most important conclusions was not made in Germany but is the brain child of the Britisher, Sir Halford Mackinder, we cannot deny either that his scheme of conquest has the characteristics of true historic greatness. Following closely Mackinder's warnings (addressed to the peacemakers of Paris, not to the German enemy), Haushofer envisaged clearly the fateful consequences of a gigantic transcontinental bloc reaching from the Rhine to the Yangtze and uniting the continental power of the U.S.S.R. and Germany.[2] Hitler, fortunately, did not listen to his would-be mentor, the former general in the Royal Bavarian Army. The mission of Hess who arrived in

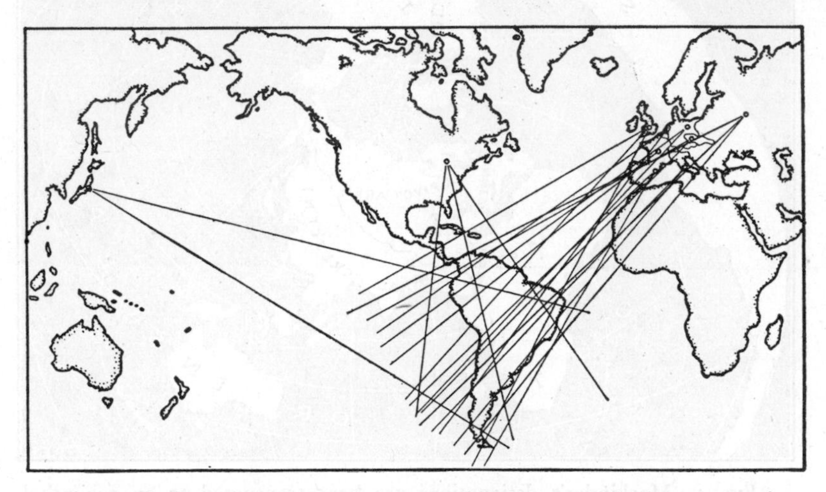

FIG. 5. A German propaganda map on Mercator's projection, purporting to show the area covered by radio beams originating in various countries and converging on South America.

[2] See the article by H. W. Weigert, "Asia Through Haushofer's Glasses," p. 395.

Scotland with Haushofer's calling card ended in failure. And Hitler's stupendous blunder in attacking the Soviet Union saved our world.

It is not with the scholars of geography in Germany nor with the appraisal, by the German geopolitikers, of the Soviet Union in world politics that we have to take issue. The point is that the Germans under Hitler, despite many successful attempts to tackle detailed problems of strategy, have utterly failed in the task to include the whole world in their vision and to apply a global view to their totalitarian strategy of conquest.

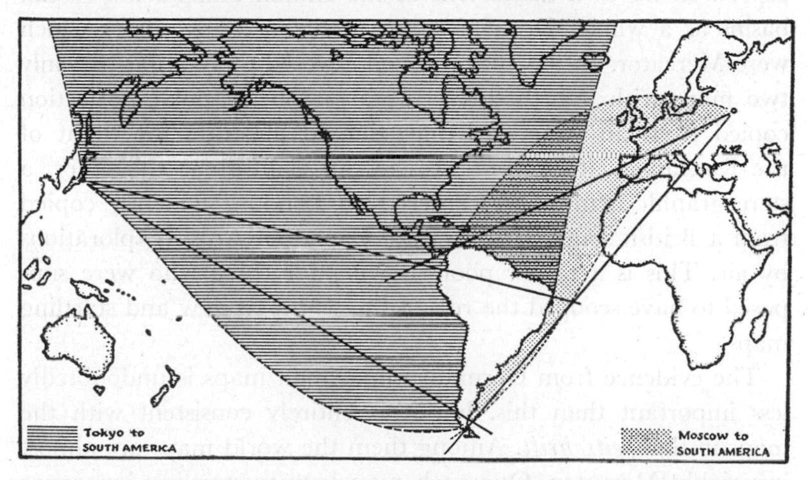

FIG. 6. The actual paths of two beams, from Moscow and Tokyo, are shown (by shading) in comparison with the straight and incorrect German version. Note that Tokyo's beam to South America also covers North America instead of being confined to the Pacific wastes.

It is of course not possible to prove this by direct evidence since we are not privy to the inner councils of the Axis High Command and do not know precisely on what maps their strategy is based. However, there are two kinds of indirect evidence, each of which gives strong support to our view: first, an examination of this kind of map used in German propaganda and in the organ of the geopoliticians (*Zeitschrift für Geopolitik*). Since Hitler's ascent to power this journal has enjoyed a high official position, and it must be remembered that General Dr. Haushofer, its editor-in-chief, was appointed head of the German Academy by the Führer. A look into its pages is the next best thing to examination of the ponderings of the General Staff. From January, 1934, to December, 1940 (the last available issue), there appeared in the *Zeitschrift* twenty world maps. One of these was on Gall's projection, two on Eckert's projection, and all the rest were Mercator. The first two can be described as projections which are similar to Mercator in that they are centered along the equator. Neither presents a new or "global" aspect. In his own discussions of the Indian and Pacific Ocean basins as a whole, Dr. Haushofer used ten maps, all of which were Mercator. In the entire period covered there appeared only two maps with unorthodox centerings: one, a polar projection copied from an American magazine to illustrate the flight of the Russian aviators from Moscow to California; the other, a stereographic hemisphere centered on London, evidently copied from a British source, to illustrate Canadian Arctic explorations by air. This is a rather poor showing for those who were supposed to have scooped the rest of the world on new and startling maps.

The evidence from German propaganda maps is undoubtedly less important than this, but it is entirely consistent with the maps in the *Zeitschrift*. Among them the world maps are almost invariably Mercator. One such map betrays startling ignorance of the properties of maps. This Mercator map (Fig. 5) purports to show how Axis radio beams blanket South America. Not a single beam follows a great circle; consequently the lines shown on this Mercator map misrepresent the true course of radio beams. Fig. 6 demonstrates how amazingly wrong the German version is with respect to the beams from Tokyo.

The first rule of cartography is that a projection must be appropriate to its use. For example, maps involving space relationships should only be shown on equal area projections. The Germans frequently violate this rule, for Mercator is anything but equal area. This is a rather common error in most countries, but it is doubly interesting here because of the German preoccupation with space and ignorance of how to portray it accurately.

The second kind of evidence to support our contention that the Axis leaders did not understand "global" strategy results from examination of their strategy as it has revealed itself in the last four years. Strategy of course is not to be confused with tactics, in which the Germans especially have frequently demonstrated clear superiority. Strategy may be defined as the *where, when,* and *with what* to fight a battle, and tactics are *how* you fight it. The paramount error in global strategy of which the German geopolitical school is guilty, concerns the geopolitical role of North America. Haushofer and his men see it as a satellite continent beyond the sphere of Eurasia. It is a view typical of a generation brought up to see the world through the eyes of Mercator.[3]

The German military seemed to share this neglect, for they made no moves except the first one (the invasion of Norway) to place themselves in a position to attack Canada or the United States. Fig. 7 is a map centered on a great circle from Berlin to Winnipeg which is near the geographical center of the North American land mass. It shows that there exists a direct route across the Atlantic via short hops from Norway to Iceland to Greenland to Baffin Island to the mainland. It is not likely that the Germans realized the existence of this direct and undefended alley to the industrial heart of its chief enemy, because at an early date they allowed themselves to be beaten to the punch by our occupation of Greenland and Iceland (with the British). They did not take advantage of the fact that Alaska is closer to Spitzbergen than the Azores are to Maine. Perhaps it is true that lack of military moves against North America was partly a reflection of their confidence in conquering the United States from within. However there is no positive evidence of any departure from the age-old flat-map strategy.

The story of Japanese strategy gives even better geographic evidence, for the Japanese opportunity to take advantage of our

[3] Cf. H. W. Weigert, *Generals and Geographers* (New York, 1942), pp. 192 ff.

ignorance was far greater and was missed more spectacularly. Fig. 8 shows the true position of Alaska between the centers of Japan and the United States. It likewise shows Japan's brilliant chance to demonstrate that our only defense of the continent (at Pearl Harbor) was in reality only a flank defense. The defenses at the center, Alaska, had been almost completely neglected in spite of the sound appraisal of its importance by

FIG. 7. Reykjavik, which Mercator minds consider pretty far north, lies on the great-circle route from Berlin to the center of North America.

many Americans, beginning with Seward and continuing through General Billy Mitchell and others. Fortunately there were enough men in Washington who realized it, and in the spring of 1942 we were feverishly trying to make up for decades of neglect. At the end of May, 1942, the Japanese, as Mercator-minded as many in this country, sent a major attack force to the Hawaiian Islands and a diversionary force to Alaska. Surprised by a handful of planes at Dutch Harbor they beat a hasty withdrawal and contented themselves with a comparatively harmless occupation of Kiska and Attu. Had they been global-minded, these forces of course would have been reversed. We were still unprepared to stop a major force in Alaska, and it is highly probable that they could have been in British Columbia by fall. This would have revealed the true position of Pearl Harbor as a naval supply base for the eastern Pacific and a steppingstone to the

Fig. 8. Dutch (not Pearl) Harbor lies between the United States and Japan.

southwest Pacific, relatively useless as a defense of our continent.

The strategy of the Japanese in the central and southwest Pacific was perfectly sound and was skillfully executed while they held the advantages of surprise and superior preparation. Perhaps it is more than a coincidence that the Mercator map, being centered along the equator, contains no serious distortion of this region.

In a voluminous collection of Japanese maps, eight maps were included which were either world maps or maps of Asia and of the Eastern Hemisphere. All these maps were Mercator projections.

In conclusion, it can be stated as one of the major lessons of this war that Axis planning, in its application of geography to actual strategy, has been unable to free itself in time from the chains of Mercator.[4] This is the main reason why both Ger-

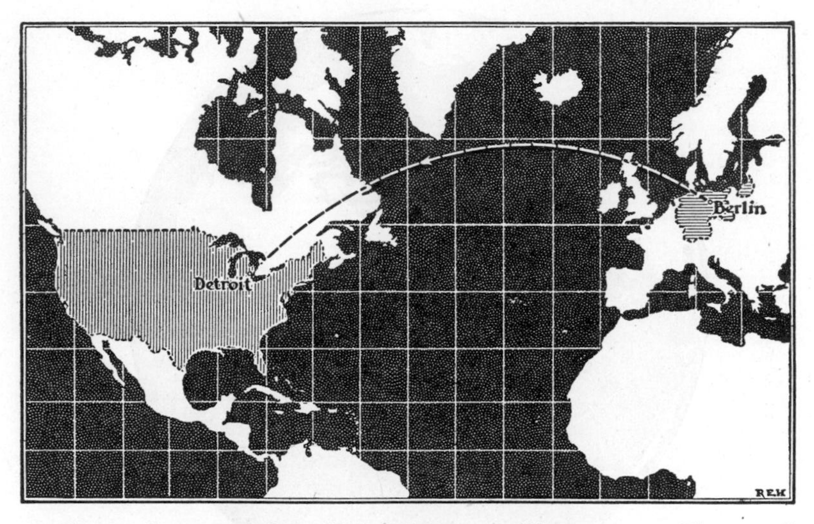

FIG. 9. Germany and the United States on a Mercator map. The curved line is the most direct line (great circle) from the political heart of Germany to the industrial heart of America.

many and Japan failed to understand the geopolitical role of North America in a world conflict. The Nazis have long seen, in Mercator fashion, the North American scene as an isolated island-continent beyond pivotal Eurasia. Japanese naval strategy

[4] In the last two years, we in this country have made great strides in breaking these chains. However, the desire of some simply to substitute another map (usually the Polar Azimuthal Equidistant projection) for Mercator is merely a jump from the frying pan into the fire and has provided opportunity for an easy rebuttal by the classicists. They have not yet fully realized that a map like Mercator's, which is perfect for navigation, cannot be used for studying world geography without causing serious misconceptions; an example is W. J. Luyten's article in *Harper's Magazine,* Oct., 1943, pp. 447–450.

in this war indicates that the Japanese, too, misjudged the American power center as it appeared to them from their own bastions. The enemies' error, in regarding American isolation and isolationism as a geographic fact, was only partly due to wishful thinking. The main responsibility for their fateful misknowledge lies with their geographic world view misled by maps not suitable for the needs of strategy in the present world conflict (Figs. 9 and 10). They are guilty of downright ignorance of the basic

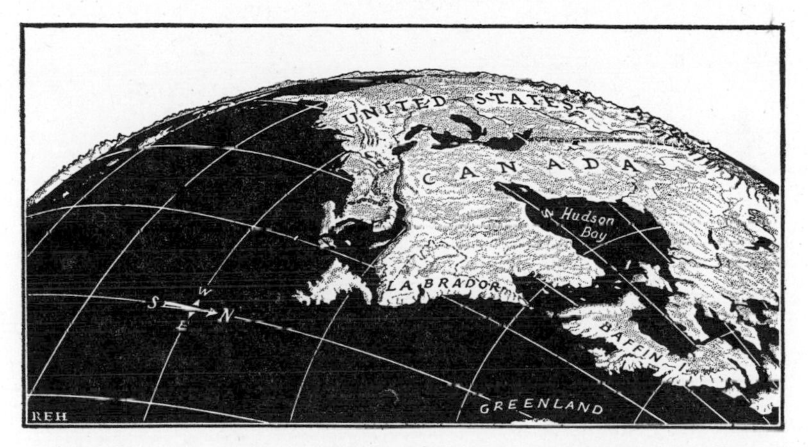

FIG. 10. A perspective view of America from the middle of the line on Fig. 9. This is actually the direct German approach. After *Fortune* with permission.

rules of a spherical and shrinking world. Their blunders are a grave reminder to us. The Hitlers and Tojos and their military staffs were not the only ones to commit strategical blunders caused by geographical misconceptions. Overemphasis of sea power and neglect of land power is the characteristic of Alfred Thayer Mahan's credo of a global naval strategy. His philosophy of sea power was to affect profoundly Theodore Roosevelt's foreign policy, and public thinking in this country in general.[5] It is not surprising to find that Mahan's geopolitics which regarded the Hawaiian Islands as vital for the security of the west coast,

[5] Harold and Margaret Sprout, *Toward a New Order of Sea Power* (Princeton, 1940), pp. 249–250; Margaret Sprout in E. M. Earle's *Makers of Modern Strategy* (Princeton, 1943), pp. 436 ff.

but neglected the pivotal role of Alaska, was entirely influenced by Mercator; all the world maps in his books which were to illustrate his global ideas are Mercator projections.

No nation possesses a monopoly of geographical wisdom. It is our good luck that the military leadership in the United Nations has learned its lessons better and earlier than the enemy. Geographical sense and geographical vision are now weapons in our arsenal. We must keep them from becoming rusty.

7

The Myth of the Continents

By EUGENE STALEY

EUGENE STALEY, born in Friend, Nebraska. A.B., Hastings, 1925; Ph.D., University of Chicago, 1928. Since 1937, Professor of International Economic Relations, Fletcher School of Law and Diplomacy; on leave at present in government service (relief and rehabilitation activities).

Author: *War and the Private Investor,* 1935; *Raw Materials in Peace and War,* 1937; *World Economy in Transition,* 1939.

The original version of "The Myth of the Continents" was published in *Foreign Affairs,* April, 1941. The United States was not yet in the war, nor was the Soviet Union. The great debate on U.S. foreign policy concerned "aid to Britain." The author has revised his study but has not attempted to remove all current allusions to issues as they presented themselves at that time. A new section on continental groupings in world organization has been added

In some of his writings Charles A. Beard reads from (or into?) American history the lesson that "continentalism" represents the predestined course of our foreign policy. Jerome Frank, writing a chapter on "Disintegrated Europe and Integrated America," argues that the basic issue in Europe, and the cause of unfortunate developments in Germany and Italy, has been "the absence of continental integration." In America, he continues, we have continental integration, "and therefore the possibility of relative self-sufficiency." Stuart Chase embroiders still further Frank's theme of "disintegrated Europe, integrated America," collects figures to explore the possibilities of various "continental economic units," and, in the last sentence of his book, urges the United States to avoid economic and political entanglements in the affairs of other nations which, "in the nature of their geographical deficiencies, must quarrel, until some day they too achieve continental unity." [1]

The Western Hemisphere complex, so conspicuous in dis-

[1] Charles A. Beard, *A Foreign Policy for America* (New York: Knopf, 1940); Jerome Frank, *Save America First* (New York: Harper, 1938); Stuart Chase and Marian Tyler, *The New Western Front* (New York: Harcourt, Brace, 1939).

cussions of American foreign policy, has often been associated with ideas of "continental" unity and "continental" solidarity. A noteworthy instance occurred in a symposium at the meeting of the American Political Science Association where Clarence Streit's plan for Interdemocracy Federal Union was up for discussion. A distinguished political scientist—a student of municipal government—based his criticism on the view that the natural political and economic grouping is the "continental" one. He therefore favored solidarity with Latin American countries as against overseas countries.

There is, of course, a tremendous literature on the theme that "Europe" must unite. Coudenhove-Kalergi's *Pan Europe;* the efforts of practical statesmen like Briand and Herriot to promote European union; and more recently a new flood of books, articles, plans, and speeches advocating a "United States of Europe" or some sort of European federation—all carry a continental emphasis. Sometimes there is an explicit argument to explain why continents, as such, must be united. Thus, H. N. Brailsford writes, "Air power has made inevitable the unification of continents."[2] More often than not, however, this point is simply taken for granted.

On the other hand, there are strong trends in current political action and thought, as well as existing economic and political connections, which cut directly across continental lines. Public opinion and official policy in the United States are today influenced very decidedly by the realization that our own ability to defend ourselves depends in no small measure on what happens in Europe and Asia. The British Commonwealth of Nations, so long as it stands, will continue to be a practical challenge to the thesis that continental units are the natural ones. The war emergency has publicized the fact that the economic affiliations of much of South America, as well as the cultural affiliations of Latin America in general, are with Europe—distinctly uncontinental. In the realm of thought about the future, particu-

[2] H. N. Brailsford, *From England to America: A Message* (New York: Whittlesey House, 1940).

larly in the discussion of war and peace aims, continental lines are as regularly disregarded by some as they are emphasized by others. Proposals like "Union Now," and the more moderate proposals of those who, while doubting the feasibility of complete federal union, nevertheless envisage some kind of permanent bond between the United States and other democratic nations, reject the continental principle in favor of an ocean-linked unity.

One general theme runs like a red thread through most of these discussions, by continentalists and noncontinentalists alike. That is the conviction that the day of the small, completely independent, sovereign national state is past. There will be in the future—and ought to be—*larger* politico-economic units of some kind. This, in the view of the present writer, has to be accepted as unquestionably sound. But is the natural progression from small, sovereign states to *continental* groupings? There is reason for making an examination of this question now, for the words "continent" and "continental" seem to be acquiring strong emotional and symbolic values which may even affect policy. Is this a well founded development, or have we here an instance of the fascination (not to say the tyranny) of certain words? What are the general characteristics that mark off continental from noncontinental, overseas, or maritime groupings? What is to be said for permanent supranational groupings of a continental sort as compared with noncontinental, maritime, or oceanic groupings? With respect to the defense problem of the United States, what are the relative virtues of a policy which stresses "continental" defense lines (admitting aid to Britain largely because it buys time for preparation), as against a policy which allies us with overseas friends in all-out resistance to the totalitarian challenge and in joint maintenance of dominant world sea power? [3]

There is only one universal characteristic which distinguishes continental from noncontinental groupings—the existence of

[3] Wherever "sea power" is mentioned in this article the term must be understood to *include* the necessary complement of air power required under modern conditions in order to hold command of the surface of the seas and in order to defend the bases—military and industrial—on which sea power rests.

land connections (or barriers) instead of sea connections (or barriers) between the members of the group. What political or economic consequences, if any, follow from this difference?

Distance has human significance only in terms of the barriers it interposes against the exchange of messages (communication), the movement of persons (travel), and the movement of goods (transport). How does *over-land* distance compare with *over-water* distance in these three respects?

Obviously, the answer depends on the character of the particular lands and seas involved (land areas differ more than sea areas in the obstacles they offer) and on the technology of the times. Nowadays, communication, which permits exchange of intelligence, impressions, and feelings, takes place over water and over land with practically the same speed, cost, and convenience. Radio waves and the air mail pay little attention to continental lines. So far as travel is concerned, surface travel on land today is swifter where there are good railway lines and highways than surface travel by ship, and it is hard to generalize about the differences in expense and convenience. But if one travels by air—and that will surely be the standard method of long-distance travel in the future—there is no important difference even today between over-land and over-water distance. Stratosphere flying will probably soon abolish what little difference does now exist. This leaves land and water distances about equally significant, in human terms, except for transportation of goods.

The transport of goods (freight) should certainly not be ranked below communication or travel in its fundamental importance for determining the "naturalness" of economic connections between different places. If freight can move easily and cheaply between two regions, their economies are much more likely to become integrated, interdependent, and complementary than if the movement of goods between them is difficult and costly. Now, it happens that for heavy, bulky goods, which are the staple items of interregional trade, water transport is much cheaper than land transport over equal distances. This has been true for centuries. It is one of the reasons why the great trading centers of the world are typically located on rivers, or lakes, or on the seacoast. It is still true today. Rumanian oil, in time of peace, moves to Germany by the long overseas route around Spain to Hamburg, instead of over the much closer "continental" connection. Italy, though linked by several railway lines to continental Europe, imported 20,000,000 tons of goods by sea in 1938 and only 4,000,000 tons by land. Coal from Germany moves overseas to Italy when there is no blockade. South American international trade, even to places on the same continent, is largely by sea.

Let us compare, in practical terms, the cost-distance from such a center as New York City to inland "continental" points and to overseas points. Using prewar rates in all cases (effective as of August 1, 1939), the "wheat-distance" between Kansas City and New York, expressed as the cost of shipping 100 pounds of wheat in carload lots, was 33½ cents to 42½ cents, while it was only 13 cents from New York to Liverpool. In mileage, Liverpool was three times as far as Kansas City; but Kansas City was nearly three times farther than Liverpool when it came to economic relations in wheat. The overseas route from Singapore to New York is more than twenty-five times longer, in miles, than the rail route from New York to Akron, Ohio. Yet the distance measured in freight cost for transporting a 240-pound bale or case of crude rubber was $1.50 from Singapore to New York and $1.03 from New York to Akron. In other words, Akron was two-thirds as far away from New York as Singapore, in "crude-rubber distance."[4]

In summary, for two places a given number of miles apart it makes very little difference under modern conditions whether land or water stretches between them, so far as communication and travel are concerned. For the transportation of heavy goods, however, which is a major aspect of economic connections, the two places would be effectively closer to each other, measured

[4] I am indebted to William M. Gavigan, of Funch, Edye & Company, steamship agents and ship brokers, for the rate data used in these comparisons.

in "cost-distance," if there were water between them than if there were land. *Given the same separation in miles, there is less economic distance across water than across land.*

But are not places on the same continent or in the same "hemisphere" closer to each other in miles than places on different continents or in different "hemispheres"? It is a temptation to suppose so. Ex-Governor Philip La Follette of Wisconsin warned his countrymen not long ago to beware lest we find ourselves fighting "not in this hemisphere where we can be supreme, but fighting with expeditionary forces four thousand miles away in Europe and six thousand miles away in Asia." Will the reader at this point be good enough to examine a globe?[5] Attach a string to a pin at Madison, Wisconsin—Governor La Follette's home town—and measure how far from home he might have to go if he were sent to defend important points "in this hemisphere where we can be supreme," as compared with other points on the supposedly distant continents of Europe and Asia. Note the following facts:

It is farther from Madison to Buenos Aires in a direct line ("great circle" distance) than from Madison to Bengasi. Ankara is about as far as Buenos Aires. Actually, by the regularly traveled routes, Buenos Aires is considerably farther away than either of these points in Africa or Asia, because of the "bulge" of Brazil.

No capital in Europe, not even Moscow, is as far from Madison as is Buenos Aires; and only one European capital (Athens) is as far as Rio de Janeiro. Again, this is direct-line distance, and by actually traveled routes Europe is relatively closer.

Gibraltar is closer to Madison than is the capital of Bolivia, closer than Tacna or Arica, and closer than any major city in Brazil or any place at all in Argentina, Chile, Paraguay, or Uruguay.

Gibraltar, incidentally, is not merely closer to the entire South Atlantic coast of South America than is Madison, but is closer

[5] This is not a rhetorical request; it is meant seriously. Illusions persist in the minds of all of us from the old schoolbook device of flat maps which break the world into "hemispheres" that have no objective existence whatever in nature.

by sea than the *nearest point* in the United States (Miami). In the same way, advanced European bases at Dakar, Bathurst, and Freetown on the coast of Africa are nearer to southern South America than our most advanced Caribbean bases.

If the Nazis had captured the British naval base at Scapa Flow in Scotland they would have been closer to Madison than Lima, Peru.

As for Asia, Manchuria is closer to Madison than is Buenos Aires. For those to whom "continental" land connections seem especially important, it may be added that a Japanese flying over the shortest route from Manchuria to Madison (a great circle via Bering Strait) need hardly lose sight of land.

Points on the same land mass may be as far apart in miles as places on opposite sides of an ocean, and may be still farther apart in economic distance measured by transport costs. On the other hand, there is likely to be a greater continuity of human habitation between them than between the overseas points. How shall we weight this characteristic in appraising the significance of continental as opposed to overseas politico-economic groupings? One might argue that the continuity permits conquest and culture to spread by easy stages, and hence that each land mass could be expected to have more political and cultural unity, more history and tradition in common, than would exist between places on separate continents. Actually, every continent has natural barriers—deserts, mountains, swamps, jungles—which are almost uninhabited, and which may be more difficult to cross than the ocean. The sea, especially in earlier centuries, has offered one of the main means of contact between peoples on the same continent, so that the peripheral areas often developed more traits in common with one another and with other continents than with landlocked regions. Thus, the political and economic system of the coast-land states of Europe spread more effectively to relatively vacant areas like America and Australia than to parts of eastern and southern Europe.

It is no accident that early civilizations developed in river valleys, and that the great center of ancient times is spoken of as "the Mediterranean world" and not the European or the African world. Nor is it without significance that Europe, having the most broken coast line, best adapted for sea-borne traffic, became the originator of modern world culture and world politics, while Africa, most "continental" of all land areas because of its smooth contours and difficulty of access by sea, remained the "Dark Continent."[6] In short, land connections, which would appear to establish easy contact between peoples on the same continent, may be barriers as well as connections, while bodies of water, appearing superficially on the map as barriers, may actually be most important connecting links. Because this has been so distinctly true in the past, the existing patterns of culture, tradition, political affiliation, and economic interdependence which confront us in the world of today are as often oceanic as they are continental.

We in this country can give the "continental" doctrine an immediate and practical test by applying it to the grand strategy of United States defense. In general, the same people who talk about "continental integration" draw a line around the so-called Western Hemisphere and refuse to concede that the United States has any vital interest outside. It should be noted, however, that our relations with the Western Hemisphere countries to the south of us are not really "continental" in any significant practical sense. A land connection is afforded by the Isthmus of Panama, but no one ever travels, or sends messages, or transports goods between North and South America *overland*. In fact, all Latin America, not merely South America, is overseas to us, with the partial exception of Mexico. Latin America is susceptible of defense by the United States only if the United States controls the sea routes, including routes which are problems of high-seas defense.

If the Western Hemisphere, then, is to be considered as one

[6] For each mile of coast line Europe has 289 square miles of surface; North America, 407; Australia, 534; South America, 689; Asia, 763; Africa, 1,420. (Derwent Whittlesey, *The Earth and the State: A Study of Political Geography* [New York: Holt, 1939], p. 308.)

unit for defense purposes, or for other purposes, it provides an instance not of continental but of *maritime* solidarity.

South America is overseas to us, and important parts of it are farther from our bases than from the bases of European Powers. The problem of defending South America is a *maritime,* not a continental problem, and if command of the seas in the South Atlantic passed to hostile Powers we could neither establish bases there ourselves nor prevent them from ensconcing themselves on the Continent. Those soporific calculations about the number of ships an invader would have to have in order to send an expeditionary force from Europe to the United States, and about the perils to which such a force would be exposed from land-based defenders, *would apply to us in reverse, once command of the South Atlantic had passed to the Axis.* For the enemy could then almost force us to launch an overseas attack in order to crush his bases and stop his infiltration in South America.

Colonel Lindbergh testified before the House Committee on Foreign Affairs that aviation has increased the vulnerability of any country to attack from forces on the same continent, but has decreased the vulnerability of a whole continent to attack from without—that is, by way of the seas. The hollowness of the argument is exposed by the considerations advanced above. The advantage of land-based aviation against sea attack is ours only if the United States can count on getting and holding and supplying bases in that distant overseas territory on the east coast of South America, and can prevent the Axis from doing so. This would be most unlikely if control of the high seas, especially the South Atlantic, passed to the Axis through the defeat of Britain. In other words, once control of the high seas passed from our friends to our enemies, we should eventually be exposed to land-based attacks by air on the vital Caribbean area of our defense system. On our side, the only remedy would be a major effort involving probably the transport of troops a long distance *overseas* in an area where the advantage of established positions and nearness to bases might be all against us.

These doubts about the security of a defense system limited to the Western Hemisphere are strengthened by consideration of the economic problems of defense against totalitarian attack. The great bargaining weakness of a Western Hemisphere economic bloc against an Axis-dominated world would arise from the surpluses of products competitive with our own which are produced in Latin America, especially in the temperate climate of southern South America.[7] In 1937 continental Europe and the United Kingdom absorbed considerably more than two billion dollars' worth of Western Hemisphere exports, principally petroleum, cotton, wheat, copper, meats, corn, tobacco, and linseed. Important Latin American groups depend for their income on selling such goods abroad. It is easy to write glibly about diverting production to products needed in the United States, disposing of surpluses by hemisphere stamp plans, raising living standards throughout the hemisphere by fostering industrial development, and creating cartels to limit production and to barter with Hitler. These are the things we would have to do if it became necessary to make a stand on the line of hemisphere defense. Some of them are worth doing anyway. But rechanneling of production takes time, and it meets social and political resistances. Messrs. Bidwell and Upgren have rightly emphasized that by stimulating Bolivian tin mining or Brazilian rubber production we would not automatically reemploy the gauchos of the Argentine pampas, or the wheat farmers of Alberta and Saskatchewan, or the tobacco growers in Virginia and North Carolina.[8]

It is not at all clear that the Latin American countries would feel inclined to undergo difficult economic readjustments for the sake of fitting into the defense plan of the United States and thereby antagonizing the Axis. Hitler, if he had defeated Britain, could probably have offered them more than we could, while demanding less in the way of readjustment of established patterns of production, and he could also have threatened them

[7] Cf. Alvin H. Hansen, "Hemisphere Solidarity," *Foreign Affairs*, Oct., 1940.

[8] Percy W. Bidwell and Arthur R. Upgren, "A Trade Policy for National Defense," *Foreign Affairs*, Jan., 1941.

more effectively. So long as Britain is in the picture, on the other hand, the economic problem of defending the Americas is much more manageable. The reason is that a large volume of foodstuffs and raw materials of a sort competitive with United States production, which we therefore do not care to import, regularly flows from such countries as Argentina and Uruguay to Britain, to be paid for in goods and services which Britain furnishes to Empire countries and to others. Some of these countries in turn sell large export surpluses in the United States (for example, rubber and tin from the East Indies), and the United States sells more than it buys in Argentina. Britain is the pivot of this triangular and multiangular trade on which the disposal of a considerable part of South American surpluses depends. Let Britain's economic life be destroyed, or let it come under the domination of Hitler's New Order, and the effect on the economic defense of the Americas is analogous to the effect the sinking or capture of the British fleet would have on the naval defense of the Americas.

A defense area limited to the Western Hemisphere has another important economic disadvantage as compared with a world-girdling defense area based on joint British and American sea power. *We should be the blockaded party.* The Nazis, controlling the overseas trade routes of the world, except those in the immediate vicinity of our bases, would have on their side the quiet, undramatic, but steady weight of advantage in economic power for defense or aggression conferred by the ability to draw upon the best and cheapest sources of materials in Europe, Asia, Africa, Australia, and the islands of the seas, and probably portions of South America. We, and not they, should have to waste part of our productive power making substitutes and adapting our industry to inferior materials. To be sure, the United States, together with the adjacent areas that our navy could protect, is better equipped than any other region to withstand a siege. But the engineers, mechanics, machine tools, materials, and inventors used to build synthetic rubber plants, or to establish our own tin smelters, or to develop *ersatz* materials could not be used at the same time to produce planes and tanks or civilian goods. The side which controls the world oceans, and which thus enjoys access by sea to allies and neutrals alike, has an inestimable long-run advantage in the scales of economic power.

A few years ago, the editors of *Fortune* captioned a pair of world charts: "U.S.A.—Compact, Easily Defended; British Empire—Diffuse, Vulnerable." The theory implied in these captions has certain commonly accepted elements of truth. But in it lurks also a dangerous fallacy—particularly dangerous under new techniques of warfare used so skillfully by the totalitarian Powers. The "diffuse, vulnerable" area, *if its communications can be maintained by dominant sea power*, is in a position to unite its allies and divide its enemies. It can nip in the bud, so to speak, threats to its position which may arise from any one of many different quarters—provided it acts resolutely and in time. The "compact, easily defended" area, on the other hand, may not be able to take action against the increasing power of a potential enemy until every ally has been "mopped up," until the enemy has gathered his forces without interference and has chosen the most advantageous moment for attack. The "diffuse, vulnerable" area, always granted it holds command of the seas, can base its military effort on the economic resources of most of the world, including the materials and the industrial man power of allied and nonbelligerent countries far out of reach of the adversary. Finally, compactness may be no particular advantage, and may even be a great disadvantage, in the psychological phases of modern warfare. There is an important psychological as well as material difference between surrounding the enemy and being surrounded by the enemy. In the case of the United States, this is the difference between joining with allies from all the rest of the world to help destroy the Axis and trying to resist an Axis combination which controls all the world except our immediate neighborhood. "Compact, easily defended —diffuse, vulnerable" tacitly assumes that the land connects, the sea divides. Such a slogan dramatizes inaccuracies of thinking that might prove as dangerous to us as the "Maginot mentality" proved to France, as little conducive to survival as the rigid strength of the mastodon in competition with the flexibility and adaptability of other animals and man.

Supranational groupings of some kind or other are bound to emerge from this war and from the peace settlement. The world is not likely to be made up in the future of fifty or sixty states claiming sovereignty and independence and acknowledging no limitations on the right to make their own decisions in matters of peace and war and economic policy. We are witnessing a continuation of the trend of centuries, under the impulse of fundamental technological changes, toward larger politico-economic units.

Should the Axis Powers win, the new supranational units would rest on conquest, and would be maintained by a monopoly of weapons in the hands of a "master people." National cultures and economies would be molded into forms befitting the particular sort of servant status ordained in each case by the conqueror, and national self-government would give place to direct rule, as in Poland, or to puppet government by men of the type of Quisling, Laval, and Wang Ching-wei. When the Axis is defeated, on the other hand, there will be one more chance for the other peoples of the world to organize themselves by voluntary consent into groupings larger than the national states of today and strong enough to deal effectively with the twin problems of security and economic stability.

Political groupings of the voluntary and democratic sort, no less than those created by conquest, must rest on an organization of power, of force. The difference is that despotism, in its ancient or modern form, is an *imposition* of power, while democratic organization represents a *pooling* of power and wide participation in its management. It is folly to suppose that democratic countries can long survive, even after an Axis defeat in this war, unless they are supported by an organization of *power,* and the power can only be provided by those peoples who have it. After this war is over, the real battle to "make the world safe for democracy" will be won or lost—as it was lost in the years following 1918—on the home front in the leading countries (not least the United States) in contest against the apostles of disunity, the narrow nationalists, the isolationists.

Supposing that isolationism can be sufficiently checked on the home fronts to permit constructive international organization for the maintenance of peace and economic stability, what should we regard as the most appropriate areas for supranational groupings? In particular, what weight should be given at a future peace conference to the concept "continent"?

It has been argued—by a Japanese writer of moderate and liberal tendencies, for example—that nationalism is being discredited and will have to be superseded by something else, and that "the substitute for nationalism—for the time being—is regionalism, a system of insuring security, order and peace, not for the whole world, as the League attempted to do and failed, but within three or four separate regions of the earth such as America, Asia, Western and Eastern Europe, etc." [9] One may question whether the League failed because it *attempted* to be universal or because it *was not* universal. In particular, it lacked from first to last the power which might have been added to it by active support from the world's largest single unit of potential economic and political influence—the United States of America. It should be recognized, as a general principle of political science, that no security system (except rule imposed by one group) can function effectively, or can avoid ultimate degeneration into open hostilities between two or more factions, unless there is a sufficiently large aggregation of power actively and resolutely interested in preserving peace and order and thwarting aggression rather than in supporting either side in a particular dispute. In other words, an organization like the League, no less than a town government, needs a large backing of powerful and rela-

[9] Iwao F. Ayusawa, in *Contemporary Japan,* July, 1940.

tively *dis*interested (but not *un*interested) support. Other things equal, a geographically small organization can meet this requirement less well than a geographically large organization.

Few will deny the merit of proposals for encouraging regional groupings of one kind and another, adapted in their structure and functioning to the local problems of the particular areas involved. But to go further, and argue that these local groupings are themselves the largest units of politico-economic organization that it is wise to attempt, is surely a mistake. The most "realistic" generalization that one can make about trends in the modern world is that continued and rapid progress in technology, causing distances to shrink from the point of view of their human meaning, will steadily force the peoples of all regions into more and more intimate relations with one another. These may be relations of conflict, or they may be relations of co-operation; but isolation and indifference will become less and less practicable. Already the world is actually smaller in significant social and economic senses than Napoleon's Europe or George Washington's United States.[10] In the next twenty-five years it will shrink much further. A postwar system which ignores this trend and attempts to divide the world into totally separate "blocs," or which relies simply on anarchic bargaining and power politics among these large units for the settlement of world-wide problems, would prove most unstable.

There are still many people who seem to think that the European security problem, for example, can be solved on a purely European basis. The kernel of the problem of security is where to find the *power* that will deter aggressors. Schemes looking toward a purely European "continental" system at the end of this war always land on the horns of a dilemma. Either they propose to keep Germany weak, so that she will not challenge the European order again—which implies subjugation and division, almost certain some day to foster a new revolt, a new Hitler, and a new war of revenge—or they propose to treat Germany

[10] Demonstrated with charts in Part I of the writer's *World Economy in Transition* (New York: Council on Foreign Relations, 1939.)

magnanimously. In this case, her great human and material resources and her capacity for organization will in time again dominate the European scene; all other Powers will feel insecure, and both sides will have to follow economic and other policies which keep them prepared for war and which encourage war. A third (theoretical) alternative is to have Germany join with her erstwhile enemies in a common federation or collective defense system; but this is manifestly unworkable until mutual trust has been established by a long period of peace—that is, until the problem has first been solved in some other way. The magic word "federation" cannot bring unity in continents or regions that, through intense conflict, have become hotbeds of disunity. In view of the deep-seated animosities which will survive this war, *the European security problem is insoluble so long as the only terms of the power equation are European.* The maintenance of order in Europe depends on some organization of power much larger than Europe in scope—so large, in fact, that the total reserve power wielded by this organization will be sufficient to overawe any single power or any coalition that may arise in Europe, and therefore sufficient to permit gradual relaxation of the fear and insecurity which would otherwise make the anti-German bloc unable for years to work out stable relations with the German people.

In 1918 Europe entered upon a postwar situation in which the power relationships had been established with the aid of extra-European support by the United States. When the terms of peace had been imposed, the United States withdrew its support and lapsed back into isolationism. This left a potentially unstable power situation, one that eventually led to an explosion, the results of which even now menace the United States with the greatest external danger in its national history. The same thing will happen again if, once more, the United States throws its tremendous weight into the balance (as we are doing, and must do, because we have such a colossal stake in seeing that the Axis does not win this war), and then withdraws when the peace is signed.

The price of avoiding a world war every few decades is committing ourselves irrevocably to some sort of intercontinental organization of power. The best and cheapest way, for us, would be to unite our sea power and air power and our economic power in some form of world-girdling combination, establishing thus the power-nucleus for a world system within which regional subgroupings might function. This, of course, would be maritime solidarity, the opposite of continental solidarity.

What of continents as a basis for regional subgroupings? In the first place, should not the fundamental principle in constituting postwar groupings be, *Different areas for different functions?* And is there any reason why there should not be a pluralistic overlapping of groups? For example, why assume that Britain should not participate at one and the same time in a European grouping for certain purposes, in a British Commonwealth of Nations for other purposes, in a British Commonwealth and United States combination for still other purposes, and in both world and regional economic conferences on appropriate problems? Could not the United States continue to be a leading member of the inter-American community, while teaming up with Britain and the Dominions for maintaining dominant sea power, and while taking part in a regional organization of the Pacific area? Within the United States itself, the boundaries of the different Federal Reserve banking districts do not coincide with the boundaries of the army corps areas or with the regions organized for irrigation and electric power developments. Similarly, it is a mistake to think of supranational groupings in rigid, single-line, inflexible terms. The touchstone should be common interest in meeting certain problems, together with some capacity to act together. On this basis, it is clear that continents, as such, have no very great claim to be regarded as the natural building blocks of a postwar order. For the major function of all, joint defense—without which peacetime economy will never be reestablished in the world—"continental integration" cannot serve, at least not alone. The fundamental necessity is a world power combination—that is, a maritime and air combination—linking and policing the trade routes and the strategic strong points of all the seas and continents.

The next most important groupings—namely, those for economic collaboration—are also more naturally maritime than continental. The distribution of resources over the earth, and the existing patterns of production and consumption, which it would be needlessly wasteful and disturbing to upset, are like an interconnecting chain—not like a collection of relatively separate regions. There is a more "natural" basis for economic association between such overseas areas as Holland and the East Indies, the East Indies and the United States, Argentina and England, than, say, between Holland and Bulgaria. The existing distribution of languages, racial stocks, and other symbols of cultural affinity likewise departs widely from continental lines. Cheap water transportation in the realm of economics, sea power and air power in the realm of military relations, easy communication in the realm of ideas and propaganda, link the continents. "Continentalism" is a myth which will have little relation to the practical possibilities of the postwar situation.

This article has explored the general characteristics of continental as distinguished from noncontinental, overseas, or maritime groupings, has examined the practical problem of defending the United States from the point of view of continental versus maritime solidarity, and has inquired into the appropriate bases of supranational grouping in the postwar period. The broad conclusion is that the notion of a continent as somehow a "natural" political and economic entity has been much overplayed. Among Americans, the continental emphasis—with the comforting corollary that Europe and America and Asia are largely separate worlds—seems to have been a last refuge for an isolationism which has been discredited in its more familiar forms by the overwhelming logic of events as well as by critical examination. Thus, we find Charles A. Beard and Senator Hiram Johnson agreeing before the Senate Committee on Foreign Relations that they much prefer to be known as "continentalists," not as "isolationists." A public opinion survey by the Congress of American Professions, which found a majority of professional people in favor of full political union with the British nations and some favoring a league of nations, asked those who *opposed* both league and union, "What plan do you suggest to promote better understanding among nations?" The most frequent suggestion was that political unions be set up on a regional or continental basis; some favored union with Canada; others proposed that the union idea be confined to Europe.[11] Continentalism thus is used as a new excuse for isolationism.

A most curious feature of the continental mythology ought not to go without mention. The mythology of continentalism and the notion of continental solidarity are most frequently applied to two areas: Europe, and the so-called Western Hemisphere lands of North and South America. Yet, curiously, neither of these areas is really continental! North and South America are overseas to each other. Europe, as a map of the world will disclose, "is a continent only by courtesy; in reality it is merely one of four huge peninsulas which depend from the southerly and westerly margins of Asia. Of the four it is the least set off from the main mass by barriers of mountain and desert, and the least differentiated by contrasts in climate and the resultant vegetation. It cannot be classed as a continent by any objective geographical test."[12]

To recapitulate, the only generally true observation which can be made about two places on the same continent is that they have land between them. But land may be a barrier as well as a connection, depending upon circumstances. As a rule, under the conditions created by modern technology, places situated on the same body of water or on interconnected bodies of water are "closer" in the senses significant for human relations than are places an equal number of miles apart which have only land between them. This follows from the fact that of the three important ways of overcoming distance—communication, travel, and

[11] *New York Times,* Jan. 26, 1941.
[12] Derwent Whittlesey, *Op. cit.,* p. 87.

transport—there is little difference between over-land and over-water distance so far as communication and travel are concerned, while water connections give a distinct advantage in heavy transportation. On the defense problem of the United States, the analysis of this article leads to the conclusion that a defense line based on overseas solidarity is a stronger defense line, if vigorously defended in time, than any quasi-continental or "hemisphere" or "quarter-sphere" defense line can be. This is particularly true under the conditions of warfare as waged by the totalitarians, where outright assault by armed forces becomes only the last step in an extended strategy that includes isolating the enemy, fomenting revolt by fifth-column activities, and disintegrating morale by psychological weapons.

Finally, on the question of the most appropriate areas for supranational organization after the war, it is suggested that the strongest and the best arrangement would be pluralistic, with overlapping groupings for different functions. All groupings would be parts of a world system in which provision would be made for functions that require universality, such as the organization of power to reinforce the authority of regional associations, and the organization of those aspects of economic cooperation that cannot well be broken down into regions. In forming the regional subgroupings within the world system, there should be no prejudice for or against continental lines. The real factors to be considered are the tasks to be performed, and the affinities of an economic, political, and cultural sort which make group cohesion possible. The physical conditions which necessitate a break from land to sea transport are important whenever they are reflected in socially meaningful consequences like cultural differences and ease of defense. But so many other factors and so many accidents of history have been at work that the "continental" myth is generally misleading and had better be discarded in careful politico-economic thinking.

8

World Airways

By Charles Hurd

Charles Hurd, former Associate Editor of *Newsweek,* has been for fifteen years a staff correspondent in Washington and Europe for the *New York Times*; he is the author of numerous articles on international politics.

"World Airways" was published in a slightly different form in *Newsweek,* March 1, 1943.

The massive air forces now determining so largely the course of the war are weaving the fabric of the future peace. Aviation is recasting our maps, rewriting our geographies, and upsetting our sense of direction.

East is no longer east; nor is west something off to the left as one faces the North Pole. Distance to far-away points is no longer miles, but something reckoned in hours and minutes.

The Arctic regions already have ceased to be only icy desolation; they are the crossroads of commerce for next year and the year after, with surfaces and climate rather well suited to their new role.

The United States is no longer a country separated by broad oceans from Europe and Asia. Our country lives next door to the world. Our former vacuum of insulating space has been filled, literally, by air and airplanes.

We are producing today, in quantity, standard transport planes that can carry six-ton cargoes about two hundred miles an hour. It is not fantastic to foresee planes that will carry one hundred tons at a speed of four hundred miles an hour; they are on the way. It is possible that postwar commercial craft will be able to maintain express schedules of three hundred miles an hour on long runs.

Most of those long runs will be in the northern half of the globe. There, 93 per cent of the world's population is found, and it therefore provides most of the traffic in passengers, mail, express, and light freight. However, because of their rich resources, South America, southern Africa, Australia, New Zealand, and the East Indies also will provide an immense growth in air traffic.

Aside from mileage—for stating global distance in miles, in relation to flight, is like giving highway distances in feet—what does a three-hundred-mile speed mean in intercontinental traffic?

It means that by the most direct routes, with allowances for take-offs and refueling stops, Chicago and Detroit are only thirty hours from Bombay and Calcutta, twenty-one hours from Ankara, and nineteen hours from Moscow; and that Tokyo and Shanghai are only twenty-three and twenty-seven hours respectively from Minneapolis.

In a world bound by land and water, the distortions of the Mercator projection were relatively unimportant. In that world, with our principal ports of foreign commerce on the seaboard, it was natural for the vast section of the nation between the Alleghenies and the Rockies to feel remote from Europe and Asia and Africa, and often to be less sensitive than the coastal states to what was happening on the oceans and beyond them. But what of a world in which bombers based on North Cape, Norway, or Murmansk are as close to Vancouver and Chicago as to Washington? in which Tulsa and Edmonton lie on the main airway from the Panama Canal to Shanghai? in which Minneapolis, Detroit, and Chicago become logical points of embarkation for the land mass of Eurasia?

These new Arctic routes are physically feasible. Their development already has gone further than the public, for military reasons, has been allowed to know. De-icing and other problems incident to the "winterizing" of planes for operation in subfreezing and subzero weather are solved or are well on their way to solution. Airfields have been built, and more can be, near the summer limits of water navigation where they can be supplied cheaply by boat.

There are, however, other reasons why the shortest Great Circle routes through the Arctic may not experience the most rapid development in the years immediately following the war.

These are economic, legal, and political. The economics of air transport has been reduced to elaborate equations. If we skip these equations, two common-sense observations may be made. First, there is no profit in empty seats. Second, there is no profit in hauling gasoline.

The first means that air transport normally will follow the routes which traffic justifies, although patently unprofitable routes may be undertaken for political reasons or with a view to longer-range economic development.

The shortest route from Chicago to Calcutta goes across Baffin Island, west-central Siberia, Sinkiang Province in western China and Tibet. This is relatively sterile territory. It is doubtful that it would provide the traffic to justify frequent, or even regular, service.

On the other hand, the route to Calcutta via London and Athens would be only twelve per cent longer than the direct Chicago-Calcutta line and would tap rich territory and great population centers. It would be fed by lines running down from Spain, France, Italy, the Balkans, and Asia Minor, and running up the length of Africa, as well as from South America. It would be a trunk line. The direct route would take forty hours as against thirty for the other, but there would be little point in a nonstop flight. With stops, the run to Calcutta might take four to six days; but, in the absence of an immense demand for a direct route via Sinkiang, it would provide cheaper and more frequent service. Likewise, in the years immediately after the war, the main air traffic between most of the United States and most of Northern and Central Europe might well go by way of England.

The second point—that there is no profit in hauling gasoline—means that all air transport will operate at less than maximum speed and over less than the maximum jumps of which planes are capable. High speeds and long jumps mean greater gasoline loads and smaller pay loads. We should not be misled by the speeds which bombing planes are now attaining with heavy loads of bombs. They are driven by tremendous power at tremendous cost. They were built to obtain military results, not to operate with economy. An air line trying to operate similar planes would go broke in a hurry. Planes can afford higher speeds on short hauls than on long because they can refuel more often.

Because there were no terminals with runways long enough, Pan American developed its flying boats for overseas work. But as better airports are developed, land planes are being substituted. Seaplanes are generally less economical to operate because of their lack of streamlining and because of the extra weight required for a stout fuselage.

If the war ends within the next two years or so, most international air transport probably will move at less than two hundred miles an hour on jumps of five hundred miles or less. The cheaper route to the United Kingdom would run by way of Newfoundland or Labrador, Greenland, and Iceland. It might carry most of the mail and light express and freight, and provide passenger service at rates not far out of line with those charged on our domestic air lines.

Domestic passenger rates are approximately five cents a mile but, in the opinion of some operators, may be reducible to three cents or less shortly after the war for comparable service.

But there will be a demand for faster and more direct service, and it can be met at a somewhat higher cost. To businessmen, a regular overnight fast mail service between New York and London would be worth cold cash because of the saving in cable tolls alone; a regular overnight passenger service, because of its saving in time. Overnight service between New York and London, with perhaps two refueling stops, is feasible. The fast transatlantic sleeper can become in air transport between London and New York what the Twentieth Century and Broadway limiteds are in railroad transportation between New York and Chicago. The same kind of fast through service can be provided between Chicago and Moscow, or between any other two points on the globe where the traffic will shoulder the costs of the dead weight of gasoline required to push multi-engined transports at high speed on long hops.

Thus after the war we may expect to see a variety of air transport services: fast through planes carrying passengers and mail at premium rates; a somewhat slower service for passengers, mail, and express which are not in quite such a hurry; and slower planes carrying light bulk cargoes and passengers at the lowest air rates. But even the slowest service will be faster than other means of transportation.

Airplanes will not, in the calculable future, supplant land-borne and water-borne transport; but they can take off the cream, and, sooner or later, they will dip down into the milk.

There is talk of a postwar rate of thirty cents per ton mile or less for domestic air express instead of the current rate around ninety cents. Officials estimate that about seven thousand transport planes of various sizes and type would be required for domestic air express alone if airplanes captured only half of this tremendous potential. In 1938 there were, in the whole world, fewer than thirty thousand civil aircraft, of which only two thousand were employed in regular commercial air services.

Before the war, the United States had the most efficient intracontinental air transport system in the world. It was building the best transport planes. And it had, in Pan American, the most extensive international air service in the world. In 1941, Pan American covered 98,582 route miles. In 1938, when the last comprehensive figures were available, United States domestic and foreign air lines flew more air miles than all the major European-owned lines put together.

Now another immense and growing factor has come into play —the Army's Air Transport Command, under Major General Harold L. George. The Air Transport Command operates more than 100,000 miles of route. This mileage is being constantly increased. The ATC flies the North Atlantic to the United Kingdom by alternative routes; it flies from the United States to Chungking, via Brazil, Africa, Arabia, and India, with spurs running up to French North Africa, Cairo, and Iran; it has developed and expanded routes to the Southwest Pacific, and through Canada to Alaska.

The ATC is about to become bigger than all the prewar international air lines of the world combined—whether the measurement be cargo carried, air miles flown, or number of planes in service. It has projected the Big Four into transocean flying and given every one of the larger domestic air lines assignments across our borders. At the end of the war it may easily have more transport planes, more experienced transport pilots, more trained navigators, and more seasoned, trained ground crews than all the other nations on earth combined—certainly more than all the United Nations combined.

Add to these the pilots, navigators, and ground crews of the Flying Fortresses and Liberators and medium bombers, who receive similar training, and their navigational instruments, and we have a reservoir of equipment, seasoned personnel, and operating experience in global flying which taxes the imagination.

But where will these pilots and navigators and planes be permitted to fly? This leads into military, legal, and political questions. We do not know how the United Nations will undertake to police the world after the war. Each country may cling to its own sphere of interest and security. There may be some overlapping or interlocking. Or there might be a truly international police force to function in certain areas. But, whatever the allocation of responsibilities, military aviation, including strategically located bases, will be essential.

It should be noted, however, that even if we should lease or retain access to military air bases on territory owned by other United Nations, we should not necessarily thus obtain landing rights for commercial aviation. We do not have the right now to use the Western Atlantic bases leased from Great Britain for commercial purposes. Moreover, the bases best for military control are not always best situated for commercial purposes—and, even if they were, it might be deemed wise, for reasons of security, to deny commercial craft access to them.

The international law of commercial aviation is governed by two principles which are related but distinguishable. The first is that every nation holds sovereign rights over its own air space. The only legally free air lies over the oceans beyond the three-mile limit. Legally, you cannot fly over any foreign nation without permission. The second principle may be called the "closed port" system, which, by unwritten international law, prevails in sea commerce. In time of peace, a ship of any nation may enter the harbor of any other nation and may sail up its rivers to the limits of navigation. Since Commodore Perry opened Japan to foreign commerce, this system has been universal. But it does not apply to air transport.

A nation might grant the right of transit by air without granting the right to land. Or it might grant the right to land without granting the right of complete transit. The air over all nations might be internationalized without the adoption of an open-port system. Or the open-port system, granting to all comers the right to land at designated airports and to take on or discharge passengers and cargo, might be universally adopted without internationalizing the complete air space which lies over land. Either type of internationalization would create problems of safety in the air and at airports. Either would involve questions of national security. And the open-port system goes to the heart of commercial policy.

Under the open-port system the United States had one period of commercial superiority on the high seas. That was when the clipper ships, by virtue of their speed, commanded premium rates. After that era, the American merchant marine languished. It has been revived periodically only with the aid of large subsidies. In fact, in recent times, international transport on the seas has tended to become an anarchic competition in subsidies.

With the present widespread knowledge of aeronautical science, it is doubtful if any one nation can secure more than briefly an advantage in airplane design over its potential competitors; and it could hold even a momentary advantage only by refusing to sell its best planes. In the air, as on the sea, American transport would have to bear the cost of higher American wage scales. In uncontrolled international competition its future would probably depend on the patient generosity of Congress in voting subsidies; and the history of the American merchant marine indicates that the willingness of Congress to appropriate large sums of money one year at a time would be a weak underpinning for American-owned and -operated international air transport.

At the same time, the present system of negotiating individual agreements with individual nations is complicated and in itself holds the danger of creating serious international trouble.

Something else, or more, is needed. Before the war, the principal European air lines realized this. They pooled the traffic on some routes and left open competition on others. This system might be extended by the formation of continental and intercontinental pools and allocations, reached through broad reciprocal agreements. An extreme possibility would be the creation of one or more international air transport systems owned and operated jointly by the United Nations. At present there is no discernible demand for such an extreme solution in any of the major United Nations. On the contrary, there are many signs of an incipient race for commercial air supremacy in which the principal competitors will be the United States and Great Britain.

At the outbreak of the European war in 1939, only six great Powers were actively engaged in international air transport. Of these, three—Germany, Japan, and Italy—almost certainly will be banned from the field, at least for some years: commercial aviation is too easily transformable into military aviation to permit nations which are supposed to be disarmed to engage in it on any great scale. The fourth is France, which is not likely to be an important factor in international commercial aviation in the years immediately after the war. The other two are Great Britain and the United States.

In addition, the Netherlands and Belgium operated intercontinental air lines before the war. The U.S.S.R. and other United Nations may wish to enter the international field for the first time.

The British have been more alert than we to the potentialities of international air transport. This is partly because of the obvious utility of the airplane in binding together a far-flung Commonwealth and Empire. Before the war, British overseas air transport developed chiefly over Empire routes. Secondly, but not less important, Britain's livelihood has come in no small part from international transportation.

Britain must get her share of the cream which the plane can skim from water-borne transport, or go into economic decline. As the British watch the tremendous wartime expansion of the American merchant marine, it is only natural for them to become apprehensive about their economic future. They know also that we are building air transport planes, whereas they are not. In fact, Germany is believed to be the only country besides the United States building them in quantity. The British feel that they should not be penalized because, for the common purpose of winning the war, they are specializing in fighter planes and truck-horse bombers (which are unsuited for conversion to commercial transport purposes), to the exclusion of cargo planes.

We, at the same time, are putting many millions of dollars into the construction and development of airfields on land within, and leading to, various parts of the British Empire and Commonwealth.

When the British Empire is restored, British planes will be able to fly around the world without once landing outside the British Empire or Commonwealth. They would have circumnavigated the globe before the war if we had not denied all foreign planes permission to land in the Hawaiian Islands. Hawaii is our trump card in commercial aviation in the Pacific. But it would be possible, if extremely expensive, for the British to skip Hawaii by one long jump from Vancouver, B.C., to Christmas Island.

Almost everywhere we go, on the other hand, we must obtain permission. To fly the short polar routes we must have the consent of Canada and, in most instances, of the Soviet Union. To fly the Great Circle from Chicago to Calcutta or Bombay, we should require permission to land in the Soviet Union, to fly its full length, to traverse Sinkiang and Tibet, and finally to land in Calcutta.

Will the Russians permit the commercial planes of other nations to fly across Soviet territory? And would the British, so long as they have any influence in India, permit a polar route from the United States through Russia to develop to the immediate disadvantage of an Empire route from Great Britain through the Mediterranean and Middle East?

We might obtain permission to fly many useful routes without dealing with either the Russians or the British, just as Pan American operates in South America. Neither has sovereign rights over any part of the route from Chicago to Ankara by way of Norway and Central Europe. In the Pacific area, we should have no difficulty in holding, recovering, and expanding our commercial air-line privileges by agreements with New Zealand, Australia, and the Dutch East Indies and China, as well as with the Philippines. We could reach the Middle East by arrangements covering the Azores, or Brazil, Liberia, French West Africa and the independent Mediterranean countries.

In a world-wide struggle for commercial air supremacy with Britain, we probably could win. But it would be at heavy cost, financially and politically, and perhaps eventually in terms of military security. It would split wide open the British-American concert which is the backbone of the United Nations, and on which the preservation of peace will largely depend. Besides, the British have within their own Empire—not counting the dominions, with which we might succeed in reaching separate arrangements—many important airfields and strategic locations for others.

At the same time, American money and energy are pouring into the construction of airports throughout the world. The exact number built or developed since the war began is a military secret. But since the ATC operates more than 100,000 miles of routes, and it is fair to presume that there is an airport for every 500 miles of operation, we can deduce that the ATC itself is operating at least 200 airports. These do not include the military and naval air bases built or developed for strategic or tactical reasons, or the airfields in the United Kingdom which Britain is providing at British expense for use by American bombers.

The ATC would like to see this herculean labor and expense turned into a peacetime commercial asset. And so that these fields may be used effectively, General George and his airmen believe the United States should have the right to establish its own radio communication and weather observation services, and that it should be guaranteed freedom from customs barriers which would prevent the free transit of freight and passengers.

We want the right to fly everywhere, but we cannot fly everywhere without the permission of other sovereign nations. If we could persuade other nations to agree on the internationalization of air space and on the application of the open-port system to commercial aviation, we would fly everywhere. But so could every other nation. The alternative to internationalization is a series of agreements between nations.

Whatever the method, the basic arrangements must be negotiated by governments. For reasons of security and trade, international air transport has become an instrument of state policy. This was openly recognized before the war by every important nation except the United States. All the others were represented in international air transport by monopolies partly or wholly owned by their respective governments. The American monopoly, Pan American, did extremely well despite its unofficial status.

It does not follow that the United States can win and hold its own in international air transport only by adopting or setting up a monopoly closely tied to the government. But the United States cannot expect to win and hold its own if competing privately owned lines are left to fight their own way against foreign monopolies fully backed by their governments. Our policy may be to allocate routes among various privately owned lines, or even to provide competition between American-operated lines on some routes. Or we may decide that we too can protect our international interests best through a single air-line company. Whatever the mechanism adopted, the government will have to negotiate the basic agreements.

In January, 1943, President Roosevelt established an Interdepartmental Committee on International Civil Aviation to study the whole question. And, as this is written, the House is discussing the creation of a separate committee to consider the air transport question. The Senate may be expected to follow suit.

It is not too soon to develop practical plans to assure the United States its proper place in international air transport after the war. If we do not have practical plans and pursue them energetically, we are likely either to get less than we should have, or to drift into a cat-and-dog fight with our victorious Allies which will knock the props from under an enduring peace.

9

The Logic of the Air

By the Editors of FORTUNE

"The Logic of the Air" is a condensed and slightly revised version of an editorial statement which, under the same title, was published in the April, 1943, issue of *Fortune.*

The statement has been made that control of the world's air routes will be the richest economic prize of the war. In the long view this may prove to be so. But there is no questioning the strategic counters at stake. Whoever controls the main strategic postwar air bases, together with the technical facilities to keep them manned, will unquestionably be the world's strongest power. In the world-to-be not one but perhaps a dozen or more equivalents of Pearl Harbor may be simultaneously possible against a dozing foe. America's air policy will be derived from our general foreign policy. But to a considerable degree our foreign policy must be derived from the logic of the air.

Questions concerning the postwar air are already agitating British and American opinion, provoking a mutual suspicion that has been more or less absent in other common dealings. It is obvious why this should be. The British realize that unless they secure a position in the air commensurate with the position they have long held on the seas, the system of communications binding them to their colonies and dominions must rapidly deteriorate. Some Americans appreciate this, too, but from a different kind of geography. We have no commercial bases except in the Pacific and the Caribbean; our problem, therefore, is not to restore the *status quo ante* but to break out.

Aside from any push of high policy, the economic pressures generated by our wartime investment in air power will force us out. The current military-aircraft programs total $30,000,000,000. The services have trained more than 2,500,000 men in various aviation skills, from piloting and navigating down to maintenance. Whole communities have seen their economic lives more or less violently changed by the aircraft business—Los Angeles, San Diego, Seattle, Wichita, Hartford, Buffalo, Omaha, Kansas City. These facilities and the skills within them will demand outlets in the postwar air. The American air is not

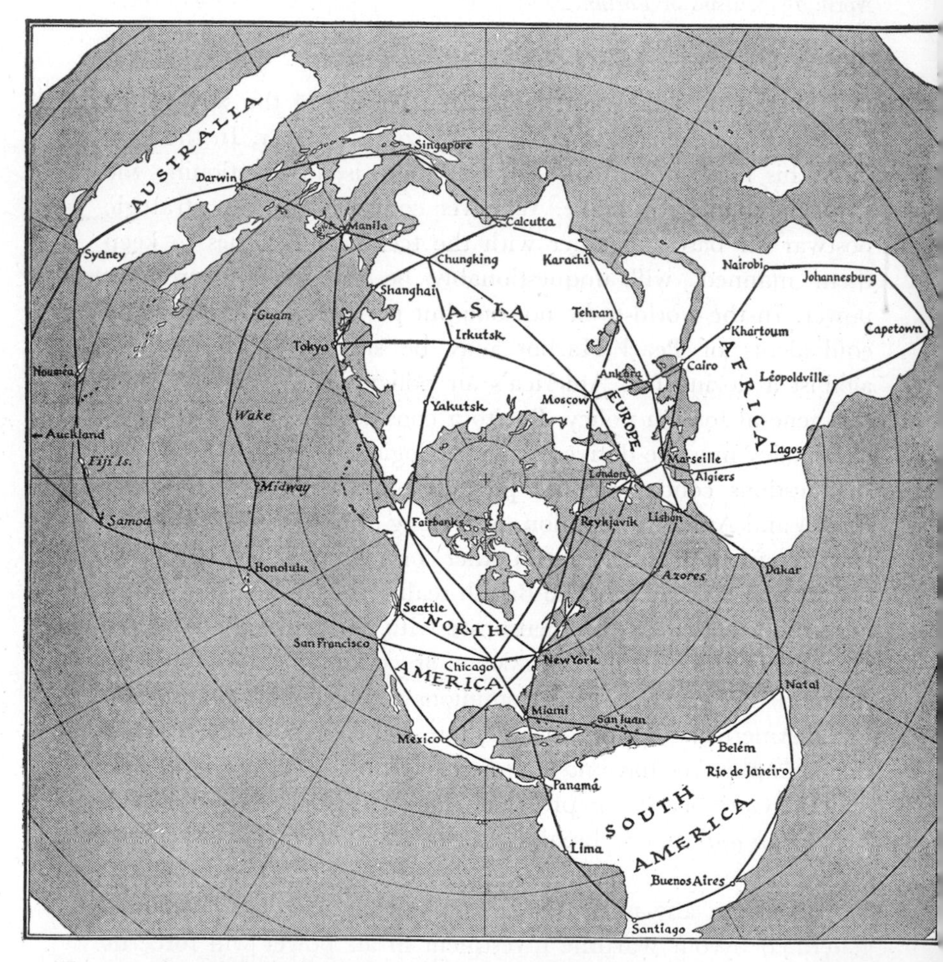

FIG. 11. On a Polar azimuthal equidistant projection is shown how the major air-traffic lanes might develop after the war. The important assumption is here made that the air will be politically uninhibited, and traffic is determined only by population centers and geographical steppingstones. After *Fortune*.

big enough to hold all that American industry will be prepared to push into it.

We have, in fact, already tasted the outer air. Under the general division of war tasks, the British have left us to build transports while they concentrate on bombers and fighters. Since the great majority of United States transports are modified commercial carriers, a tremendous postwar advantage will accrue to us during the conversion period.

Again, for military purposes, the British have opened to us international routes never before flown by United States carriers. These rights lapse shortly after the cessation of hostilities. Meanwhile, however, aircraft of the Army Air Transport Command together with the Navy and their United States contract commercial services, plus the Pan American fleet, are reaching almost every nation in the world, except those under the Axis. The once powerful international competition of the German Lufthansa, Air France, the Dutch KLM has evaporated. Even the British Overseas Airways Corporation (BOAC), although still plying the North Atlantic and the All Red Routes of Empire to Africa, India, and Australia, is severely handicapped by the lack of new equipment.

The present size of ATC's operations is naturally secret, but a few months ago it was flying 60,000 miles of route, and more are being added all the time. ATC is operating in and out of scores of airports all over the world. More airports are being built for it by Army engineers in Canada, Greenland, Iceland, South America, Africa, the Middle East, and China. In all areas it has its own radio and meteorological systems and repair crews.

Although ATC, as a military organization, must get off the world routes when peace comes, United States contract operators will not want to quit. But neither will our allies docilely let them exploit the routes—not over their sovereign earth. In December, before the House of Commons, Captain Harold Balfour, Under Secretary of State for Air, made plain that our present military rights on British routes carry no commercial franchises. "All bets," he said, "are off at the end of the war."

Shall we withdraw? Or shall we insist upon our right as a great Power to fly anywhere? And whose air is it, anyway?

Politically and strategically, two extreme choices appear to lie before us. The first is called "freedom of the air." The British have another term for it: the "open sky." Under this doctrine—freedom of the high seas made three-dimensional and universal—any nation equipped to do so would be free to fly at will in the international air. Like a merchant ship, a commercial aircraft, regardless of nationality, would be allowed to call at airports anywhere, without prior notice, subject only to the usual nondiscriminatory local regulations.

The other apparent choice is called "sovereignty of the air" or the doctrine of the "closed sky." Under it every nation has unrestricted authority over its upper air, clear to infinity. Air travel between or over countries is possible only through the nations' indulgence; any unauthorized passage is an act of trespass. This doctrine, before the war, had become a basic principle of international law, obviously for military reasons.

Emotionally, these terms appear to denote a choice in the air between absolute internationalism and absolute nationalism. So they would, in their extreme meanings. And because of the ideals associated with these catchwords in other connections, many who now utter them for the first time have been misled into thinking that the air demands a clear-cut either-or choice.

Freedom of the air, in the airman's language, means many things. It can mean the separate right of any aircraft to fly unhindered through the atmosphere of any nation. It can mean this right, plus the right to land for repairs and fuel and to take refuge from weather. These privileges, when applied to private as distinct from commercial aircraft, are sometimes called the right of "innocent passage." Finally, freedom of the air can mean these two things plus one more: the right to pick up passengers and trade. For a nation to give away any of these rights could mean a technical impairment of its air sovereignty; yet, unless at least the first and in many regions the second are given, international air travel is inhibited.

Nearly all nations have at some time extended one or two or all of these rights to the commercial air operators of other nations, yet without relinquishing political sovereignty in their own air. This was managed through separate bilateral agreements between governments, or unilateral agreements between governments and operators. Thus, in the practical sense, the air-sovereignty doctrine has not prevented international air operations, although the individual state reserved the right to interrupt them at its discretion.

The present argument over the political air is really the continuation of an old one. At a meeting of the Institut de Droit International in Brussels in 1902, a year before the Wright brothers flew, a French lawyer, M. Paul Fauchille, introduced a resolution incorporating the famous principle that subsequently became the doctrine of air freedom. "The air," M. Fauchille decided, "is free. The states have no authority over it in time of peace or in time of war other than that which is necessary for their own preservation."

Few could have imagined then that the air held any serious menace to a nation's "preservation," yet four years later an Englishman, John Westlake, visualized the dangerous implications of that clause. At a later meeting of the Institut he offered a counterresolution proclaiming: "The state has a right of sovereignty over the aerial space above its soil." This established the gospel for the air-sovereignty school, based on national security.

In 1919 the high-pressure development of the airplane in World War I forced the question before the Paris Peace Conference. The strange outcome of the test of doctrines was recently described before a congressional committee by one of the United States delegates, Colonel Edgar S. Gorrell, head of the Air Transport Association of America.

"At the close of the last war I sat at international council tables representing our nation on vital matters affecting aeronautics. Yet my colleagues and I had been given only a few days—almost literally only a few hours—to prepare. And across the table sat representatives of our allies who had been preparing for months and even years. On our side we had nothing but our native intelligence—a slender reed indeed upon which to rest our country's welfare. . . . Practically everyone at that convention wanted freedom of the air. . . . America wanted freedom of the air. . . . But one nation said that it would not let so-and-so fly across its borders and look down and see its military works. Therefore all of the rest said, 'If you will not let us fly over your country, you cannot fly over ours.' That resulted in a decision that each nation had sovereignty in the air above its land and territorial waters. . . . Glamorous 'freedom of the air' remained just a phrase. The doctrine fell and will not rise until someone effectively challenges the monopoly of the air. He who challenges monopoly of the air must, if necessary, be able to back up his challenge with force."

The important fact is that in the first big test unlimited freedom lost out. It lost out because the war had demonstrated the importance of the airplane as a military instrument. The Paris Convention was the work of practical airmen, many of whom had fought in the air; with them national security took precedence over everything else.

However, the idea of unlimited freedom refused to die, and the Dutch, a maritime nation with a rich but remote colonial empire, persisted—with good logic—as its strongest advocate. At the 1929 meeting of the International Commission for Air Navigation the Netherlands, the United States, Great Britain, and Sweden were the only four nations out of thirty-one to vote for freedom of passage for international commercial aircraft.

The United States, which had signed but did not ratify the Paris Convention, in 1928 finally undertook to formulate a hemispheric air policy. A Pan American Convention on Commercial Aviation, somewhat resembling the Paris model, was drawn up at Havana. It provided that each country grant "in time of peace freedom of innocent passage above its territory to private aircraft." The Air Commerce Act of 1938 left no doubt as to the United States' attitude toward our own atmosphere. This says categorically that the United States possesses "complete and exclusive national sovereignty in the air space" above its territory.

The net effect of this and other declarations was to leave only the air above the high seas free for unhindered trade. Yet within this strait jacket, world-wide air routes managed to get strung. The BOAC reached thirty-one countries; Pan American, thirty-eight. But the diplomatic dealing and double-dealing required to obtain rights unquestionably kept international air transportation from developing as fast as it might have done.

The prewar maneuverings of air diplomacy were often reflexes of high national policy. The classic example is to be found in a defunct air line called Deruluft. Formed in 1921, when their relations were friendly, it was jointly owned by the U.S.S.R. and Germany. For fifteen years Deruluft flew regularly between the two countries. Then the Germans wanted to fly across Russia to China; but Hitler had come to power, and the Soviets rejected the scheme and subsequently washed out Deruluft. In 1939, when the Nazi-U.S.S.R. nonaggression pact was signed, Deruluft was revived, and once again its planes flew across the frontiers—until Hitler broke the truce.

Similarly, the dangerous track over mountains and deserts stipulated by Iran forced powerful British Imperial Airways (predecessor of BOAC) to shift its eastern Empire route to the southern shore of the Persian Gulf. Turkey's refusal to admit international air carriers blocked all European lines from direct access to the short route to the East. This put Greece in a strategic position. She compelled all air lines to land at Athens and wangled from the British permission to fly to Malta and Cyprus.

Sovereignty was also a trump that big countries played against one another. The British refused to let Pan American, which had got as far as Manila, land at Hong Kong, thereby blocking it from the Asiatic continent. However, Pan American persuaded the Portuguese to let its Clippers into near-by Macao; their trumps having proved worthless, the British turned around and let Pan American into Hong Kong. On our side, in deference to the Army and Navy, the United States Government refused to let either the Dutch or the British extend their proposed Pacific services to Honolulu. This of course shut them off from the United States and Canada. In their turn, the British and the Australians barred us from Australia. True, the New Zealanders allowed Pan American into Auckland; but the rights can be terminated if the United States refuses reciprocal privileges for the counter service that the New Zealanders may one day wish to launch.

Air diplomacy generated plenty of hard feelings, but it also made international operations possible. In Europe, where national rivalries were intense, the French, Germans, and Scandinavians took the lead in pooling arrangements: the French with the Dutch on the far eastern routes, C.S.R. (Czechoslovakia), and with the Belgians in Africa. A trade association known as I.A.T.A. (International Air Traffic Association) worked out the mechanics of international air traffic.

Contrastingly, the United States, the U.S.S.R., Turkey, China, and Japan discouraged or directly forbade international operations into or over their territories. The American prewar air policy, on the whole, was negative. The government held down encroachment upon our own sovereign air.

In 1939 the State Department stated that further negotiations for transatlantic rights "should be a matter . . . between the government of the United States and the foreign government concerned." This policy, which the Europeans have long followed in the air, is almost certain to apply in all postwar air deals.

It is plain that the issue between sovereignty and freedom, for practical purposes, long ago ceased to be the clear-cut choice between extremes that many imagine it to be. So the real postwar issue is how much more freedom or how much less sovereignty may be required in the world's air to guarantee the full development of commercial aviation. What international understandings will be necessary to guarantee it?

For us, a policy of exclusion—a closed sky—can end only in our being excluded. At the present maximum economical range of aircraft (about 2,000 miles), we cannot reach Asia or Europe without flying over or refueling at at least one foreign-held base. The same holds true on the great-circle approaches to Africa, the Middle East, and India. In Latin America our present advantage, made almost monopolistic by the complete elimination of Axis interests, depends upon the continued good will of sovereign governments.

The prime geographical counters lie in the hands of other empires, particularly the British. If the British were to rely upon Commonwealth associates alone, quite aside from any arrangements with old allies, they could manage a workable, if awkward, round-the-world air system. The one big gap would be in the Pacific between Australia, New Zealand, and Canada, where possession of Hawaii gives us control of the eastern Pacific.

The aircraft ranges possible in the next few years suggest that to reach Europe it will not be necessary for American aircraft to fly over or land in Canada, Newfoundland, Bermuda, or the Azores. Similarly it should be possible to reach China without crossing Soviet or Canadian sovereignty.

An alternative has been advanced: internationalization of the commercial air. This was a favorite prewar thesis of the French, who proposed it at the Disarmament Conference of 1932. It has been revived in various forms by European thinkers—ranging from a proposal for a joint Anglo-American corporation to develop civil aviation, to a scheme for putting all international operations within an international corporation, modeled on the Suez Canal affair, in which all governments would hold shares. In between is a suggestion by a British aviation expert that all European air trunk lines be internationally controlled. In this country only one government official, Vice President Henry A. Wallace, has come out for internationalization. In an article published by the *American Magazine,* Mr. Wallace suggested the founding of a "United Nations investment corporation," which as "the very first order of business" would set up "a network of globe-girdling airways." Just how this United Nations air combine would work, and what relationship it would bear to the existing commercial operations on the international routes, Mr. Wallace does not explain. He refers to it hopefully as an instrument to be "operated by the air arm of the United Nations peace force." He justifies it on the ground that "the cost of subsidizing the United Nations airways would be less than the cost of maintaining a military air force in idleness."

That it is in the American interest to make the international air reasonably free is self-evident. It is necessary for our trade. It is the only way to assure a world market for our huge aircraft industry, which the national interest demands shall be maintained at a level second to none. And finally, the unique importance of the airplane in the rapid diffusion of ideas and commerce requires that it be liberated to the fullest possible extent.

Yet, since whatever the government does about the postwar air will be inseparable from whatever is done about the conventional ground institutions, it is important to see how the logic of air power fits into the framework of the various general diplomatic approaches. There are four.

The first is a *Festung* or fortress policy. As part of a national policy of isolation, we would close off the American air and rim it with a circle of defensive air power. No intelligent citizen wants that. We are in the world to stay.

The second policy is one of diplomatic twit and twaddle. Along with the other problems, the air would be delivered to the diplomats for solution according to stately ritual. Politics would go on, diplomacy would go on, and the citizen would be conscious of a vague disquiet until the unresolved politics of the air exploded around him in the resolved chemistry of a block buster. No one can want that.

The third is the extreme if vague brotherhood-of-man policy. Because the conception of the air is inextricable from the conception of a more unified world, many writers are convinced that air power makes total internationalism inevitable. It is argued that the logic of the air makes for a world authority and that the logic of a world authority makes for a world control of the air. The President and Congress of the United States would be, in all vital respects, subordinate to an all-powerful ruler of the world.

It may turn out that way. But in the absence of a universal desire to go to world federation in a single leap, no American can be expected to hand over his civil or military air power to an international trust, any more than he can be expected to throw away his national independence like a worn-out suit.

The fourth is a policy of American leadership. Since we shall end up as the world's strongest air power by far, many say it is our responsibility to open up the international air. They would prefer to have this done within the general framework of post-war agreements. But where the logic of the air does not fit into conventional formulas, they want the air dealt with separately by specialists, as a problem in itself.

Under this policy the American approach to the air would not be from Geneva but from somewhere inside the United States. The American premise would be an international agreement on the right to fly not *everywhere,* but anywhere that trade and national security justify. It means, for example, letting other nations into the American air, at specified landing areas or through specified atmospheric channels. But it does not mean letting foreign nations fly at will over a country, trading along domestic routes, spying out the military situation. Sovereignty is not given away—only the right of limited access in return for the same right elsewhere.

The necessary understandings might be reached inside the United Nations. But if the U.S.S.R. should choose to revert to a policy of isolation, they can and must be reached among ourselves, Great Britain and the Dominions, and China. In collaboration with them, together with what we can count on elsewhere, we shall have, for purposes of commerce and defense, plenty of air to fly. Yet our approach must be from a positive and enlightened sense of both the national and the world interest.

The American assumption should be that the air shall be a reasonably free ocean for commerce in which all nations shall participate according to their responsibilities and technical abilities. Toward that end, five conditions are minimal:

(1) *The postwar air map must be drawn in terms of geographical realities.* In view of the range and speed of aircraft, it is unthinkable, for example, that the air map of Europe should be drawn in terms of Wilsonian principles of self-determination. This could only end in a "Balkanizing" of the air. The sovereign power could be used selfishly to block through passage in the upper air or to hinder local passage with insupportable tariffs, landing fees, technical regulations, and other restrictions that would frustrate air commerce and inevitably excite rivalries and wars.

The British Royal Institute of International Affairs, in a recent bulletin, stated that as a prior condition for the fullest possible development of civil air transport, "the prewar restrictions of international air services at the whim of each state will have to be modified." This is sensible. It applies particularly to small sovereignties whose geography may confer disproportionate advantages. But it also applies to the ranking Powers.

(2) *Every nation is entitled to trade in the air, subject to reasonable conditions of national security.* This may involve setting aside certain free-zone landing areas on the logical international routes. Similarly, appropriate channels might be allocated for through foreign-flag traffic. Under such conditions the right of international air carriers to refuel, make repairs, take refuge from weather, and draw upon the meteorological and communications systems of national states should be fundamental.

(3) *The preservation of the air for all people may well require*

the internationalization of or a strong trusteeship over certain strategic areas.

Some believe in the possibility that peace in the air can best be guaranteed by some sort of United Nations air police. A more practical step would be to bring under international control, or under the trusteeship of one or several Powers, certain strategic areas on the international air routes, now either weakly held or in the possession of aggressor Powers.

The west coast of Africa, commanding the European approach to South America, is such a place. Greenland and Iceland, on the great-circle course between North America and Europe, are others. In the Far East there are a number of key islands—Formosa, the Gilberts and the Marshalls, and New Caledonia.

(4) *Military security requires that the world's air traffic be divided by international agreement.*

Merely because the United States is in the most favored position productionwise to exploit the *post bellum* air is no justification for its doing so. It is to be hoped that the senior partners of the United Nations—China, the British Commonwealth, the United States, and the U.S.S.R. will approach the problem on the basis of equality of interest.

Oppositely, Germany, Italy, and Japan, which had strong commercial air fleets, should be ruled out—for a period to be decided. This would prevent their using civil aviation to build up air striking power, as Germany did after Versailles.

The only reasonable premise for an American foreign air policy is that the international division shall be on the basis of trade and natural interest. Probably the wisest course for this nation will be to deal separately with the sovereignties on the needed routes, arriving at clear-cut understandings on rates, number of schedules, technical standards, and the sharing of costs of navigational aids.

In the North Atlantic, for example, we would deal with Great Britain, Canada, the U.S.S.R., and the other European nations, according to a formula based on trade. Britain's paramount interest must of course weigh heavily. It need not follow as a condition of reciprocity that the United States match with a schedule of its own every transatlantic schedule of a European Power, or even the sum total of their schedules. In the Pacific, the trade must be shared with China, Australia, Canada, New Zealand, and the Netherlands.

Intimately related to this problem of division is the problem of colonies. Unless the United States chooses to underwrite the colonial status quo in every part of the world, it can scarcely recognize that "owning Powers" shall be entitled to full rights for themselves as deriving from their colonial possessions. The point is made here merely to indicate how the air problem is bound up with all the basic problems of the future ordering of the world.

(5) *Subject to the overriding concerns of inherent national security, United States air policy should encourage the fullest possible competition in the international air.*

Many believe that unregulated foreign competition will drive our aircraft out of the sky. And many citizens mistrust the prospects because they imagine that national rivalries will lead to staggering subsidy wars, which in turn will lead to monopoly.

That a powerful position in the air will take subsidizing, heavy subsidizing, is fairly certain. That it may lead to monopoly is also possible. Conditions may dictate that the government should run all foreign air operations, as the other major world Powers do, through what Europeans call a "chosen instrument." Or it may turn the whole show over to a private operator to run as a utility. It may allocate zones to separate operators, as many foreign governments once did, or it may allocate several to the same zone.

But recognizing the possibility of heavy subsidies and the "chosen instrument" brand of monopoly does not imply that American air policy accepts either as desirable. With respect to both foreign and American-flag competition our leadership should be directed toward making international air transportation as nearly self-supporting and as free as possible. It will have to be a regulated freedom, as our internal air freedom is now. But if the others choose to play a subsidy game, they must realize that the United States can also play that kind of poker, with more chips.

Far from being afraid of competition (a shameful posture, surely, for Americans), we should encourage fair competition under equitable conditions. Among the four major United Nations Powers (to say nothing of the others) a wide discrepancy exists in air assets and liabilities. The United States lacks steppingstones around the world. Great Britain will lack equipment until a tedious conversion takes place. China, of course, does not possess the technical plant to build aircraft. Yet its air potential may be as great as any nation's.

Obviously, the need for fast communication in the first postwar year cannot be allowed to go by default merely because one country or another is unable to supply its quota of transportation. It would be desirable for the United States to supply equipment to other countries to the extent that they are prepared to do a serious and efficient job of air commerce. That policy should apply to a nation as technically well equipped as Britain. And it should apply to such a country as China. Any attempt to throttle the development of aviation in Asia would be as hopeless as it would be ungenerous.

Of course, low-wage competition from countries with low standards of living will rise to plague the international air. However, this is a fundamental question, not peculiar to air power, and therefore no basis for exclusion. In fact, owing to the high technical requirements and the high ratio factor of fuel to total operating costs, many airmen argue that wage differentials are not controlling in air economics.

Furthermore, all kinds of tricks can and will be played in this international air game, from manipulating currencies to slandering the technical repute of a rival. And because so much about the possible political and economic consequences of the air is unknown and unpredictable, no statesman can be expected to know all the answers. Wisdom therefore suggests that the agreements we make with other Powers should be flexible. If our outlook is liberal and our technology does not fall rusty, the international air should hold no terrors. We can do nothing else than fly it.

American Air Transport Faces North

By William A. M. Burden

William A. M. Burden, born in New York City. A.B., Harvard, 1927. Officer and director of various aviation and industrial companies, 1930–1940. Aviation consultant to the Coordinator of Inter-American Affairs, 1940–1941. Vice President, Defense Supplies Corporation, in charge of the Division of American Republics Aviation, which was responsible for the elimination of Axis air lines from Latin America, 1941–1942. From 1942 to 1944, special Aviation Assistant to the Secretary of Commerce, supervising Civil Aeronautics Administration. Now Assistant Secretary of Commerce.

Author of *The Struggle for Airways in Latin America* (New York, 1943).

The impact of the airplane on man's existence during the years of this war has been so violent and terrible that we can almost forgive those of us who dwell in the past for hoping that aviation may not play so dominant a part in human affairs in the future. However, such thoughts are the exception; the majority of mankind realizes that the progress of mechanical invention is certain to continue, and it is generally accepted that the Air Age, far from being a thing of the future, is already here.

The next decade or two will see the airplane reach a position of great importance in at least three vital fields of human activity. In war it is likely to become the dominant weapon, outweighing surface armies and navies. In transportation it will play a really major role, carrying practically all long-distance passenger and mail traffic except for that small proportion which can pay only the lowest possible tariffs, and gradually increasing its share of high-value merchandise transport. Finally, the airplane will win wide acceptance as a privately owned vehicle for individual transportation, perhaps much more general acceptance than conservative aeronautical engineers are now inclined to believe.

The tremendous acceleration of travel and transport which will result from this development will make itself felt in many fields and will require corresponding changes in our educational system. Aviation will profoundly affect the subject matter of geography, sociology, economics, physics, mathematics, city planning, and half a dozen other fields of major importance. It is no wonder that most thoughtful men are now convinced that, as the primary task in winning the war has been to train our youth to use air power, so the greatest essential in constructing a civilized postwar world will be to condition our entire population to the air point of view.

Even a superficial study of the broader problems posed by commercial and military aviation makes it clear that one of the important fields of human knowledge which will be greatly affected is geography. Because of its unique ability to overcome geographical obstacles the airplane has always carried within itself the germ of a geographical revolution. By throwing off the shackles of seaboard ports of call and the dependence on canals, straits, and other ocean bottlenecks which have moulded ocean transport for centuries, it is capable of changing the whole structure of international transportation and ultimately the relative importance of the strategically situated cities which have in the past constituted the key points of the surface transport network. Such basic changes in our transport system and in our military strategy require a new geographical approach—an approach far less stifled and narrow than that to which most college graduates of the past generation have been accustomed. Even in primary and secondary schools geography can no longer be a matter of Mercator's projection maps and the memorizing of "principal ports, principal rivers, and principal products." Because the airplane can traverse almost every part of the world with ease and follow great-circle courses regardless of whether they are over land or water, different parts of the earth will become important to us as United States citizens; it behooves us to become familiar with those areas and their relation to the rest of the world. This requires progressive geographical teaching.

Our geographers have risen to the challenge, and during the last year there has been an outpouring of popular articles and pamphlets on cartographical subjects which has probably never been equalled in history. In fact, one must go back to the time of Columbus to find an equivalent interest in matters geographical. The bulk of this interest has naturally focused upon the northern hemisphere, where 90 per cent of the world's population and almost all our important industrial concentrations are located; there is a well founded feeling that the transportation routes in this hemisphere are about to undergo revolutionary changes.

It is time to take a balanced view of the situation and try to forecast seriously the lines which postwar air routes will actually take. It is only from such a study that we can judge clearly what parts of the world will become of increasing importance to the United States and therefore deserve increased attention in our schools. It is well to begin by reviewing the process by which transport aviation reached its present state of development and the technical and other limitations under which it still labors.

The airplane has taken forty years to reach its current degree of perfection, and the believers in air transport have waited two decades for the practical realization of its potential capacity to overcome geographic obstacles. The first postwar crossings of the Atlantic (1919–1920) by dangerously overloaded airplanes carrying only a single pilot or at best a crew of three or four were almost universally recognized in informed circles for the reckless adventures they were. However, the spectacular transoceanic flights of British and later German airships in the early 1920's gave a brief hope that long nonstop commercial flights with a significant pay load might at last be feasible. These flights were quick to arouse the imaginative geographers of the world, and as early as August, 1922, Vilhjalmur Stefansson published a very farsighted article in the *National Geographic Magazine* on the importance of transpolar air routes in commercial air transport,[1] an article which was based largely on the performance of lighter-than-air craft. The dirigible development came to naught, however, despite the impressive scheduled operations carried out by

[1] The article was titled "The Arctic as an Air Route of the Future." See also same author's *The Northward Course of Empire*, New York, 1922, especially the chapter "Transpolar Commerce by Air."

the *Graf Zeppelin* and the *Hindenburg* in 1930–1936. Structural failures in American and British airships and the inability of the Germans to obtain helium precluded the development of any substantial volume of airship operation.

In the case of the airplane, progress toward the development of really long-range craft was extremely slow until comparatively recently. As late as 1935 the longest scheduled nonstop flight on any American international service was 700 miles.

LONG SCHEDULED NONSTOP FLIGHTS ON
PAN AMERICAN AIRWAYS SYSTEM

Year	Route	Approx. Distance
1933	Kingston-Barranquilla	500
1935	Antofagasta-Santiago	700
1936	San Francisco-Honolulu	2,400
1939	Bermuda-Azores	2,000
1939	Botwood-Foynes	2,000

Ranges far greater than this were necessary for successful trans-oceanic operation along the world's principal trade routes. A study of the map shows that 2,000 miles is the critical figure as far as the ocean barriers between continents are concerned. It is 1,900 miles across the South Atlantic from Dakar to Natal, 1,995 miles across the North Atlantic from Botwood to Foynes; the longest single jump on the transpacific route is the 2,400 miles from San Francisco to Honolulu.

In the late 1930's, thanks to the initiative of Pan American Airways, American designers produced two types of flying boats —the Martin M-130 (1936) and the Boeing 314 (1938)— which had a range of 2,000 to 2,500 miles with a reasonable fuel reserve although they were capable of carrying only a relatively small pay load over such distances.[1] During the same period

[1] The Boeing 314, the larger of the two airplanes, will carry a pay load of about 10 per cent of its gross weight over a 2,000-mile range. In domestic operations where the operator can to some extent control the length of the flight in relation to the carrying capacity of the aircraft, a pay load of 20–25 per cent of the gross weight is considered desirable and up to 1942 there were no nonstop hops of over 720 miles on the United States domestic air-line system—a sure indication that the extremely long-range airplane must still pay a very heavy economic penalty.

American designers were developing the Boeing B-17 and the Consolidated B-24 long-range four-engined bombers which are playing a vital part in the present war. These bombers have ranges for ferrying purposes (without bomb load but with a reasonable reserve for headwinds) of 2,500–3,500 miles.

Actual scheduled transoceanic passenger service was thus possible for the first time. Pan American opened its transpacific service in 1936, and in 1939 the extremely important North Atlantic route between the United States and the British Isles was inaugurated. However, at the beginning of the present war both services were still in the very early stages of development from the commercial standpoint. The volume of operation was in fact incredibly small. Despite the impressive route mileage of international air lines there were only eight commercial airplanes in the entire world capable of carrying a significant pay load nonstop over a 2,000-mile range.

Thus, though the technical seed had been sown, it had not yet borne fruit; the amount of transoceanic operation was as yet too small to have an effect upon world policy or upon the thinking of the average man. A serious reappraisal of world geography in terms of the airplane had to wait until under the pressure of war long-range air transport really began to develop on a large scale.

The scope of wartime operation has been literally tremendous. Long-range transports are being built by the thousands, and long-range bombers by the tens of thousands. Of more permanent importance, very large numbers of airports have been constructed throughout the world. All the strategic routes traversing countries under United Nations control are now provided with landing fields spaced at reasonable distances which are suitable for large aircraft. Many of these airports are located on hitherto inaccessible islands, and their construction has been very expensive. The total airport investment must run into hundreds of millions, a far larger sum than purely commercial reasons could have justified for many years to come. The basic groundwork for a very extensive international air transport system has thus been laid in advance.

Moreover, the tremendous volume of intercontinental flying carried out by the armed services and by civilian air lines under contract with them is providing a vast amount of invaluable operating experience in a relatively short time. By the end of 1943 the operations of the Air Transport Command alone were ten times larger than those of all the air lines in the world in 1940. The increase in purely transoceanic operation was even greater; the total volume of airplane traffic across the North Atlantic in 1943 being over a hundred times what it was in 1939. The war's final contribution will be the development of new, much larger bomber and transport types capable of carrying really large pay loads over longer distances than the standard long-range bombers and transports of today.

When peace comes, the air transport executives, statesmen, and generals who will be the architects of the world's postwar air transport system will lay down the routes which will constitute the basic framework of air-line operation for some years to come. How will that network differ from the old ocean transport system and from the air transport network which was beginning to come into existence before the present war? In particular, how will it affect our geographical outlook and our national policy? Any prediction as to air transport development must be carefully qualified in terms of time; what will be true in a generation will not necessarily be true in the first five years after the war.

The choice of routes to be flown in commercial service in the immediate postwar period will be governed by two types of factors which will be contradictory, to some degree. On the one hand, because of its flexibility air transport can follow more closely than ocean transport the short great-circle routes in the northern hemisphere. More important, these routes are largely overland and therefore permit shorter hops and increased pay loads. From the standpoint of mechanical efficiency it would seem desirable to follow the shortest routes as closely as possible. On the other hand, the great-circle routes between the United States and Europe and the United States and the Far East trend very far to the north, where population is quite sparse (Fig. 12) and weather somewhat more severe and certainly much less well known than along the century-old steamship tracks. Moreover, those to the East all pass through the U.S.S.R., which has not permitted foreign-owned air lines to cross its territories. It should

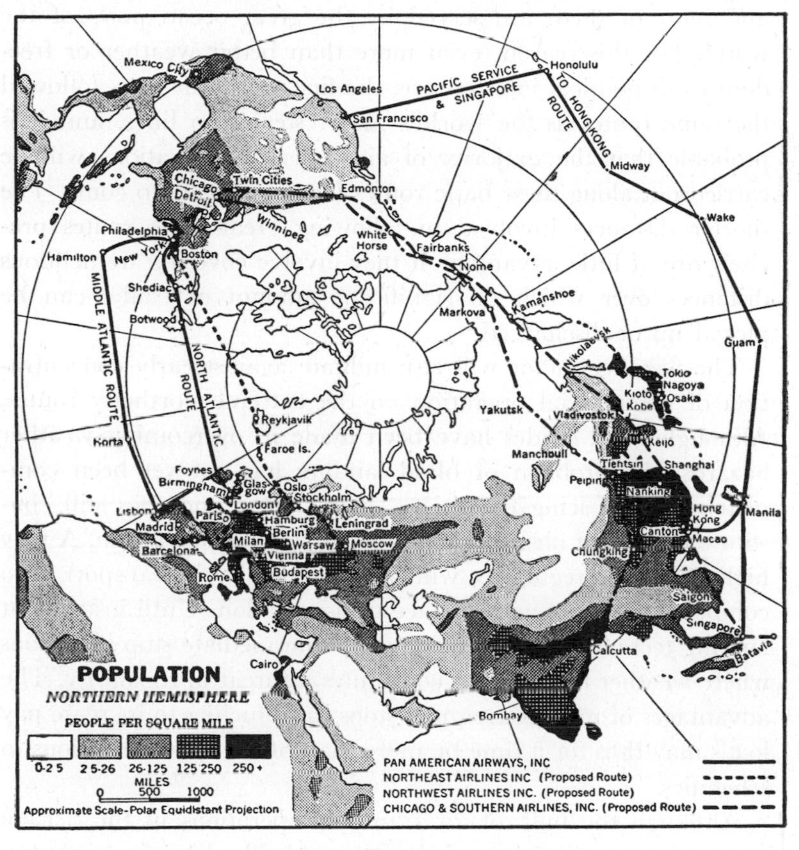

FIG. 12.

be noted that overland routes in general have been more subject to political interruptions than overseas routes, and will doubtless continue to be so unless the principle of innocent passage for commercial aircraft becomes universally accepted.

All these considerations, however, are secondary to population distribution, which seems certain to be the controlling factor in the choice of air routes. Air transport is primarily a business; it must tap the densely populated centers of the earth if it is to develop sufficient traffic to be commercially self-supporting. As Fig. 11 shows, these centers are concentrated on the coast lines, and most of them are served by the great ocean ports of the world. For this reason, even more than better weather or freedom from political interference, the first world air lines followed the same routes as the world's major steamship lines, and it is probable that the majority of air transport operations will be carried out along these basic routes for many years to come. The shorter distances involved in following great-circle routes precisely are of little advantage if they involve covering tremendous distances over which no significant amount of traffic can be picked up or discharged.[2]

The weather factor will also militate against early concentration of commercial operation on the extreme northerly routes. Although great strides have been made in overcoming weather hazards, the problem of blind landing has not yet been completely solved; icing conditions, high winds, and fogs still constitute important obstacles to regular scheduled operation. A very high degree of regularity will be necessary if air transport is to compete effectively with surface transportation. Until instrument landing technique is perfected, every intermediate stop in regions where weather is uncertain constitutes a threat to regularity. The advantages of making frequent stops for refueling to increase pay loads may thus for a time be more than offset by interruptions to schedules.

Although the bulk of air transport operations in the decade after the war will follow at least roughly the historic steamship routes of the past, the fundamental attraction of shorter nonstop hops and shorter over-all distances will result in a certain amount

[2] For example, the great-circle steamship route from San Francisco to Yokohama (which passes not far from the Aleutians) is roughly 1,090 miles shorter than the southerly route via Honolulu. Nevertheless, the volume of steamship operation via the Hawaiian Islands has always been much greater than on the northern route because Hawaii is a very important traffic center.

of operation connecting important population centers along approximate great-circle routes; these will pass so far north as to be within the confines of the Arctic Circle. Three such routes are shown in Fig. 12; they represent actual route applications before the Civil Aeronautics Board. All three deviate substantially from true great-circle courses, as any practical air transport route must, in order to reach as many large population centers as possible and to pass through points where adequate landing fields are or will be available. For example, the proposed Chicago and Southern route from San Francisco to Singapore (8,969 miles) is only 515 miles shorter than Pan American's route between the same cities (9,484 miles) via the mid-Pacific. However, as a result of being almost entirely overland, the Chicago and Southern northerly route has a maximum nonstop flight of 1,098 miles (Kamenshoe-Nikolaevsk) as compared with a maximum nonstop flight of 2,402 miles (San Francisco-Honolulu) on the Pan American route.

Because of these short nonstop distances the early development of a route of this general nature seems likely, and a northerly route to Europe stopping in Newfoundland or Labrador and possibly Iceland is also more than a probability.[3] In addition to these northerly runs certain actual transpolar routes may be inaugurated for political or military reasons before they are justifiable commercially; a direct service between the Soviet Union and the United States across the Polar Sea, for example, is quite possible.

So much for the situation in the first few years after the war. As air transport technique improves to the point where safe and regular operation regardless of weather becomes practical, the far northern routes may begin to carry a much larger proportion of the total traffic. Any very large increase in the volume of air

[3] In the opinion of most air transport economists a stop at Newfoundland or some other halfway point will be almost essential for a sound commercial operation between New York and London. The increased pay load possible on such an operation should permit fares 40–50 per cent lower than a nonstop service. On the other hand, many experienced operations men believe that nonstop service will be so much more regular that its greater appeal to passengers will more than offset the higher cost.

travel will accelerate this trend. At present it would be uneconomic to support an elaborate ground organization along a transpolar route say from London to Tokyo; the relatively few passengers who make this trip direct could better be routed along a longer route (such as London-Montreal-Seattle-Tokyo) which would also serve other traffic centers. However, the transport airplane is a relatively small unit (perhaps 100–150 passengers in the immediate postwar period) and if enough traffic developed, direct routes linking important centers across the Arctic might be justified despite the lack of important cities in between. It is also possible that over the very long term the population density of the extreme northern areas of the world may increase.

Thus, although the immediate outlook for actual transpolar air lines is less spectacular than the enthusiasts would lead us to believe, there will undoubtedly be a substantial amount of commercial operation over northerly routes within a decade or so after the war. This development is bound to have an important effect on the orientation of our national interests. Since the founding of the republic our orientation has been largely toward the Atlantic, with our trade, our cultural relations, and our diplomatic interests all centered upon Europe. We have had, to be sure, a considerable interest in the Far East beginning in the nineteenth century; but our communications with the Orient were by sea, and our interests therefore did not extend to the countries bordering the Pacific on the north. In the last decade or two our horizons have broadened, and there has been a sharp increase in our commercial and cultural interchange with Latin America. It has taken the development of air transport, however, to open our eyes to the lands which lie to the north of us. Even today the geographical links between North America, the U.S.S.R., and China and between the United States and Europe along the northern routes are very little known. Northwest Canada, Alaska, and Siberia on the one hand and Newfoundland, Labrador, Greenland, and Iceland on the other are still terra incognita even to well educated Americans.

If we are to play an intelligent part in the world of tomorrow, this ignorance must be dispelled. The educational process is already under way on a peculiarly personal basis. Many tens of thousands of our citizens have flown these northern routes as crews or passengers on military aircraft, and in so far as censorship permits, their families are learning of their exploits. It no longer seems odd to these men, educated though they were to the ocean-conscious world of Mercator's projection, that one should normally stop at Iceland on the way between New York and England, or that Alaska should be a regular way station on the direct route between San Francisco and China. Their curiosity as to the life, habits, and history of the northern lands is effectively aroused. That curiosity will be intensified in their children and their children's children. Our schools and colleges must rise to the challenge so that future Americans may face northward with the same resolute confidence with which their ancestors faced the West.[4]

[4] Cf. "The Northward Course of Aviation," by Graham M. Grosvenor, article 20, p. 312; also "Arctic Supply Line," by Vilhjalmur Stefansson, article 19, p. 295.

CHAPTER III

Reflections on the Heartland

II

Heartland, Grassland, and Farmland

By J. RUSSELL SMITH

J. RUSSELL SMITH, born Lincoln, Virginia. B.S., University of Pennsylvania, 1898, Ph.D., 1903. Professor of Economic Geography, Columbia University, 1919–1940. President of the Association of American Geographers, 1942.

His standard works include the following titles: *Industrial and Commercial Geography; Commerce and Industy; Human Geography; North America.*

H. J. Mackinder wrote a book at the close of World War I launching the term "Heartland." The book may fairly be called a tract addressed to the Peace Conferees at Versailles.

Mackinder's Heartland may be roughly defined as southeastern Russia and Central Asia north of Persia and west of China. Mackinder's point was that this area, beyond the reach of naval power, is central to the Eurasian land mass as Germany is to West Europe. Germany's central location gave her, while on the offensive, the chance to strike in any direction; if Germany and Russia should unite they could from this central location dominate the Eurasian land mass. With the control of this they could dominate the world.

Mackinder was talking about the future. If we take the trouble to examine the past we find striking evidence that his thesis had already been quite convincingly in operation for several thousand years. The grassland that stretches from the Carpathians to the mountains of Central Asia and from the Siberian forest to the Plateau of Iran was the place of origin of horse culture. Most of this area is nonagricultural land fit only for pastoral nomadism. The combination of nomadism and horse culture made the most mobile society the world has ever seen; and armed mobility and conquest are almost synonyms.

In the second millennium before Christ the Central Asian horsemen overran the original seats of complex cultures in Egypt, Mesopotamia, and the Indus Valley. Also they overran the secondary cultures—Cretan-Aegean, Hittite, and Chinese. In the Roman period and succeeding centuries they kept it up.

The horseman with a crossbow was the greatest "blitz" before gunpowder. The crossbow brought the horse to his Golden Age, to his zenith as an influence in the affairs of man. From the beginnings of cavalry with the Scythians, about the ninth century B.C., to the date of the effective use of gunpowder more than two thousand years later, the cavalrymen of the Eurasian grasslands almost continuously harassed the settled cultures upon the grassland rim and often smashed them at will. Thus the horse, the great contribution of the Eurasian grasslands to history, *had several millennia* during which his relation to sedentary societies was not primarily in the field of economics, but in the field of war; not primarily at defense, but rather the war of offense. The horse was an instrument of conquest and destruction of peoples, cities, governments, and social organizations.[1]

In the Chou Kingdom in China, 1000 B.C., the Minister of War was known as the Master of the Horses. The Chous had no currency. Taxes were collected in kind, and the chief taxgatherers were known as "bullock drivers." For many centuries over wide areas in three continents, kingdoms were measured by the number of chariots they could put in the field. (See King Solomon.)

A recent writer, Bates, emphasizes the acute shortage of power among the Romans on both sea and land. This power shortage led to the use of the galley slave at sea and of slaves to turn the mill and to do other drudgery on land. Bates alleges that Roman wars were often little more than slave-gathering expeditions.

In the ninth century after Christ someone, apparently in

[1] Carl W. Bishop, *Origin of the Far Eastern Civilization* (Smithsonian Institution Publication No. 3681, 1942), p. 26.

France, invented the horse collar and traces. A horse could then pull a load. Then as Bates tells us, horses could really work and enter the economic realm. Horsepower became cheaper than slave power, and slave power and slavery gave way to serfdom. As mechanism improved, serfs became freemen. Inventions gave man equipment that permitted him to emerge from the slave age, as at a much earlier time inventions had ushered in the Stone Age. Important inventions usually change man's relation to some part of the earth.

The horse, especially the horse bearing grassland man upon its back, seems to have carried destruction to ancient societies in a way that suggests a strong resemblance to the work of the airplane today.

CHINA AND ITS RELATION TO THE GRASSLANDS

The relations of China with the grasslands of Central Asia fall into two epochs. In the first epoch China *received culture elements.* In the second epoch China *received conquerors and destroyers.*

Considerably before 3000 B.C. Babylonia had a well developed culture which included writing and a complete mastery of work in bronze. Babylonia also had wheeled vehicles, ox-drawn plow, wheat, many other crop plants, and all of the common domestic animals except the horse.[2]

There is no evidence that China had knowledge of metals before 2000 B.C.; but five hundred years later peoples ruled by the Shang Dynasty in the central and lower Yellow River Basin had a mature and developed system of writing evidently homegrown. These peoples also had a skilled technique for working in

[2] Bishop, *op. cit.*, p. 14. For further light on early Asiatic origins of complex culture see Carl W. Bishop, *Origin and Early Diffusion of the Traction Plow* (Smithsonian Institution Publication No. 3477, 1937). See also *Journal of the American Oriental Society*, Dec., 1939, Supplement, *The Beginnings of Civilization in the Orient*: Hermann Ranke, "The Beginnings of Civilization in Egypt," p. 3; E. A. Speiser, "The Beginnings of Civilization in Mesopotamia," p. 17; W. Norman Brown, "The Beginnings of Civilization in India," p. 32; Carl W. Bishop, "The Beginnings of Civilization in Eastern Asia," p. 45.

bronze. Bishop says, "Bronze working was carried to a pitch of technical and esthetic excellence hardly if ever equaled in later times in any land." Much of this craftsmanship was undoubtedly borrowed together with many plants and animals from the Near East. It had taken the Mesopotamians several thousand years to develop these things.

Before Chinese contact with the Near East the Stone Age man of the loessial area, on which Chinese culture is believed to have developed, was a sedentary agriculturist. He lived, at least for the colder part of the year, in a pit house which gave unusual opportunity for the preservation of archaeological records. These pit dwellers had dogs and many domesticated pigs. As early as the fifth millennium B.C. they cultivated millet and some leafy plants (Goodrich).

There is no sign of fortification about their villages until culture elements from the Near East appear—sheep and bronze or copper arrow tips. The need for defense has come. The villages of the pit dwellers now have earthen walls. These tillers of the loessial lands are learning unpleasant things from the west whence they have derived so many useful things.

About 1050 B.C. (according to Bishop), the Shangs were conquered by the Chous, assisted by rebellious Shang subjects. The Chous came from inner Asia—conquerors from the grasslands. About this time, also, other outsurges of steppe peoples went into Europe, Southwest Asia, and Egypt.

Ellsworth Huntington will smile with satisfaction at the mention of the Chinese tradition to the effect that the Shang dynasty came to its end during a period of protracted drought, for which the king was held responsible because he had neglected to observe the proper rites. Bishop states that the conquering Chous had a culture much like that of the Aryans who invaded India about 1200 B.C.

Shang refugees fleeing before men from the grassland carried their culture eastward and southward to outlying regions hitherto barbarous. The oft repeated process of culture spreading is now being repeated as the educated Chinese from the westernized east coast of China move their colleges and industries to the conservative western uplands to escape the Japanese destroyer.

In the first millennium B.C. this process of grassland invasion and eastern culture dispersal was repeated several times. The unification of many kingdoms into one Chinese empire is commonly attributed to the fact that about 300 B.C. one of the western kings adopted a new technique of warfare from the barbarian enemies of the steppes. This was the mounted bowman: an irresistible blitzkrieg much superior to the lumbering chariot—the preceding blitz.

The Great Wall of China rose as a tribute to the marauding horsemen of the steppes. One might almost say it is a monument to the horse. This, the greatest structure in volume reared by man, was built steadily during the seventh, sixth, fifth, fourth, and third centuries B.C. and extended thereafter even as late as the middle of the eighteenth century. Although the wall was designed to keep the nomads of the steppes out of the farm lands, it was only a limited success—as is shown by the conquests of China by Tatars, Mongols, and Manchus. These cavalrymen from the steppes could conquer China. They spread terror and rapine and made periods of chaos. The conquerors established dynasties. The dynasties melted away. The Great Wall still remains, fourteen hundred miles of it, in varying degrees of decay or ruin. But the nomad conquerors that rode through the wall in shouting triumph have disappeared completely, having been absorbed by the great mass of the Chinese people. Meanwhile the Chinese peasant still keeps on with his not yet so greatly modified neolithic type of agriculture.

ROME AND THE NOMADS FROM THE EAST

The unfortunate experiences of the late Roman Empire with the seminomadic Germans and the Huns (Turanians, not Indo-Europeans) of Asia and Mongolia are a standard part of school history. Bands of marauding horsemen, recognizing no law but the power of conquest, came out of the land north of the Black

Sea, crossed the Danube, harried without mercy the Eastern Empire, and collected tribute from Byzantium itself.

Eastern Goths, Western Goths, Vandals, Huns, Alans, Bulgars in turn punished the provinces of Rome both east and west for having been prosperous enough to produce material worthy of pillage.

The Bulgars remain as a name—their language has been absorbed by that of the Slavs whom they conquered and ruled. The Alans melted away as the Scythians had done in the fat lands of Mesopotamia a thousand years earlier, and as the Mongols did in China a thousand years later. Many of the Huns of Attila's empire merged with the conquered, but one group went back to the grasslands of South Russia. Some four hundred years later they returned to the Plain of Hungary, where today they are the only remaining citadel of their language.

THE ARABIAN GRASSLAND EXPLODES

The seventh and eighth centuries of the Christian Era witnessed the entry of the Arabian grassland into the history of Eurasia in a large way. It was not the first time that Arabia had played a part in the history of lands beyond its border. One of the first recorded conquerors of Mesopotamia was Sargon the Akkadian, 3800 B.C. Sargon was a Semite, presumably from Arabia. Arabia is regarded as the original Semite nest.

In Roman times, succeeding generations of Arab horsemen harried the Roman Empire. As the seventh century opened, Arabia was a political chaos of independent oasis settlements and endlessly quarreling nomad tribes.

A genius appeared upon the scene in the person of Mohammed, who preached patriotism and religion. He used the sword to advance his precepts, and when he died in A.D. 632 Arabia was united.

The followers of Mohammed started a career of wider conquest. The Arab horsemen and camel men rode east, west, and north. In a few years they had conquered Mesopotamia, Persia,

Palestine, Syria, and Egypt. In less than a century they had crossed the Ganges and the Pyrenees, conquering all the lands between. Their defeat at Tours, France, in 732 by Charles Martel, who drove them back into Spain, is one of the very important turning points of history.

THE MONGOLS AND THE TATARS

The eruption of the Arabs from their grassland was unrelated to happenings in the greater grassland of the present Russian domain. The central grassland of Eurasia kept on producing horses and men and marauders. In the ninth century a Russian chronicler recorded one of their many pillaging raids. "Whence they came," he lamented, "God only knows, and whither they went, God only knows; but while they were here they were terrible."

Unfortunately later generations of eastern and southeastern Europeans knew more than this about the Mongols and the Turks. These sons of the steppes came and remained to rule.

Genghis Khan, "Perfect Warrior" (1162–1227), son of a Mongol chieftain, was a supreme genius. He was probably the greatest cavalryman that ever lived. In thirty years Genghis the Cavalryman spread his empire eastward to the Yellow Sea and westward to the Adriatic and the Baltic.

Medieval Europe salved its sore vanity by saying that Genghis overwhelmed by myriad numbers. Not so. He won by discipline, strategy, and tactics. He was a master of speed. The armies he defeated were usually much larger than his own, but he had more men at the point of combat than the enemy—"the mostest men there fustest" (Forrest, C.S.A.).

In one forenoon Genghis left 70,000 Europeans dead on the plain of Hungary, and then "reduced three quarters of Hungary to ashes."

It is reported that the strategy and tactics of Genghis Khan have been most carefully studied by Hitler and company. Equipment may change, but the effectiveness of strategy and surprise remains. Genghis seems to have been a true Nazi. He softened up prospective victims by propaganda, got information by spies, and attacked because he thought he could win. Details of his equipment and effective methods stand in reference books for those who wish to read them.

These Mongols conquered cities but camped without, in tents, as nomad warriors should. As he walked through a gutted Russian

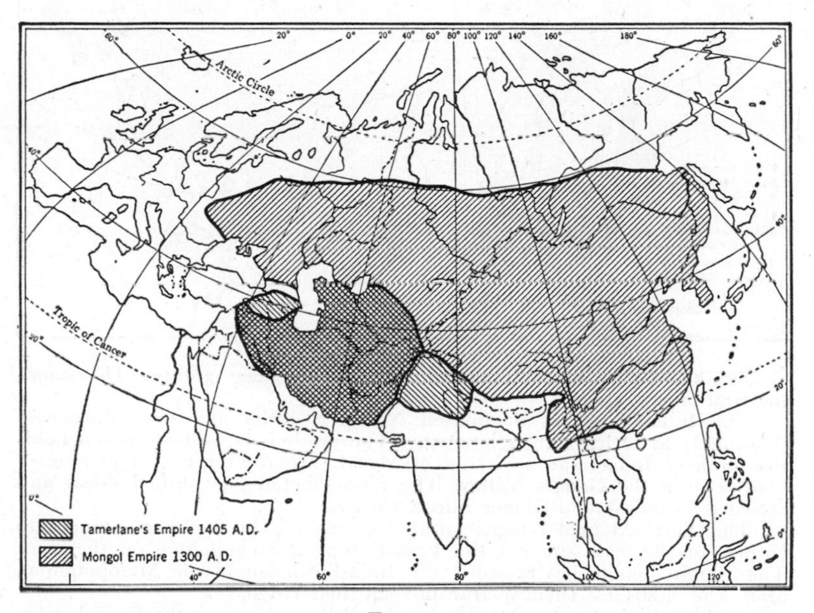

FIG. 13.

city a Mongol warrior kicked a bag of gold coins out of thc way, remarking as he walked on, "A heap of good it did him."

It is said that Genghis's gcncrals urged him to cleanse North China by massacring the millions of agricultural human vermin who inhabited it. Genghis said No, but his successor slaughtered the entire population of Baghdad, perhaps 700,000 in number.

If Russia has been somewhat backward in comparison to some other European countries in recent generations, we should remember its complete submergence beneath the Mongol horde nearly a thousand years after the Roman Empire had its some-

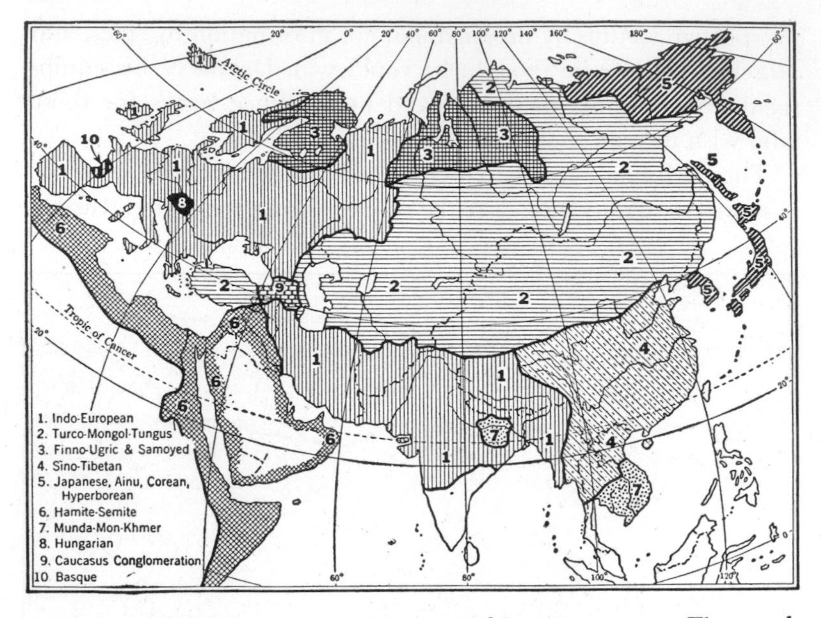

FIG. 14. (After Louis H. Gray) Areas of language groups. They mark the trail of migrations.

The Indo-Europeans dominated Northern India and even Burma so thoroughly as to leave their language. The original Dravidian speech holds the south of India; and an island of Munda-Mond-Khmer (Indo-Chinese) holds out in the Ganges Valley. The Sino-Tibetan has pushed down and crowded Munda-Mond-Khmer into a corner.

The Turco-Mongol-Tungus group has pushed the Japanese group into corners on the east and cut the Indo-European area in two on the west. The Hamite-Semite has crowded the Indo-European in the Mesopotamian area. The Arabs left Islam in Iran but not their language.

The Indo-European block holds nearly all Europe except the Finnish area, the Hungarian remnant, and the Basque and Caucasus areas. The Caucasus Mountain area seems to have been an island of human refuge in the sea of migrations. It contains much linguistic and human flotsam and jetsam. It is said that seventy-two languages are spoken in Tiflis.

In summary, the Indo-European of the western Grassland spread his language to the Mediterranean, the Atlantic, the Arctic, and the Bay of Bengal. Then the Turco-Mongols with their later outbreaks spread their language from southern Russia to the Arctic and the Pacific.

what similar but less thorough destruction at the hands of mobile horsemen from the steppes.

Parts of European Russia are still inhabited by several groups of the descendants of these Mongoloid Asiatic invaders. Their number runs into millions. We might call them, and the Hungarians and the Finns, Asia's return for the settlement of Indo-

Europeans in southwestern Asia. The Turks continued this reciprocity ferociously.

THE TURKS

The Whang Valley seems to have been the center of peoples who are called Mongoloid. Central and north central Asia was the center for peoples called Turanian. The names Turki, Turcoman, and Turk have been variously applied to a dozen or more ethnic groups living west of the Great Wall and close kin to Mongol and Hun.

The mobility of these horsemen of so-called Turkish stock was so great that in a short period they were to be found at Lake Baikal and also in Morocco, seven thousand miles distant. When the Russians took Merv less than a hundred years ago, the Turcomans of the near-by steppes were known by their neighbors as "the man-stealing Turks."

The Turkish group that conquered Constantinople has repeated the southwest Asia historical cycle with variations. They came from Turkestan, crossed a corner of Persia, and settled in Asia Minor. There they increased, organized, and crossed the Bosphorus. Passing the walls of Constantinople, the invaders established themselves in southeastern Europe in the early 1300's. After generations of war they took Constantinople in 1453 and extended their empire into Hungary and south Russia. In 1683 the Turkish siege of Vienna was raised by John Sobieski of Poland.

If you look at the map and locate Tours, the northernmost reach of the Arab invasion, and Vienna, the westernmost reach of the Turkish invasion, you will see that Christendom was subjected to a menacing pincers movement. Fortunately, the different sides pinched in different centuries.

If anyone is inclined to criticize the Balkan peoples, for cultural or political shortcomings, let him remember that for five hundred years the Balkan peoples were subjected to the tyrannous misgovernment of the Turks. The Turks ruled a wide empire of many peoples, but were able to establish their language only in Anatolia.

RUSSIA TAKES THE STEPPES

Gunpowder with muskets and cannon ended the career of the horsemen of the steppes after an undisturbed independence of unknown duration, and after about four thousand years during which they overran almost at will their more civilized neighbors on the east, south, and west. In 1580 the Russians with muskets, cannon, and wagons crossed the Urals. In three hundred years they subjugated the whole of Central Asia and all its horsemen right down to the mountain walls of Persia, Afghanistan, and the outer provinces of the old Chinese Empire.

The tables were turned. The mobile grassland horseman found himself dominated by a machine-using sedentary man from beyond the grassland border.

It is interesting to contemplate the almost unchanging continuity of two culture types. East of the Great Wall, in the good farm land of the Chinese plain, the man with the hoe, the mud village, the brick temple. He was, and is, a peace-loving creature untempted by the lure of conquest, praying to be let alone in his garden. Instead he has been the victim of oft-repeated pillage.

West of the Great Wall the grassland man, riding a horse; living in a tent; menaced by perennial uncertainty of supplies of grass and water. His temptation to maraud was strong and oft repeated. The mobile existence of the grassland man made it easy for him to raid and pillage. The grain bags of the man with the hoe offered an easy objective. Thus for four thousand years grassland culture changed but little, and the raiding nomad never ceased his attacks. Almost any year cavalry could muster on the plains, and in irresistible numbers appear unannounced in the farm land beyond the mountain.

Thus civilization after civilization and empire after empire developed in the farm lands and fell before the man from the grassland.

Perhaps we have here an example of working of the Darwinian "law" of the survival of the fittest. It is probable that there have been 40 or 50 centuries, perhaps more, of nomad horse culture, one hundred and fifty to two hundred generations of nomad horsemen. Is that time enough to develop a psychological type?

Grassland society permitted and encouraged military power, often unlimited except by the whim and fancy of him who wielded it. Temptation by the power lust was more frequent in the grasslands than in other environments. The power lust is unique among man's desires. The gratification of the desire for food, drink, sex, the pleasures of the chase, of workmanship, of the intellect, of creative art—the exercise of all these leads to satiety and sleep. But in terrible contrast, the lust for power grows by gratification. It runs away with the human spirit. At times it unbalances the mind. The Romans with the pitiful record of Emperors before them had a word for it—"Imperial Madness."

History furnishes abundant illustrations. To read *Mein Kampf* and contemplate the actions of the Nazis proves the present and continuing menace of unchecked power.

The dangerous thing is that the power lust is born in all individuals. It is even shared by some of the quadrupeds.

If the turbulent history of the Eurasian grassland has any message for this generation of men it is an imperative command to organize our affairs so that no race, nation, or group can get into a position of unlimited power over other large groups.

Gunpowder and the railway reduced grassland man to impotence. They made him the vassal of the man from outside whose mechanisms could outrun the horse and outshoot the horseman's bow or rifle.

But what about this Eurasian grassland as a *stage and base of operations* in the world of tooth and fang, but equipped also with plane and bomb?

Mackinder pointed out at the end of World War I that land-based air power would soon make the Mediterranean untenable to any kind of shipping. Here he showed himself a most true prophet.

The same reasoning applied to present and prospective techniques seems to make the rest of Mackinder's prophecy also true. For example, take a modern air force and let it fly the distance covered by the force that flew from Egypt to the Rumanian oil fields in August, 1943. Base such a force on present Russian territory and it can bomb the Suez Canal and Bombay. Also it can bomb all of Japan and North China down to Shanghai and Hankow. And it would be a bold prophet indeed who would say that the limit of bombing range has been achieved. The old jealousy of the British Lion and the Russian Bear about the Afghan passes and their eager courtship of Afghan governments has become a back number in the air age.

If the Russians should wish to continue the expansion of their domain, nothing could prevent an air force backed by ground force from taking the Mongolian and Central Asian plateaus. Railroads could then be built and air bases equipped within effective bombing range of Hong Kong and South China.

I suspect that Mackinder's fears are still with him, and that they have grown a bit. He feared an effective alliance between Germany and Russia to produce a dominating weight of equipment. I wonder what he now thinks since he has seen what Russia alone has done, and contemplates what those hundred and eighty million people might do in another quarter-century if the germs of the old grassland conquest fever should rise up out of the grass and infect them with the desire to dominate Asia—and then . . .

History both ancient and recent has vindicated Mackinder. It has also vindicated Woodrow Wilson's dictum that, if any people or nation is not safe, no nation is safe. Immensely strengthened is the argument for world organization to outlaw war. If our intelligence is any greater than that of the sheep or the cow we will strive for international organization that is equipped for—

(1) the removal of international tensions before they make explosions, and

(2) the treatment of any international war as we now treat smallpox and rabies.

12

The Round World and the Winning of the Peace

By SIR HALFORD J. MACKINDER

THE RT. HON. SIR HALFORD J. MACKINDER, P.C., born in Gainsborough, England. Formerly Reader of Geography, the University of Oxford, and Professor of Geography, University of London; Member of Parliament, 1910–1922.

Author: *Britain and the British Seas,* 1901; *Elementary Studies in Geography* (eighteen editions); *Democratic Ideals and Reality,* 1919, 1942.

"The Round World and the Winning of the Peace" appeared in slightly different form in *Foreign Affairs,* July, 1943, pp. 595–605.

I have been asked to carry further some of the themes with which I have dealt in my past writings, and in particular to consider whether my strategical concept of a "Heartland" has lost any of its significance under the conditions of modern warfare. In order to set that concept into its context, I must begin with a short account of how it came to take shape.

My earliest memory of public affairs goes back to the day in September 1870 when, as a small boy who had just begun attendance at the local grammar school, I took home the news, which I had learned from a telegram affixed to the post office door, that Napoleon III and his whole army had surrendered to the Prussians at Sedan. This came as a shock to that generation of Englishmen who still moved mentally in the wake of Trafalgar and the retreat from Moscow, but the full effect of it was not realized until some years later. Britain's supremacy on the ocean had not yet been challenged, and the only danger she saw at that time to her overseas empire was in the Asiatic position of Russia. During this period the London newspapers were quick to detect evidence of Russian intrigue in every rumor from Constantinople and in every tribal disturbance along the northwest frontier of India. British sea power and Russian land power held the center of the international stage.

Thirty years later, at the turn of the century, von Tirpitz began to build a German high seas fleet. I was busy at this time setting up the teaching of political and historical geography at the universities of Oxford and London, and was noting current events with a teacher's eye for generalization. The German movement gave obvious notice that the nation already possessing the greatest organized land power and occupying the central strategical position in Europe was about to bid for sea power strong enough to neutralize British sea power. At that time the United States was also rising steadily to the rank of a Great Power. As yet, however, that rise could be measured only in statistical tables; although in my childhood someone in my house must already have been impressed with American resourcefulness, for I remember in our schoolroom a picture of the battle between the *Merrimac* and the *Monitor*, the first armored ship and the first turret ship. Thus Germany and the United States came up alongside of Britain and Russia.

The particular events out of which sprang the idea of the Heartland were the British war in South Africa and the Russian war in Manchuria. The South African War ended in 1902, and in the beginning of 1904 the Russo-Japanese War was clearly imminent. A paper which I read before the Royal Geographical Society in January of the latter year, entitled "The Geographical Pivot of History," was therefore topical, but it had a background of many years of observation and thought.

The contrast presented by the British war against the Boers, fought 6,000 miles away across the ocean, and the war fought by Russia at a comparable distance across the land expanse of Asia, naturally suggested a parallel contrast between Vasco da Gama rounding the Cape of Good Hope on his voyage to the Indies, near the end of the fifteenth century, and the ride of Yermak, the Cossack, at the head of his horsemen, over the Ural range into Siberia early in the sixteenth century. That comparison in turn led to a review of the long succession of raids made by the nomadic tribes of Central Asia, through classical antiquity and the Middle Ages, upon the settled populations of the crescent of subcontinents: peninsular Europe, the Middle East, the Indies, and China proper. My conclusion was that, in the present decade we are for the first time in a position to attempt, with some degree of completeness, a correlation between the larger geographical and the larger historical generalizations. For the first time we can perceive something of the real proportion of features and events on the stage of the whole world, and may seek a formula which shall express certain aspects, at any rate, of geographical causation in universal history. If we are fortunate, that formula should have a practical value as setting into perspective some of the competing forces in current international politics.

The word Heartland occurs once in the 1904 paper, but incidentally and as a descriptive and not a technical term. The expressions "pivot area" and "pivot state" were used instead, thus:

> The oversetting of the balance of power in favor of the pivot state, resulting in its expansion over the marginal lands of Euro-Asia, would permit of the use of vast continental resources for fleet-building, and the empire of the world would then be in sight. This might happen if Germany were to ally herself with Russia.
>
> In conclusion, it may be well expressly to point out that the substitution of some new control of the inland area for that of Russia would not tend to reduce the geographical significance of the pivot position. Were the Chinese, for instance, organized by the Japanese, to overthrow the Russian Empire and conquer its territory, they might constitute the yellow peril to the world's freedom just because they would add an oceanic frontage to the resources of the great continent.

At the end of the First World War, my book *Democratic Ideals and Reality* was published in London and New York.[1] Clearly the "pivot" label, which had been appropriate for an academic thesis at the beginning of the century, was no longer adequate to the international situation as it emerged from that first great crisis of our world revolution: hence "Ideals," "Realities" and the "Heartland." But the fact that, even when additional criteria were brought to bear, the thesis of 1904 still sufficed as the background for an estimate of the position fifteen years later, gave confidence that the formula sought had been found.

We turn now to the main object of the present article—the

[1] A new edition, with text unaltered, was published in 1942 by Henry Holt and Company, New York.

drafting of an interim estimate of the value of the Heartland concept in a survey of the world preliminary to the coming settlement. It must be understood that I am dealing with a strategical idea which might influence policy in peacetime no less than in wartime (see Figs. 2, 3, pp. 76, 78).

The Heartland is the northern part and the interior of Euro-Asia. It extends from the Arctic coast to the central deserts, and westward to the broad isthmus between the Baltic and Black seas. The concept does not admit of precise definition on the map for the reason that it is based on three separate aspects of physical geography which, while reinforcing one another, are not exactly coincident. First of all, we have in this region by far the widest lowland plain on the face of the globe. Secondly, there flow across that plain some great navigable rivers; certain of them go north to the Arctic Sea and are inaccessible from the ocean because it is there cumbered with ice, while others flow into inland waters, such as the Caspian, which have no exit to the ocean. Thirdly, there is here a grassland zone which, until within the last century and a half, presented ideal conditions for the development of high mobility by camel- and horse-riding nomads. Of the three features mentioned, the river basins are the easiest to present cartographically; the water divide which delimits the whole group of Arctic and "continental" rivers into a single unit does isolate neatly on the map a vast coherent area which is the Heartland according to that particular criterion. The mere exclusion of sea mobility and sea power, however, is a negative if important differential; it was the plain and the grassland belt which offered the positive conditions conducive to the other type of mobility, that proper to the prairie. The grassland traverses the whole breadth of the plain eastward and westward but does not cover its entire surface. Notwithstanding these apparent discrepancies, the Heartland provides a sufficient physical basis for strategical thinking. To go further and to simplify geography artificially would be misleading.

For our present purpose it is sufficiently accurate to say that the territory of the U.S.S.R. is equivalent to the Heartland, except in one direction. In order to demarcate that exception—a great one—let us draw a line, some 5,500 miles long, westward from Bering Strait to Rumania. Three thousand miles from Bering Strait that line will cross the Yenisei River, flowing northward from the borders of Mongolia to the Arctic Ocean.[2] Eastward of the Yenisei lies a generally rugged country of mountains, plateaus and valleys, covered almost from end to end with coniferous forests; this I shall call Lenaland, from its central feature, the river Lena. Lenaland Russia has an area of three and three-quarter million square miles, but a population of only some six millions, of whom almost five millions are settled along the transcontinental railroad from Irkutsk to Vladivostok. In the remainder of this territory there are on the average over three square miles for every inhabitant. The rich natural resources—timber, water power, and minerals—are as yet practically untouched.

West of the Yenisei lies what I shall describe as Heartland Russia, a plain extending twenty-five hundred miles north and south, and twenty-five hundred miles east and west. It contains four and a quarter million square miles and a population of more than one hundred seventy millions. The population is increasing at the rate of three millions a year.

The simplest and probably the most effective way of presenting the strategical values of the Russian Heartland is to compare them with those of France. In the case of France, however, the historical background must be the First World War, while in the case of Russia it is the Second World War.

France, like Russia, is a compact country, as long as it is broad, but not quite so well-rounded as the Heartland and therefore with a rather smaller area in proportion to the length of boundary to be defended. It is encompassed by sea and mountain,

[2] The rounded estimates of distance in this paragraph are apparently based on two Great Circle arcs, the one from Yeniseisk to the East Cape on Bering Strait and the other from Yeniseisk to the Dniester River at the point of meeting of the Russian, Polish, and Rumanian prewar frontiers.

except to the northeast. In 1914–18 there were no hostile countries behind the Alps and the Pyrenees, and the fleets of France and her allies dominated the seas. The French and allied armies, deployed across the open northeastern frontier, were therefore well defended on either flank and were secure in the rear. The tragic lowland gateway in the northeast, through which so many armies have surged inward and outward, is 300 miles wide between the Vosges and the North Sea. In 1914, the line of battle, pivoting on the Vosges, wheeled backward to the Marne; and at the end of the war, in 1918, it wheeled forward on the same pivot. Through the four years' interval the elastic front sagged and bent but did not break even in the face of the great German attack in the spring of 1918. Thus, as it proved, there was space within the country sufficient both for defense in depth and for strategical retreat. Unfortunately for France, however, her principal industrial area was in that northeastern sector where the unceasing battle was waged.

Russia repeats in essentials the pattern of France, but on a greater scale and with her open frontier turned westward instead of northeastward. In the present war the Russian army is aligned across that open frontier. In its rear is the vast plain of the Heartland, available for defense in depth and for strategic retreat. Away back, this plain recedes eastward into the natural bulwarks constituted by the "inaccessible" Arctic coast, the Lenaland wilderness behind the Yenisei, and the fringe of mountains from the Altai to the Hindu Kush, backed by the Gobi, Tibetan and Iranian deserts. These barriers have breadth and substance, and far excel in defensive value the coasts and mountains which engird France.

It is true that the Arctic shore is no longer inaccessible in the absolute sense that held until a few years ago. Convoys of merchant ships, assisted by powerful icebreakers and with airplanes reconnoitring ahead for water lanes through the ice pack, have traded to the Obi and Yenisei rivers, and even to the Lena River; but a hostile invasion across the vast area of circumpolar ice and over the Tundra mosses and Taiga forests of Northern Siberia seems almost impossible in the face of Soviet land-based air defense.

To complete the comparison between France and Russia, let us consider the relative scales of some parallel facts. Heartland Russia has four times the population, four times as wide an open frontier, and twenty times the area of France. That open frontier is not disproportionate to the Russian population; and to equal the breadth of the Soviet deployment Germany has had to eke out her more limited manpower by diluting it with less effective troops drawn from her subject countries. In one important respect, however, Russia began her second war with Germany in no better position than France occupied in 1914; as with France, her most developed agriculture and industries lay directly in the path of the invader. The second Five Year Plan would have remedied that situation had the German aggression been delayed a couple of years. Perhaps that was one of Hitler's reasons for breaking his treaty with Stalin in 1941.

The vast potentialities of the Heartland, however, to say nothing of the natural reserves in Lenaland, are strategically well placed. Industries are growing rapidly in such localities as the southern Urals, in the very pivot of the pivot area, and in the rich Kuznetsk coal basin in the lee of the great natural barriers east of the upper Yenisei River. In 1938 Russia produced more of the following foodstuffs than any other country in the world: wheat, barley, oats, rye, and sugar beets. More manganese was produced in Russia than in any other country. It was bracketed with the United States in the first place as regards iron, and it stood in second place in production of petroleum. As for coal, Mikhaylov makes the statement that the resources of the Kuznetsk and Krasnoyarsk coal basins are each estimated to be capable of supplying the requirements of the whole world for three hundred years.[3] The policy of the Soviet Government was to balance imports and exports during the first Five Year Plan. Except in a

[3] N. Mikhaylov, *Soviet Geography* (London: Methuen, 2nd ed., 1937).

very few commodities the country is capable of producing everything which it requires.

All things considered, the conclusion is unavoidable that if the Soviet Union emerges from this war as conqueror of Germany, she must rank as the greatest land Power on the globe. Moreover, she will be the Power in the strategically strongest defensive position. The Heartland is the greatest natural fortress on earth. For the first time in history it is manned by a garrison sufficient both in number and in quality.

I cannot pretend to exhaust the subject of the Heartland, the citadel of land power on the great mainland of the world, in a short article like this. But a few words should be devoted to other concepts which balance it.

From Casablanca there came lately the call to destroy the ruling German philosophy. That can be done only by irrigating the German mind with the clean water of a rival philosophy. I assume that for, say, two years from the time the "Cease fire" is sounded, the Allies will occupy Berlin, try the criminals, fix frontiers on the spot and complete other surgical treatment so that the older generation in Germany which will die impenitent and bitter cannot again misrepresent history to the younger generation. But it would obviously be worse than useless to set alien teachers to work in Germany to inculcate the theory and practice of freedom. From native sources, however, the polluted flow of German life might be swept clear if it were controlled by strong embankments of power on either hand—land power to the east, in the Heartland, and sea power to the west, in the North Atlantic basin. Face the German mind with an *enduring* certainty that any war fought by Germany must be a war against two *unshakable* fronts, and the Germans themselves will solve the problem.

For this to happen it will be necessary in the first place that there be effective and lasting cooperation between America, Britain, and France, the first for depth of defense, the second as the moated forward stronghold—a Malta on a grander scale—

and the third as the defensible bridgehead. The last is no less essential than the other two, because sea power must in the final resort be amphibious if it is to balance land power. In the second place, it is necessary that those three and the fourth conqueror, Russia, be pledged together to cooperate immediately if any breach of the peace is threatened, so that the devil in Germany can never again gets its head up and must die by inanition.

Some persons today seem to dream of a global air power which will "liquidate" both fleets and armies. I am impressed, however, by the broad implications of a recent utterance of a practical airman: "Air power depends absolutely on the efficiency of its ground organization." That is too large a subject to discuss within the limits of this paper. It can only be said that no adequate proof has yet been presented that air fighting will not follow the long history of all kinds of warfare by presenting alternations of offensive and defensive tactical superiority, meanwhile effecting few permanent changes in strategical conditions.

I make no pretense to forecasting the future of humanity. What I am concerned with are the conditions under which we set about winning the peace when victory in the war has been achieved. In regard to the pattern of the postwar world, now being studied by many people for the first time, it is important that a line should be carefully drawn between idealistic blueprints and realistic and scholarly maps presenting concepts—political, economic, strategic, and so forth—based on the recognition of obstinate facts.

With that in mind, attention may be drawn to a great feature of global geography: a mantle, as it were, hung around the north polar regions. It begins as the Sahara Desert, is followed as one moves eastward by the Arabian, Iranian, Tibetan, and Mongolian deserts, and then extends, by way of the wildernesses of Lenaland, Alaska, and the Laurentian shield of Canada, to the sub-arid belt of the western United States. That mantle of deserts and wildernesses is a feature of the first importance in global geography. Within it lie two related features of almost equal significance: the Heartland, and the basin of the Midland Ocean

(North Atlantic) with its four subsidiaries (Mediterranean, Baltic, and Caribbean seas); outside are the Great Ocean (Pacific, Indian, and South Atlantic) and the lands which drain to it (Asiatic Monsoon lands, Australia, South America, Africa south of the Sahara, and the west coast of North America).

Archimedes said he could lift the world if he could find a fulcrum on which to rest his lever. All the world cannot be lifted back to prosperity at once. The region between the Missouri and the Yenisei, with its great trunk routes for merchant aircraft between Chicago–New York and London–Moscow, and all that the development of them will stand for, must be the first care, for it must be the fulcrum. Wisely the conquering of Japan has waited for a while. In due course China will receive capital on a generous scale as a debt of honor, to help in her romantic adventure of building for a quarter of humanity a new civilization, neither quite Eastern nor quite Western. Then the ordering of the Outer World will be relatively easy, with China, the United States, and the United Kingdom leading the way, the last two each followed by its trail of a commonwealth of free nations—for though their histories will have been different the result will be similar. But the first enterprise undertaken in economic rebuilding will surely have to be within the area encompassed by the desert mantle, lest a whole civilization should deliquesce into chaos. Pity that the alliance, negotiated after Versailles, between the United States, the United Kingdom, and France was not implemented! What trouble and sadness that act might have saved!

And now, to complete my picture of the pattern of the round world, let me epitomize my argument thus far and add very briefly two concepts to the three already visualized. For the purposes of what I see described in American writings as "Grand Strategy," it is necessary to build broad generalizations in geography no less than in history and economics.

I have described afresh my concept of the Heartland, which I have no hesitation in saying is more valid and useful today than it was either twenty or forty years ago. I have said how it is set in its mantle of broad natural defenses—ice-clad Polar Sea, forested and rugged Lenaland, and Central Asiatic mountain and arid tableland. The mantle is incomplete, however, because of an open gateway, a thousand miles wide, admitting from Peninsular Europe into the interior plain through the broad isthmus between the Baltic and Black seas. For the first time in all history there is within this vast natural fortress a garrison adequate to deny entry to the German invader. Given that fact, and the defenses to the flanks and rear which I have described, the very breadth of the open gateway is an advantage, for it provides the opportunity of defeating the enemy by compelling him to make a broad deployment of his manpower. And upon and beneath the Heartland there is a store of rich soil for cultivation and of ores and fuels for extraction, the equal—or thereabouts—of all that lies upon and beneath the United States and the Canadian Dominion.

I have suggested that a current of cleansing counter-philosophy, canalized between unbreachable embankments of power, may sweep the German mind clear of its black magic. Surely no one is going to be mad enough to set foreign teachers to exorcise the evil spirits from the soul of the conquered German nation. Nor, after the first inevitable punitory years, do I have sufficient trust that the conquering democracies would maintain garrisons of the necessary spirit and number *stationed in the vanquished lands*; for there is no use in asking democrats to persist in an attitude contrary to the very spirit and essence of democracy. The cleansing stream might better be released to flow from some regenerate and regenerating *German* source, between the embankments of power I have named, the one within the Heartland and the other within the territories of the three amphibious Powers, American, British, and French. The two friendly forces facing each other across the flow of the canal would be of equal power and should always be equally ready for necessary action. Then Germany would live continuously under the threat of immediate war on two fronts should she be guilty of any breach of the treaties which prohibited either physical preparation for war or the misleading of youth which is another way of preparation for war. The democratic garrisons in their home countries would be, by force of example, the teachers.

On this proposal follows my second geographical concept, that of the Midland Ocean—the North Atlantic—and its dependent seas and river basins. Without laboring the details of that concept, let me picture it again in its three elements—a bridgehead in France, a moated aerodrome in Britain, and a reserve of trained manpower, agriculture, and industries in the eastern United States and Canada. So far as war-potential goes, both the United States and Canada are Atlantic countries, and since instant land-warfare is in view, both the bridgehead and the moated aerodrome are essential to amphibious power.

The three remaining concepts I shall do little more than sketch, and only for the sake of globular completeness and balance. Girdling the twin unit just described—Heartland and the basin of the Midland Ocean—there appears on the globe the mantle of vacancies, constituting a practically continuous land-space covering some twelve million square miles—that is, about a quarter of all the land on the globe. Upon this vast area there lives today a total population of less than thirty millions, or, say, one seventieth of the population of the globe. Airplanes will, of course, fly along many routes over this girdle of wilderness; and through it will be driven trunk motor roads. But for long to come it will break social continuity between the major communities of mankind on the globe.[4]

The fourth of my concepts embraces on either side of the South Atlantic the tropical rain-forests of South America and Africa. If these were subdued to agriculture and inhabited with the present density of tropical Java, they might sustain a thousand million people, always provided that medicine had rendered the tropics as productive of human energy as the temperate zones.

Fifthly, and lastly, a thousand million people of ancient orien-

[4] Some day, incidentally, when coal and oil are exhausted, the Sahara may become the trap for capturing direct power from the sun.

tal civilization inhabit the Monsoon lands of India and China. They must grow to prosperity in the same years in which Germany and Japan are being tamed to civilization. They will then balance that other thousand million who will be living between the Missouri and the Yenisei. A balanced globe of human beings. And happy, because balanced and thus free.

13

The Influence of Geography and Climate Upon History

By Ellsworth Huntington

Ellsworth Huntington, born in Galesburg, Ill. M.A., Harvard, 1902; Ph.D., Yale, 1909. Research Associate, Yale University. From 1903 to 1908, member of expeditions to Russian Turkestan, Persia, Chinese Turkestan, China, Siberia, and India.

Dr. Huntington is the author of three types of books, relating to (1) the effect of climate and its changes; (2) problems of racial character and eugenics; (3) geography in its human and economic aspects. Among his most important books are *The Pulse of Asia* (1907), *Civilization and Climate* (1915), *The Character of Races* (1924), and *Principles of Human Geography* (with Sumner W. Cushing; 5th ed., 1940).

"The Influence of Geography and Climate upon History" includes quotations from the concluding chapter of *The Pulse of Asia* (Houghton Mifflin, Boston).

The human geography of Central Asia sheds light on German geopolitik. It provides a key to the problem of the Heartland which has occupied so great a place in recent German thinking. It reveals two important conditions which were not sufficiently recognized by Mackinder in his original statement about the Heartland, or by Haushofer in his later elaboration of Mackinder's ideas. First, the character of the Heartland people themselves has not been sufficiently emphasized. Second, the driving power of the dry phases of climatic pulsations has also been underrated.

Pastoral nomads have long been the most influential inhabitants of the grasslands and deserts of Asia. The essential point as to their character is well summed up by Liddell Hart.[1] He says that there is no good ground for the common view that the victories of the Mongols under Jenghiz Khan and his successors were due to overwhelming numbers. The character of the people, rather than their number, was the reason for their amazingly rapid suc-

[1] Article "Mongol Campaigns," in *Encyclopædia Britannica*, 14th ed., Vol. XV, pp. 705–707.

cession of victories. They alone among the people of their time grasped some of the most vital principles of military strategy and tactics.

This agrees with conclusions drawn from a study of pastoral nomads in many parts of Asia and Africa.[2] Wherever nomads possess good riding animals, whether it be in the Old World, or among Apaches in North America, raids are practically certain to be an essential part of the mores, or established habits. In times of drought the mother animals stagger and die for lack of water and grass, and children, as well as young animals, die for lack of milk. Raids are practically the only means of gaining new animals and additional food wherewith to keep the children alive. Hence they have become a noble exercise to be practiced at all times, and to be carried out in deadly earnest whenever there is a drought. The spring of 1909, for example, was so dry that four Arab raids on the borders of the Syrian Desert took place while the author was present.

The successful nomad must have innate qualities such that he can arouse himself to intense exertion if need be, endure great privation and weariness when animals stray for mile after mile, when wild beasts attack the flock, when he himself goes on a raid, or when other tribesmen attempt to drive off his animals. It is even more important that he possess the power of leadership, ability to make quick decisions in an emergency, and the capacity to obey his leaders unquestioningly and to cooperate fully with his comrades. Lack of these qualities spells failure in the great crises of life. Hence the social ideal of pastoral nomads is the man who is a good raider, no matter how idle he may be ordinarily. Young men who fall too far below the ideal—cowards or those whose comrades cannot rely on them—have for ages been expelled by public opinion and forced to go to the oases or other agricultural regions. The youth who approaches the ideal, on the contrary, gets the prettiest, healthiest girl for a wife. He later gets other wives, and has many children. Thus a drastic

[2] Ellsworth Huntington, *The Character of Races* (New York, 1924), chap. VIII "The Asiatics Who Dwell in Tents"; Huntington, *The Pulse of Progress* (New York, 1926), chap. V, "The Dominance of Nomads."

selective process tends to produce a certain definite innate type of temperament wherein self-reliance, boldness, versatility, military capacity, and power of leadership are well combined.

The regular routine of ordinary life also exercises a profound selective effect on the women and children. During the migrations from one pasture-ground to another they must often endure the hardships of cold, snow, floods, or burning sun. Many a death takes place in fording icy floods, climbing steep crags to rescue lambs, or merely from sleeping unprotected in the cold after undue exertion. Few people who have not participated in such a migration from lowlands to highlands, for example, realize how many hardships are involved, how strong the women and children have to be, and how intense is the selective process which weeds out the weaklings. Nomadic groups are in danger of extinction unless they possess a high degree of physical toughness as well as self-reliance, power of leadership, and ability to work with others toward a common end. Thus for untold generations the nomads of the Heartland, especially those who dwell among mountains as well as plains, have been subjected to a rigorous biological selection which has produced a definite type of bold, soldierly, and dominating people.

Before the days of modern highways, railways, motorcars, and airplanes, the dominating quality of the nomads of the Heartland was reenforced by a degree of mobility far exceeding that of agriculturists. This helped to make it possible for a few nomads to conquer a vastly greater number of sedentary people. Then the nomads' innate powers of leadership helped them to establish themselves as rulers of these same "tame" agriculturists. This helps to explain the dominance of four nomad dynasties for centuries in China. It also throws light on the outbursts of the Huns, Mongols, and others from Central Asia, the existence of the Moghul Empire in India, the Osmanli empire in Turkey, and many other instances of nomadic aggression such as the Shepherd Kings of Egypt, and the empires of the Medes and Persians. This brings us to the mistake which seems to have been made by both Mackinder and Haushofer. The mere control of the Heartland is of relatively little importance. The greatest secret of the unquestionable historic importance of that region lies in the selective effect arising from thousands of years of life in the grassland environment.

The second neglected factor in the usual interpretation of the role of the Heartland is the great variability of the climate by reason of its highly continental character. Because Central Asia and the surrounding steppes are so far from the sea and so cut off from oceanic influences, all types of climatic variation tend to assume an extreme form. Violent rains and marvellously sudden floods alternate with long periods of no rain at all. Extremes of heat and cold are great. Summer and winter differ to an extraordinary degree. The climatic cycles which all meteorologists now recognize as universal assume an unusually intense form. The longer and more severe the cycles, the greater has been their effect in creating unrest, raids, and unusual migrations among the nomads. Such events often have repercussions which endure for decades or generations, especially if an unusually able group, such as the Mongols of Jenghiz Khan, is uprooted from its moorings. One migrating or conquering group upsets another; this group in turn forces still a third to move away from its accustomed round of camping places. A series of years with droughts at unusually frequent intervals is enough to set the whole Heartland in commotion and to let loose disruptive influences which continue for centuries. Climatic changes have been one of the great factors in influencing the course of human progress. This conclusion applies primarily to Central Asia; but there is strong reason to believe that it is equally applicable to Western Asia, North Africa, and Europe. Apparently, the same is true of America and of the continents of the southern hemisphere; but it is impossible to consider them here.

The geographic basis of history, as distinguished from the nonphysical basis, with which we are not now concerned, consists of what may be called permanent facts, on the one hand, and changeable facts, on the other. The permanent facts—which are permanent historically but by no means geologically—are exemplified by the relief of the lands, the distribution of water, and, above all, the great difference in temperature between the cold polar regions and the warm torrid zone. The changeable facts include not only accidental occurrences, such as earthquakes, volcanic eruptions, the swing of rivers into new courses, and hurricanes, but also changes of climate of longer or shorter duration, which are vastly more important than the others.

Few people doubt the importance of the permanent facts of geography in influencing the course of history; although, as it seems to me, their relation to human character needs greater consideration than is usually given to it. The main movements of population have been east and west in Eurasia because mountains and deserts interpose barriers in the other directions. England's commercial supremacy is due not only to the character of her people, but also in part to her insular position on the border of the comparatively narrow sea between Europe and America, and in part to the presence of coal and iron in close proximity. France and Austria have often battled in the valley of the Po because narrow gaps at either end of the Alps gave both countries ready access; and the outcome of more than one battle has depended on the ability of one of the contestants to entrench its army behind a river flowing southward from the Alps to the Po. Napoleon said that the cold of Russia and the heat of Syria were the most unconquerable enemies that he ever met.

The illustrations just given relate to the physical side of the geographic control of history. A far deeper and more important aspect of the subject is found in the influence which physiographic environment exerts upon human character. Consider, for example, the effect of the deserts, steppes, and plateaus of Central Asia on the character of nomads, such as the Mongols and Khirghiz, in contrast to the effect of the neighboring oases on their agricultural population. The nomadic life accentuates certain characteristics, such as hardihood, hospitality, laziness, morality, and family affection. The oases of the basin floors, on the other hand, are particularly fitted for intensive agriculture, such as is practiced by the Chantos. The sheltered easy life, thus made possible, seems to encourage weakness of will, cowardice, immorality, and the weakening of those ties between parents and children which lead to careful training of the growing generation. Religion and other cultural conditions play an equally or more important part. Nevertheless, much of the difference in character between the nomads and the agricultural people is closely related to the contrast between the physical conditions in which they respectively live.

This is probably true of all races. Not that a single individual's character in a civilized community is directly influenced to so great an extent by the inorganic world around him. He inherits, or receives through childhood training, most of what he is. Nevertheless, inheritance, both biological and cultural, is merely that which is left after a long series of inappropriate qualities have been eliminated by selection. The selection is the result of either physical or social environment; the training of the average man is strictly in accordance with the social order in which he is born; but the social order owes much of its character to the sea, the plains, the forest, the mountains, or the water power by which the occupation of the majority of the people is determined. Those who belong to the so-called upper classes of society are apt to forget that the average man is limited by physiographic conditions much more closely than they; and the limitations become closer the farther back we go toward the savage state. When all this is considered, it becomes almost impossible to assign limits to the influence of physical environment upon character.

The philosophical historian recognizes more or less completely that history is the record of human character as expressed in action. A migration is not a mere unrelated event; it is the expression of a spirit of discontent, or of a desire for something unattainable under existing conditions. Probably no leader, however gifted, has ever persuaded a thoroughly contented people to abandon all that they love and migrate to the unknown. The wars of Rome, her wide conquests, and her laws loom large in history; but after all, they are outward signs. Rome was invincible, and her leaders were great in war and peace because her people, her average men, were strong in body, resourceful, brave, temperate. When they became cowardly and self-indulgent, Rome fell. The people of the United States do not speak English today solely because England lies on the European border of the Atlantic Ocean. Spain, Portugal, and France also lie in highly favorable positions. At first they dominated America; but there was something in English character, a tenacity of purpose and a degree of energy, which outstripped all rivals. In these and countless other cases history is fundamentally the expression of human character. In these instances, as in Central Asia, the development of character has probably been deeply influenced by geographic environment. Therefore, geography must be reckoned with in attempting to understand not only the outward details of history, but the great events which express the character of races.

The evidence of long climatic cycles which is widely found in the Old World seems to render it probable that in each great country at the time when it rose highest in civilization and power there prevailed a climate which approached especially close to the ideal for the stage of cultural progress then prevailing. Therefore, we may conclude that long-continuing cycles of climate have been one of the controlling factors in the rise and fall of the great nations of the world. The Dark Ages, at first sight, do not seem to correspond to this conclusion. Climatic conditions in central and northern Europe were apparently more favorable than today. Accordingly, we should expect to find rapid progress of civilization in northern Europe; but only in Ireland is our expectation realized. The discrepancy is easily explained. At the beginning of the Christian Era, the vast plains of Central Asia appear to have supported widespread hordes of nomads. When the plains began to grow drier, the inhabitants must have suffered sorely. According to Hahn, a rainfall of twenty inches a year in New South Wales makes it possible to keep over six hundred sheep on a square mile of land; with a rainfall of thirteen inches only about a hundred can be kept; and with ten inches only ten sheep. During the short space of a thirty-five-year cycle, meteorological records show that the rainfall at certain Siberian stations near the center of Asia may vary in the ratio of two and three-tenths in the good years to one in the bad years. Therefore we can scarcely be exaggerating if we assume that during the great and relatively sudden desiccation in the early part of the Christian Era, especially in the fifth and seventh centuries, the average rainfall decreased in the ratio of two to one. If it fell from thirteen inches to six or seven in a given steppe, the nomads would have been able to find pasture for only one sheep where formerly they found it for fifteen. If the rainfall fell from twenty inches to ten, the number of sheep would decrease from sixty to one. Manifestly, if such a change took place in the course of a few generations, most of the inhabitants would be obliged to migrate. As the nomads pressed outward from the drier central regions of Asia, we can imagine how they were obliged to fight the neighboring tribes whom they tried to dispossess. The old inhabitants and the newcomers could not live together; new migrations would be a necessity; and confusion would spread in every direction. Meanwhile, northern and western Europe, after a long period of blighting cold and storminess at the time of Christ was becoming relatively warm and habitable, and the migrants pressed into it, tribe after tribe. No one tribe could stay long in its chosen abiding place, for new bands of restless nomads pressed upon it. Rome fell before the wanderers. Nothing could stay their progress until the turn of the tide.

Perchance, though this is only vague conjecture, the legends of King Arthur and his knights bear a hint of what might have occurred all over central Europe if it had not been for the influx of barbarians. England, in its remote corner of Europe, far from the dry plains of Asia, responded at first to the influence of improved climatic conditions, until it too was reached by the migrating hordes of invaders. Only beyond another ocean barrier in Ireland did a relatively warm dry climate and freedom from barbarian invasions permit a notable outburst of culture. There the Tara culture was well-nigh the most advanced of its period. Ireland adopted Christianity and sent missionaries eastward to what are now the most advanced parts of Europe. Meanwhile, in the most densely populated part of Arabia, another movement of the nations had begun, presumably due in part to the distress arising from rapid desiccation. The Arab migrants carried with them the fanatical faith of Mohammed, and were inspired by it to remoter conquests.

When the progress of desiccation was stayed in Asia, and the desert lands began to grow slightly more habitable, no further impulse of this kind caused migration, and Europe was largely freed from further invasion. At last, at the beginning of the Middle Ages she was free to develop in response to the relatively warm and favorable climatic conditions which had come upon her. Christianity and the civilization to which it gave name and form found a fruitful field of development, one which has continued to expand. Climate, however, varies in long cycles. Hence Mohammedanism, too, was able to progress for a time, because increased rainfall seems to have led to the expansion of the habitable areas of Persia, Syria, and other parts of Central Asia and North Africa. Mohammedan civilization under the Caliphs progressed more rapidly than Christian Europe, but soon the desert climate ceased to be favorable, and increasing desiccation apparently led to stagnation in the twelfth and thirteen centuries. Northern Europe's turn to suffer climatically came in the stormy fourteenth century, when England and northern Germany suffered from famines due to excessive storminess and violent oscillations of rain and drought, heat and cold.

Today, the strongest nations of the world live where the climatic conditions are most propitious. Japan, Russia, Germany, England, the United States, and southern Canada, all occupy regions where the climate appears to be most favorable to progress among people who have risen to a stage of culture such that they can protect themselves from cold stormy weather. Much as these nations differ in race, ideals, and type of civilization, they all agree in possessing a high degree of will-power and energy, and a capacity for making progress and dominating other races. Throughout the course of history, similar conditions of climate seem to have prevailed wherever a nation has displayed these qualities. With every throb of the climatic pulse which we have felt in Central Asia, the center of civilization has moved this way or that. Each throb has sent pain and decay to the lands whose day was done, life and vigor to those whose day was yet to be.

The full significance of climatic changes becomes evident only when the effect of climate on human beings is clearly understood. Ordinary experience makes it clear that climate and weather affect people in two distinct ways, direct and indirect. The indirect ways are much better understood than the others. Every intelligent person knows that warm and cool climates in different parts of the world are the basic reason for a vast number of differences in food, clothing, shelter, disease, occupations, transportation, labor, standards of living, recreation, and many distinctive features of the social system. Similar, although less extreme, differences are associated with summer in contrast to winter, and even with one day in contrast to another.

Direct climatic influences take the form of an actual alteration not only in the ordinary physiological processes—such as breathing, the circulation of the blood, and the composition of the bodily fluids—but in psychological attitudes. Some kinds of weather tend to make people not only inert and susceptible to disease, but also inattentive, pessimistic, and disinclined toward mental effort and concentration. Others make people vigorous, resistant to disease, and also mentally alert, optimistic, eager for work, and able to concentrate intently. Diet and disease also play a vital part in creating psychological contrasts of a similar kind, but throughout most of history their geographical variations have been so closely related to those of climate that all three have generally worked together. Thus human vigor, both physical and mental, owes its geographical variations more largely to climate than to any other one cause, provided we disregard racial or other innate human differences. Such qualities as inventiveness, social responsibility, and the power of constructive leadership find full expression only where people have surplus energy over and above what is needed to get a living. Such a surplus is common only in regions with a stimulating climate. Hence the degree to which a climate approaches the optimum for physical health and mental vigor is one of the major factors in determining the rate of human progress.

The optimum climate appears to be substantially the same for all of the world's main races, but varies considerably according to the stage of civilization. Europeans, Chinese, Javanese, and Negroes, if similarly dressed and housed, feel most comfortable, work best, and have the best health under practically the same climatic conditions. They feel most comfortable at temperatures ranging from about 68° Fahrenheit in winter clothing where there are no drafts up to about 77° in light summer clothing with a little movement of the air. They have the best health when the average temperature for day and night together ranges from about 65° to 73°. They work best when the average is about 60° to 70°. This sounds as if the optimum climate for all kinds of people were semitropical with an average temperature of about 60° to 73° for day and night together, and with midday temperatures of about 65° to 78°. This is not true, however, because a uniform climate of this sort lacks two kinds of stimulation which are a great incentive to human progress and of high value in promoting health and vigor.

One of these two climatic stimuli is changes from season to season. Such changes, if not too severe, increase people's resistance to disease, improve their health, and add to their vigor. They also provide a most valuable indirect stimulus because they place a premium upon the kind of inventiveness and forethought required in preparing food, clothing, shelter, and so forth for unproductive seasons. Changes of weather from day to day provide the second type of stimulus. They act in much the same way as the seasons. Ordinary storms illustrate this. When a storm comes to an end with cool, sparkling air and an almost universal sense of well-being, almost everyone has more energy and initiative than before the storm when the air felt "heavy" and "dead." Up to a certain optimum level the net effect of storms is an increase in energy. Indirectly also, storms have long been a great stimulus to forethought and energetic action because they bring rain, frost, and other conditions which oblige the farmer or animal husbandman to be alert and active if he wishes to avoid loss. Storms of the kind here considered are common in the United States, Europe, and Japan, but rare in most parts of the rest of the world.

The existence of an optimum climate seems to make it almost inevitable that the level of civilization in the various parts of the world should be greatly influenced by the type of climate. Few people would question this general statement. The debatable point is how far the level of civilization depends upon the indirect effect of climate through agriculture, diet, disease, transportation, migration, and so forth, and how far upon the direct impact of the weather upon man's physical and mental activity. Although the indirect effects are extremely powerful, the direct effects are probably equally important in the long run. In all parts of the world the general type of culture appears in due time to become adapted not only to the external influences of the geographic environment upon occupations, diet, clothing, shelter, transportation, resources, and so forth, but to the internal effect of climate, diet, and disease upon the energy and activity of the people.

Another great historic fact which depends upon climate is the gradual shifting of the centers of civilization from Babylonia and Egypt to northwestern Europe. This change in the location of the main centers of civilization may be defined climatically as a stormward and coldward march. It began in regions such as Ur of the Chaldees and central Egypt. There during the three winter months the average temperature is approximately 50° to 55°, and the rainfall only one to five inches. In the three summer months the temperature averages 85° to 90°, and there is no rain. Today the main centers of European civilization are located in regions within a few hundred miles of the North Sea, where the three summer months are only a little warmer than the winter months in the earlier centers. They average about 63° with seven inches of rain. The winter on the other hand averages about 36° with five inches of rain.

These climatic figures represent the last stages in a process which began when *homo sapiens* acquired the climatic adaptations which we now inherit. He was then presumably fireless, unclothed, and without knowledge of artificial shelters from rain and cold. Therefore, the best climate for him was one where the coolest month averaged no lower than about 70°. That was the kind in which his general health, vigor, and comfort during the year as a whole were greatest. The stimulating quality of such a climate, both directly and indirectly, is low because there is only a little seasonal change and practically nothing in the way of storms which bring frequent rain and masses of cool air from higher latitudes. As time went on, man learned to protect himself against both cold and rain or snow by means of clothing, shelter, and fire. For tens of thousands of years, however, these methods were of little effect. Even in ancient Babylon and Egypt clothing was ornamental rather than protective. Fire did not help much in keeping warm, because it was kindled directly on the floor with no means of getting rid of the smoke except through the open door, or possibly a tiny unshuttered window. Nevertheless, the dry climate made it possible to construct little huts of sun-dried clay which were fairly effective as a protection against cold nights and against the comparatively small rainfall of the short rainy season in winter. Thus the Babylonians and Egyptians were able to keep reasonably comfortable during a winter which was considerably cooler than the optimum. Of course disease and death ran riot, as they do today where people live under such circumstances. Nevertheless, when both direct and indirect influences are considered, the physical and mental stimulus of such a winter more than overcomes its handicaps. Thus in the early centers of civilization during about half the year the people were stimulated to activity by temperatures below the optimum for comfort. They also had to exercise forethought and do much work in order to provide food and shelter for a long season when no crops ripened and cool nights were uncomfortable. This must have tended to make them much more active and progressive than the people who lived in warmer regions. Such people not only were impelled to do as little as possible in order to avoid the discomfort of being too hot, but did not need to do much because food was available more or less at all seasons and little protection from the weather was needed.

From that day to this, there has been a gradual improvement in man's ability to protect himself from cold and rain and snow. Each step of progress has enabled people to live with greater comfort and better health in regions cooler, more stormy, and hence more stimulating than the previous centers of civilization. In harmony with this gradual change in human culture the center of civilization passed from Babylonia and Egypt to Assyria, Syria, and Crete, four or five degrees of latitude farther north. Then Greece took the lead—another two or three degrees to the north and farther to the west, so that its climate is both cooler and more stormy than that of the previous leaders. Rome, still farther north and west, came next. The westward part of this movement is significant not only because it means increased storminess, but because it indicates a tendency for the centers of civilization to keep away from the great continental interior where the winters are extremely cold. One wonders whether modern Russia will reverse this latter tendency.

During the Dark Ages, with their great barbarian invasions and recession of progress, the lead passed to Constantinople in the east, and curiously enough to Ireland in the far west. Then the northwestward march was resumed, and the center of progress moved to northern Italy with Venice, Florence, and Genoa in the van. These in turn gave place to Vienna, Paris, and minor cities still another five degrees to the north. Even here the northwestward progress did not stop, for London, Amsterdam, and Berlin represent regions which came to the forefront still later. Last of all, in our own day Stockholm, Copenhagen, and Edinburgh represent extreme northwesterly regions where remarkably high standards of living are universally recognized.

This great migration of the centers of progress for twenty-five hundred miles from Babylonia to the North Sea is the result of the combined action of many factors; but it cannot be rightly understood unless the climatic factor is given full weight. The first essential is to recognize that there is an optimum climate from the standpoint of the direct effect upon human vigor and also from that of such indirect climatic responses as diet, disease, and the stimulus exerted by the necessity to take thought for seasons of physical discomfort and scarcity of food. The second essential is that in general, although not always, the direct and indirect climatic optima both become different as man attains greater ability to protect himself against vicissitudes of weather and season by means of such things as tight-walled dwellings, fireplaces, chimneys, stoves, furnaces, window glass, clothing, and methods of storing and transporting food in all kinds of weather. Because of this intimate relation between climate and culture the centers of human vigor and hence of progress have hitherto migrated coldward and stormward with the growth of civilization. The best climate for primitive, naked savages is one where no month is cooler than the optimum, or so rainy as to be detrimental. The best for people higher in the scale is a climate with the following qualities: (1) a good degree of storminess at all seasons, (2) a temperature close to the optimum during a long summer, but low enough in winter for a good measure of seasonal contrast, and (3) no weather so cold or stormy that people cannot adequately protect themselves.

This brings us back to climatic changes. If the preceding analysis is correct, it is clear that climatic cycles must have a tendency to shift the climatic optimum first one way and then the other. The most variable climatic element is storms with their great movements of vast masses of air. During the historic period there is no evidence that the average temperature of either summer or winter in any part of the earth has varied more than about five degrees, but there is abundant evidence of considerable variation in storminess and rainfall during cycles with a length of hundreds, or thousands of years. A true picture of the influence of climate upon history includes the idea of a shifting of the centers of human progress in response to either advance or retrogression in man's control over nature, and also in response to climatic cycles.[3]

[3] The theory of history outlined above has been fully developed in a book which will soon be published, probably under the title *Mainsprings of Civilization: Heredity and Geography in Relation to Culture and History.*

14

Geography and World Power

By James Fairgrieve

James Fairgrieve, born in Saltcoats, England. M.A., Oxon; B.A., London. Late Reader in Education with special reference to Geography in the University of London Institute of Education; Head of the Department of Colonial Education, 1927–1935. Author of the standard works *Geography and World Power, Geography in School,* and *Human Geography,* and of numerous other books and papers connected with the teaching of geography.

The following essay is a slightly revised version of a chapter in *Geography and World Power,* 8th edition (University of London Press).

Within the last generation or two, thanks largely to increased ease of communication, the world has become a single system with no part really independent of any other part. The world is, indeed, an organic unity, though the organization of this comity is far from complete, even on the material side.

We must then consider the modern world as a whole, rather than its separate parts. The world organism is much too complex to be represented by a simple formula; but there are one or two ways of looking at it which may at once indicate how organization has taken place—and therefore energy saved—and the lines along which it may proceed. Each conception has its value.

One of the simplest ways of regarding the distribution of land is to think of the land masses as two great islands, the Old World parallelogram and the Americas, set in a greater ocean. The Americas came only late into the story. But in the Old World there developed three ancient settled civilizations: the European in the belt of lower and partly submerged ground across the land mass, the Indian and the Chinese on the ocean border.

The Old World parallelogram is divided by the Sahara, even more effectively than by the water belt of the Mediterranean-and-Red-Seas–Persian-Gulf, into two unequal portions—the African, without a history, and the Euro-Asian. Within the great land of Euro-Asia lay the plain, steppe to the south, backed by forest and unnavigable ocean, now Russian but long the home of pastoral nomads ever emerging into the borderlands. Round this plain, and partly separated from it by high plateaus or mountain chains, were the coast lands, organized as various states, and to a great extent protected from the black peril by the barrier of the Sahara. The central area, partly plain, partly plateau, organized or unorganized, occupies, from the very fact of its effective centrality and size, a unique position in the world ancient and modern. Not only out of touch with, but independent of, the ocean, this land could most easily be unified by the railway; but from the fact that its centre tends to be steppe, if not desert, the unification is most naturally to be effected from an excentric position near its margin, to east or south or west, and, in fact, this heartland has been organized for longer or shorter periods and in different ways, all autocratic, from the Altai in the east, from the Turan in the south, and last, and most effectively of all, from Muscovy in the west.

In the periphery of Euro-Asia are the lands in touch with the sea, the ocean border. The inhabitants of most of these, on the European sector, have at one time or another dominated the seas. Arabs, Phoenicians, Greeks, Italians ancient and modern, Spaniards, Portuguese, French, British, Dutch, and Norwegians have had sea power or ocean power depending, some almost entirely, others to a less extent, on the ease, cheapness, and certainty of water carriage, and on a certain knack of the sea, bred of familiarity and use. On the Asiatic sector only the Japanese have found any part of their destiny on the ocean. India and China remain essentially different from the Western lands: they are open to the influences from the ocean, and yet have never made any attempt to play a part on it.

With the organization of the Heartland and the Sea Powers, a crush zone of small states has gradually come into existence between them. These states are largely survivals from an earlier time when political and economic organizations were on a smaller scale, and each has characteristics partly acquired in that earlier time and partly natural. With sufficient individuality to withstand absorptions, but unable or unwilling to unite with others to form any larger whole, they remain in the unsatisfactory position of buffer states, precariously independent politically, and more surely dependent economically. This zone of states, with small populations, has varied in position from time to time with changing conditions, but it has included Finland, Sweden, Norway, Denmark, Holland, Belgium, Luxemburg, Switzerland, Poland, the Balkan States, Iran, Afghanistan, Siam, and Korea. Finland is remote and essentially only a shore belt capable of cultivation, backed by forest and marsh, and inhabited by those who differ in many essentials from all their neighbours. Scandinavia and Denmark have much in common, but are occupied by peoples who differ—and feel strongly that they differ—in history and in habits. The Low Countries again are occupied by peoples, Dutch and Belgian, who are comparatively few in number but value their distinctness from each other: the Dutch seafaring and agricultural, the Belgians commercial and industrial. Together with Luxemburg, Alsace-Lorraine, and Switzerland, the Netherlands represent the ancient Lotharingen, the land between the east and the west of Charlemagne's empire. Switzerland is the only land of the Alpine mountaineers to retain independence; it sprang from the league of the four cantons, which held the great crossroads within the Alps above Andermatt, and occupied a position more suited for defence than the other Alpine states, in that the dwellers in the mountain valleys could easily meet on the lower ground to the north and still be behind the wastes of the Jura and the moats of Geneva and Constance. The Balkan states —of mountain shepherds, valley farmers, and merchantmen on the sea—are Slav and Greek, Catholic, Greek Church, and Mohamedan, as befits their history, and yet have feelings for national groupings which correspond to geographical conditions. Farther north are states sprung from the peoples of the plains, possessing doubtful boundaries, some in favourable situations with independent histories that date back for centuries, others carved from the forest, never yet able or allowed to stand alone. Eastward is Turkey, Greek or pre-Greek, Roman, Byzantine, and Turkish, with doubtful limits yet fixed in Istanbul or Constantinople, while essentially based on Asia Minor. Armenians on the heights, Persians on the plateau, have remembrance of ancient glories, military, intellectual, and spiritual; yet Persia is so devoid of recognized authority that only with difficulty can it be given even the semblance of a state. Afghanistan and the other Himalayan states, though less civilized than the smaller states of Europe, have something more of real independence because they are more remote and more difficult of access; but they have even less power of resistance against organized attack.

In some sense Germany and even China belong to this belt. Central Europe, unorganized and broken into small and antagonistic communities, essentially belongs to the crush zone; but, organized and powerful, it is in a very different position. In touch with the sea and tempted on to the ocean, Germany is one of the sea powers, while her situation on the western and most populous margin of the great heartland makes her, at any rate, a possible centre from which that heartland might be organized.

The larger China, the land of the Chinese, roughly corresponds to the Chinese Empire at its greatest extent. This China, again, a world in itself, is far too great and homogeneous to be crushed, though parts of it may be exploited by men of other lands. Unwilling—quite naturally, as we have seen—to become seamen in any numbers, the Chinese are yet in touch with the sea, and reap advantages which they are ready to take from that position; and again like Germany, to an even greater extent than Germany, China is in a position to dominate the heartland with little possibility of interference from others. It must not be forgotten that a very considerable portion of the plateau steppe even as far west as Kashgar and Zungaria has been under some kind of Chinese rule, and is permeated by Chinese culture. China, then, though immobile as a state, has yet a situation of peculiar importance.

India is in an even more extraordinary position. Few of her peoples are seamen or even rivermen, and yet, as part of the British Commonwealth, India shares in the advantages of ease and safety of communication on the sea. With no real unity, and composed of numbers of diverse and rather hostile states, India might be expected to belong to the crush zone; and yet under British control she is more nearly unified than she has ever been.

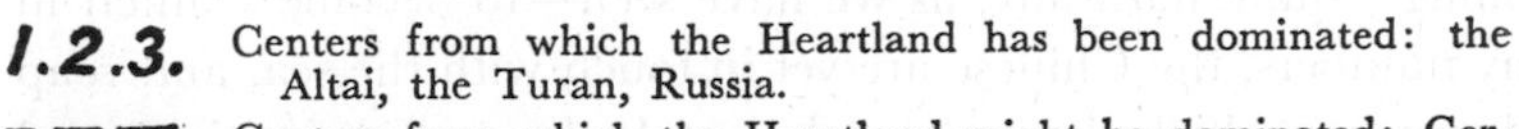

1.2.3. Centers from which the Heartland has been dominated: the Altai, the Turan, Russia.

I.II.III. Centers from which the Heartland might be dominated: Germany, China, India.

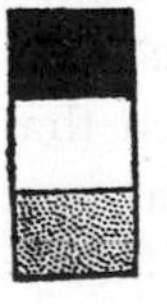

Lands of the Sea Powers.

The Crush Zone.

The Heartland.

FIG. 15. The Old World System

Nearest of the lands of the ocean border to the margin of the heartland, it would be natural for India to take a foremost place in dominating that heartland; and yet since the dawn of history, while there has been a continuous movement from the interior to India, there has been no reverse process. Only in the very earliest times of man on the earth is there a suggestion that the human stream flowed in any effective way from India to the interior.

The conceptions of the central Heartland, the Sea Powers, and the crush zone do correspond to actual facts. There is order, but it is an order which comes from growth; and with changing conditions the heritage of the past is knit into the present scheme. There is no rigid arrangement.

And this Old World system does not stand alone. The New World takes its place in a larger *Orbis Terrarum*. Here the geographical conditions and the past history provide little that corresponds in any way to the states of the Old World. In the New World heartland and sea power are not separate: there is no crush zone; the United States dominates the stage. Indeed, the United States might conceivably be the seat of an ocean power, and play the part on a vaster scale which Britain played in earlier times. Removed, but not far removed by an ocean moat, from the direct effects of Old World strife, with power of all kinds, material and economic and moral, the United States can claim to be arbiter in world disputes.

With the rise of the United States to the position of a great Power a new condition appears in the world, or rather, the condition which Columbus made significant acquires a new significance. The earth is round. It was because the earth was round in the days of Columbus that there was another way from the west of the Old World to the east. The earth is round now, and the United States lies *between* the west and the east of the Old World. The west of the United States is nearer to the east of Asia than is the west of Europe, and yet not so very much nearer. Look at a globe and try to realize the distance across the Pacific Ocean, especially from southeast to northwest. It was this distance across the Pacific that prevented any real use being made of the western route from Europe to the Indies, so that till the rise of the United States the New World was but a land of no great consequence, lying at some distance to the west of Europe.

The United States is outside the system which has hitherto mattered, compact and coherent, with enormous stores of energy, facing Atlantic and Pacific, having relations with east and west of Euro-Asia, prepared by a fortified Panama Canal to fling her one fleet into either ocean, and attempting to secure the approaches to that Canal by the formulation of a Monroe Doctrine which forbids control of any lands of the New World by Powers of the Old, but is effective at present only in those small and comparatively unimportant states lying round the seas through which vessels using the Panama Canal would pass. Here, unlike the disunited states of Europe, in which men speak many languages and remember that through the long past years they have been at enmity, we have a vast land where people speak one language, with no long history of discord behind them—the *United* States.

But this conception of the arrangement of land masses is not quite complete; we have left out of account some important features of the greater land distributions. Just as in Africa south of the Sahara, and in Australia, there are indefinite fringes of the Old World largely dominated by the Sea Powers, so South America may be regarded as a fringe to the United States. The position of these lands and of Australia in the present world system may be made clearer by looking at the distribution of land on the globe in another way. It is only one-half of the truth to say that there is an Old World system and a New World system.

With the rise of the United States the distribution of the great masses of land on the round world has come to have further significance. The importance of Russia and that of the marginal lands remain; but there is something more. In what appears to be a disorderly distribution of lands there is yet some order. Round the South Pole there is a great continent, round the North an ocean. Round the southern continent there is an unbroken ring of ocean, while round the Northern Ocean there is an almost unbroken ring of land; from the ring of land there run southward three tapering land areas, separated by three oceans tapering northward.

Partly owing to the fact that the greater proportion of land is thus in the Northern Hemisphere, it is in the Northern Hemisphere that there are those large areas of desert where the early civilizations began, and following on this that other civilizations have developed between 30° and 60° north latitude, with the most energetic of mankind north of 35° N. The Southern Hemisphere has neither such large desert areas nor such areas of land as have hitherto been suitable for settlement by men who have learned elsewhere how to save energy. We thus see that, with the exception of a few isolated communities in the south of South America, in South Africa, and in Australia, all those which matter lie on an almost continuous belt round a central area, which is unsuited for settlement because of cold. These communities, being what they are, naturally desire communication with one another, and the rise of North America to world power thus makes it possible not merely to have a back-and-forth service across the Atlantic and across Euro-Asia, but to have a continuous circular service, in some parts better, in some parts worse, giving to the inhabitants of every place on this belt better facilities for movement at less expense than they would have if they were not on this belt. There are fewer termini and dead ends; every place is on the way to somewhere else.

Transcontinental lines across North America and Siberia are thus seen to have an importance, not merely because they save an enormous detour by ship, but because they are several parts of a circular route with no final termini, while routes like the proposed Cape to Cairo line are seen not only to be in competition with the sea on either hand, but to lead nowhere at the southern end. Cape Town as a land terminus is a dead end. New York and Montreal, Vancouver and San Francisco, equally with Tokyo, Nagasaki, Omsk, Moscow, Shanghai, Colombo, Alexandria, Berlin, Paris, and London, are seen to lie on these main routes by sea and land and air.

In the Northern Hemisphere there is, then, a continuous route, because the lands are fairly continuous, and because there are great areas north of 30° N. suitable for modern civilizations. In the Southern Hemisphere there is little land south of even 30° S.,

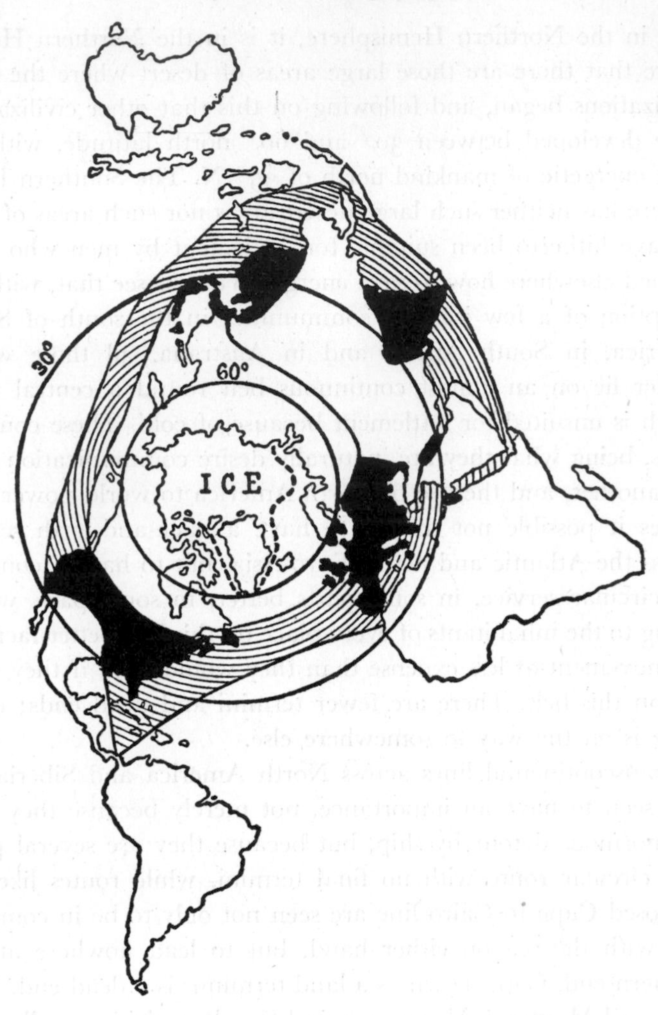

FIG. 16. The Northern Belt of Settlement and Movement.

and the corresponding communities on the southern fringes are but offshoots of those to the north.

The southern lands themselves are curiously alike in structure, possibly the result of the fact that they are remnants of an ancient plateau continent of which there are remnants in South Africa, in the east of South America and the west of Australia, bordered on the two latter by the fold mountains of the Andes and the Eastern Chain, and separated from each other by sunken lands in the Atlantic and Indian oceans.

They are also curiously alike in climatic conditions, there being no great variations of climate introduced by the existence of great land masses. The areas where white men may live are largely desert in the west and have only an eastern coastal belt, this being especially noticeable in Australia. Producing the same commodities, they have little opportunity for intertrade, and are isolated even more from one another than from the northern belt. There is, in fact, no southern circular route. Tristan da Cunha lies directly between Buenos Aires and Cape Town, Kerguelen directly between Cape Town and Melbourne; yet it is the rarest thing for ships to see either, while the few islands between Australia and South America bear names that are never heard of.

As long as Suez and Panama remained uncut, and world traffic was largely water-borne, traffic of considerable importance, though of no great volume, did pass through Magellan Strait and round the Cape; and South America and South Africa, especially the latter, had the advantage of lying on main through routes; but with the building of railways on a continental scale and the opening of the great canals, these have lost in relative importance. Australia never had even the advantages which these lands possessed. Detached from the lands of Asia by broad stretches of sea, so that there was no necessity to round it when the world was circumnavigated, it was undiscovered till late, and lies, and must lie, away from all important trade routes. South America, Australia, and still more New Zealand, lie literally at the ends of the earth. It is possibly connected with this fact that the aborigines of Australia are few and of a very primitive type. South Africa has lain more open to stimuli, and in addition to the fact that it extends only as far as 35°, it is occupied by native races. Australia, then, left undiscovered till the period of British supremacy on the sea, is entirely British and fervently "white," all the more because it is largely vacant and more readily accessible from the lands to the north than from the far isles in the Atlantic.

Southern Africa, occupied comparatively late though discovered early, is governed by the Sea Powers but has a large native population, while South America, occupied in the first flush of the discoveries, is essentially Spanish and Portuguese in culture, and economically related to the northern belt.

It is evident, then, that the important lands of the world, hitherto organized in countries, lie on a northern belt of settlement and movement, and that attached to this belt are relatively unimportant fringes; whether men are organized in states or by occupations, whether the cleavage is horizontal or vertical, national or international, the same fundamental distribution holds.

And here we must note the significance of another geographic fact, in some ways the most important of all: the distribution of the air. The facts that the amount of air decreases upwards, and that there are air currents or winds, have directly or indirectly affected the distribution of man on the earth. There is a more important and more fundamental fact still, that the atmosphere is continuous all over the surface of the earth.

For millions of years the air has been there; its movements brought rain to the land; its storms have brought destruction. Without air, life of any kind would be impossible, as it is in the moon. The existence of air has through all time allowed of life on this planet. But man has himself done very little with it; he has used sails for his ships and for windmills, but that is about all. Now sails and windmills have almost disappeared just when the continuity of the air all over the earth has come to have further significance. Land surfaces are discontinuous; the oceans are continuous, but they do not cover the earth as does the atmosphere; the sea allows of movement from one land to another but, obviously, ease of movement on it stops at the water's edge. Also both water and land are frozen for a considerable distance round each of the poles and movement on either in these areas is carried on only with extreme difficulty. On the other hand, movement in the air, when it is found to be possible at all, is possible in any direction and for any distance. Nor are there any obstacles in the air; so a direct route, *i.e.*, by a great circle, can be followed, and the ancient barriers of water, marsh, desert, forest, and highland are of much less, if they are of any, account. Movement by air, whether in war or in peace, is scarcely hampered by these at all.

This is not to say that movement by air is everywhere equally easy or desirable; the distribution of inhabited lands and of the great oceans has its influence. There must be bases for aeroplanes as for other forms of transport, and air routes, as other routes, lie between places where there are most people. These routes necessarily follow the northern belt of settlement and movement with extensions southwards to the southern continents. But there are naturally modifications of these routes to suit air conditions. For one thing the Arctic is no longer closed to movement, and the longer great-circle air routes in the Northern Hemisphere tend to keep much farther north than those by land and water and to pass over frozen areas. The effective distance between British Columbia and Britain is nearly halved, and Britain is approached much more nearly from all round than formerly; and, no longer kept inviolate by a moat held by her sea power, these islands, for good or ill, are more really in the centre of the lands of the world than ever before.

Nor is this all. The speeds that are possible in the air are so much greater than those by land and water that distances have become effectively less; and though heavy transport must remain on the old ways, yet the fact that planes in peace or war may fly from any point on the earth's surface to almost any other point in a day or two, and in most cases in a few hours, implies that very many of the conditions that have controlled events in the past, whether in the Old World or the New, no longer have the same influence as they have had in the past. The world and every part of it has shrunk, and every part is in effective contact with almost every other. New routes are possible for passengers and mails; direct communication may take place not only between lands in the Northern Hemisphere but between the southern continents and specially between the southern portions of these, and in general air routes of greater or less importance run crisscross over most of the lands and oceans of the globe. The world has in fact become a unity as never before.

This new unity of the world is strengthened by the fact that the atmosphere can now be used not only as a means whereby material things can be taken from place to place; it is also the medium whereby ideas and news can be conveyed by the human voice with an expenditure of energy only a minute fraction of that necessary for any other method, and all over the world practically at once. When Big Ben is heard by a listener in the antipodes sooner than by one standing underneath the clock tower at Westminster the time lag has been eliminated. With the discovery of the atmosphere the world is effectively one in time and space.

The world, in fact, however one looks at it, is now a single system. When all people depend on the efforts of all the rest, when in a single day an inhabitant of Britain utilizes directly or indirectly the labour of tens of thousands of people, not only in his own land but over the whole world, when even the Eskimo depends on the factories of the industrial lands for his tools, and the Negro of Central Africa depends on the same lands for his cloth, it is impossible to consider individual independence as an ideal in itself. The real problem is not how to live separately but how to live together. The aim still is to obtain as much energy as possible, natural or human, and use it as economically as possible; but not only is energy slowly obtained by individual as well as by collective action, it may be wasted by collective as well as by individual action. The waste of energy in great wars is beyond belief. Coal, crops, the going concerns of towns and industries, the potential powers of human lives—all wasted. It would take something like one-fiftieth of all the coal in the globe to make good the material losses of 1914–18, and the losses in the Second World War have been many times larger. Even in peace the waste of all sorts is extraordinarily great. Whether we like it or no, some kind of political world organization is imperative. We are all in it, and we have to stay in it. There can be no contracting out. That is the fundamental fact of geopolitics.

15

The United States and the "Shatter Zone" of Europe

By RICHARD HARTSHORNE

RICHARD HARTSHORNE, born in Kittanning, Pa. Ph.D., University of Chicago, 1924. Professor of Geography at the University of Wisconsin.
Author: *The Nature of Geography* (1939), "A Survey of the Boundary Problems of Europe" in *The Geographic Aspects of International Relations,* ed. Charles C. Colby (1938), and articles on political geography.

Of all the areas of the world, none presents such a multiplicity of territorial problems as the belt of Eastern Europe lying east of a line from the Baltic to the Adriatic, including in 1938 some thirteen countries situated between Scandinavia, Germany, and Italy on the one hand, and the Soviet Union and Turkey on the other. Although we have heard much of this area as the "shatter zone" of Europe, in the words of German propaganda of the interwar period, most Americans other than the several million who emigrated, or whose parents emigrated, from those countries have little familiarity with it. Normally it seems too remote to require our direct attention. But for the second time in a generation we are engaged in a war that originated in that belt. Why should the United States in these two wars be concerned with an area that was of so little importance to us through over a century of our national life, an area in which we have had relatively minor economic relations, whether of trade or of competition, an area that has never produced a political or military power that could seriously endanger us?

Since it is natural for people to think of the history of any foreign area primarily in terms of our interest in it, we tend to think of the history of this belt of Eastern Europe as though the year 1914, or 1917, were its base-line. Common thought among Americans therefore tends to assume that the situation in Eastern Europe prior to the First World War was more or less satisfactory so far as this country was concerned, but that after we were drawn into that war along with Western European countries our representatives joined theirs in committing the blunder of dividing large unit areas into a great number of individual independent states, in mistaken obedience to the principle of nationality. This division ignored the necessities of modern economic geography; the structure was therefore unsound, and in less than a score of years collapsed—one is almost led to suppose—from its internal difficulties. Hence, it is thought by many, a more secure system for this part of the world must not be based upon the bankrupt principle of nationality.

That this line of thought is false to very recent, as well as more remote, history should not require demonstration. In one respect, however, it contains a germ of truth; namely, this is an area where international events of major importance are determined from without rather than from within. It is hardly possible to conceive of any political development intrinsic to this belt producing results within it that could ever endanger the United States. What does concern this country is the fact that while political instability is characteristic of this zone, as it has been for centuries, it offers a tempting opportunity to any large state in the neighborhood to expand its territory and thereby augment its military power.

The expansion of any land Power in Europe was never of major concern directly to the United States, as long as that Power was limited to the land areas of Europe. In 1815, therefore, it was of no direct concern to the United States that the Congress of Vienna divided all Eastern Europe among four land Powers—Russia, Turkey, Austria, and Prussia. Likewise the rising movement of nationalism that immediately began to undermine this imperial structure and continued to attack it for over a century concerned us only in terms of political ideals. For none of the naval powers of Atlantic Europe could effectively exploit this unstable situation to secure mastery of the continent, and then consider transatlantic attack on the United States. Domination of the continent was never possible for Britain. The one great attempt of France, under Napoleon, had failed before many

Americans could realize that it might well have proved serious for us. Spain had ceased to be a major naval Power and had long since been eliminated from territorial control in Central or Eastern Europe. Obviously none of the smaller western countries, such as Holland or Sweden, could play a major role in Eastern Europe.

The formation of the German Empire in 1870–1871 made it finally impossible for any Atlantic Power to exploit the insecurity of Eastern Europe for its own enlargement. At the same time, however, this created the more real danger that the new Germany, a land Power which began also to develop naval power, might be able to utilize the opportunity to secure domination in Central and Eastern Europe. But any German ambitions for such a course of conquest in the east were checked by the "balance of Powers"—more particularly by the opposition of those great Powers that bordered directly on Germany. In allying herself, in this situation, with the Hapsburg empire of Austria-Hungary, Germany became a supporter of the imperial status quo in the very area where national disintegration might have provided her with easy opportunity for expansion. It was true that the alliance might be converted into a tool for conquest, but it could be only a cumbersome and unreliable tool, both because of the independence of Austria from Berlin and because of the large degree of independence of Hungary from Austria.

In the First World War this situation was changed in ways that presumably no one had anticipated: while Germany by the end of 1916 had been able to conquer large areas of the opposing states on both the east and the west, her allies, Turkey and notably Austria-Hungary, had been so weakened by internal disintegration under war pressure, as to open up a real possibility for expansion of a German Power far into the southeast—and simultaneously there developed the unexpected chance to destroy British sea power by strangulation of its base through submarine warfare.

The failure of the submarine campaign saved the old order in Western Europe; but that of Eastern Europe could not be saved, even had the enemies of Germany and Austria-Hungary wished to save it, for it was already destroyed from within. Since Germany itself escaped disintegration, the new geographic situation in Europe established by the peace treaties was one which made a German conquest of Europe relatively easy—once Germany had time to recover from the immediate effects of the war and to escape from the military limitations imposed by her opponents.

From the Baltic to the Aegean, the new system in Eastern Europe included no obstacle to German advance comparable with the Hapsburg empire of Austria-Hungary. This could have been accomplished only by a close combination of the several units into which it had split. Because these included the former dominators with those who had been dominated, any such combination was politically difficult if not impossible. Further, the freed peoples had mutual enmities that were almost as great. All these animosities were increased by the numerous minority problems inevitable in a region where it is impossible to draw boundaries mutually satisfactory even to reasonable people.

Theoretically there was one basis on which security might have been established in this region of small states—namely, the maintenance by the three great Powers bordering it of a large buffer zone against one another, like the maintenance by the Powers of Western Europe, each for its own purposes, of the independence of the Netherlands, Belgium, and Switzerland. But none of these neighboring great Powers—Russia, Germany, or Italy—had had a major hand in setting up the new system, and each had reasons of its own for favoring change, with hope that such change might be to its advantage, rather than to the others'; and finally, in each of them there came to absolute power a government committed to attack on the status quo.

In contrast with the neighboring great Powers opposed to the status quo, the Powers interested in maintaining it—France, Britain, and, so far as we recognized our interest, the United States—were geographically and psychologically so remote that they gradually lost interest. The continuous difficulties, inevitable in any new structure of young states, made the people of the western Powers more and more ready to wash their hands of Eastern Europe as time enabled them to forget its dangers to them—even though those were actually increasing.

That the new politico-geographic system of Eastern Europe would inevitably face great difficulties was certainly not unknown to the statesmen who took part in its establishment. Just because it was almost completely new, they recognized that for a long time it would suffer the insecurity of immaturity. But they were dealing with a part of the world that had never known political security, that had never developed mature, well established states loyally accepted by the peoples included in them.

Unlike Western Europe, Eastern Europe had not experienced a long continuous evolution of states each based on the national loyalties of its people, but rather had endured a meaningless series of conquests with more or less peaceful interludes marked by opposition of the many national groups to whatever imperial Power had conquered their territories. If any developmental trend could be read in its history, it was that of the rising authority of national units in opposition to imperial rulers, which had increased progressively for over a century. Most of these national groups, however, had attained to actual governmental control but very recently—some as early as 1830, but over most areas only as a result of the series of Balkan Wars that began in 1912 and terminated, apparently, in 1918. (From the point of view of Eastern Europe the war of 1914–18 can be considered as simply a widely extended "Third Balkan War.")

Consequently all these new states were cursed with the ills of youth, as well as handicapped by lack of strength.

Because the cultural geography of Eastern Europe—as revealed in maps of languages, or religions, or economic standards, or of such social factors as literacy—is so much more confused than that of Western Europe, it was impossible to represent the different national units by simple national states of internal integrity. Save for the remnant of defeated Austria, all were plagued by linguistic minorities, accentuated in many cases by religious and other social cleavages inherited from previous political divisions, and aggravated particularly by the socio-economic problem of landownership in a region emerging belatedly from feudalism.

In nearly all the new states German minorities provided an ever-ready tool for German expansion propaganda. Had the number of German minorities been reduced by applying the principle of nationality where it favored Germany, the result would have given Germany—as it later did give her—a stranglehold over the westernmost states bordering Germany, and thereby indirectly over the others.

Finally, both the location of all these states in relation to the western half of Europe and the agricultural character of their economy provided a basis under which Germany was naturally the single largest factor in their foreign trade. Once the German government established rigid control of all German foreign trade, it was relatively easy for it to extend economic domination over the individual small states trading with it.

In brief, the ultimate change in the politico-geographical situation caused by the conflict of 1914–18 was that Germany, by extending the struggle to the utmost, caused the destruction of its ally Austria-Hungary, so that the peoples of southeastern Europe, after a short period of life under small national states, were exposed to piecemeal conquest by a reorganized Germany.

It is extremely unfortunate that the period of grace granted the new states of the shatter zone was too short to permit of much change in inherited feelings or to develop new habits and associations. For a nation is an entity that must be developed through common political life. Even where the territory of the state is homogeneous in culture, this requires time. For the new states of Eastern Europe, each with its various minority problems, several generations of time were needed.

Indeed the period has been too short even for experimental purposes: to demonstrate whether or not the system set up could be made lasting. For it is essential to remember that great as have been the problems within each of these new states and the animosities between them, their current destruction has not been caused by these forces but plainly and simply by conquest from an outside state that would not have hesitated in its conquest had all those difficulties been absent. In other words, the present war, in demonstrating that Germany could conquer Jugoslavia—or for that matter Denmark—tells us nothing that was not obvious before.

On the other hand the experience of the new states during the twenties and thirties does emphasize certain conclusions which though not unknown in 1919 were not sufficiently recognized by those in authority. Of these, perhaps the most important is that the identification of the national political unit with an independent economic unit cannot work effectively in a region where national areas are so small. In other words, the necessary economic basis for anything approaching well-being of the peoples of Eastern Europe cannot be attained in a system of small states each operating its economy independently and, most often, in opposition to the others. But as long as security is based on the complete sovereignty of each political unit, such economic independence is essential for national security. Consequently, it was obvious, long before the war broke out, that in this part of Europe two things were incompatible—economic well-being and national security based on national sovereignty. The war has merely demonstrated a more obvious point; namely, that national sovereignty for these small states provided no national security.

If, however, these conclusions are sound for the small states of Eastern Europe, are they not equally sound, and equally significant, for the states of Western Europe? Indeed, in Western Europe, the conclusions appear to hold no less for the large states than for the small. The larger states suffered more from the economic nationalism than the smaller ones and, excepting for Great Britain, found no greater degree of national security.

Is there any reason to hope that the peoples of Europe and the rest of the world will have learned lessons from the present struggle which they failed to learn from the last? We should remember certain major differences in the development of the two conflicts. With one or two minor exceptions, no state in the

First World War experienced the catastrophe that has overwhelmed a dozen states of Europe today, including one of the most powerful. Indeed, for all the states of Europe that lie between Russia and Britain, the concept of "national security" is completely bankrupt. Under these circumstances, it does not seem too much to hope that a political concept that has long been antiquated in terms of economic geography will no longer be regarded as the essential basis for political organization.

At the time of America's entry into the war in December, 1941, the European situation presented two alternative possibilities. If the Axis Powers could secure peace without retreat, they could establish their control over all, or nearly all, of Eastern Europe. As a restoration, on a larger scale, of imperial power in Eastern Europe of earlier centuries, this in itself would be nothing new. Neither have we any reason to suppose that it would be permanent: Nazi control is no more skillful in developing the essential element to permanence—the loyal consent of the peoples—which their predecessors were ever unable to attain. But if we may call temporary a control that may last only a century or so, that is long enough to be of utmost concern to all living. But what would have been new in history was that a single Power would simultaneously have controlled the greater part of Eastern Europe and dominated Western Atlantic Europe as well as Africa and could easily have become the sea Power of first magnitude in all history. That, in brief, is what the *Anschluss*, the acquisition of Sudetenland, and the invasion of Poland meant to the United States.

We may now look with confidence to the other alternative, defeat of the Axis by the United Nations. This carries obviously the responsibility for us of taking part in planning what can be done with this most difficult part of the world. The consideration of that problem must recognize the reality of three major factors, the combination of which presents such apparently insurmountable difficulties that anyone attempting to solve the problem is tempted to ignore one or more of them. But we should consider sceptically, if not immediately dismiss, any plan for settlement that does not give due consideration to each of these factors.

The first is so widely recognized today that there is little likelihood that anyone will ignore it, as many no doubt did in 1918. Whatever criteria are used for determining nationality, the national map of Eastern Europe does not permit of division into clear-cut national states comparable with the system of national states in Western Europe. If anyone charges the statesmen of 1919 with failure in this part of Europe, he must realize that the error was not in having failed to establish *just* boundaries, for that is impossible in this region, but rather in failing to recognize this fact and therefore to attempt an entirely different basis of state construction.

Those who are most impressed by the first postulate might wish to ignore the second; namely, that, however impossible it is to draw clear-cut boundaries between the national units of Eastern Europe, each of a large number of national units is a definite reality possessing a strong geographic core area, and no politico-geographic system can be expected to succeed that does not give expression to each of these national areas, that does not permit each national group the exercise of those functions of government in which cultural differences are vitally important. Space does not permit further demonstration of this proposition than the bare statement that every government in this area that has ignored it has been able to rule its domain only by the elimination of all the freedoms we regard as essential to decent human life. And where these freedoms are denied, we can expect no political security.

The third postulate is that the area of German nationality—at least as large as the Germany of 1920—by reason of its location, resources, economy, and population, possesses permanently the power to destroy whatever political structure is set up in Eastern Europe, unless the structure is effectively designed to prevent that outcome.

The politico-geographic structure established at the end of the last war was in no way equipped to prevent its own destruction. The one major alliance within the area, the Little Entente, was directed not at Germany but only at another small state, Hungary, which is now also a victim. The support of the system depended almost exclusively on the western Powers, whether in terms of direct alliance, as with France and—too late—with Great Britain, or in terms of the League of Nations, which was helpless when abandoned by the Powers that had established it (the United States, Great Britain, and France), or in terms of the disarmament of Germany, to maintain which the western Powers were not willing to fight.

To be sure, the fact that in this case the western Powers failed to maintain the necessary support does not prove that, after learning the disastrous effects of that failure, they would act the same way again. But the peoples of Eastern Europe will indeed be blind if they again place their security in the hands of many small national states supported only by remote Powers.

In sum, the problem of security as well as the requirements of modern economy demand a more effective organization of large blocks in this part of Europe, blocks large enough to impose some considerable obstacle, checking any potential new effort of German expansion.

Undoubtedly any union or federation of the peoples of this part of Europe, where the mutual animosities seem more powerful than any animosities directed toward the outside, presents so many difficult problems as to appear soluble only in dreams. But we cannot hope to establish a secure system in this part of the world unless we have the imagination to construct something new.

In seeking ideas for a new solution, however, we need not waste our energies on a dream from the dead past. That the Hapsburgs had the opportunity, at least as late as 1848, to establish a genuine federal nation in the mid-Danube lands, is probably true. But certain it is that they completely failed, not merely to accomplish it but even to perceive its possibilities. The imperial emblem which all groups in the empire abandoned in October,

1918, is hardly the symbol with which to bring them together again.

On the other hand, something like the territorial basis of the former empire in the mid-Danube realm *could* provide the basis for a federated state, sound in its economic geography and in its external geopolitical relations, difficult though the internal problems would be.

To present this our major geographic suggestion, is to raise a host of geographical questions: Is Austria to be separated from Germany once more—and, if not, can such a mid-Danube state operate successfully without its key focus in the Vienna basin, and with its western front exposed to the German salient in the eastern Alps? If all the Balkan area could be considered as physically oriented on the mid-Danube region, and therefore to be federated with it, what of Poland and the peoples of the Baltic coast?

Likewise a host of questions are raised if one actually attempts to consider the internal structure of such a federation. What national components are sufficiently strong, in terms either of mere numbers or of intensity of national feeling, as to require major territorial recognition? If it can be agreed that any political system for this part of the world must recognize the national integrity of the areas of Poles, Czechs, Magyars, Serbs, Rumanians, and Greeks, what of the secondary groups such as Slovaks, Croats, Slovenes, and Albanians? One approach to this question should, I think, involve a detailed mapping of linguistic areas, not in terms of majorities, but for each cultural unit, in terms of the percentage of its people to the total population of each district, in order to establish the core areas; the significance of these may further be demonstrated by a study of the history of political life of each such core.

Finally, we may point to certain more general political questions that are raised as soon as one attempts to consider the possibilities of federated systems of government. Since the elimination of the feudal system as a form of federation, do we know any federal system that does not require a considerable degree of democracy—and, if so, are the peoples of this part of the world able to govern themselves by anything approaching democratic methods?

This is not the place to attempt to answer these questions. Whatever the difficulties, answers must be sought. So long as there is a threat of domination of Europe, a farmer in Iowa cannot consider himself secure. So long as the shatter zone of Eastern Europe is unstable, the possibility exists that Germany could utilize that area to gain mastery of Europe. Stability in the shatter zone cannot be achieved by absorption from the outside, whether from west or from east, nor by the reestablishment of free but hopelessly small units, but only by integration into a free association of free peoples, capable of providing a major element of its own defense. Such an organization within this area is not in conflict with plans for a larger-scale organization of the states of Europe, or of the world, but on the contrary would be supplementary to it. A world organization should not be called upon to solve the endless number of local problems involved in the community life of the many individual peoples living in this area. On the other hand, the addition to a European, or world, organization of an additional large federal state would give strength where the addition of a dozen small states would only give confusion.

CHAPTER IV

The Northward Course

16

The North American Arctic

By VILHJALMUR STEFANSSON

VILHJALMUR STEFANSSON, A.M., PH.D., LL.D., was born in Canada, but his family moved to the United States when he was a year old. Since 1932 he has been adviser on northern operations to Pan American Airways; since 1935 more than half his time has been devoted to writing manuals, guidebooks, and reports on northern subjects for the United States Army and preparing for the Navy pilot books of northerly countries.

He is author of numerous books—among them, *My Life with the Eskimo,* 1913; *The Friendly Arctic,* 1921, 1943; *Hunters of the Great North,* 1922; *The Northward Course of Empire,* 1922; *The Adventure of Wrangel Island,* 1925; *Iceland,* 1939; *Ultima Thule,* 1940; *Greenland,* 1942; *Arctic Manual,* 1944.

"The North American Arctic" was published originally as "The American Far North" in *Foreign Affairs,* April, 1939; it took the present revised and lengthened form in November, 1943.

Men of white skin have trespassed upon the Arctic more during the last twenty years than during the previous two hundred. The main reasons are that knowledge of geography and climate has grown, and that the former complete dependence on surface transportation, whether on land or on sea, has been modified, for now we are also flying.

The climate of the Arctic and sub-Arctic is continental on the mainlands and oceanic over the polar sea. This means that midsummer temperatures frequently reach 90° Fahrenheit in the shade on the continents north of the Arctic Circle (there is one Arctic Weather Bureau record of 100° in the shade), and that in winter the readings drop to 80° below zero, or even lower. Still, the greatest midwinter cold of the Arctic mainland is not quite so intense as that of the north temperate zone. The Cold Pole in

North America is at least 100 miles south of the Arctic Circle, while in Siberia it is 100 miles still farther south.

Sir John Richardson, the first explorer of the Arctic North American mainland whom we could classify as a scientist, wrote that he had "never felt its [the sun's] rays so oppressive within the tropics as I have experienced them to be on some occasions" in the Arctic. Such heat enables vegetation to grow with tropical speed. There is no chill of night because there is no night; plants work twenty-four hours a day, so that one Arctic day is as good to them as two tropical days would be. This explains why it is that, in spite of the shortness of the Arctic summer measured in days of the calendar, the season is still so long in hours of daylight that wheat has been successfully cultivated, without artificial means, fifty miles north of the Arctic Circle in Canada, and still farther north in Siberia. Because it needs clear skies and a brisk heat, wheat goes farthest north in districts that are farthest removed from the influence of warm ocean currents.

So the Arctic land is not the wasteland of our inherited beliefs. Nor is the Arctic sea barren. The world's greatest commercial fishing grounds are on the fringes of the Arctic, with life abundant throughout polar waters.

The Arctic has violent local gales wherever high land faces open water, as in Greenland. Otherwise the northern mediterranean, as De Long noted in 1880 and as Nansen confirmed a decade later, is one of the least stormy regions in the world. Though it is windier over the land than over the sea, the winds on the average are no worse than in Illinois or Kansas. Fogs are rare over both land and sea during the Arctic winter. Exceptions are such transitional belts as the Bering Sea, which is near the Japan Current, and the southern edge of the Arctic north of Europe, which borders the Gulf Stream.

The temperatures most hostile to flight are neither extreme heat nor extreme cold, but the intermediate range near the freezing point. Those are the levels at which ice, by gathering on planes and dirigibles, changes their aerodynamics and weighs them

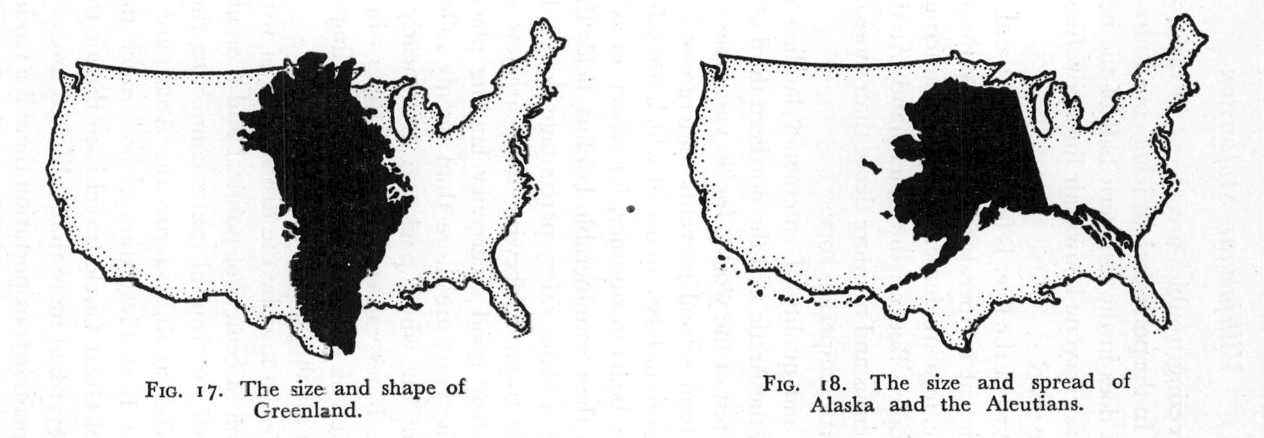

FIG. 17. The size and shape of Greenland.

FIG. 18. The size and spread of Alaska and the Aleutians.

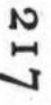

down. Such freezing troubles are absent in the tropics except at high altitudes. In the polar regions icing constitutes less of a flying hazard than it does in the northern half of the north temperate zone—where, as everyone knows, air lines now function regularly throughout the year.

Another enemy of the flyer is fog. Like sleet and "warm" snow, it changes to ice at temperatures just below the freezing point. On the average, fogs are denser and more numerous in the Arctic than in the tropics. But, on the other hand, Arctic fogs are less deep, less numerous and no more dense than those in the northern part of the north temperate zone.

In number and quality of emergency landing places, an important factor, the Arctic and the northern third of the temperate zone excel the rest of the world; for on vast areas of the northern lowland the frozen subsoil prevents underground drainage, thus producing millions of lakes, many of which are safe landing spots for pontoons or boats in summer, for wheels or skis in winter. It is in the main these innumerable landing fields that have given northern flying a better safety percentage than is found in other zones, even the tropics. Likewise, there are few sections of the Arctic pack where good emergency landing places, during the cold part of the year, are more than twenty miles apart, while the average for the whole pack, an area nearly as big as the United States, is several every twenty miles—in fact, there is usually a choice of two or more within gliding range if one's engine stops at an altitude of a mile or over.

If one studies on a globe the distribution of world population and the location of centers of political and economic power, one sees at once that the tropical routes connecting them are usually roundabout, whereas those across the Arctic are usually direct. This, of course, is an illustration of how much more applicable the principle of Great Circle travel is to the air than to the sea, where it has never had more than a limited use.

Under competitive transportation there is a tendency to shorten routes, to cut corners. At first, Chicago, San Francisco, and other western American cities will be satisfied to send their European mail by way of New York. But the time is bound to come when these cities will resent the delay involved in shipping around two sides of a triangle. They will want to ship direct to Europe, and they will do so whenever the traffic is enough to load a plane in the Mississippi Valley or on the Pacific Coast for London, Moscow, Paris, Berlin, or Rome. The shortest line from Illinois to Iran will have a midway stop in Iceland.

One of the recent developments in North American geographic thinking is to realize that all of South America is farther east than Chicago; but not many realize that the easternmost tip of Greenland is so much farther east than South America that a line drawn straight south from it passes 44 miles east of Iceland, which many think of as the easternmost part of the American Far North. This southward line barely misses the coast of Portugal, and slices through Africa so as to leave several hundred thousand square miles of that continent to the west of it.

The section with which we deal, then, stretches from easternmost Greenland, which is farther east than western Africa, to the westernmost Aleutians, which are only a little east of the easternmost Japanese islands, the Kuriles.

By the Canadian doctrine of sectors laid down by Senator Poirier through a speech in the Parliament at Ottawa in 1907, and which the chief nations seem to have accepted, a new island will belong to the North American Arctic if it is discovered in the sea to the north of Alaska, Canada, or Greenland. Just in the unlikely case that a further island is discovered, we say that our part of the Arctic is wedge-shaped, with its apex extending northward to the Pole. The southern boundaries are irregular and arbitrary; for we customarily include all of Alaska, all of Yukon Territory, as well as the Northwest Territories of Canada, Hudson Bay, the Ungava Peninsula, Labrador, and Greenland. We do not discuss Iceland in this paper, for though American it is a land of an ancient European-type civilization, and its problems are not those of frontier lands.

GREENLAND

Although a part of Greenland is more easterly than any spot in Iceland, which brings this island continent close in miles to the Old World civilization of Europe, still Greenland is commercially the least developed of the circumpolar countries.

As of just before the war, the prime concern of the Danish Government was to keep Greenland's 17,000 Eskimos alive and in good health. (There were about 500 whites in the country, mostly Danish civil servants.) The natives were encouraged to retain their traditional diet, consisting almost exclusively of flesh, for it seems best adapted to their physiological needs and has the further advantage of keeping them self-supporting and thereby self-respecting. The principal imported foods were "staples" like cereals and sugar. An excellent medical service carried on preventive as well as therapeutic work. There were local Eskimo-language schools, where Danish was also taught. Eskimo books were printed in Denmark and in Greenland, while an annual, printed in Eskimo by and for Eskimos, has been published in Greenland since 1861.

To supplement the Eskimo's main dependence upon hunting and fishing, the Government was considering the introduction of reindeer and the domestication of the musk ox. Several years ago sheep were introduced; as yet they number only about 10,000, but the climate and vegetation have proved well suited to sheep raising. There is also a small dairy industry capable of a limited expansion. Gardens are being cultivated in a few places, and doubtless could be in others. These developments are chiefly on the southern third of the west coast.

We know from school geographies that "most of Greenland is permanently ice-covered." How, then, is it possible to graze animals and cultivate gardens? The answer is that, although Greenland is perhaps 84 per cent snow-covered in midsummer, the snow-free 16 per cent amounts to some 130,000 square miles, an area larger than that of the British Isles. One of Greenland's largest snow-free regions is at its north tip—the northernmost land in the world. In summer this land, named after Peary who discovered it, is green with grass and bright with flowers, and is inhabited by numerous birds, insects, and mammals. The birds migrate south each fall, the insects survive as eggs that germinate in the heat of the next summer, the mammals stay the year round, feeding on grasses, sedges, lichens, small brush, and other vegetation.

Since many of us are still in the traditional frame of mind which brings astonishment on reading in Peary's narrative that he saw bumblebees and butterflies on the northernmost shore of the northernmost land in the world, only a little more than 400 miles from the North Pole, we might say here in passing that the life is not peculiar to the grasslands of the shore but continues out into the sea and is found at all levels, from the surface down to the ooze in the bottom of the sea. Until a few years ago this was a mere deduction from the reports of travelers, who had always found life when there was a reasonable chance to see it, no matter how far north they had been.

The diehards fought this conclusion, clinging to the ancient theory of a northern limit beyond which life does not go. But there is no place farther north than the North Pole, and the Papanin expedition, who came there by airplane in May of 1937, found polar bears wandering around on the ice, with cubs so young as to indicate that they were born in the vicinity. These bears were living on seals that swam around in the leads between the ice floes, feeding on shrimps. Applying the technique of the marine biologist, the Papanin group lowered traps to greater and greater depths, and always brought up plants and animals similar to those which would have been found at a corresponding depth, or at some other depth, in the Atlantic—which is, of course, logical, since the Arctic Mediterranean is, as you see on a globe, merely a gulf running out from the northern Atlantic.

Except for marble quarries, from which stone has been exported in small quantities, Greenland's only significant mineral development is the cryolite mine at Ivigtut which has been successfully operated for several decades by a Danish company. The mine is located on a reservation from which Eskimos are excluded in accordance with the Danish Government's quarantine program for hindering the spread of white man's diseases among the native population. A similar reservation has been established for the Faroese fishing fleet in order that it may exploit the rich West Greenland fisheries.

No Arctic district outside the Soviet Union has had such thorough scientific study as Greenland, where large Danish endowments, as well as the Government, maintain research workers in practically every branch of the natural and social sciences. Both Danish and foreign scientists have made extensive use of the airplane to explore the country. Americans, notably through Pan American Airways of New York, were foremost in prewar study of Greenland from the aeronautical point of view.

Greenland is in a position to play a unique role in the development of trans-Arctic flying. The practically level top of its icecap forms a vast and, except for the crevassed belt along its margins, almost level emergency landing field. True, this is not without its drawbacks, for it is hard to take off after a forced landing because of the rarefied atmosphere at a 10,000-foot altitude, and then this high plateau facing the sea causes local gales along the coast. However, practicable coastal base stations can be selected. On the whole, Greenland's climate is not prohibitive to local flying, and it is no serious handicap to a through air service.

As brought out elsewhere in this volume, the most direct routes from Chicago, San Francisco, Vancouver, and other western North American cities to Paris, London, Berlin, Rome, and Moscow lie across Greenland. When the air lines are ready to begin running planes along these routes, Denmark will have received Greenland back, according to the promise of the United States Government, and she will then have to decide whether or not to maintain her former quarantine. Perhaps the flying companies could be given reservations for radio stations and landing places along the coast from which the natives would be excluded as they now are from the Danish mining reserve at Ivigtut. Radio and supply stations will probably also be required at one or more inland points along the 600- to 700-mile route across the icecap. These stations could easily be maintained, as was shown by the British and German expeditions that wintered there in 1930–31 (at 8,600 and 10,000 feet and at 67° and 71° North Latitude, respectively).

CANADA

Canada has been less interested in her Arctic domain than one might think; yet the reasons are not far to seek. The Dominion has only some eleven millions with which to people a territory the size of the United States, and most of these live in the country's southern fringe, separated from the Arctic by a broad intermediate belt that has not been colonized. She has felt no immediate need for her Arctic region, and has thus far shown little interest in settling even the intermediate belt. Take the case of the Hay valley.

Hay River, which flows north from Alberta into western Great Slave Lake, could be served by an extension of the railway from Peace River station. Dr. D. C. Coleman, President of the Canadian Pacific system, reports that a survey of this valley by his company showed the district to be well suited, climatically and otherwise, for wheat and mixed farming. He adds that a railway into the Hay would not merely open the valley itself to agricultural colonization but tap the Mackenzie River just north of Great Slave Lake and thus facilitate communication with the Canadian Far North. He feels, nevertheless, that such a railway would not pay, and that private enterprise cannot be expected to undertake its construction.

In this, of course, he is quite right. The only possible sponsor for nonpaying lines is the Government. The Dominion, however, is not at present in the mood to construct any railroads that will open up new wheat lands, for the farmers of southern Canada are making little enough money as it is and they do not want to be taxed, or to have the national credit pledged, for a railway that would pour additional millions of bushels of grain onto the market every year.

Experimentally, without the use of hothouse methods or other trickery, wheat has been grown more than 300 miles north of the Hay at Aklavik, just within the limit of the forest more than 100 miles north of the Arctic Circle, on the most westerly branch of the Mackenzie delta. This may or may not have ripened. Mature wheat has been demonstrated where the Thunder River

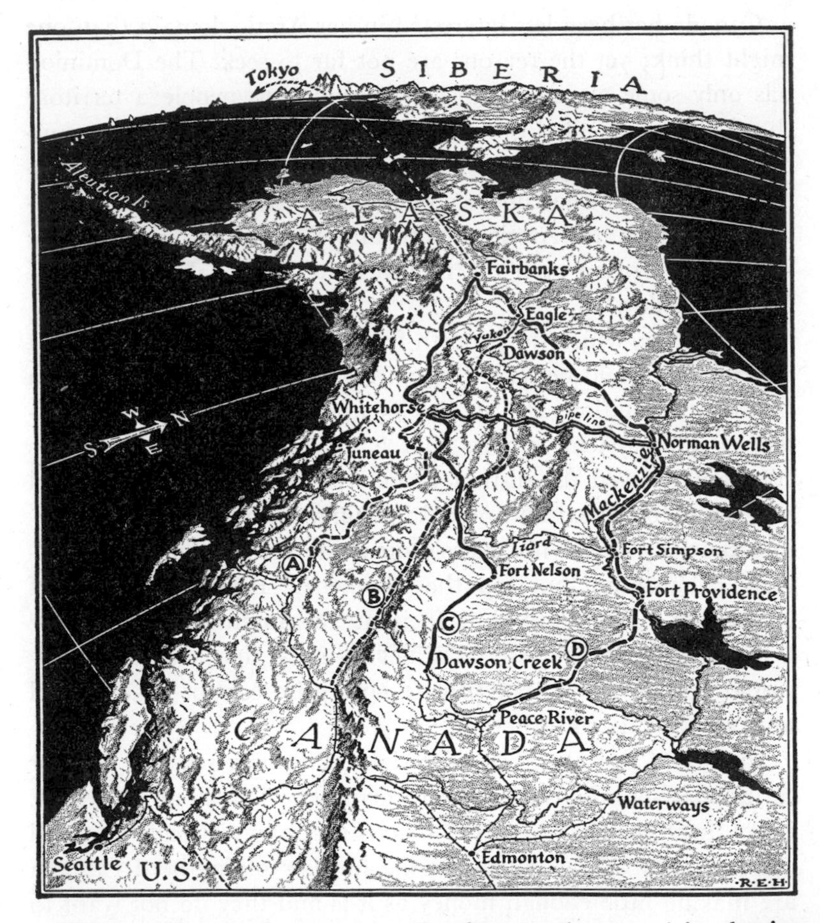

FIG. 19. How northwestern America faces northeastern Asia, showing that the Mackenzie and Yukon valleys, connected by a pass from Norman Wells to Eagle, are in effect one valley leading from the Chicago-Winnipeg region toward Siberia, China, and Japan. Highway C, a solid black line; highways A, B, D, broken lines. After *Fortune* with permission.

enters the Mackenzie, about 60 miles north of the Arctic Circle. It would seem, then, that where the soil is good wheat could be extended along the Mackenzie basin practically to the Arctic Circle. At any rate, it could be extended to Fort Good Hope, about 25 miles south of the Circle, for the station has been a garden center of the Roman Catholic missions and the Hudson's Bay Company for more than half a century. Potatoes from these gardens have been shipped not only northwestward down the Mackenzie but also southeastward, upstream.

While Canadians are fearful that a northward extension of farming will depress grain and meat prices, they do not have the same feeling about minerals. For instance, they take national pride in the radium-bearing ore mined practically upon the Arctic Circle on Great Bear Lake which reduced the price of radium in a few years from $50,000 to $25,000 per gram.

One of the greatest triumphs of commercial aviation was scored on the Canadian frontier. Because there was no competition from railways and trucks, more tons of freight were being carried in 1938 by air in the northern two-thirds of Canada, which has a population of less than a million, than in the entire United States. Loads sometimes consisted of such bulky things as teams of oxen or pieces of machinery weighing several tons. Even more striking, thousands of tons of ore were flown, in some cases hundreds of miles, from mines to river or rail transportation. Mining in the Canadian North is almost wholly dependent on aviation for its prospecting work. A large part of the furs taken in that region, including the remote islands north of the mainland, is carried out by plane.

Only one important business is more active in northern Canada than in Alaska, the fur trade. That oldest trading organization, the Hudson's Bay Company, still one of the world's greatest, maintains posts all over the Canadian mainland and on some of the islands. There are, too, a number of "free traders"—small fur dealers who compete with the great Company and usually go broke in a few years, only to be replaced by newcomers who think fortunes are to be won in furs.

The first exploitation of the northern half of North America was through the fur trade. The largest single agency in that development was and still is the Hudson's Bay Company, which celebrated in 1920 the first 250 years of success. The full, official name indicates its program: "The Governor and Company of Adventurers of England Trading into Hudson's Bay." At that time the northern half of the continent seemed to the British, and indeed to the whole of commercial Europe, most easily and logically accessible through the bay and strait that were named for Henry Hudson.

The Hudson's Bay Company had no difficulty in navigating Hudson Strait and Hudson Bay, and this was popularly and correctly looked upon as a short and satisfactory route for two hundred years. By it the Company expanded to the Pacific Coast, where now are our western seaboard states and the province of British Columbia, and by it, and by following the river system named after Sir Alexander Mackenzie, later of the Company, it expanded northwestward in the direction of China. The route was logical, not merely because it led straight toward where the Company wanted to go but also because natural conditions were favorable.

Gradually, with the increase of population in southeastern Canada, and in what were later called the Thirteen Colonies, began a shift of traffic to the St. Lawrence valley, and Montreal developed that economic and political strength which is even now paramount in Canada. There was for this change the additional logic, from the Hudson's Bay Company's point of view, that it was trading down into the present United States, having posts, among other places, in New York, California, and Oregon.

By the 1840's, roughly one hundred years ago, the Company had become so Montreal-minded that Sir George Simpson was suspected of collusion in the murder of his nephew Thomas Simpson, the chief reason for the suspicion being that the nephew was ambitious to open up a sea highway around the north of North America and was believed to be on the verge of success.

There was so much glamour about the Northwest Passage at

the time that Sir George was no doubt right in thinking that if the feasibility of the northern sea route were announced it might not be possible to prevent its becoming a rival to the St. Lawrence and Great Lakes route. Sir George would not have minded this if he had felt sure the Company would be able to control the northern seaway; but he was already worrying about what finally did happen, in 1869, when the Canadian nation deprived the Hudson's Bay Company of its exclusive privileges for northern Canada, and he felt that this event would be hastened if a northerly commercial route were developed, leading to a wider and more rapid colonization of the whole vast region between. Moreover, the Company was then exclusively engaged in the fur trade, and it was obviously to its disadvantage to promote any development in Canada other than that of trapping.

This is a complicated matter which we can here no more than indicate; but through the efforts of Sir George, and through many other circumstances, the Northwest Passage, which was actually discovered by Thomas Simpson before his tragic death in 1840, failed to reach commercial use until a few years ago.

Just as the Soviet Union works the Northeast Passage around Siberia chiefly by sending vessels in both from the Atlantic and from the Pacific Ocean to various centers of commerce, some of the ships nearly or quite meeting and then each returning to the ocean from which it came, so the Hudson's Bay Company now has vessels which pick up goods from river steamboats at the mouth of the Mackenzie and take them east around the north of Canada to Bellot Strait, where they meet other ships that come from the St. Lawrence by way of the North Atlantic. Each ship usually turns back, after they have exchanged greetings and certain items of cargo at Fort Ross.

The Northwest Passage around America and the Northeast Passage around Asia are probably about equally difficult, mile for mile; but the Northeast Passage is twice as long and in that sense twice as difficult. It is used extensively, however, because (for many reasons) this is the policy of the Soviet Union. The easier because shorter Northwest Passage is used very little; and as yet only one of its possible five routes is employed, the one that mainly follows the continental shore, where a line of the Company's trading stations furnishes the ports of call.

Many reasons are given to explain the lack of enthusiasm in Canada for the development of this northern seaway, among them, that everybody wants the transcontinental railways to pay dividends, and that the Northwest Passage would be a competitor.

More worrisome than the Northwest Passage to Montreal and the rest of southeastern Canada, at least for the moment, is the possible resumption of commerce through Hudson Bay and Strait. In the teeth of southeastern opposition, a struggle toward this had been carried on by the Prairie Provinces for more than half a century, and finally there was at least apparent success while the Dominion was war-minded during the First World War, to the extent that a nationally financed railway was authorized from The Pas in Manitoba to Churchill on the Bay, with great works at this terminal, among them one of the largest wheat elevators in the world. The central idea then was to take the grain of the prairies directly, cheaply, and quickly to Liverpool. It is said by those who favor the use of this route that through the dozen years since its completion the short transport highway from the Canadian West to Europe has been kept inactive by a Great Lakes and St. Lawrence "conspiracy" for the use of the roundabout Winnipeg-Montreal route.

A large element in the struggle between the St. Lawrence and Hudson Bay routes has been disagreement as to the length of the navigation season in Hudson Bay and Hudson Strait. The house organ of the Hudson's Bay Company, *The Beaver,* published in March, 1941, an article by A. D. Bajkov which divided into four groups the navigators and scientists who have made enough of a study of the bay and strait to hold an opinion that is not derived from the opinions of others. The views represented are: (1) that both bay and strait can be navigated between July 15 and October 15; (2) that they can be navigated from July to November; (3) that navigation can begin as early as April; and

(4) that the bay and strait are open to navigation the whole year.

It appears upon study that the above four groups are about equal in experience and general standing; moreover, among those who believe that both bay and strait can be navigated during the whole year are experienced representatives of the Hudson's Bay Company itself.

But of still greater consequence than a summertime Northwest Passage or an all-year service through Hudson Strait and Bay, is the development of that inland highway to the Far East which can be provided by combining the use of the valleys and waters of the Mackenzie and Yukon rivers.

If you look through a good collection of old maps, you learn it is only during the last hundred years, approximately since 1850, that Europeans, and their intellectual cousins the Americans, have been thinking of the earth as if it were flat, from which have come such strange ideas as that the nearest way to China from the United States is west, that it is logical to fly the Pacific on your way to China, and that places like the Hawaiian Islands lie on a nearly direct road between the two countries.

The realistic conception that the earth is spherical, and that the near way from Europe to the Far East is by way of the north, was strong when the Hudson's Bay Company received its charter in 1670, and when it began to spread out from Hudson Bay in every direction that promised furs.

The charter stipulated that the Company was to seek the Northwest Passage; and it did seek this by what was to it a logical route. It moved west from the bay to the headwaters of the Mackenzie and then directly toward the Indies down the Mackenzie. Along the eastern foothills of the Rockies it kept to that highway of water nearly to the Polar Sea, where the mountains on the west practically disappeared so that it was easy to cross the low and narrow strip that separates the great Mackenzie from the almost equally great Yukon, along which it might continue in the direction of China.

At this stage, during the first half of the nineteenth century, there were three Powers that wanted northwestern America: Russia which had it, Great Britain which desired it partly because of its contiguity with the lower Mackenzie, and the United States which looked at the question with a Pacific Ocean and northerly slant, for British dominions separated us from Russian America and the seaway north along western America was the only road we could freely use.

Under the inspiration of that builder of the fur empire and of the British Empire, Sir George Simpson, the British penetrated as far in the direction of China as the junction of the Porcupine with the main Yukon. There they were stopped by the Russians; there Alexander Hunter Murray built for the Company its farthest outpost in 1847, Fort Yukon.

At first the Mackenzie was a canoe route; then came the York boat, and later cheap flat-bottomed scows which drifted, some of them, nearly 2,000 miles downstream from the vicinity of Edmonton, and which were dismembered and used for building lumber or firewood, each at its own destination. Next came the period of steamboats. Built at Fort Smith, nearly 500 miles north of Edmonton, the winter 1885–86, the *Wrigley* made her first voyage across Slave Lake and down the Mackenzie as far as Simpson in September, 1886; her first complete voyage down to the Mackenzie delta was made in 1887. She was more or less of ocean-going or Great Lakes type, with a screw propeller and drawing six feet of water. Despite occasional stormy weather on a lake so wide that you see no land when in the middle of your crossing, the *Wrigley* type was replaced in 1907 by the top-heavy *Mackenzie River* and her sort, flat-bottomed stern-wheelers.

Across the divide from the lower Mackenzie the development of steamboating on the Yukon had been slower. It came with a rush in the Gold Rush that followed 1897. From the start Yukon boats were stern-wheelers, drawing four to five feet of water.

Before the turn of our century, then, you could go down the Mackenzie by steamer, walk across the portage and board a Yukon steamer. That is what I did in the years 1906–7. This would take you by fresh water considerably farther west, and nearer to Japan, than if you went by ocean steamer to Hawaii.

Simpson, in the terms of his day, thought of the combined Mackenzie and Yukon as highways for boats in summer and for sledges in winter, with the portage between them crossed in summer by men carrying packs, in winter by dogs pulling sledges. The late nineteenth century was an era of railways, and several plans were advanced for construction down along the bottom lands of the Mackenzie, the low pass to the Yukon, and down the Yukon valley, some of them with a tunnel to pass under Bering Strait and a continuation of the railway through Siberia. One of these plans got so far that rails were actually laid 250 miles north from Edmonton to the head of navigation of the Athabaska branch of the Mackenzie at Fort McMurray. This took from 1914 to 1926 and got no further for lack of money, but it has been of great value in the present war as a connecting link between the railway network of the United States and southern Canada on one side and Mackenzie river traffic on the other.

There were known to be deposits of coal in the Mackenzie basin, and on these the railway promoters counted for fuel. Some of them, at least, foresaw the coming of the oil-burning locomotive, and the Mackenzie had been known as an oil region from 1789, when Sir Alexander Mackenzie, whose name it bears, got his footgear soiled with "mineral tar" along its banks. The basin was also known as a gas reservoir; on the mentioned journey down the Mackenzie in 1906 we saw gas wells that had been blazing uncapped for many years.

In 1927 the first oil developments started at McMurray in the Athabaska "Tar Sands," which are now considered by the appropriate government departments to contain "not oil shales but oil itself" in quantity greater than has been used by man from the start of the industry to the present day. The Geological Survey of Canada values the Tar Sands at 100 billions of barrels; the United States Bureau of Mines says 250 billions. For comparison, the petroleum used from the beginning of the industry to the start of the Second World War has been reckoned at 81 billions.

But perhaps even more significant for the development of extreme northwestern Canada, and of Alaska, was the bringing in of the first successful well at Norman Wells, about 900 miles downstream (northwest) from McMurray, a mere 100 miles south of the Arctic Circle, and just about abreast of Fairbanks, Alaska. This was in 1920. The operator was Imperial Oil of Toronto, Canadian subsidiary of Standard of New Jersey. The first few wells showed that oil could be struck at from 1,400 to 1,800 feet, that most tries were successful, that the drilling was cheaper per well than in most oil fields anywhere in the world, and that average production ran better than 100 barrels per day per well.

This immediate oil region was roughly described in a government report as extending about 100 miles along the Mackenzie on both banks and being at least 60 miles wide. However, later investigations seem to indicate that there is a territory similar geologically, and with equal promise, wider than sixty miles and extending several hundred miles from the locations now being worked to the head of the Mackenzie delta. It would seem, then, that we have here, strategically located on the road to Japan and China, one of the more promising known oil regions.

Norman Wells, the producing section of this oil region, is about halfway from New York to Japan, and the field lies in the most direct air route between them, the great circle route. As it comes out of the ground, this oil is closer to Japan than if it were in Honolulu.

Norman oil proved to be rich in gasoline, and so fluid that the crude would move through a pipe at 50° below zero. In its native state it was just about right for trucks, tractors, boats, and mining machinery, and was used to help build up the mining industry, first at Bear Lake and later far upstream along the Mackenzie basin, as at Yellowknife. Refining was started in 1939 with the production of 82 octane aviation gasoline and a series of heavier grades, down to bunker oil. At first the local market was only about 40,000 barrels per year, which was produced in a few weeks each season, the plant being shut down for the rest of the year, pending the need for longer operation through an increased demand.

The first airplane service down the Mackenzie was started by Canada's great aviation pioneer, James Richardson of Winnipeg, a director of the Canadian Pacific Railway, thus affiliated with large-scale transportation, for the Canadian Pacific was then and still remains the longest privately owned railway in the world. Richardson founded Canadian Airways in 1930. He had sporadic competition, and eventually a serious competitor in Mackenzie Air Service, organized by Leigh Brintnell of Edmonton.

Thus there were for several years before the war two main services down the Mackenzie, with a great deal of other flying. The planes, when they continued to the Yukon basin, crossed over from the lower Mackenzie and headed either for Dawson or for Fairbanks.

Work of the Geological Survey of Canada and the reports of travelers indicated that, since it would be desirable to have a trucking road to parallel an airway, the best place for crossing to the Yukon would be from the lower (northwestern) end of the Norman Wells oil region at or downstream from the mouth of the Carcajou River, heading for the vicinity of Eagle, Alaska. A narrower crossing was available farther south, going up the Keele River and down to Mayo on the Stewart, and some favored this route for a motor highway and oil pipe line. Here the divide is only about 300 miles wide, but it may go as high as 3,000 or 4,000 feet. The Carcajou-Eagle divide seemed better although 400 miles wide, for it was believed that pipe and road might cross without going above the tree line, which in this region is somewhere around 2,000 feet.

The building of a road down the Mackenzie, over this divide, and then down the Yukon was proposed at least as early as 1940 by the Province of Alberta through its Minister of Public Works, the Honorable W. A. Fallow. When the clouds were gathering for the Second World War he attempted to interest the United States and Canada in developing a route at nearly water level (except for the just-mentioned low Yukon-Mackenzie divide) by which supplies, and particularly oil, could be sent cheaply and easily in great quantity as far as Bering Sea—where, as said, they would be considerably nearer to Japan than at the Hawaiian Islands, and where we could have a port free from ice twelve months in the year, on Bristol Bay. This project came to be known as Route D.

Mr. Fallow recommended a course from Edmonton by rail to the town of Peace River and then by the Grimshaw Highway, which his department had already built as a winter road,[1] to the Mackenzie where it emerges from Slave Lake—avoiding the Slave rapids, storm delays on Slave Lake, and the annual delay of three weeks or so in the spring due to the persistence of ice on the lake. Thence he proposed to use at first a winter road (steamers in summer); later an all-year road would run parallel to the Mackenzie, east of it, as far as the Norman oil region, then cross to the Yukon by the most feasible divide. This portage was also to have at first only a winter road, later an all-year road.

Mr. Fallow urged that an all-season freighting road could be built more quickly and at a lower cost in money, man hours, and strategic materials by his route than by any other, not only because of the level topography and the favorable dry climate but also, and chiefly, because of the Mackenzie, on which steamboats and scows could freight in from railhead supplies for the construction at a tiny fraction of the cost on the proposed highway through the mountains toward Alaska. A final argument was that the Mackenzie route, alone among those proposed, could furnish

[1] In northern Canada and Alaska, when the frost has hardened swamps and converted lakes and rivers with strong ice, they are used for sledging and tractor roads. Trees are pushed over with heavy machinery and then removed from the right of way, or are chopped off level with the ground. Such highways, according to Mr. Fallow, cost his province less than $400 per mile. Their usefulness begins not earlier than November and ends, in different parts of the North, at various dates between early March and early May. These winter roads carry tens of thousands of tons of freight in every direction through country that is practically impassable during summer. The same effect of frost accounts for the mobility and great activity of armies in winter on the Soviet-Finnish front, and even considerably farther south.

its own petroleum both during construction and in later operation; on any of the other routes fuel for planes and trucks would have to be brought in either from the outside or from the Mackenzie oil fields.

Three other highways, called A, B, and C, were proposed.[2] Roads A and B, favored by the cities of the Pacific coast, were to run north from Seattle through Yukon Territory to Alaska; but these were vetoed by the military as being so near the Pacific that they might be cut by enemy raids. Highway C was advocated as the shortest, and far enough inland to be safe from enemy raids. It would run from Mr. Fallow's own city, Edmonton, to railway terminal at Dawson Creek and thence, not parallel to any navigable river but through increasingly mountainous country, by way of Fort Nelson, Watson Lake, and Whitehorse, to Fairbanks.

It was said that Route C, measured from Edmonton to Nome, Alaska, was about 100 miles shorter than the road proposed by Mr. Fallow; others claimed 200 miles. But this, it appeared to those who favored the river road, was only an apparent saving; for the Nelson-Whitehorse road would have to wind about so much between mountains, seeking passes, that most if not all of the saving in mileage would be used up; there would remain the handicap of more bridges, tunnels, and grades.

It was objected by some that the river road would need great bridges; for the tributaries of the Mackenzie were wide near where they entered the main stream, and it would be necessary to cross the Mackenzie itself twice: near Slave Lake, and near the refineries in the Norman district. But those who favored the water level route countered that bridges would not be needed because these rivers, being wide, are sluggish: ferries could be used in summer, and the ice in winter.

The river road faction urged, too, that for the maximum saving of cost, and the quickest possible utilization of the route, con-

[2] For discussions of Routes A, B, C, and D see Richard Finnie, "A Route to Alaska through the Northwest Territories," *Geographical Review*, July, 1942; and Vilhjalmur Stefansson, "Routes to Alaska," *Foreign Affairs*, July, 1941. (For map showing routes see p. 224, *ante*.)

struction should be limited at first to the improvement of the Grimshaw Road from railhead to the Mackenzie at Providence, and the building of the portage highway from Carcajou to Eagle. For in summer steamboats, scows, and tugs could be used on both Mackenzie and Yukon; and in winter tractors could draw sledges on the river ice—a practice common on the great rivers of the Soviet Union and, indeed, also in the middle north of Canada and in certain parts of Alaska.

A chief argument by those who favored the river route was that it would traverse a country which was being developed rapidly for the sake of well known and great resources certified by government departments, and that a road would have to be built now or later to serve a growing community. Chief detail in the resources argument was the local petroleum supply.

Around 1939 and 1940 there was a great deal of newspaper and other public debate between the Pacific coast mountain routes A and B on one side and the mountain route C on the other; but only in a few scholarly journals (such as the *Geographical Review* of the American Geographical Society and the *Foreign Affairs* of the Council on Foreign Relations) was there discussion of the river route, our Route D. Then came from the blue the announcement that the road which would be built was the one the Alberta government had been opposing, even though it started in the provincial capital, Edmonton—the northwestward mountain route would be built, and not the northwestward river route.

It seems to be agreed that we shall not know until the war is over, when an investigation will be permissible, the inner and dominating reasons for the choice of the mountain road—"America's Burma Road" as the enthusiasts for spectacular scenery have called it. Superficially, the course of events is known.

After the Mackenzie air route had been preempted by the Richardson and Brintnell interests, as described above, a third airway was financed, known as Yukon Southern, and promoted by Grant McConachie. It flew approximately the route we have called C, by way of Fort Nelson and Watson Lake to Whitehorse. The press told in wide publicity that it was the shortest route to the Orient, with plans of expansion to Asia.

It is agreed on all sides that Yukon Southern was promoted with great energy and ability. But it does not seem that anyone familiar with transportation history and conditions in northwestern Canada had in those early promotion years any thought that a trucking highway was likely to be built along this airway. True, it was direct, saving something between 100 and 200 air miles between Edmonton and Bering Sea, as compared with the river route flown from Edmonton by way of Peace River, Simpson, Norman Wells, and Fairbanks to Nome. But it had to go through comparatively bad weather when passing over the mountains which filter the moisture from the Pacific breezes and give the Mackenzie basin its clear skies and light precipitation. In crossing those mountains it passed above a terrain where a trucking highway would have to twist and turn, dip and climb. Then the precipitation which meant bad flying weather aloft would mean comparatively deep snow on the road in winter, with problems of plowing and snow sheds, succeeded by spring freshets from the melting snows that would be hard on bridges and other roadwork as they tore down their gullies. Obviously a road paralleling Yukon Southern would cost several times as much to build as one paralleling the Richardson-Brintnell airways. Moreover, Highway C, later named Alcan (Alaska-Canada), would be costly to operate; for, in addition to the problems of grades, curves, and snow, fuel would have to be brought from outside for the construction and also for the operation of the road when completed, or else, as said, it would have to be piped or trucked from one or more of the Mackenzie valley oil fields which lie along the right of way of Route D.

Clearly these drawbacks must have been counterbalanced by weighty considerations, as yet unrevealed, or a trucking highway paralleling Yukon Southern would not have been built. The reasons published in the United States have not so far been very explanatory. They are chiefly that Route C was the shortest, that it was far enough from the Pacific to be reasonably safe against

Japanese attack, and that it had been selected by the Canadian authorities. We have dealt with the first of these reasons. The comment on the second is that Route D, farther from the Pacific, would have been even safer than Route C. The third explanation, that the Canadians selected the route, merely shifts responsibility.

Although at first, in Canada as in the United States, there was a good deal of criticism of Alcan on the score that it ran through a country which was not merely unsuitable in topography but also comparatively devoid of natural resources, there followed a period of boosting by films in the theaters, by articles and news stories in the press, and by talks on the radio. According to this publicity, Alcan would tap great resource areas which would bring a great era of postwar colonization and development.

This praise went so far that it began to worry the friends of the highway, and apparently not least the Dominion Government. To indicate what seems to be their position as we go to press, we quote by permission of *MacLean's Magazine*, Toronto, extracts from an editorial printed in its issue dated November 15, 1943:

> Applications are now being received in Ottawa for hamburger, barbecue and filling station concessions along the Alaska Highway when the war is over and the tourist business is restored.
>
> Department officials are perturbed over such optimism; feel that much of the ballyhoo concerning the highway's postwar potentialities is premature and overdone . . .
>
> After Dawson Creek for hundreds of miles the highway runs through scenically dull territory. The dust is so terriffic that truck drivers often wear masks. Many years must elapse before the surface can be oiled or paved.
>
> Concerning postwar transportation of commercial goods by truck to the Yukon and Alaska, officials think that so long as ships are available trucking would be uneconomic, expensive and slow.
>
> Nor do they think that the existence of the highway will facilitate anything like the amount of settlement that has been forecast.
>
> It seems apparent that before the Canadian stretches of the highway could become a realization of the rosy dreams of many people, a great deal of additional money would have to be spent on it, and years of improving construction. And whether or not the results would justify the expenditures is a matter in which there is room for considerable difference of opinion.

If this editorial gives the view of the pertinent departments of the Canadian Government, as seems implied, it would appear they are already taking at Ottawa a position common with men who are working on the Alcan Highway, that it will fall into disuse, "go back to the wilderness," as soon as the war is over. This does not mean, of course, that the road could not be kept in service if we were willing to go on pouring into it government money; it means only that many feel public moneys will cease to flow so freely when Japan has been defeated and that things will then presently shake down to their natural level—which will be the level of two other roads, B and D.

For there will, no doubt, be a revival of the drive to construct along Route B a railway or trucking highway, likely both; for these, in connection with ocean traffic, would serve Vancouver and Seattle in their attempt to maintain for Pacific Coast cities a monopoly, or at least a hegemony, in the commerce of the Yukon and Alaska. The competitor will be a route down the Mackenzie River, substantially Route D, and will in part represent the effort of midcontinental centers, like Minneapolis, Winnipeg and Edmonton, to cut into the business of Yukon Territory and Alaska by entering through the back door.

The inevitability of Route B depends in part on topography and on the present location of railways and northerly coastal centers of distribution; but it rests more upon the energy and business foresight of the three Pacific Coast states and the province of British Columbia. The inevitability of Route D has less of present-day commercial awareness behind it, for the midcontinent cities are still somnolent, and it depends chiefly on natural conditions—on the combined transporting power of the Mackenzie and Yukon rivers, on favorable topography for railway and highway construction, and on resources along the right-of-way, chief of them the string of oil fields.

For if the realities of Mackenzie oil are half as good as the government and private geologists now believe, nothing is going to stop the great oil companies from crowding into the Mackenzie region when the war is over. The likelihood is that the first series of big northerly developments will radiate from Norman Wells. With an oil center, even if not quite a Tulsa, springing up in Canada right abreast of Fairbanks, there will of necessity be roads between. And by them we shall have a beginning of that through traffic on Route D, and of that commercial rivalry of inland with coastal cities, which Vancouver and Seattle evidently fear.

Whether there was any reasonable chance that the Mackenzie could produce sufficient oil for a pipe line of considerable diameter, justifying a large refinery, was in 1940 an issue between pessimism and optimism.

There were many pessimists in many quarters, but enthusiasm for Mackenzie oil was known to have been shown by certain private oil men, and by some government geologists. There was, for instance, Dr. Charles Camsell, Deputy Minister of Mines and Resources for the Dominion, a distinguished geologist born on the Liard branch of the Mackenzie and brought up on the Mackenzie itself, who had done in the very section under dispute much of the field work which made him prominent, and who had at his command, because of his official position, every resource toward knowledge possessed by the Canadian Government. He had said, for instance, in a paper "The Unexplored Areas of Continental Canada":

"Oil springs have been noted on the shores of Great Slave Lake and at several points in the valley of the Mackenzie and on Peel River . . . the region is believed to be one of the largest areas of possible oil-bearing country yet unexplored on the face of the earth."

This statement had been made by Dr. Camsell in 1916. Since that time a beginning of the demonstration that he was right had been made by the Standard Oil Company of New Jersey when, through Imperial Oil of Canada, they developed Norman Wells, following 1920, with its successful refinery.

In war, where chances must be taken, this oil region, halfway from New York, practically on the direct road to Japan, and right at the best inland gateway to Alaska, was something to try out, the optimists felt. They recommended energetic drilling in the Norman Wells field and wildcatting in the general region, believing there was a reasonable chance of producing large enough quantities of oil to be significant toward defeating Tokyo. While the drilling and the wildcatting were going on there would proceed a survey of the divide between the Mackenzie and Yukon rivers to determine where to run a pipe line, if the drilling showed oil prospects to justify it.

At this stage it was assumed, by both sides to the dispute, that if a pipe line were laid it would run to Fairbanks. Whitehorse had been mentioned as being something like 20 per cent closer; but this met no favor with those who knew the country and who agreed with the chief Canadian Government explorer of the region, Joseph Keele, who had written that the district between Norman and Whitehorse probably contained "the greatest mountain group in Canada." Winding in and out among those peaks would lengthen the pipe line by at least enough to cancel the 20 per cent saving, and then there would be the other difficulties of mountain construction.

So presumably the destination of the pipe would be Fairbanks, for a combination of reasons: it was in effect nearer to the oil field than Whitehorse, because of the more favorable topography; it was already the Alaska center both for civilian and for military aviation; it was a city of considerable size in a mining, agricultural and potentially industrial region that could use the oil to advantage when the war was over; and it was the focus of a distributing network of rivers, railways and roads.

There was discussion of alternative methods of transportation from Norman to Fairbanks. If there were only 2,000 or 3,000 barrels of oil per day obtainable, the processing would be done at Norman by expanding the present unit refinery, and the gasoline would be flown to Fairbanks. If production was somewhat more, a 400-mile winter trucking road would be constructed to the Yukon River (at an estimated cost of between $200,000 and $500,000). Only if the Norman field proved rich would there be a pipe line to Fairbanks.

But this discussion turned out to have been quite beside the mark. For high authorities in Washington decided not to prospect extensively before building a pipe line, not to lay a big-diameter pipe, not to run oil westerly in the direction of Fairbanks and Tokyo; but instead to lay in advance of prospecting a small-diameter (four-inch) pipe, and to run it southerly, toward Whitehorse. This became known as the Canol Project.

As this is written (November, 1943) the United States press has just started carrying notices of a proposed Congressional investigation of the Alcan project, now frequently referred to as the Alaska Highway or Military Highway to Alaska. In Canada the report is that the support of this route by the Dominion Government, in preference to another route, is going to be one of the issues of the next election, which may come in 1944.

But it looks as if the dispute would center, both in the United States and in Canada, not so much upon the Alcan Highway itself as on what some think of as a side issue, the said Canol (Canadian-Oil) project. This is the building of a construction road and the laying of the small-diameter pipe line from the Norman field to the Alcan at Whitehorse. The press has given the length of pipe at 560 miles.

One side to the dispute maintains that Canol is truly and solely a method of local fueling of the Alcan Highway; the other side maintains Canol is at bottom a plan for side-tracking and defeating what to them is the chief thing that ought to be desired, to bring into Alaska by a sensibly laid and big-diameter pipe line, and through Alaska to a point near the war front, a material part of the oil needed for the defeat of Japan. This group charges, in effect, that when it proved beyond the strength of the opposition to block all use of Mackenzie oil in the Japanese war, then they hit upon the scheme of nullifying this development by laying the wrong kind of pipe line, and in the wrong direction.

It appears that in the early stages of the discussion at Washington the issues were fairly clear cut, and that there were but two sides. One side desired a large-diameter pipe laid from the Norman field westerly to the Yukon with a view to the construction of a refinery in Alaska, either where the pipe struck the Yukon River or, more likely, at Fairbanks, with enough petroleum handled so that it would have a substantial bearing upon winning the war. The size of the pipe and refinery was to be determined jointly by the authorities of Army, Navy and Lend-Lease and with the object of utilizing all petroleum products, from the heaviest oils and lubricants to the required grade of aviation gasoline. The other side wanted no Mackenzie development, no pipe line or other transportation of petroleum from the Mackenzie toward Alaska and Bering Sea, but favored instead tankers runing from a Pacific port of the United States, with storage in Alaska. This plan rested on the assumption that there would be plenty of tankers and that our Navy and other forces could keep Japan at such a distance from Alaska that stored fuel would be in no danger from bombing raids.

The contention that storage tanks in Alaska were almost of necessity beyond Japanese bombing reach, and that we had plenty of tankers, disappeared with the news of Pearl Harbor. Then, for a time, opinion swung from an underestimation to a corresponding overestimation of Japanese strength. At this stage of the pendulum swing it was decided to make use of Mackenzie oil.

But the pendulum was to swing back, in something under two years; and once more the feeling grew that storage tanks in Alaska were safe from enemy depredations and that we had enough tankers. People now began to criticize the expenditures in connection with Mackenzie oil, on the ground that tanking California oil and storing it would have been cheaper. These criticisms we do not consider, except for a passing reference in another connection, because we feel they are related to a side issue, to mere economizing and to such hindsight as we all find easy when sufficient time has elapsed. So we devote ourselves here to what we consider the main issue, whether Mackenzie oil should have been used on a large or on a small scale, and where the refinery should have been located.

Those who want to use Mackenzie oil in great quantity as a

basis for shortening the war, and as a foundation for development of northwestern North America when the war is over, say that a pipe of the required diameter—be that ten, fifteen, or twenty inches—should have been laid in the direction of Japan, which would be westward from the downstream end of the Norman oil region through the low Eagle Pass to the town of Eagle, and as far as desired beyond, perhaps all the way to a permanently ice-free southwestern port. They maintain that the Canol project, using a four-inch pipe, is of negligible significance for shortening the war, no matter in which direction it is laid; and then, instead of going in the direction of Japan, it goes in the direction of Seattle; instead of going through a country of known resources, that could be developed after the war, it goes through and into a section of no known special resource.

Anyhow, the critics say, if the planners wanted to fuel a road with Mackenzie oil, then why didn't they build the road by way of the Mackenzie oil fields in the first place?

Enough to show the complexity of the problem, and the difficulty of forming reasonably sound opinions in advance of a full postwar investigation, we review the current pro-and-con discussion of the Canol project.

A charge which is not usually denied, but rather explained away, is that one reason why the pipe line was run to Whitehorse, a Canadian town, rather than to Eagle, Fairbanks, or another point in Alaska, is the opposition of Alaskans to the entry of Canadian oil under the guise of military necessity when, it is alleged, the real purpose of the Canadians no doubt is to corral the Alaska market so as to keep the territory flooded with cheap Canadian oil when the war is over. This flood of cheap foreign oil, it is said, the Alaskans do not want because they desire to produce oil from their own fields and are afraid that the Federal Government would not give adequate support in this if Canadian oil were already coming in through such a cheap and efficient means of transport as a large pipe.[3]

[3] There is going the rounds a suspiciously amusing explanation of why the pipe line terminal is in Canada, to the effect that those who determined the routing thought that Whitehorse, the destination they themselves fixed for

It is conceded that a good deal of prospecting in Alaska has not thus far shown much chance of rich fields in southern or central parts of the Territory; but it is claimed, and is beyond reasonable dispute, that prospects are good on the north coast of Alaska, as indicated on the petroleum map, page 338. (The difficulty is that this northern field cannot be developed in time for use against Japan unless, indeed, the war continues past 1945. But that apparently is secondary with at least those Alaskans who are opposed to a direct and capacious pipe from the Mackenzie primarily on the ground of postwar economic strategy.)

Another charge of a similar nature is that the Canol pipe is of such small diameter, and was run through such difficult terrain to a terminal in Canada, because the Pacific coast states did not want a pipe into Alaska that would lessen or destroy their chance to control the Alaska oil situation both during the war and after. The Pacific coast reply would appear to be that Alaska is United States territory, and that they do frankly believe they are justified in clinging to this market.

A charge frequently heard is one of extravagance in dollars, man power, and strategic materials. The papers have said that $134,000,000 has already been appropriated for Canol, and that this will not be enough for completion, including the pumping stations en route and the terminal facilities. To this it is countered that while the price is high, in all three elements of expenditure, the Canol does deliver to the Alcan Highway petroleum from a Mackenzie River source, thus leaving us free to use in other theaters all the oil available along the western seaboard of the United States and Canada. It is added that an extension of the

the pipe, was under United States jurisdiction. Specifically, it is charged by critics of Canol that a memorandum accompanying the U. S. Army directive for this project contains instructions that the terminal refinery should be located "at Whitehorse, the Yukon, Alaska." Though strange, this would not be without precedent. There was, for instance, the attempt by the United States Treasury to collect an income tax from Jan Welzl, the alleged author (he himself denied he was the author) of the best-seller *Thirty Years in the* Golden North, a Book-of-the-Month Club selection. Welzl, at the time that the Treasury made this attempt, was living at Dawson, Yukon Territory (not so far from Whitehorse). This tax matter was dropped by Washington when an attorney pointed out, on behalf of Welzl, that Dawson is not in Alaska but in Canada.

pipe from Whitehorse to Skagway permits us to deliver to the Pacific any surplus there may be.

The critics charge that the Canol pipe line goes through mountains where some passes are about 5,000 feet above sea level, which would mean that an extremely costly route has been chosen, and one which puts a terrific strain on the pumping stations so that these are liable to go out of order, leaving the Alcan Highway without fuel supplies until repairs can be completed. The reply is that the Canol project was entered into after so much construction work had already been done on the Alcan Highway that the routing could not be shifted, and that the 400-odd miles of Canol construction, crow-flight distance,[4] is the shortest and most practical way of reaching the highway from the Norman oil field.

It is charged that a 400-mile pipe line west from the lower end of the Norman oil region over comparatively low and flat land to Eagle would have cost only a third or a quarter as much as the 560 miles of rugged mountain construction to Whitehorse. The reply is that a line westward, in the direction of Japan, would be on a theory with which neither the Alcan nor the Canol people have anything to do. They are merely road and pipe line transportation men, concerned with fueling trucks, airplanes, and other machinery on an established route. To them the wrangling about sending oil in the direction of Japan is irrelevant, or worse —an attempt to confuse by mixing two issues.

It is charged that a large part of the Canol project is the building from the Norman region to Whitehorse of a road which is at right angles to any foreseeable traffic and cannot therefore have any other use than servicing the pipe line; while a road west from the oil region to the Yukon would have been at once a service road and an important link in a practical freight highway between the Mackenzie and Yukon. But again the reply is that this

[4] The 400-odd mile crow-flight distance mentioned, Norman Wells to Whitehorse, is taken from the map. That the pipe actually is 560 miles is taken from newspapers. Apparently the difference represents the turnings and twisting of the pipe in finding its way through the mountains to Whitehorse.

is beside the point; that the Canol project was intended solely to fuel a previously constructed highway, and that whether there should or should not be a freight highway connecting the two rivers where they approach each other, or a pipe line following that highway, is beside the point.

The charge is made that taking oil through a meager four-inch pipe from the Norman field to Whitehorse has no bearing on large plans for postwar development that will take care of some of our returning soldiers. Once more the reply is that a side issue is being injected.

There is publicity in the newspapers, which is not too fortunate in its bearing on the good-neighborliness of the two countries, to the effect that the Canadian Government inveigled the United States Government into building a pipe line from a Canadian oil field to a Canadian terminal, instead of what these critics allege should have been built, a pipe line from a Canadian oil field to a United States (Alaska) terminal. It would appear that this criticism of the Canadians is based upon a misunderstanding, for few things seem clearer than the passive opposition to Canol by the Dominion Government. They do not appear to have been active in opposition, seemingly taking the position that they wanted to do whatever the United States Government asked them to do; but when Canadian officials were asked for opinions by the United States Government they appear to have pointed out, usually if not always, the difficulty of the proposed routing, emphasizing their doubt that such a construction along such a route to such a destination would be worth while.

And, so far as the record is as yet available, a reluctance corresponding to that of the Canadian Government is equally clear upon the part of the Standard Oil Company of New Jersey, although their reluctance applied rather to the development of the Norman field than to the routing of the pipe. Their passive resistance to the development was so well known that it occasioned comment and questions on why the company was so backward about accepting government encouragement of the development of its property. The only reply made by the company that is personally known to me was to the effect that they wanted to be sure the record would carry throughout its own evidence that they had not been painting rosy pictures or in any way "promoting" the Government into a Mackenzie oil project, though, at the same time, assuring the Army that they were willing to cooperate, in case the military came to the conclusion the project was worth while from a defense standpoint.

Then we come to a whole group of charges which the defenders of Canol feel are unworthy of serious rebuttal. It is suggested, for instance, that powerful oil companies did not want the use of Mackenzie oil on the Japanese front because they could make more money selling California oil and transporting it by tanker, making a reasonable profit not merely upon the quantities sold at the refinery but also upon the transportation, including a fair percentage on any tankers that happened to be destroyed by the enemy, with opportunity of further sale to replace oil so lost. It has even been suggested that destroyers, cruisers, and aircraft that protect the tankers while crossing the Pacific are themselves burning oil, upon which the companies receive a fair profit. The answer to all this is that such objections come from men who are out of sympathy with our American way of life, socialistically if not communistically inclined.

This brings us to a second group of innuendoes that deal with socialism by name. It is charged that an antisocialist Dominion Government has been unsympathetic to the rapid development of Mackenzie oil, particularly at the Athabaska Tar Sands, because the province of Alberta has a Social Credit government, thought of as socialistic by the rest of Canada. It is said to be felt in Ottawa that Alberta voters might be the more inclined to reelect their socialist government if a great wave of prosperity were to strike the province during its tenure. Here it is being replied that this is merely a political canard; but the charge seems to be taken seriously enough in Canada for a fight to be made along this line by the Cooperative Commonwealth Federation, a body of liberals frequently thought of as the Canadian equivalent of the New Deal.

Basic to these innuendo-type arguments is the mentioned theory that laying a small-diameter pipe line in the direction of Seattle, as against a larger pipe line in the direction of Tokyo, is not a bona fide attempt to fuel the Alcan Highway, but is instead basically a way of seeing to it that Mackenzie oil does not play any important part in the present war.

But lest we succumb readily to the innuendoes, and the reasoning and alleged facts which support them, we should keep steadily in mind the fundamental question under debate: Has the Mackenzie, or can it have in time for use in the present war, enough oil to justify a large-diameter pipe line from somewhere near the Carcajou mouth to Eagle or to Fairbanks? If so, there must be arrangements at Norman to produce gasoline needed for blending with the crude to guarantee the westward flow of crude at the lowest winter temperatures, and great refineries in Alaska and a distribution system, probably based on Fairbanks, including pipe lines thence to ice-free harbors westward at Bristol Bay and southward in the Anchorage-Kodiak region. Remember well that, while some insist all the technical problems of the fabulous Tar Sands have been solved, there are others who maintain the solution will require ten years; and that, while there are some who claim you can get from the Norman region oil in proportion to your willingness to drill, there are others who maintain two hundred Norman wells are not going to produce much more than one hundred, the quantity and area being (they contend) so limited.[5]

[5] After this was set in type the newspapers carried pertinent statements by officials of the Standard Oil Company of New Jersey, and others, on Norman Wells. These reports are to the effect that, while the Norman region probably is not one of the fabulous oil discoveries it is nevertheless certainly important. One of the statements is that 4,000 acres in the immediate vicinity will produce 200,000,000 barrels. This would mean enough oil to keep the present 3,000-barrel-a-day pipe line to Whitehorse busy for more than 175 years.

If, as many feel, it is not yet too late for taking advantage of the favorable topography between Norman and Fairbanks, and of the strategic location of that city as a refining and distributing center, we might perhaps go ahead and spend a quarter as much as has already been spent on Canol (let us even say half as much) and run a large-diameter pipe through the Eagle Pass to a refinery at Fairbanks. A 20,000-barrel-a-day pipe would be occupied with the estimated 200,000,000 barrels for 25 years, but so small a diameter

Moreover there is the censorship, on compliance with which the Edmonton newspapers and others in Canada pride themselves. For all we know, perhaps some of those things are being done in 1943 or 1944 which the critics of Alcan and Canol think should have been done in 1940 or 1941. If so, these critics would agree on better late than never. Certain rudimentary airports existed along the Mackenzie River prior to the war, and we can only surmise as to whether or not these have since been extended and developed and roads constructed. If so, it is possible that this work has been undertaken in direct relation to oil developments in the Norman district and may well affect the post-war situation in this region. Pilots along the airway that parallels the Alcan Highway are reported to say that while having difficulty with the mountain weather on that route they constantly hear of much better flying conditions over the lowlands of the Mackenzie, and that they feel they could have saved delays and difficulty by going that way. Still more often we hear what a blessing it is in thick weather to be able to follow such a great river as the Mackenzie or Yukon; for the planes may safely keep almost on the river's surface if the fog is thick, because the stream is wide and the land on either side is low as compared with the deep and sometimes canyonlike valleys which the planes attempt to follow under certain conditions along the Alcan. It may be that such reports and opinions are gradually bringing about a rehabilitation of the flying route pioneered by Richardson and Brintnell.

Finally, closing the discussion, we emphasize what has already been implied, that high statesmanship and broad considerations of world strategy may be the reasons why no defense of Alcan or Canol has yet been published that seems to meet the attacks made upon them. The attackers have the advantage that they

would be unreasonable in view of the near certainty that there is much good oil land in the region beyond the 4,000 acres which have been "proved."

A daily piping to Fairbanks of 40,000 barrels for the next twelve years might not be forcing Norman Wells too much. A 60,000-barrel-a-day output might be high for the good of the field, but would perhaps be justified under the stress of war conditions.

So far as oil geologists at present understand, the Norman Wells oil field is but one in a large and probably important oil region. See the article in this volume by Wallace E. Pratt, "Petroleum in the North."

are outside governments and without formal responsibility; the defenders are handicapped by military and political considerations of reticence.

ALASKA

Most Americans will recall having seen one of those maps where Alaska is superimposed on the United States. Then the southeastern tip of the Alaskan Panhandle lies along the Atlantic seaboard in Georgia; the western end of the Aleutian chain reaches the Pacific coast in California; on the north Point Barrow is found up in Canada, beyond Minnesota.[6] In area, however, Alaska comes to only about one-fifth of the forty-eight states—it is roughly as large as all the states east of the Alleghenies. As for extremes of climate, Barrow, at the northern tip, has a minimum winter temperature about ten degrees higher than the coldest spots of Montana or Wyoming, while in central Alaska the maximum heat of summer is about equal to that of New York City.

Alaska is prairie throughout its northern fifth and over considerable areas along its western side; the central portion is forested, mainly with spruces, birches, alders, and cottonwoods; the southern fifth, the most mountainous part, has forests of giant trees comparable to those of Washington and British Columbia.

The Arctic and sub-Arctic prairies will eventually produce great quantities of meat through the reindeer industry. The forests in the central zone are chiefly of local value, but those on the southern coast offer great possibilities for the export of lumber and pulp. The river and coastal fisheries are among the richest in the world, while both the prairie and the forest are still large producers of valuable furs. The territory is famous for its gold, discovered in nearly all parts; it contains extensive deposits of numerous other minerals, including coal. There are prospects for oil, particularly along the north coast, as discussed hereafter. Wheat and a variety of other agricultural products find both the

[6] Our own map, on page 217, departs from the usual in placing Alaska farther south, whereupon (also perhaps because of greater-than-average accuracy) the farthest Aleutians are out in the Pacific beyond California.

soil and the required climate along the southern coast and in the Yukon and Kuskokwim basins.

To visualize the lines along which Alaska may develop it is perhaps best to think of it as a greater Scandinavia, which it resembles closely in many respects, with an area somewhat larger, a climate similar, and resources on the whole greater than those of Denmark, Finland, Iceland, Norway, and Sweden combined. As everyone knows, the Scandinavians were at the start of the war among the most advanced countries in the world, economically and socially, supporting in better than average American well-being some seventeen millions.

Alaska north of the Arctic Circle has few people, most of whom live for at least a good part of the year near the coast. On the great inland prairie the population is sparse. Fifty years ago this plain was inhabited by ten times as many Eskimos as now, perhaps even twenty times as many. While this decrease has been taking place in Alaska, the Eskimo population of Greenland has had a steady increase comparable to that of white populations elsewhere. The disparity is in part due to the divergent policies of the United States and of Denmark. The Danes enforce a quarantine to protect the Eskimos from outside influences, and they encourage natives to retain their old economy and culture. The American authorities have, until recently, taken but few leaves from Denmark's book of experience.

However, a change seems coming. Secretary of the Interior Ickes pointed out in his Annual Report for 1937, and has continued to do so in later reports, that the nicely balanced economy of the Alaskan natives has been upset both physically and psychologically by encouraging them to trap for the whites or to work for wages, and that as a natural consequence native culture has decayed. "More and more," his report says, "a people which once was self-sufficient has become dependent upon external forces which are totally disregardful of their needs." After referring to the natives as Alaska's greatest resource, he goes on to say: "The whites of Alaska cannot continue to profit at the expense of the natives. Constitutionally suited to life in the Arctic, the Eskimo and the Alaska Indian must form the foundation to any long-range planning for the development as contrasted to the exploitation of the Territory." He then states that the Education Division of the Indian Office is undertaking a "program which will capitalize the native virtues and at the same time adapt the natives for necessary contacts with their white associates."

In Arctic Alaska the Government maintained at the start of the war eight schools (out of one hundred three in the whole Territory). There were also five Weather Bureau stations scattered about this vast region, and a hospital at Barrow. Aside from this, there has been little governmental activity north of the Arctic Circle. The United States Geological Survey, for instance, did no work there from 1927 to 1941. As for nongovernmental activities, such as commerce, there are practically none in Arctic Alaska except for the coastal fur trade.

The southern three-quarters of Alaska was, on the other hand, the scene of what will be to many surprising activity. Here the Territorial Government, and even more the Federal authorities, have been energetic, intelligent, and liberal. Two of the most interesting enterprises in this region have been the construction of the Alaska Railroad, from Seward on the south coast to Fairbanks in the Yukon valley (a distance of 470 miles), and the establishment of the Matanuska Colony.

Twenty years ago, when the railway was new, three out of four people one met along the Yukon River maintained that the railway to Fairbanks had done harm to interior Alaska by competing with river traffic just enough to ruin the steamboat companies without supplying an alternative service adequate to take their place. That may be so. Still, the railway is to many Alaskans a sign that our competitive civilization, once successful in conquering the wilderness in the States, has not wholly lost its vitality. They point out that since 1937 the Alaska Railroad has made a profit.

Among Alaskans there is much debate about the Matanuska Colony. Some defend it as it is and where it is. Others accept it as right in conception but maintain that it should have been located farther north. The fact is that July temperatures are not so high at Matanuska as they are on the Tanana River near Fairbanks, two hundred miles northward. If, therefore, it was the purpose of Matanuska to supply the district north of the mountains with farm produce, there seems to have been a miscalculation.

The Department of Agriculture reports areas in the Tanana, Kuskokwim, and Yukon valleys, and along the south fork of Fortymile River, that could be cultivated. Fortymile, which is over a hundred miles north of Matanuska, is said to contain 750,000 acres of arable land and is described as likely to "prove one of the most productive in Alaska."

The Alaska Railroad and the Matanuska Colony are the outstanding governmental interests in Alaska. But others, although less publicized, are important. The petroleum deposits on the north coast have been set aside as a reserve for the armed forces; most of southeastern Alaska has been made a national forest; the commercial fisheries along the southern coast are regulated to prevent a depletion of the salmon supply; the fur seals of the Pribilof Islands are protected against extermination (only a small percentage is killed each year)—all in the name of conservation.

People as well as natural resources are being conserved. The Territorial Government maintains health services which include the care of communicable diseases, maternal and child welfare, public health laboratories, and engineering. In its labor legislation Alaska is more progressive than many of the states; and it maintains high standards for the teachers in its schools and in the university at Fairbanks. There are special industrial schools, and traveling medical and dental units.

During the eleven years between 1892 and 1902, long before the New Deal, 1,280 reindeer were brought to Alaska from Siberia on the theory that the white men, and the weapons given to the natives by the whites, had so far reduced the wild reindeer, called caribou, and other game that a domestic meat substitute was needed for the Eskimos. These animals doubled in three years and continued at that rate until it became obvious to forward-looking Alaska businessmen that here was a great natural industry, and they decided to go in for it.

From this point on, the matter is so complicated that a book would be necessary, and even at the close of such a volume you would probably find in agreement with you only those who agreed with your point of view in the first place. We hesitantly summarize, trying to steer halfway between the emotional extremes and realizing we are going to please nobody.

It was Sheldon Jackson, a Presbyterian missionary, and other paternalistic and evangelistic people, who originally got the industry started; and one of their ideas was to limit its direct benefits to the natives. The Government also took this position. However, the gold country of Alaska is the happy hunting ground of the big-time lawyer, and just as soon as the white men realized that here was a new source of big money, the lawyers pointed out that it was unconstitutional—class legislation or something of the sort—to try to hog a natural resource for the benefit of a certain group, to wit, the Eskimos and perhaps the other Indians of the Territory. So business went in for reindeer, facing the hostility of both the missions and the Government.

The industry continued to prosper; the deer multiplied nearly or quite according to schedule, and finally New York money from people who controlled millions became involved. Reindeer meat was a success in the big cities, and was sold with a luxury slant—it might be cheaper to raise a pound of reindeer beef in Alaska and deliver it to New York than to raise a pound of shorthorn beef in Wyoming and deliver it to the same market, but it was considered unwise to make this the basis for selling reindeer cheap, for then the idea would spread that it was a poor man's food, whereupon even the poor would avoid eating it. The plan used was to sell reindeer as a delicacy for those who could afford the price, and this plan was succeeding when the promoters overstepped the mark.

The beginning of the end was when the Lomen interests,

under the name Lomen Reindeer Corporation and under several other names, arranged with the Great Northern, Northern Pacific, and Milwaukee railroads to serve reindeer steaks, chops, roasts, and stews on their dining cars. The splurge and fanfare with which this began aroused the cattle and sheep men of the West, who, like many another citizen of the States, looked upon Alaska as a foreign country, or acted as if they did, and arose as a man "in the defense of the American farmer and rancher." Mass meetings were held, chambers of commerce passed resolutions, there was even resort to vigilante methods.

These were only a few of the many elements of the campaign against the introduction of "cheap and inferior imported meat" into the United States market. The farm lobby is notoriously strong in Washington, and cattlemen have their share of the power. The Government had been hostile, anyway, to the Alaska whites' taking over of the reindeer as an industry, and the missions remained in opposition, partly because their share in the monopoly had been slipping out of their hands, and partly because of the belief (less well-founded in Alaska than in most other places) that the white man is likely to rob the native.

The market for reindeer meat declined, and the financial backers of the industry saw the writing on the wall. Money was no longer available for herding and other care of the reindeer, including protection from wolves; the natives who had reindeer herds were no longer able to sell their meat, since the white buyers had lost all the money they could afford and were withdrawing.

From a high point, some ten years ago, of anywhere between 350,000 (estimate of the Government and others opposed to the private ownership) and 1,000,000 (contended by the private owners), the number of domestic reindeer has gone down steadily.

One factor in the decline is that the difference between reindeer and caribou is one of name only; we speak of them as reindeer if they are domestic, as caribou if they are wild. One source of increase in the domestic herds was a few caribou that joined the reindeer—which brought not merely a numerical gain but an improvement of the breed, since the caribou were on the average larger. Now the process was reversed; when the care of the herdsmen was relaxed the domestic animals wandered off and joined the wild herds. Wolves were increasing; for their chief food is the caribou or reindeer, and the reindeer were less on guard against predatory beasts and were more easily killed when not protected by man.

So the opposition to the reindeer grew in strength—in the Government at Washington, and among the wolves in Alaska. They worked together so effectively that the reindeer decreased in number faster than they had increased, until by 1943 there were said to be fewer than 100,000 left, not counting some on islands in Bering Sea, where the wolf does not exist and where the sea takes the place of the herdsman.

As a footnote, it should be said that there has been nearly as much opposition to the reindeer within Alaska as without. The people who own the newspapers and control the radio, the members of chambers of commerce, the men of local influence, are in the main importers and exporters. They export gold, other minerals, fish, and fur; they import beef, lamb, all the things that the white Alaskan eats. These businessmen are frequently affiliated (in fact, are practically always either directly or indirectly affiliated) with businessmen in Seattle and other Pacific states. It is to the common interest of the Seattle wholesalers, the Seattle longshoremen, the Seattle-Alaska transportation companies, the Alaska longshoremen, and the Alaska wholesalers and retailers that the food eaten in Alaska shall be an Oregon roast of beef and an Idaho potato rather than an Alaska potato and a reindeer steak or roast. (We speak of the period just before the war; the feelings, and the facts, seem to be changing under war conditions.)

Immediately before the war, in spite of the world depression, the main commercial enterprises in Alaska, except the reindeer, were showing material gains over 1928. The newest of these, aviation, made the greatest strides, and with reason; for on the frontier, where there are few railways and roads, the plane is the cheapest means of long-distance travel. It is so cheap that even an Eskimo who owns his own dog team, and to whom time is of no value, cannot afford to travel by sledge between such points as Nome and Fairbanks; the cost of food for himself and for his dogs, plus his lodging fees en route, would amount to several times the price of an airplane ticket.

Flying in Alaska is as safe as in New England, and as pleasant. Pan American Airways, the largest single operator, finds that on the average its pilots are as well satisfied with their jobs in Alaska as in Brazil, that over half the pilots on its Alaska lines prefer January to July, and that (assuming like equipment and ground service) schedules can be maintained through the midwinter period with an average regularity at least as good as that of the northeastern United States.

Air mail was started in 1924 by that most famous of Alaska flight pioneers, Carl Ben Eielson; since then it has expanded fitfully. Air-line operators increased from four in 1928 to forty in 1937, planes from eight to one hundred, passengers from 2,171 to 20,958, freight and express from 94,701 pounds to 2,940,757. In 1938, 30,000 passengers were carried. By June 30, 1938, there were 155 planes in operation. Freight carried by air during 1938 totaled 3,415,759 pounds. This means that just before the war the 70,000 or 80,000 Alaskans, about half of whom were whites, created nearly 70 per cent as much air freight as did all the 130,000,000 inhabitants of the forty-eight states.

Since the war began, Alaskan aviation is known to have made vast progress, but the details are not available for publication.

By implication, and occasional direct mention, the petroleum situation of Alaska has been discussed in our preceding section on northern Canada; but a few remarks may be added.

As indicated by the map on page 338, the great oil region of median North America, which contains in sub-Arctic Canada among others the oil districts of the Athabaska Tar Sands and of Norman Wells, extends along the eastern side of the northerly continuation of the Rockies to the mouth of the Mackenzie and then west along the north coast to and beyond Point Barrow, keeping north of the mountains as they curve westward.

Petroleum ("mineral tar") was discovered by Thomas Simpson just back of Cape Simpson in 1837. There have been many reports since, and now the Barrow section is an oil reserve of the United States Government. This is considered to be by far the likeliest oil region of Alaska. There have been no steps toward development—perhaps because our people did not adequately visualize the coming of the war; but that would appear to be a lesser reason, for there has been rather persistent and widespread search for oil in the rest of Alaska. It must be acknowledged, even by the northward development enthusiasts, that the Barrow region, and particularly the section east of Barrow, are in about the least accessible part of the North American continent.

A pipe line south from the Barrow oil region would have to go through several mountain ranges of the Brooks chain, which rise in places above 10,000 feet (according to belief rather than measurement), and the passes of which are little known. The engineering difficulties are formidable, and the amount of strategic materials required would be great, at least in comparison with that required for bringing in petroleum from the Norman region, as indicated in the preceding section.

There is the possibility of sea transport, but the years are few in which the first ships get east beyond Barrow before early July, and there are not many in which conditions are favorable past September. When west, northwest, or north winds blow, the summer navigation may be interrupted at any time and for any length of time.

The Government in its encouragement, whatever that may have been, and the private companies in their speculative efforts, have therefore been quite right in trying for oil not beyond the mountains on the eastern north coast, where it was practically known to be plentiful, but instead through the Yukon and other basins of rivers emptying west into Bering Sea, and along the south coast.

One section here is geologically rather hopeful: the district which includes the mouths of the Kuskokwim and Yukon rivers and runs northeasterly. But for some reason this section does not appear to have been drilled for oil, at least not before the cloud of war secrecy descended.

There had been a good deal of drilling by various companies in other sections of the Alaskan interior, but particularly on the south coast, all without leading to much encouragement, some companies withdrawing after extensive and expensive operations. But there distinctly is hope for Alaska as a whole, which you see clearly by a study of Mr. Pratt's article in this volume.

In the section on Canada were given the arguments for and against a program which, if successful, would lead to making Fairbanks a center for the refining of Canadian crude oil brought by pipe line from the Norman vicinity and either produced at Norman or brought there by downstream navigation from fields higher up the Mackenzie—if necessary, from as far south as the Athabaska Tar Sands that are at the head of navigation just above Edmonton. That presentation admitted the possibility that the Norman region might not be as rich as its advocates believe, and that there might be more difficulties than they think about refining the Tar Sands product; but we probably left, on the whole, small doubt in the mind of a reader who depended solely on our material that Alaskans were being penny-wise and pound-foolish in so far as they opposed the entry of Canadian oil.

But there is the saying about two sides to a controversy; we were going to hedge further in the Canadian part of our discussion, but are doing it here instead: if there had been good work on the hopeful district around the mouth of the Yukon, oil might have been found there, as on the Mackenzie, and refineries might be making high octane gasoline and other products. To that extent we should perhaps sympathize with those Alaskans who resent the slow internal development of their territory and show it in what may nevertheless be unwise opposition to working hand in glove with Canada on petroleum, and on the related problem of a cheaply built and capacious rail, river, and trucking-road system through an eastern gateway leading to Fairbanks.

For one thing, it is a pertinent and common view that a number of the abandoned gold mines around Fairbanks, and indeed along the entire Yukon basin both in Yukon Territory and in Alaska, could be reopened if fuel costs were materially cut. This is one of the postwar development opportunities which some Alaskans eagerly desire to make good through Canadian oil; others prefer to take a chance on the development of local oil.

Basic to a discussion of the future of Alaska, as of any other country, is whether people enjoy living there. Take Fairbanks, one of the larger cities, typical in climate of the Yukon basin, a region of forest, cold winters, and hot summers that includes half of Alaska.

In November, 1940, Fairbanks had perhaps 5,000 people but was comparable to a city of 10,000 in Vermont or Montana. Its people had come from every state in the Union and from nearly every country in the world. Its children were growing up in homes similar to those of our midwestern and far western states.

For real first-hand opinions, go to youngsters: their elders may be swayed by theory and propaganda. For a just view of how a typical American likes a typical northern climate you could do no better than take a vote of the school children of Fairbanks, where the extreme heat of summer, according to the Weather Bureau, is 99° in the shade, and the extreme chill of winter, 72° below zero. The summer climate is, then, not very different from that of New York City or of the northern peninsula of Michigan, both of which claim to be summer resorts. In January weather the comparison is to states like Montana and Wyoming. The Fairbanks midwinter extreme is six degrees lower than the minimum recorded within the States, at Riverside Ranger Station, Wyoming, 66° below zero.[7]

It was important in the Fairbanks vote that there should be no previous discussion to create a bias. Accordingly, I did not

[7] The Alaska minimum is six degrees lower than that of Fairbanks, for the Weather Bureau in 1941 published 78 degrees below as the Alaska minimum, at Fort Yukon which is about 125 miles farther north than Fairbanks and is, in extreme temperatures, both the coldest and hottest spot in Alaska; the top record there is 100 degrees in the shade.

mention the plan for a ballot until I was lunching with W. H. Bloom, Superintendent of the city schools. After lunch we went to the central school together. He summoned the teachers and instructed them. They were to go back to their own classes and, without other discussion, were to impress upon the children that the teachers did not care one way or the other, and that nobody cared, whether they enjoyed better midwinter or midsummer, whether they disliked more 99° in the shade or 72° below zero; but that the teachers were keen to know their real preferences. Then the children voted, with result as you see by the following letter from Mr. Bloom:

FAIRBANKS PUBLIC SCHOOLS
W. H. BLOOM, SUPERINTENDENT
Fairbanks, Alaska

November 15, 1940

Dr. Vilhjalmur Stefansson
Nordale Hotel
Fairbanks, Alaska

DEAR DR. STEFANSSON:

The tabulation below indicates the replies we received when our pupils were asked to express their preference as to the winter and summer seasons in Alaska.

Elementary Grades

Boys		*Girls*	
Prefer Summer,	57	Prefer Summer,	58
Prefer Winter,	105	Prefer Winter,	86

High School

Boys		*Girls*	
Prefer Summer,	34	Prefer Summer,	23
Prefer Winter,	21	Prefer Winter,	32

A few did not vote because they had no preference, and several had not spent both a summer and a winter in Alaska.

Very truly yours
(Signed) W. H. BLOOM

It surprised many in Fairbanks that the liking for winter was stronger among high-school girls than among high-school boys; but nevertheless it appeared in the wide discussion which followed the vote that parents were divided much as the children, and that the women averaged a higher preference for winter than the men.

A reason assigned by some for the preference for cold weather by the high-school girls was that on the average they were fonder than the boys of winter sports, like skating, skiing, and snowshoeing. This was said to have some relation to the particularly attractive and comfortable sports costumes. And here you have one of the main keys to the situation—one does not like any place unless he is comfortable in it; the children of Fairbanks, well dressed for the cold, were more comfortable in January than in July, for you cannot protect yourself similarly from heat. But the July of Fairbanks is the kind of July that many of us like and all of us are used to, which should mean a good deal when we evaluate their testimony on the comparative likability of the different seasons.

There are three chief climate areas in Alaska—the north coast, the Yukon basin, and the south coast. Only on the south coast, where the summers are never as hot as in Fairbanks and the winters never as cold, are you likely to find a majority in any town who prefer summer.

Wherever you go in Alaska, a majority speaks well of the climate as a whole, but a fairly strong minority is in some places vociferous against it.

It can be inferred from other sections of the present volume, and from the general evidence, that between 1920 and 1940 the Soviet Union accomplished so much more than Greenland, Canada, and Alaska combined in the study and development of the Far North that comparisons are practically impossible. Still we attempt a few:

During the twenty or so years between the two wars no Alaska town north of the Arctic circle grew materially. In that period the largest Arctic town of Canada's largest river, Aklavik on the Mackenzie, grew from a few dozen to something between 200 and 300. In the same period the Arctic village of Igarka, on Siberia's comparable river the Yenisei, grew from less than 100 to more than 20,000. Just before 1940 more than 100 steamers were plying the Arctic coasts of the Soviet Union—more than 20 of them going all the way through the Northeast Passage between Atlantic and Pacific. On the Arctic coast of North America there were a half-dozen steamers, and none went through the full Northwest Passage. In a single year a dozen or so different Canadian airplanes crossed the Arctic Circle and flew there a total of a few hundred miles, and the like was true for Alaska; more than a thousand airplanes were then operating in the Soviet Arctic, flying several hundred thousands of miles.

There are of course for these differences many reasons of geography, economics, and foreign relations—naturally, for otherwise the differences would not exist.

An explanation, put forward no doubt chiefly to sound clever but containing more than a little truth, is that one of the main reasons for the difference between the northward policies of the United States and Canada on one side, and those of the Soviet Union on the other, lies in the exile system as handled by the Czars. There was a subversive character named Josef Stalin, and he was banished to the lower Yenisei, on the verge of the Arctic, where he had to spend three years. Now, if Warren Harding and Robert Borden had had the good sense to exile Franklin Roosevelt for three years to Fort Yukon and Mackenzie King for three years to Aklavik they might have formed conceptions of northern development and strategy not unlike those of Stalin, and there might then have been in North America for some time before the war a northward surge of development not unlike the grand-scale poleward movement of colonization and exploitation that was carried out by the Soviet Union under the second and third Five Year Plans.

Failing the benefit of exile for our prospective rulers, we may gain through the lessons of war a concept of the earth as round *for practical purposes* and of the Polar Sea as a World Mediterranean. With these key understandings we may begin to see many specific reasons for us to develop our northern resources and to spread our population northward so that we shall have on our side of the polar basin a development comparable to that of the Soviets.

But such development on our side is perhaps unlikely to follow close upon the first day of world peace. For we may prove overly tax-conscious, and there can result a period of economy and retrenchment. And should there be, from exhaustion or any other cause, a similar period of letdown in the northward trend of Soviet development, then it would seem likely that several decades might pass before North Americans ceased trying to exploit the North at a distance through a sort of colonial policy, using Alaska for the benefit of the forty-eight states, northern Canada to profit southern Canada—in both cases, no doubt, chiefly through furs, mining, and fisheries.

However, there is certain to develop (through the sphericity of the earth, and the apposite location of great cities across the polar basin from each other) a network of trans-Arctic air commerce. This will bring about an education in the qualities of the Arctic and sub-Arctic not so dissimilar to the Yenisei schooling of Josef Stalin. So the postwar decades should not be many before absentee control in the North American Arctic is replaced by the direct use of northern resources by people who live there. Then will the basin of the Arctic Mediterranean at last come into its own, judged by its real merits and demerits, no longer by folk beliefs which we have inherited from our intellectual ancestors, the subtropical Egyptians, Hebrews, Greeks, and Romans who dwelt around the Old World's lesser mediterranean.

17

The Aleutians

By Anthony J. Dimond

Anthony J. Dimond, born in Palatine Bridge, New York. Delegate from Alaska to Congress since 1933; author of numerous articles on Alaska.

"The Aleutians" was published in the *New York Times Magazine,* November 18, 1942.

The Aleutians have as many moods and are, in turn, as calm, as smiling, as vivid, as charming, as irritating, and as torturingly destructive as any of the women of fact or fiction, and the changes may occur with almost startling suddenness. The vision of the Aleutians that will be with me the longest is that of flying over many of them at a height of approximately eight or ten thousand feet, with visibility clear and unlimited, and looking down on these islands, the smaller ones reminding me of nothing so much as green pancakes on a griddle of stainless steel. Some of them from the air seemed to be exactly round. Some of them were sprawled out in one direction or another as if the batter had run a bit before congealing.

To worshipers of preconceived opinion, it may seem almost like sacrilege to say it, but the sun does shine in the Aleutians. My own personal recollections of that area are not ones of appalling combinations of cold and gusty Arctic winds driving sheets of even colder rain or snow, but rather of marvelously green islands set in clear and untroubled sunlit seas. The beauty of the picture is enhanced by the memory of slender mountains or volcanos like those of the Islands of the Four Mountains, or of Mount Vsevidof on Umnak Island, each an almost perfect cone, luxuriant grass growing high up the sides, snow-covered at the top.

Of course, rain and snow fall in the Aleutians, and winds blow there; the combination is sometimes too sadistic for human comfort, or even complete tolerance, and one can understand how bitter such experiences may be to soldiers who are stationed on those far-flung islets, constantly on watch against a powerful and ruthless enemy, and without any of the ordinary means of mental or physical recreation which might be afforded in more populous areas.

Not from individual recollections but as a result of day-after-

FIG. 20. This is the map General Mitchell might have used to illustrate his famous remark that Alaska is the Achilles' heel of America.

day observations we know that the Aleutians enjoy sunshine for some period of the time on at least three-fourths of the days of the year. On many of those same days wind or fog or rain, or some combination of the three, engulfs one part of the area or another. If variety in climatic conditions has any attractions, then the Aleutians are among the most climatically seductive places in the world. So, the Aleutians enjoy—or suffer from—what may be called marine climate, which means, I suppose, a climate somewhat more moist than that which is to be found in the great plains of the continent or in its western desert.

After all, despite the fictionized ideas which so many people entertain about the Aleutians, the climate of that area is not Arctic or even sub-Arctic. The islands, having an over-all length from east to west of eleven hundred miles and an area approximating four million acres, lie well within the North Temperate Zone. If—without shifting them a single inch from the north or to the south—we could slide them bag and baggage east between the parallels of latitude which embrace them, across the intervening Pacific waters, the Dominion of Canada, and the Atlantic Ocean, they would first pass over southern Ireland between Cork and Carrick, over southern England between Dover and Lancaster, over the Netherlands, southern Denmark, northern Germany, the center of Poland and then come to rest, if it were so stipulated, in central Russia a bit north of Stalingrad and a bit farther south of Moscow. In fact, the southernmost border of the Aleutians is not more than one hundred fifty miles north of the boundary between the United States and Canada.

To some extent at least, the climate of the islands is benefited by the near-by presence of the Kuroshio, or Japan Current, which originates in the tropics, flows northeast along the eastern shore of Asia, on both sides of the Japanese Archipelago, and thence, after looping one branch into the Okhotsk Sea, turns eastward south of the Aleutians and bathes and warms a large part of the southern coast of Alaska as well as the shores of British Columbia, Washington, Oregon, and California. While not so warm as the Gulf Stream, the Kuroshio unquestionably benefits with its heat all the lands along its course.

Like many other earthly circumstances, fog may lose its terror, and even its discomfort, as one becomes accustomed to it. When our airmen first went into the Aleutians the fog must have seemed baffling to them; but the late reports indicate that they have triumphed over the fog, and are now daily either ignoring or making use of the same kind and variety and quantity of fog in bringing death and destruction to the enemy no longer entrenched on Kiska Island. The fog at first so much complained of is being turned to our advantage as we gain mastery of it. It is no longer a "one-way" affair.

With the removal of the aboriginal native population from the Aleutians, no human being can be found there except those in military or other Government service, our own troops on the easterly three-fourths of the islands, and the Japanese on the westerly group embracing Kiska, Agattu, and Attu. This condition is a far cry from that which existed when the Russians discovered and took over the islands in the late 1700's, for then, according to the best information, 25,000 healthy, sturdy native people, of Stone Age economy, called Aleuts lived in comfort in the Aleutian Archipelago, without steel or bronze tools and with weapons no more deadly or dangerous than bows and arrows.

A Japanese journalist is reported to have said the Aleutians could support five million people, and that is probably a fair estimate. That the islands are not economically worthless is known to practically everyone except the majority of the residents of the forty-eight states. While it is true that the Aleutians are mountainous and really constitute the summits of a range which has its bases deep in the adjoining seas, the hills and the lowlands have a sufficient covering of soil to grow grasses and grains of many kinds, as well as ordinary garden vegetables. Nowhere have I seen more sturdy or nutritious grass than in the Aleutians. This has been measurably proved by the successful sheep-raising experiment on Umnak Island. Starting with a few head only, the herd has increased until it numbered, last spring, about 14,000. No wolf or other predatory animal is to be found on any of the Aleutians west of Unimak Island and, therefore, one can foresee clearly a satisfactory economic future for the islands if devoted to stock raising alone.

It is true that the Aleutians are unique. That is one of their attractions. Bogoslof Island, which may be considered as a part of the Aleutians, has the amusing habit of disappearing beneath the surface of the sea and then arising above it. It is set down on the charts at a certain place, but the experienced mariners of that region know that it may show up somewhere near by. It is an evidence, of course, of the volcanic and, therefore, unstable character of a considerable part of the area, which was illustrated a few years ago when one of the volcanos of the mainland, named Katmai, virtually exploded and blew into dust about six cubic miles of its upper story which was distributed for hundreds of miles over the surrounding area, in some places many feet deep.

The waters surrounding the islands are rich in fish of various types. I vividly recall the occasion when we put into the harbor of Nikolski, on Umnak Island, working our way among reefs which must have been a nightmare to the skipper. When finally anchored, the cook and one of his helpers put a number of hooks and lines overboard and inside of twenty minutes we had on deck at least fifty fat codfish of texture and flavor unsurpassed.

The exceptional importance of the Aleutians in world strategy is proved not by the opinion of any person, military or layman, but by the irrefutable facts of geography. Unless and until the Aleutians are bodily shifted to some other area on the world's surface, they are bound to be of the highest consequence in all military planning of the nations which front on the Pacific Ocean. This is because the direct and short line, which is called the Great Circle route, between the western coast of the United States and Japan, lies directly through the Aleutian Islands. No one can really grasp this by looking at any map in which some portion of the area shown thereon is always distorted. The distortion is greatest for northern countries on a Mercator map.

A single glance at the North Pacific area on a globe, especially if helped with a piece of tape, will show that the highroad between the northwestern United States, and the great Japanese cities of Tokyo and Yokohama, by sea and by air, drives directly through the Aleutians, while the approach to Tokyo through the Hawaiian Islands is fourteen hundred miles longer. In the Aleutians, the United States approaches closest to Japan, the distance between our Attu Island and Paramoshiri Island, site of a great Japanese sea and naval base, at the northern end of the Japanese archipelago, is 716 statute miles. It is, therefore, sufficiently obvious that when the day comes for winning the war, in which we must carry the fight to Japan, the natural and inevitable advance of our forces will be made on the short route through the Aleutians, in which we have a succession of firmly based, permanent, and non-sinkable airplane carriers in the individual islands of the Aleutians, the last one of which is within easy striking distance of the forces which Japan is bound to bring into action to defend her own territory. Futile it is to contemplate an advance against Japan over a route ten to twelve thousand miles long, from San Francisco to Sydney, or the Solomons, and thence north to the Dutch East Indies, to Singapore, the Philippines, and Tokyo, as against a five-thousand-mile journey from Seattle to Yokohama through the Aleutians, where we already have an air base, according to recent information, in the Andreanof Islands, within twenty-three hundred air miles of Tokyo.

That the Japanese early recognized the strategic value of the Aleutians seems beyond question. Their studies of the islands extended over many, many years: not only of the climate but of the terrain, the depth of the waters, the harbor facilities, the outlines of the coast, and all the physical surface and subterranean aspects of the adjoining seas. These accurate studies of the Aleutians, we permitted without more than an occasional protest. Many reports were made of seeing Japanese vessels in close proximity to the islands, and even of seeing their men on shore, apparently engaged on surveys of the land and the adjacent waters. There is sound reason for believing that at the outbreak of the war the Japanese knew more about the waters surrounding the Aleutians than we, and that they had better charts of that area.

The vivid realization by the Japanese of the importance of the Aleutians was evidenced in 1922, when at their vigorous insistence we agreed in the Treaty of Naval Limitations not to place any fortifications or military forces in the Aleutians. The pity of it is that after the Japanese denounced that treaty, and it became no longer binding on anyone, we did not immediately establish in the islands such strong military forces and fortifications as effectively to deter the Japanese, in view of the proximity of the Aleutians to their own territory, from making war upon us.

Any man who says the Aleutians are of no strategic consequence disregards the facts of geography, and ignores not only the eternal principles of strategy which have prevailed from the time of Alexander the Great until the present day, but equally the insistent and compelling demands of plain common sense.

18

Canada's Role in Geopolitics[1]

By Griffith Taylor

Griffith Taylor, born in Walthamstow, Essex, England. D.Sc., University of Sydney, 1916. Department of Geology, University of Sydney, 1905–1906; University of Cambridge, 1907–1909; Antarctic Research, 1910–1913; Physiographer, Commonwealth Service, 1914–1920; Professor of Geography, University of Sydney, 1921–1928; Professor of Geography, University of Chicago, 1929–1934; since 1935, Professor of Geography, University of Toronto.

Author of more than twenty books and of many articles in professional journals. *Economic Aspects of Australian Physiography,* 1911, four eds.; *Australia, (University text),* 1940, three eds.; *Australian Meteorology,* 1920; *Australia: A Geographic Reader,* 1931; *With Scott: the Silver Lining,* 1916; *Antarctic Adventure and Research,* 1930; *Environment and Race,* 1927; *Environment and Nation,* 1936; *Environment, Race and Migration,* 1937.

President, Section E (Geography), British Association for the Advancement of Science, 1938. President, Association of American Geographers, 1941.

"Canada's Role in Geopolitics" is a condensed version of a booklet, published under the same title by The Ryerson Press in Toronto (1942), under the auspices of the Canadian Institute of International Affairs.

Certain areas in the world are clearly the best suited for the development of large numbers of vigorous peoples. These areas will possess an attractive climate, with the temperatures neither too hot nor too cold; and an adequate rainfall. In Fig. 22 the isotherms of 40° F. and 60° F. are charted. These lines include the homelands of the important nations in Europe, where they support a population of about 500 millions with a European culture.

Let us see how Canada and Australia fit into this picture. As I have pointed out elsewhere, Australia lies in latitudes *too hot*

[1] Haushofer and his school seem to imply that Geopolitics necessarily includes discussions of world domination and of racial superiority. To the present writer these are arbitrary and unnecessary extensions of the term Geopolitics. The latter may be defined as the study of the outstanding features of the situation and resources of a country with a view to determining its status in World Politics.

for the easy development of a large European population. (It may be that widespread "central cooling" will help in this respect in the future.) So also almost all Canada lies in the latitudes which are *too cold* for the easy development of a large proportion of her area. Latitude 50° N. runs through Winnipeg and Anticosti Island; hence most of the present population—though not the bulk of Canada—lies just south of latitude 50° N.

FIG. 21. Orthographic projection centered on Canada

It has often been pointed out that there are four major areas of population and power. The first of these is Europe; in which 500 millions of vigorous (largely industrial) folk live, in a continent which is now essentially "saturated." The second area is in Eastern Asia, where live about 500 million folk with a low standard of living. Of these the Japanese are highly industrialized, but China is almost unexploited in the modern industrial sense. It is the aim of Japan to obtain control over this vast region of potential wealth.

The third major area is India, with a population of about 300

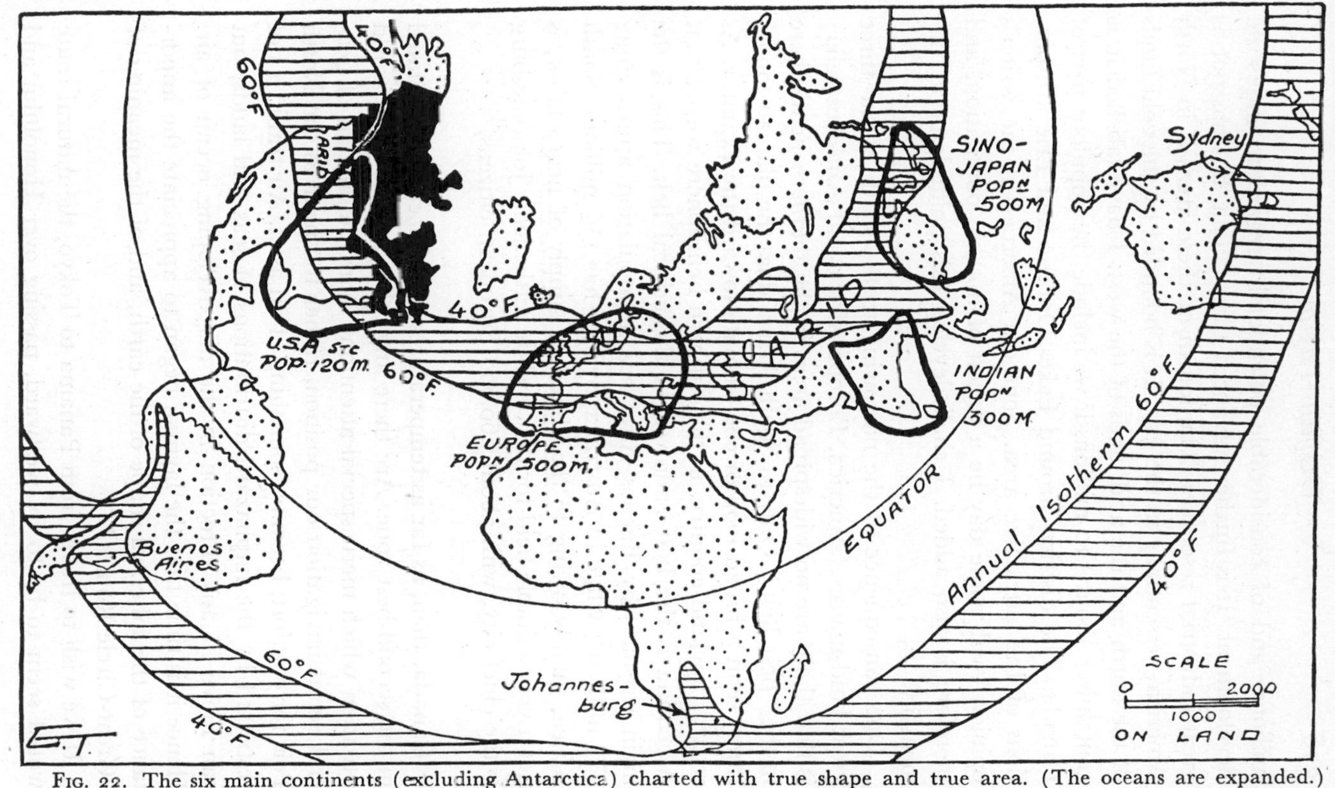

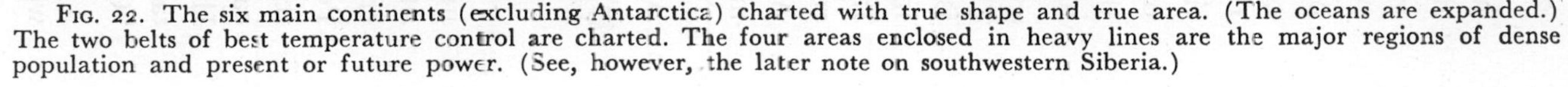
FIG. 22. The six main continents (excluding Antarctica) charted with true shape and true area. (The oceans are expanded.) The two belts of best temperature control are charted. The four areas enclosed in heavy lines are the major regions of dense population and present or future power. (See, however, the later note on southwestern Siberia.)

millions; and of considerable potential in regard to industrial development. It is further advanced than China, but has not as great industrial resources. The fourth of these areas is in North America—essentially in the east. It is bounded by the cold lands of the north and the arid lands of the west. I have labelled it as containing about 120 millions if we include the populous part of Canada. The districts around Lakes Ontario and Erie are portions of this attractive area. Southern Alberta—in the writer's opinion—will some day be a region of notable population, and therefore is also added. I shall develop this point later in this memoir.

One consequence of the narrowing to the south of the three great land-masses (America, Europe-Africa and Asia-Australia) is that there are no widespread areas in the *southern* hemisphere in the "Best Belt." Only in South Africa does the plateau-topography send a broad loop of cool climate toward the Equator. As regards lowland country, in the southern hemisphere we see that Argentina is the best endowed in the critical belt. This is the main reason why Buenos Aires has a population approaching 2½ millions; while in Australia, Sydney has 1½ millions. South Africa, mainly owing to the abundant supply of negro labor, is not a very suitable field for dense white settlement. Johannesburg is the chief city, with about 260,000 European citizens.

Canada, then, as far as temperatures are concerned is situated in the second-best zone. Are there any other aspects of its world situation which merit special attention? With the advent of general aerial navigation our position, rather too near to the North Pole for comfort, becomes something of an asset. Air traffic is not restricted by the haphazard distributions of seas and lands, but can move in any direction in the all-enveloping ocean of air. Hence it is time that the layman began to appreciate the importance of the spherical shape of the earth, and of the meaning of "Great-Circle Routes."

If we wish to travel from Panama to Tokyo, the natural route would seem to be to fly westward, passing over Honolulu, and ultimately reaching the coasts of Japan. We can test this idea by referring to a globe. Let us stretch a piece of elastic between the two ends of our journey. We shall find that the shortest track is nowhere near Honolulu, but passes over Yucatan and along the Rio Grande, to Seattle or thereabouts. Then our plane would fly near the coast of British Columbia to the end of the Alaskan Peninsula, along the Aleutian Isles, down the coast of Siberia, and finally along the Kurile Isles to Japan. (We can here see why the Japanese were so anxious to conquer the Aleutian Isles; and why Alaska is so important a land to military strategists.)

Coming nearer home we find that the cold polar lands of Canada are certain to be of great and increasing importance as air travel replaces land and sea travel for the longer journeys of the globe. It is not easy to construct a true map which will show these features accurately. We are faced with the usual problem of representing a spherical surface by the flat sheet of paper. However, if we simplify our problem, it is possible to show much of what we want on an accurate chart. I have attempted to do so in Fig. 23.

The shortest route between any two places on the earth's surface is the great circle. Our test with a piece of elastic gave us such a great circle passing through Panama and Tokyo. All circles on the earth's surface with centres at the *centre of the earth* are great circles. The Equator is the most familiar example. But the meridians, which mark out longitude, are also great circles. They all pass through the North Pole; and if we lived at the North Pole, these meridians would show us how to choose our shortest path to any other place. But such a map would be of no use for any other place on earth (if we except the South Pole). Our problem then is to choose a spot from which our air traffic is likely to be most abundant, and make a sort of "North Pole" of this central air-station. In Fig. 23 I have drawn such a map.

In this map the centre of the chart (i.e., the centre of the plane of projection) is the little town of Massena on the Saint Lawrence, and in the state of New York. It is on the 45° N. latitude, and 75° W. longitude. More importantly to us, it lies between Ottawa, Montreal, Kingston, Syracuse (N.Y.) and Albany (N.Y.); and so our projection will serve well enough for planes starting from any station in or near these towns. Indeed we may assume that Ottawa is the center of our projection plan.

The chief fact in Fig. 23 is that the broken lines radiating from Ottawa are all "great circles," and therefore represent the paths

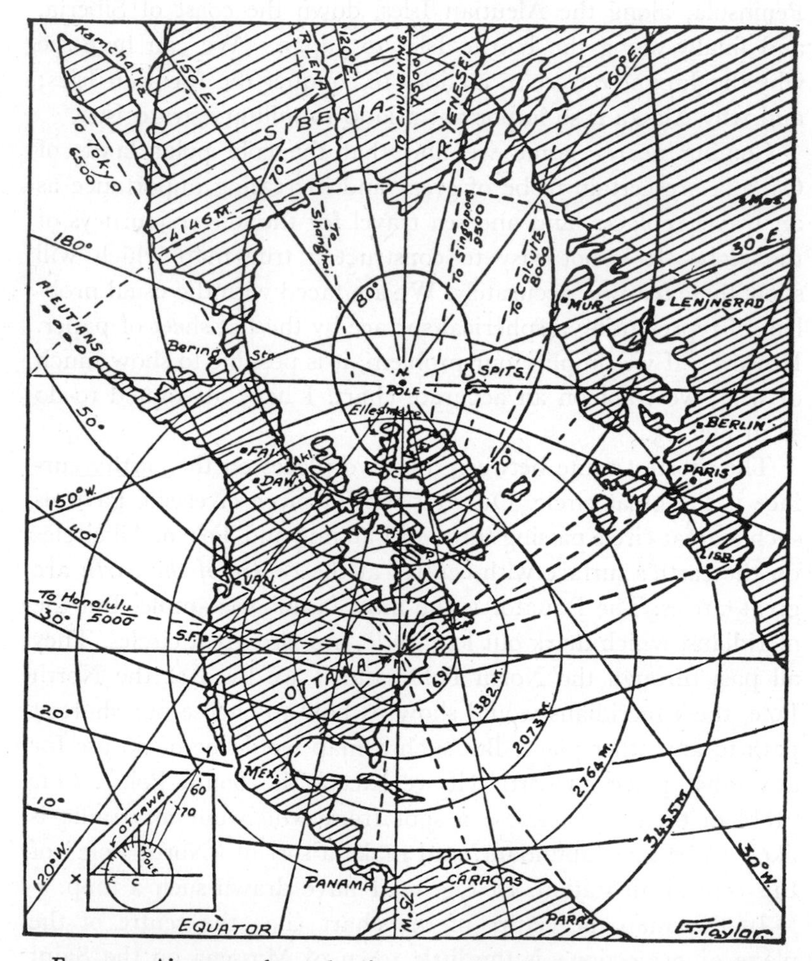

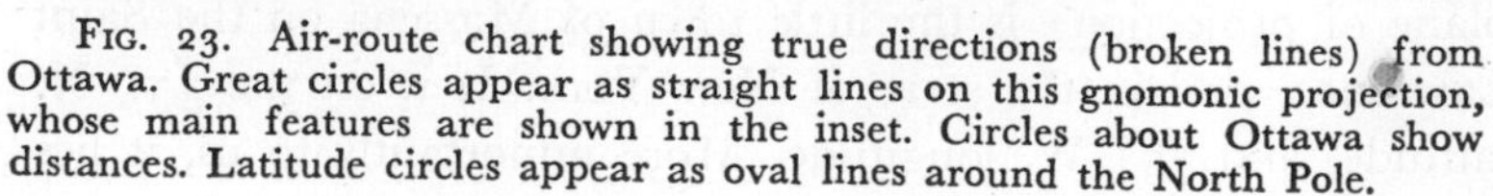

FIG. 23. Air-route chart showing true directions (broken lines) from Ottawa. Great circles appear as straight lines on this gnomonic projection, whose main features are shown in the inset. Circles about Ottawa show distances. Latitude circles appear as oval lines around the North Pole.

which airplanes will follow in the traffic of the future. The path to Honolulu goes to the west, across the Pacific, as we should expect. The path to Tokyo, however, will not pass anywhere near Honolulu; but will pass over Churchill (on Hudson Bay), and then over Aklavik (at the mouth of the Mackenzie), and so down the coast of Siberia to the islands of Japan.

There is nothing novel in the tracks to Central Europe. They will always traverse the Atlantic; though the tip of Greenland may some day be a useful way-station, adding little to the great-circle journey. But as regards Russia, the air-route is clearly over Greenland and Iceland. As for the air traffic of the future, which we may be sure will develop between the great manufacturing regions of North America and the huge populations of China, Japan, and India, it is clear that this future traffic brings our Canadian Polar lands very much into the picture. I show by broken lines the air-routes from Ottawa (or Pittsburgh, or New York) to Shanghai, Singapore, and Calcutta. The two former routes across over Ellesmere Land, where the Canadian Police have a permanent station at Craig Harbour (C. in chart) only seven hundred miles from the North Pole. In Baffin Land are several police and trading stations; of which one, Pang-nirtung, is shown (as P.). In Greenland the permanent settlements of Etah (E.) and Godthaab (G.) will also be of importance on these polar air routes.

The circles drawn on the chart (Fig. 23), with Ottawa as centre, give the distances in statute miles from the airport at Ottawa. It will be noticed that all places at the same distance from Ottawa are situated on a circle; but the length (on the chart) of the mile increases as we move further away from the centre of our projection (Ottawa). The normal lines of latitude are shown as heavy lines. They form closed ovals near the Pole, but become less and less curved as we approach the Equator. Since the Equator is a great circle, on our projection it appears (at the bottom of the chart) as a straight line, as do all other great circles. The true meridians radiate as straight lines from the North Pole in this form of projection.

Owing to its particular latitude Canada possesses certain resources which enable it to take an important place in world economics. The great belt of Coniferous Forests (Taiga) occurs precisely in our latitudes; though of course the same favourable conditions are found in the Old World also. Hence Canada will always be an important producer of lumber, paper pulp, newsprint, etc. Since this is a reasonably watered part of the world, it is rich in water power during a large part of the year. Of less importance today are the obvious treasures of the fur trade.

On the borders of our particular temperature belt are found the great areas of spring wheat. They flourish in the short hot summer of the interior of the continents. Here again our rival in spring wheat (in addition to the United States) is in the heart of the Old World in Russia and Siberia. The great ocean fisheries also occur in the cooler latitudes, where conditions in the coastal waters are favourable.

It is, however, in the mineral field that the resources of Canada stand out. In Fig. 24 the extent of the vast area of ancient rock which is known as the Canadian Shield is clearly indicated. It covers more than half the four million square miles of the Dominion. It is one of the great geographical problems of Canada to decide on the best way to develop this vast area of the Shield. Opinions as to its possibilities have varied considerably. It was the great source of the fur trade, but at first seemed to have few other possibilities. In Australia I shared the current opinion of many geographers that it was essentially a mass of gigantic rock only sparsely covered with soil. On my first journey across large areas of the Shield I decided to take detailed note of the *forested* portions! Very soon I found that it was essentially all forested, and that bare rock was the exception. I have obtained the opinion of geologists who have travelled all over the Shield, and they state that the amount of bare rock (south of the Barren Grounds or Tundra) is less than 10 per cent of the whole. This cuts two ways. As regards prospecting for valuable minerals the tree-cover greatly impedes investigations. But agriculture and forests are more permanent assets than mines; and the writer is more optimistic of the ultimate value of much of the Shield than are some of the writers who deal with the future of Canada.

Let us, however, confine our attention for the present to the great mineral wealth of the Shield. Almost all minerals are derived from the denser lower portions of the earth's crust. In gen-

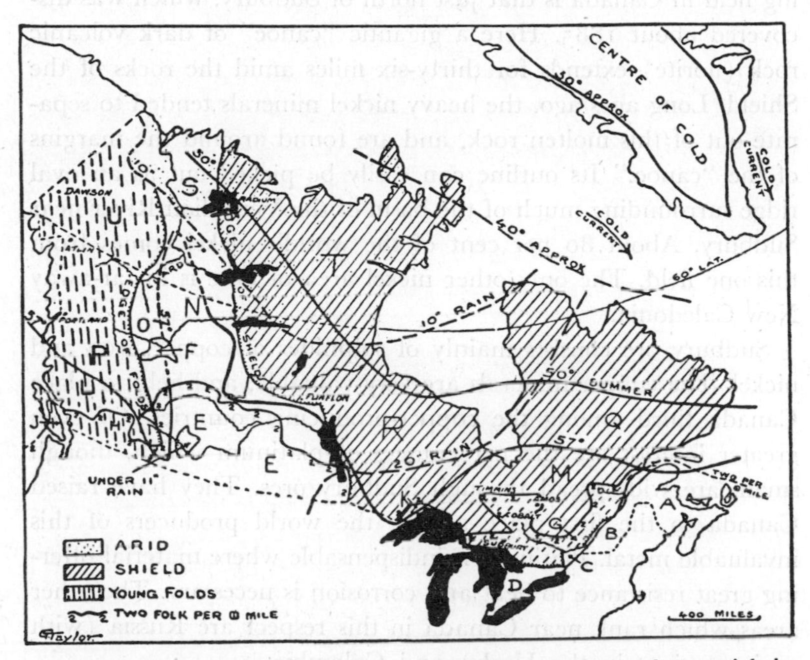

FIG. 24. An analysis of Canadian population, present and potential, in terms of geographic controls. Areas A to K already have over two people per square mile. (Courtesy of the *Canadian Geographical Journal.*)

eral, the *younger* geological deposits do not contain metals, etc., unless there has been marked volcanic action affecting them. (This has been the case in the Selkirks and Coast Ranges of British Columbia.) In the oldest rocks, where there has been most erosion (removing younger deposits) and most faulting (i.e., cracking) of the crust, there are the best chances of finding metals, i.e., where they have been deposited by waters or vapors deriving from the deeper layers of the earth.

One of the spectacular discoveries of recent times was that made only twelve years ago on the eastern shore of the Great Bear Lake. This field so much increased the world's supply of radium as to cut the price in half. The reducing plant at Port Hope near Toronto is one of the chief sources for the world's supply of radium. As everyone knows, the most interesting mining field in Canada is that just north of Sudbury, which was discovered about 1885. Here a gigantic "canoe" of dark volcanic rock (norite) extends for thirty-six miles amid the rocks of the Shield. Long ages ago, the heavy nickel minerals tended to separate out of this molten rock, and are found around the margins of the "canoe." Its outline can easily be picked out as an oval ridge surrounding much of the basin of the Vermilion River near Sudbury. About 80 per cent of the world's nickel comes from this one field. The only other nickel area of note is in far-away New Caledonia.

Sudbury ore consists mainly of sulphides of copper, iron and nickel. The copper minerals are very valuable, and help to place Canada third among the copper-producing countries. Of even greater interest are the percentages of platinum which, though small, are widespread through Sudbury ores. They have raised Canada to the first place among the world producers of this invaluable metal. Platinum is indispensable where material offering great resistance to heat and corrosion is necessary. The other areas which rank near Canada in this respect are Russia (with various mines in the Urals) and Colombia.

Probably the field of greatest importance after Sudbury is the adjacent gold field on the borders of Ontario and Quebec. Here are the three great mines of Porcupine, Kirkland Lake, and Noranda. The value of the metals (chiefly gold) much exceeds that at Sudbury, but there are several other gold fields in the world still more important; whereas there is no other "Sudbury." This great gold field dates from 1909, when the Hollinger Mine at Timmins in the Porcupine district was discovered. In 1912 equally rich ore was found to the east at Kirkland Lake, and in 1920 the adjacent area in Quebec near Noranda was found to contain rich gold veins. As a result Canada ranks next to the Rand Field of Johannesburg among the world's producers of gold. It is but fair to say that the U.S.S.R. and the U.S.A. are treading close on its heels for second place.

The third great mine in Canada is the Sullivan Mine at Kimberley, British Columbia. It was discovered in 1892, but was not fully exploited till 1920. It is one of the greatest lead-zinc mines in the world, resembling the Broken Hill Mine in Australia. Canada is fifth in zinc production, following the United States (Joplin and Franklin Furnace), Belgium, and Germany in this metal. In lead it is fourth, being surpassed by the United States, Australia, and Mexico. In silver the Sullivan Mine has raised Canada to third place, following Mexico (Guanajuato) and the United States (Idaho). We have seen that Sudbury gives Canada a great deal of copper. Another famous mine is Flinflon, on the western margin of Manitoba just on the edge of the Shield. This is a copper-zinc mine; and Noranda also is an important copper producer. As a result Canada takes fourth place in the world production, being surpassed by the United States (Bisbee, Utah, and Butte), Chile (Chuquicamata), and Rhodesia.

There are two non-metallic minerals of considerable importance which remain to be discussed. The first of these is asbestos. This is a fibrous silicate which can be woven like cotton, and has many uses based mainly on its non-inflammable character. The best supplies in the world are found in the folded rocks of Quebec in the vicinity of Thetford. For a time Quebec produced about 80 per cent of the world supply, but of recent years it has a serious rival in asbestos mined in Rhodesia.

Possibly of all the mineral products of Canada the last to be discussed will in the long run be the most important. This is the vast coal field of southern Alberta. The coal is of Cretaceous age, and is not equal in quality to the Carboniferous coals of Nova Scotia or of the United States. But it is more valuable than the brown coals of Europe, which the Germans are using to a tremendous extent in modern industry. Around Lethbridge and

Drumheller it has been estimated that there are about 600,000 million tons in reserve. This is considerably more than the combined coal supplies of Germany and Poland, which have led to the growth of huge industrial populations in those countries. The sole rivals of Alberta, if we accept the figures quoted, are to be found in the United States, which has vastly greater supplies (near the Rockies, and around Illinois) and China (Shansi) and Siberia. The Russians claim to have larger deposits than those of Alberta near Kuznetsk and the Tunguska rivers. Since coal means "heavy industry," it is difficult to see how Canada can leave her colossal Alberta resources almost untouched much longer.

In various publications I have pointed out that the geographer may, in some sort, be likened to a "town-planner," in that he examines the development of the nation's resources, and tries to show the best way in which future settlement should take place. Indeed, in this respect he may perhaps have some right to be called a "nation-planner." In Fig. 24 a map of Canada is given in which the country is divided into a score of more or less homogeneous regions. Some of these are fairly well exploited already; some are only partially exploited; others are very much in the pioneer stage; yet others do not seem to offer any large possibilities for future settlement.

The fringelike character of the Canadian population is well brought out in Fig. 24. Here we see a line labelled 2,2,2,2; this is the isopleth (line of equal abundance) of two people per square mile; and bounds on the north all the important population of the Dominion. The three densest areas are, of course, around Montreal, Toronto, and Windsor, where considerable districts contain more than forty-five persons to the square mile. These are not, however, especially designated on the map. The largest area of fair population is the newly-settled prairie region; here the unlimited supplies of Alberta coal will, in all probability, produce the densest Canadian population of the future.

The three main divisions, as has often been pointed out, are topographic. They comprise the Shield in the east (shown by close ruling); the relatively level area of the Prairie lands, with their extension of somewhat similar formations along the Mackenzie River almost to the Arctic Ocean; and lastly the complex series of folds and uplands which together form the Rockies and the Coastal Ranges of the Yukon and British Columbia. These latter are shown by broken lines.

The soils of the Shield, with the exception of the Great Clay Belt are poor. They are much more widespread than most people believe; and I see no reason why they should be worse in general than similar lands which have led to a fair amount of settlement in such a country as Finland. The best of the three terrains is, of course, the second of the three just mentioned. In the third major region the land available for close settlement is confined for the most part to the lower part of the various basins (such as that around Prince George) or to the terraces along the rivers in the narrower valleys of the interior. Unfortunately, much of this region with a reasonable temperature is very dry. For instance Ashcroft (120 miles north-east of Vancouver) has less than eight inches of rainfall in the year.

Perhaps the most vital isopleth for Canadians is that showing a summer temperature around 57° F. This is charted approximately in Fig. 24. It includes only the southern coasts of Newfoundland; runs well north of the Saguenay, through Moosonee and across to Fort William. Thence it sweeps to the north-west nearly up to Norman, near Great Bear Lake. The cold ranges of the Rockies produce a cold loop extending south to the border; but in British Columbia it again runs to the north-west to the coast somewhere near Prince Rupert. (Of course with so confused a topography in the West such isotherms cannot yet be charted with any accuracy.) It seems likely that south of this line the climate is warm enough for grains like oats and barley, and for potatoes, to be grown quite successfully. However, it is quite useless to try to settle large numbers of farmers on these marginal lands as long as the better areas are by no means saturated.

In the following table I have classified the score of regions

(A, B, C, etc., to U) in four groups. In the first group are all the districts which today have over two people per square mile. We may be sure that they are the most attractive. The presence of valuable minerals has, of course, hastened settlement in certain areas, such as that around Timmins. In the Great Clay Belt are comprised about thirty-six million acres of soils, which are much better than the general run of those on the Shield. These fine silts were laid down in a gigantic ice-age lake, ponded back by the ice-front on the northern edge of the Clay Belt for a very long period. There are many difficulties facing the farmers of the Clay Belt. Bad drainage, summer frosts, difficulties of transport, distance to markets, the poor character of some of the settlers; all these disabilities have to be overcome. But they are inherent in a "pioneer fringe," and to the writer, since the climatic and soil conditions are reasonably good, success must follow sooner or later. The geographer, as I have often said, is the long-range forecaster. He bases his conclusions on what has happened elsewhere in earlier-settled lands with similar environments. Similar considerations have determined the order in which the districts are arranged in the following table. Wise policies of development will leave the later-placed districts alone until the earlier groups have become very much more settled.

CLASSIFICATION	EAST	CENTRE	WEST
I. Over 2 folk per sq. mi.; and south of 57° F.	A, Maritimes, B, C, D, St. Lawrence G, Taiga* (mines and pulp)	E, Prairies F, Mid-Peace River	H, Okanagan, etc. J, Vancouver, etc.
II. Potential settlement south of 57° F.	M, Clay belts in the Taiga	N, Athabasca-Laird Taiga	L, Upper Fraser to coast
III. Transition		O, Fort Nelson Taiga	P, Skeena Area
IV. No notable settlement, except mines	Q, R, Northern Taiga	S, Lower Mackenzie T, Tundra*	U, Yukon

* Taiga is the Coniferous Forest and Muskeg region, south of the "Barren Grounds" (Tundra).

No principle of geography as applied to Canada is more important than that which teaches us to watch carefully the projects and research of the Soviet Union. Their problems are in large measure our problems. I have tried in Fig. 25 to show the similarity of the two vast regions. The climatic data are not yet very well known, while soil surveys are absent in most of the vast areas. But as a first approximation, we can see fairly clearly that Russia has large areas with reasonable rainfall and with temperatures above 56° in July, much like Canada. These areas are shown to the same scale in Fig. 25.

The population of the Soviet Union is 170 millions today. Somewhere about 14 million Russians have settled in Siberia in the last thirty years.[2] I have added to the map of Siberia the isopleth which shows where the population exceeds 16 per square mile (it is labelled 16 P.). In Canada this line (at present) would include only regions C and D, and the western half of B, in Fig. 24. These are too small to be shown on the map of Canada in Fig. 25. Yet I expect the density lines to spread in Canada much as they have done in Siberia.

The Russian birth rate is very high, which is, of course, a factor that does not depend directly on geographic controls. Some Russian publicists confidently expect a population of about 340 millions by the year 1975; though the present war may considerably modify this figure. What I wish to point out is that Canada, which has about half the Russian area of "potential-settlement country," cannot possibly be "saturated" with a population of eleven millions. The writer has been publicly denounced for encouraging such optimistic ideas as to the future population of Canada—just as formerly he was denounced for damping the enthusiasm of Australians, who held his estimate of a future 30 millions to be libel of the fair name of the southern land! In the next section I will endeavour to explain how an objective picture of future populations may be obtained.

[2] Possibly the "dense area" in Europe (Fig. 22) should be extended to the east to include part of south-west Siberia.

Many years ago I worked out a scheme for obtaining a first approximation to the "saturation" populations for the "empty lands" of the world. This research is often quoted, so that I may

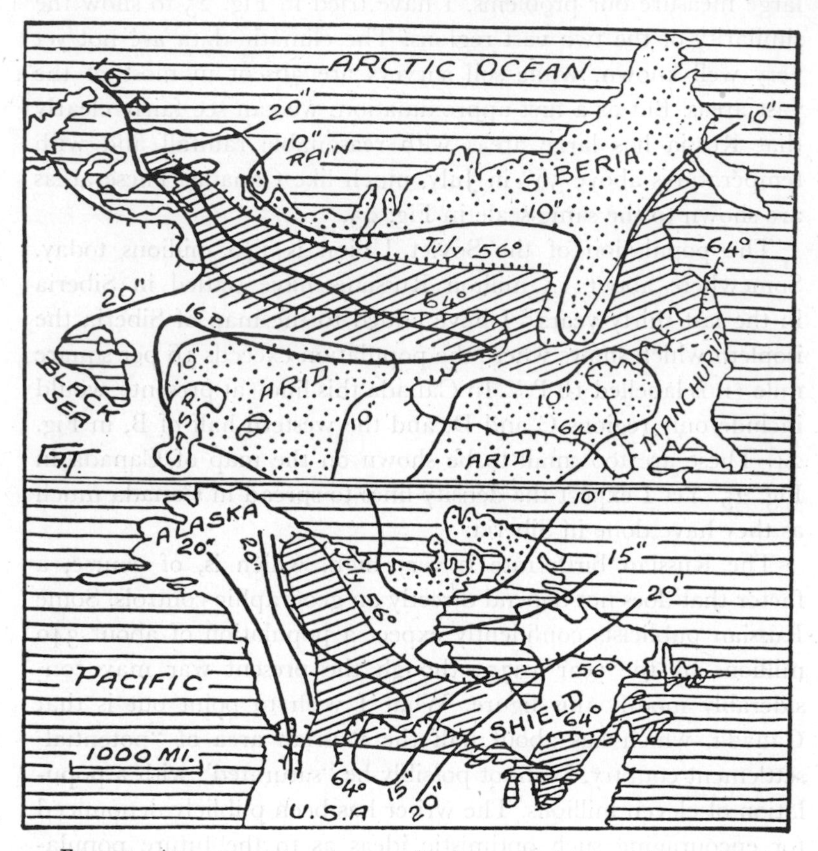

FIG. 25. An attempt to compare the future settlement of Canada with that taking place in Russia and Siberia. Here with somewhat similar environments a population of 170 millions has grown up. Regions ruled diagonally have similar conditions of fair rainfall and temperature in both countries. Notice the heavy line (16 P.) in Siberia including densities over 16 per sq. mi. Dotted areas are arid.

be allowed to explain the essential features in this memoir. Europe is the sole continent where the white populations are relatively "saturated" and stable. The population-pattern of Europe is diverse, but is quite definitely due to the controls exercised by the environment. Of these temperature, rainfall, and coal seem to be by far the most important. Elevation was a fourth factor which I took into account. Many minor factors, such as oil and hydro-electric power, could only indirectly be considered in the research.

The chief feature of this attempt to derive future population densities is that the comparisons are always referred to Europe as a criterion. I divided the world into seventy-four economic and more or less homogeneous regions. Each of these regions is tabulated in terms of the four dominant controls (temperature, rainfall, coal, and elevation). A quadrangular graph (the econograph) is constructed for each region. The area of each graph is found to represent approximately the "habitability" of the region concerned. Lines of equal habitability (isoiketes) are drawn on a map of the world (as in Fig. 26). With the present European populations of the corresponding European regions as criteria, it is possible to convert the former "habitability map" into a map showing *potential densities per square mile*.

The reader must refer to the original description for details as to the method of obtaining the econographs. (The whole process is described in Part IV of my book *Environment, Race and Migration,*[3] 1937, Toronto.) A reference to the original map will show that certain econographs are large and kite-shaped; such as those near London, New York, and Sydney. This means that the regions are very well endowed as regards all four controls. In South America are a number of econographs (such as that near Buenos Aires) which lack the right half of the "kite." Hence the right-hand axis is wanting. This means that the region lacks coal, and is not likely to become a very important industrial region. Certain others, as in the deserts, are very tall and thin. This means that the rainfall factor (left-hand axis) is not at all satisfactory. When the areas were measured, the figures came out as follows (maximum 100 per cent): Britain, 77; the region around New York, 75; North China, 77; region around Buenos Aires, 31; North American Tundra, 1.5; Sahara 1.0.

[3] The resources of Canada are also discussed in five chapters in this book.

These units of habitability are translated into potential populations (on European standards) according to the tables shown at the bottom corners of Fig. 26. The isopleths of potential population are drawn on the map in Fig. 26. The regions around China and India are treated in the same way, though clearly the question of large European populations settling within the heavy

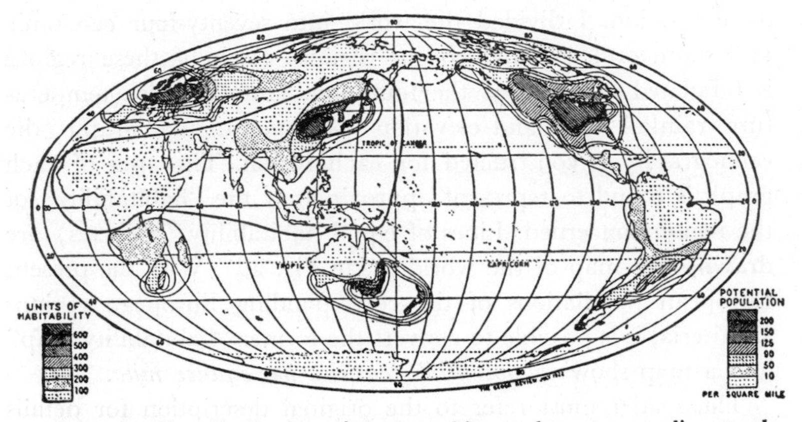

FIG. 26. The distribution of future white settlement according to the economic value of the world regions. The area within the heavy black line is not available for white settlement, but has been treated uniformly here. The facts of the distribution shown in this figure may be expressed by degree of habitability, shown by "isoiketes" (see legend to the left) where the optimum of habitability is 1,000; or by the corresponding potential population density (see legend to the right). The potential population of Siberia is greater than here represented. (From *Geographical Review,* 1922.)

black line in Fig. 26 is entirely academic, since they are already "saturated" with non-European peoples.

It is not difficult, using Europe as a guide, to estimate what these lines denote in actual populations. Assuming the rather low standards of living which obtain in Europe in general, we get figures somewhat as follows for the lands with which we are most concerned.

Europe (accepted as standard and "saturated"), 500 millions.

Canada, 100 millions	Australia, 60 millions
U.S.A., 500 millions	Siberia, 200 millions
Argentine, etc., 100 millions	S. Africa, 80 millions

In my original estimate I did not, I think, make enough allowance for the poor quality of much of the Canadian Shield. Nor, at that date, did we know much about the enormous mineral resources, especially the coal fields, which are now known to be present in Siberia. Still the final map gives one some idea of the relative values of the empty lands of the world.

The data deduced in this research on future population are so often quoted inaccurately that I may be excused for commenting on them further. First, the hypothetical millions are reckoned not on American, but on the *much lower European* standard of living—say one-half or one-third as costly as the present American standards. If we prefer to keep the present standards, our potential 100 millions for Canada is at once halved.[4] The Silesian farmer farms 40 acres successfully; the Canadian prairie farmer (in a pioneer stage) farms 400 acres. Here is a possibility in the future of placing ten farms where one exists today. The great populations of central and north-west Europe are based on exploiting the coal for fuel and power. Its utilization has about doubled the populations of the regions affected. We may some day use our Alberta coal in the same way. Thus in the distant future if we decide to lower the standards (which I do not advocate), to split up the large farms, and to develop the coal to its utmost; then a figure of 100 millions seems to the writer to be not altogether visionary.

We may now turn to other aspects of Canada's position among the larger land masses. It has often been pointed out that the British Empire forms a kind of broken zone around the margins of the Old World. This is suggested in Fig. 27 by the areas marked by the open ruling. As regards the oceans it is obvious that the Indian Ocean (surrounded by South Africa, India, and Australia) is almost wholly in British control. In the south-east corner of the Indian Ocean (south of Perth, Western Australia) is the *antipodes* of Ottawa. As Professor C. B. Fawcett has pointed out

[4] Around 1914, before the great wars, the population of Canada was doubling in about 37 years. If this rate is maintained after the Peace (which is not likely), then Canada would reach 50 millions about the year 2030.

in his *Political Geography* (London, 1933), this means that Canada is the Dominion furthest from the centre of gravity of the British Empire, which would seem to centre somewhere near India.

We may for a moment digress to consider the remarkable position of the Soviet Republics in relation to the British Empire. Unlike our British Empire, which has grown up in scattered lands along the edge of the Old World, the Russian territories form a compact oval mass of land, which contain more of the favored belt (shown in Fig. 22) than any land except the United States. Unfortunately, much of this favored belt is the rather *arid* inland region. However, from the point of view of "interior lines," it is clear that the U.S.S.R. will be in a very satisfactory position when it has weathered the present storm, and increased its eastern population somewhat. It is well for the Allies occasionally to contrast the small area so far overrun by the Germans with that in the hands of our friends. Yet if the Japanese should obtain control of China and India, and Germany maintain her hold upon most of Europe; a glance at the four heavy black rings in Fig. 22 will show that only one of the four great "potentials of power" —that in the United States—will remain firmly in the hands of the Allies.

The teaching of Geopolitics seems to be that if the British maintain friendly relations with the U.S.S.R., as all the dictates of reason would seem to demand, then the two forces of the Empire and the Soviets have a strangle-hold on the Germans and Japanese. In a sense the latter are between the upper and the nether millstones, as is quite clear from a consideration of Fig. 27.

There is one last concept which is suggested by the world chart given in Fig. 27. If we group together those nations which have a completely European culture, as distinct from an Oriental or partly non-European culture; then Canada seems to lie in the middle of this "European-culture bloc." The writer is a strong protagonist of a future "world-state," with all nations free and equal. He sees no reason why in a relatively short time we should not live quite harmoniously with any racial or cultural group which will adopt the "four freedoms" as their guiding principles.

It is, however, not completely impossible that there will be a prolonged cultural and economic (but, one hopes, peaceful)

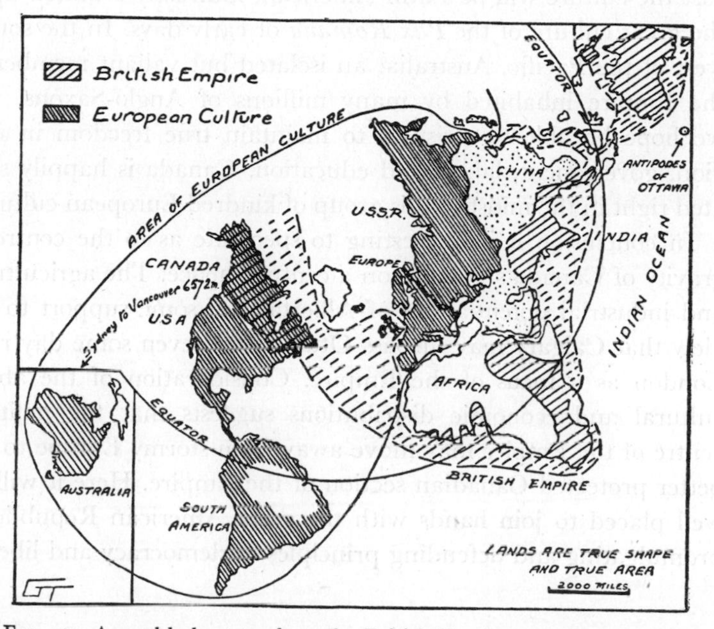

FIG. 27. A world-chart to show the British Empire as a "zone" about the Old World. It is shown by open ruling. Notice the central position of the solid area of the U.S.S.R. in regard to the British Empire. Canada is seen to be the central area in a group of lands with "European culture," extending from Siberia to Australia. The dotted area is mostly under Asiatic control.

struggle in which Occidental will be ranged against Oriental. It is interesting to note that Canada may be less affected by this rivalry than almost any other region. In a sense we may say that the Arctic Ocean and most of the Pacific are surrounded by folk who profess the European cultural way of living. These areas are shown by the close ruling in Fig. 27. Along the north coasts of the Old World this culture will be mostly a Slav culture, though western Europe will always make great contributions in the Old World.

In the New World, Canada will dominate on the northern ocean, while around the Pacific she will also play her part in the north-east. Here the wealth and progress of the United States will no doubt dominate the Pacific in the future. To the south-east the culture will be Latin American, indirectly founded upon the great culture of the *Pax Romana* of early days. In the south-west of the Pacific, Australia, an isolated but valiant member of the Empire inhabited by many millions of Anglo-Saxons, will we hope be able to assist us to maintain true freedom in religion, government, labor, and education. Canada is happily situated right in the midst of this group of kindred European cultures.

In conclusion it is interesting to speculate as to the centre of gravity of Canada's population a century hence. The agricultural and industrial potentialities of Alberta lend some support to the view that Calgary may surpass Ottawa, and even some day rival London as a focus of the Empire. Consideration of the above cultural and economic distributions suggests that the political centre of the Empire may move away from stormy Europe to the better protected Canadian section of the Empire. Here it will be well placed to join hands with the great American Republic in promulgating and defending principles of democracy and liberty.

19

Arctic Supply Line

By VILHJALMUR STEFANSSON

VILHJALMUR STEFANSSON, A.M., PHD., LL.D., was born in Canada, but his family moved to the United States when he was a year old. Since 1932 he has been adviser on northern operations to Pan American Airways; since 1935 more than half his time has been devoted to writing manuals, guidebooks, and reports on northern subjects for the United States Army and preparing for the Navy pilot books of northerly countries.

He is author of numerous books—among them, *My Life with the Eskimo,* 1913; *The Friendly Arctic,* 1921, 1943; *Hunters of the Great North,* 1922; *The Northward Course of Empire,* 1922; *The Adventure of Wrangell Island,* 1925; *Iceland,* 1939; *Ultima Thule,* 1940; *Greenland,* 1942; *Arctic Manual,* 1944.

"Arctic Supply Line" was published originally in *Fortune* magazine for July, 1942; it took the present revised and lengthened form in October, 1943.

The most important geographic fact of World War II is that it is being fought mainly in that northern temperate zone which, on a spherical earth, lies in a circle around the Arctic. The capitals of all the great warring powers, with the exception of China, are closer to the Arctic Circle than to the Equator.

The so-called Arctic Ocean has the nature of a mediterranean sea: the land masses of Europe, Asia, and North America are grouped around it somewhat as Africa, Europe, and Asia surround the sea that bears the name Mediterranean. Thus the shortest flying routes between most of the north temperate zone nations cut through the Arctic Circle, and many of them cross the Arctic mediterranean. We see this at once when we look at a globe, which truly represents distances and direction relationships. Only when we look at maps that give the impression the earth is flat, or cylindrical, does it seem reasonable to fly east and west between north temperate zone countries, or to cross wide oceans.

But even when we grasp this key to the future trend of world aviation our thinking may remain confused by a set of inherited views on climate. For it was a nearly universal belief until twenty years ago, and is a common belief even now, that Arctic flying conditions are so bad that the plane is unable to capitalize upon the roundness of the world to shorten aerial transport routes. It is only beginning to sink into our consciousness that the flying weather averages better over Arctic lands than between New York and Cleveland, and over the Arctic mediterranean than over the Atlantic between Newfoundland and Ireland.

Even after we have rid ourselves of these factual handicaps to realistic thinking we still have difficulty in visualizing the Arctic as an important crossroads of international travel. We have been looking so long at world maps which represent the earth as flat or cylindrical that we cannot readily use in our thinking the spherical-earth knowledge which we do possess.

For instance, we are so used to world maps of Mercator projection that most of us feel as if a direct flight from Washington to Manila would go approximately by way of San Francisco and Hawaii. We reason subconsciously that because Manila is farther south than Washington we should head a little south of west on leaving the District of Columbia; it is hard for us to realize that our best mileage-saving course would be nearly at right angles to what the Mercator chart appears to show, that the correct routing is northwest through Canada, that we cannot cross the Pacific en route to the Philippines unless we are willing to go out of our way to do so, and that near the middle of our journey we find ourselves over the Polar Sea about a hundred miles north of northwestern Siberia, near Wrangel Island.

On a nonstop flight from San Francisco to Berlin a flat-earth thinker might expect to cross Missouri and leave the eastern seaboard around New York or New England, in a direction a little north of east. But the true direction is a little east of north. You fly diagonally up through California, across Oregon and a corner of Washington, and enter Canada to fly over Alberta. The flight continues north of Hudson Bay, across Baffin Island and Greenland, touching the northeastern corner of Iceland, the southwestern corner of Norway, arriving at Berlin from a little west

Fig. 28. Half the world, three-fourths of the land, nine-tenths of the population, are north of the Equator. The capitals of all the great military powers, except Chungking, are nearer to the Arctic Circle than to the Equator. In an air age the Arctic Mediterranean is the hub of world power. After *Fortune* with permission.

of north. Instead of passing over New York, the line of flight is more than 1,000 miles north of Montreal, thereby saving about 1,000 miles in total flying distance.

That Iceland dominates the North Atlantic was recognized by William Henry Seward, Secretary of State in Lincoln's and Johnson's cabinets. He considered that we needed both Iceland and Greenland for dominion over the North Atlantic and should buy them from Denmark; and that we needed Alaska for dominion over the North Pacific and should buy it from Russia. He made good on Alaska in 1867. Thereafter the military atmosphere faded from Washington, and we soon forgot about Greenland and Iceland and about the military reasons that had prompted the Alaska purchase. But around 1939 we once again began to see clearly the importance of dominating both the North Atlantic and the North Pacific.

Iceland had become an independent nation in 1918 and so could not be purchased. Greenland was still a colony and theoretically at least might have been bartered or sold. The British first, and the United States later, took military possession of Iceland for the duration, following the German occupation of Denmark and Norway. The United States borrowed Greenland from Denmark. In both cases assurances were given that these lands will remain as self-governing during the war as is compatible with military use, and that all troops and restraints will be withdrawn when the war is over.

During World War I, the British studied Iceland carefully from a naval point of view. During World War II, British battleships have been constantly steaming out of Icelandic ports in blockade and convoy operations, and in connection with such battles as the *Hood* and the *Bismarck*. Today the air challenges the sea as a highway of war, and again Iceland has clear advantages, with her many fjords, almost any of which could be used as a seaplane base, some of which also have land-plane facilities.

Flying conditions are about the same in Iceland as in and

around Scotland. This was demonstrated first by an Icelandic subsidiary of the German Lufthansa, then by the studies of our own Pan American Airways, and finally by the all-year operation of a small Icelandic flying company, using American Waco planes. The harbors of Iceland are numerous and never freeze. The midwinter temperature of Reykjavik is about the same as that of Milan or Philadelphia, but with more rain and wind. The summer climate is somewhere between that of Seattle, Washington, and Aberdeen, Scotland. Fogs are about as in Scotland, but very rarely is there a fog on both the north and the south coast at the same time. Even though the island is 20 per cent larger than Ireland, it is possible to have two airports well within 200 miles of each other, one of which is practically sure to have good visibility if the other has bad. From Iceland, even with the small cruising range of fighter planes that were building at the start of World War II, not merely the 180 miles to Greenland but most of the 500 miles to Scotland can be covered. With bombers of medium range this is still simpler, and thus the full width of the North Atlantic is under control.

When the present war started no people in the world, not even the Icelanders themselves, knew that country as well from a military standpoint as did the Germans. Before the war, Iceland was of all the Scandinavian countries the most sympathetic to the German people, although the most decidedly anti-Hitler. Still, during the early part of Hitler's tenure, the Icelanders permitted a German air survey of their country. No one now doubts it was a most thorough study, particularly in military aviation. For this survey the Germans used glider flying as a pretext. They brought glider planes and helped the Icelanders build others. Basic to the sport, they said, must be a careful survey of the entire country, which they carried out in two airplanes.

Apart from its landing fields, seaplane and naval bases, Iceland has some militarily useful resources. Because of high mountains and heavy precipitation, waterpower is so well developed that the island uses more electricity per capita for domestic purposes than any other country.

Volcanic heat is another military asset. In several parts of Iceland it is possible to get an artesian flow of water that is just below the boiling point. Reykjavik public buildings have been heated in this way for a decade. Equipment for heating private buildings now being installed will include facilities for heating certain buildings used by the armed forces of the United States.

Iceland can supply our troops with some butter and cheese, and with a good deal of fresh milk. Icelanders can raise most standard vegetables, sweet corn and tomatoes being two exceptions. Mutton and lamb are obtainable, but no appreciable amount of beef, since the cattle are chiefly dairy stock. Egg production has hitherto been for local use but can be expanded rapidly.

The volcanic hot water has long been used to supply through hothouses what normal gardening does not furnish—vegetables such as tomatoes, and flowers of many kinds, from orchids down.

The only food that Iceland can supply in unlimited amounts is fish. It has long been a popular sport-fishing country; the ocean production of fish is about the greatest in the world. Much of the herring that has been eaten in America under a Swedish label came from Icelandic waters; much of the cod that has gone to Brazil as Norwegian came from Iceland.

Greenland is the most easterly of the countries on the American side of the Atlantic, for a line drawn straight south from its northeast corner will pass 44 miles east of the easternmost point in Iceland. Cape Farewell in Greenland is about as far south as the Shetland Islands, thus considerably farther south than any part of Iceland. The harbors of the southern Greenland west coast never freeze over, so that there is an all-year base for surface craft, submarines, and flying boats. It was once believed that vessels could not reach Greenland except in summer, but gradually the practical navigation season on the southwestern coast was expanded by the Danes to start in March and close in October. Now we are beginning to wonder if the reason for the October closing may not have been that the Danish skippers wanted to spend Christmas at home with their families.

The winters of Greenland are colder than those of Iceland, but not so cold as most people imagine. For instance, Commander Donald B. MacMillan once spent three consecutive winters in northwestern Greenland, more than 800 miles north of the Arctic Circle, and $-42°$ was the coldest moment, a temperature that has been equaled in twenty of our states. Ten states have recorded temperatures colder than $-52°$.

It was also formerly believed that the east coast of Greenland could be approached only for a brief period in the late summer. But Dr. Jean Charcot, the great French polar explorer, advanced the view in 1936 that the east coast, especially the northern half of it, is easier to reach in winter than summer, the easiest period being probably February to April. Many now agree with him.

True, the harbors of northeast Greenland are frozen in winter, but that is not a serious drawback to those used to cold-weather technique. A ship bound there could sail north through the Atlantic, passing east of Iceland and east of Jan Mayen Island. Although Jan Mayen is 300 miles north of Iceland, even there ice is usually not seen until after midwinter. So the vessel can proceed north through nearly or quite iceless water until she is a little north of her proposed landing point in Greenland; then she steers toward shore. When twenty to forty miles away she waits, if necessary, for an offshore wind. Most Greenland winds blow offshore, and the wait would not be long. The conditions right, the ship noses up to the edge of the landfast ice, which may be anywhere between a few hundred yards and a few miles from shore. She then ties up broadside, unloads upon the ice as if it were a dock, and supplies are taken ashore by tractor-drawn trains of sledges.

Apart from its value as a base for submarines, surface craft, and aircraft, Greenland has a special value in weather forecasting. It is about a three-quarter truth that weather comes from the west. So it is one of the trump cards of the United Nations that they control reports from Greenland, Iceland, and Labrador. Supposedly they know what the weather is going to be if they bomb Germany tomorrow night; and supposedly the Germans can only guess what the weather is going to be if they plan an attack on London.

The Germans, however, have been suspiciously accurate in their weather forecasts, as we can tell not merely from their bombings in Scotland and England, but especially from the escape of their warships from a French harbor, when they were able to slip into and through the English Channel under cover of the thickest weather of several months. The general opinion is that they drew up these obviously good weather forecasts from weather reports sent in by their submarines, scattered over the Atlantic. But it is at least possible that they were getting them from Greenland, by a technique that they themselves and the British were joint leaders in developing.

In the fall of 1930, young Augustine Courtauld, a member of the British Arctic Air Route Expedition, wintering near Angmagssalik, was taken by his companions up on the Greenland Icecap, 140 miles from its eastern margin, about forty miles north of the Arctic Circle, and 8,200 feet above sea level. He was left there alone for five winter months to take weather observations. By the published account, he suffered no particular hardships.

Parallel with Courtauld's work, the Germans established in 1930, under the leadership of Alfred Wegener, a well rounded scientific Inland Ice observatory, with a staff of three scientists. They spent a year near the center of Greenland, nearly 300 miles above the Arctic Circle and about 10,000 feet above sea level. This was followed some years later by similar studies, although for only two months, made by Professor Ralph Belknap of the University of Michigan Expedition, 180 miles east from the western margin of the Inland Ice, some 560 miles north of the Arctic Circle and about 8,840 feet above sea level.

Nothing is known to indicate that the Germans cannot have done in this war what their scientists did in peacetime. They may have used, for instance, a combination of two previously successful methods. In May, 1937, four four-engine Soviet airplanes delivered in a single flight to the geographic North Pole, from one of the Franz Josef Islands, a distance of more than 500 miles, a total pay load of ten tons. This was food and scientific and other equipment for Ivan Papanin and his three companions, and included a windmill to generate power, an engine for supplementary radio power, and petroleum for the engine, for cooking, etc. The members of this Soviet expedition drifted on their ice floe eight months and still had a lot of supplies when they were picked up. In 1938 Lauge Koch, the Danish explorer, made a base in Spitsbergen about 280 miles east from northeast Greenland and from there flew nonstop twice to Peary Land and back.

Assume, then, that the Germans, like Lauge Koch, took off from a natural landing field in Spitsbergen, and that, like the Papanin expedition, they carried supplies. They could have delivered them to Peary Land by making ordinary wheel or ski landings, or they could have dropped men, machinery, and supplies with parachutes, methods used by the Germans for landing troops and supplies on mountain glaciers during the invasion of Norway. Once in Peary Land, and having erected their main base, the Germans would move supplies south along the spine of Greenland by airplane, or by motor sledges, perhaps driven by airplane propellers, which has been one of the Soviet techniques. One man at each of these southward stations would be enough, according to Courtauld, but more likely there would be two or three. Stations would be 200 or 300 miles apart along the north-south median line of the island continent. Each would be equipped with a very weak radio sender of the beam type, and would communicate only with the station immediately north of it. The accumulated information would reach the northernmost main station up in Peary Land, from which, by a more powerful beam radio, it would go to the north of Norway.

It might be thought that stations on the Icecap would be readily detected by scouting airplanes, but the contrary was true in the case of Nobile, camped out on the sea ice near Spitsbergen in 1928. The numerous airplanes searching for him knew his location almost exactly, knew that he was living in a red tent and that he was spreading dirty rags out on the white ice to make as big a dark patch as possible. Even so, several airplanes were seen by Nobile during several days before any of them saw him. Secret weather stations on the Inland Ice of Greenland would look to it that everything around the camp was white, and would avoid anything that cast a shadow. Courtauld was so well hidden in his subterranean dwelling that his own companions, who had delivered him there, had to organize two different search expeditions before they found him.

Or the Germans might, of course, rely in part or wholly on shore stations which they would conceal in one or another of the ramified fjords of East Greenland. These would be easier to discover for us, but not so very easy. Besides, the Germans sacrifice men rather freely, and they might think it worth while to sacrifice a dozen or so here and there on Greenland's coast on the chance that some at least of the groups might be able to smuggle weather reports through for a few weeks or months.

From Greenland to that territory which on Seward's advice we finally bought from Russia for $7,200,000, runs the Northwest Passage, used by the ships of the Hudson's Bay Company and of the Royal Canadian Mounted Police. But more important to World War II, because more used, is the Northeast Passage developed by the Soviets. In addition are the river highways of our Arctic which, used in conjunction with those of Asia, shorten the distance between the United States production centers and our allies in the East by many thousands of miles.

Because of the Gulf Stream the ice of the Arctic Mediterranean has been pushed over onto the Alaskan side, so that the middle of the region too icy for a steamer to penetrate is not at the geographic pole but about 400 miles from it in the direction of the Bering Sea, the so-called Pole of Inaccessibility. For several hundred miles around it is ice so steady that although it moves constantly one can camp upon it for months without evidence of motion except by astronomical determination of latitude and longitude.

Members of my expeditions and I have spent an aggregate of more than a year traveling and camping on moving sea ice, and in our opinion the risk of camping on the pack is negligible, except near the margins. The Papanin expedition, starting its drift from the North Pole, was safe for more than six months in its elaborate camp; during the eighth month it got so near the margin of the ice that it was in danger, and had to be picked up by a ship. If its base had been established 300 miles from the North Pole *in the direction of Canada*, it would not have drifted toward the Atlantic and the Gulf Stream, but rather first south toward the mouth of the Mackenzie River, then westward parallel to the coast of Alaska, and finally in a very wide spiral, northward and westward, gradually getting farther from the Siberian coast until its floe reached the gap between Norway and Greenland, there to melt and disappear. Papanin was nearing the end of his rope after six months, but an encampment such as we have described might take six years to reach a place of corresponding danger. The most obvious use of such an encampment is as a weather-reporting station. But it could also be a gasoline depot.

To those unaccustomed to thinking that ice is useful, the advantages of the liquid part of the Polar Sea may be a good deal more obvious than those of the central ice area. The Soviet Government in its First Five Year Plan included a program of developing a reliable freighting waterway around the north of the Old World. Fifteen years ago most scientists probably thought, as I did, that this route would not be of real value, that cargo ships would get through it only about one year in three. But after 1936 the Soviets were successful, under the Third Five Year Plan, in bringing to fruition the program of the first plan. Just before the war, well over a hundred freighters used the northern route in a single year. A few of them came from the Pacific, went halfway west along the north coast of Siberia, and returned to Vladivostok or Petropavlovsk. The greater number came from Murmansk and Archangel, went halfway east and returned. These steamers exchanged cargoes with river boats, some of which descended 2,000 miles from the interior of Asia, bringing lumber, grains, and other produce.

For complete through traffic the Northeast Passage was probably never used before World War II by more than about twenty ships in any one year. Only one round trip is known to have been made in a season, from Atlantic to Pacific and back.

The success of the Northeast Passage has depended not so much on the development of powerful icebreakers, or other specially constructed ships, as on radio reports of ice character and ice movement. These reports came from observatories on every strategic promontory—mainland or island—and from airplanes that swarm everywhere along the 3,000 miles of the Northeast Passage during the three months' navigation season. Ice forecasting, which combines meteorological with ice studies, enables the commander of a fleet of freighters or warships to plot on a map every day the location of ice on the entire passage, with its character and speed of movement. The forecasters can even tell him approximately where the ice that is here today will be tomorrow or the day after. A fleet may have to go several hundred miles out of its course; but in this way it may avoid even seeing an ice field which would block the most powerful icebreakers.

There are actually five Northwest Passages around North America. The route in use by the Hudson's Bay Company and the Royal Canadian Mounted Police follows the mainland coast, servicing the trading posts. Western freight goes to Edmonton, Alberta, and by rail 250 miles north to the head of navigation at McMurray. Then it moves by steamer down the Athabaska, Slave, and Mackenzie rivers (actually segments of the same river). At the Mackenzie delta the freight is taken on by ocean-going ships and carried east as far as Bellot Strait, where it is met by other freighters coming in from Montreal and the East.

Part of the Northwest Passage is subject to ice difficulties, but this segment is only half as long as the ice-infested stretch of the Northeast Passage. And since the Soviets have been able to make one round trip a season, two round trips should be possible between the North Atlantic and North Pacific around Canada.

This may be of value in moving freight or troops; it could be of even greater value in shifting a battle fleet or a school of submarines. Not merely would the voyage from the North Atlantic to the North Pacific be only a third as long as via the Panama Canal, but there would be two additional advantages: immunity from observation by the enemy and immunity from submarine and airplane attack.

Through the use of rivers to supplement railways and other land highways, freight from all the great American centers of war production can reach, and can be transported along, the Northeast and Northwest passages between Atlantic or Pacific. A generation that tends to think lazily in terms of railroads, ships, and trucks has almost forgotten the value of river traffic. In North America the Mackenzie River, second only to the Mississippi system, is little considered as yet in the present war, but it is the historic commercial highway of northwestern Canada. It begins to be navigable at the head of rail north of Edmonton, and flows almost straight in the direction of Japan and China.

The Mackenzie does not go to that Bering Sea which spreads nearly to Japan, but the Yukon River does; and the Yukon is the third longest river highway of the North American continent. It could be coordinated with the Mackenzie and the two rivers used practically as one. For the Mackenzie, 400 miles from its mouth, is only 400 miles from the Yukon. All that is needed is to cross a low divide, perhaps best from the downstream end of the Norman oil field by the pass that runs toward Eagle, Alaska; and the Yukon will then carry forward the transport to Bering Sea. Construction of a road by this low pass would give us a 3,000-mile highway extending in the direction of Asia from rail head just north of Edmonton—in summer a liquid highway for steamboats, in winter an automotive road paved level and hard with ice. At the western end of this highway, on the east shore of Bering Sea, you are a good deal nearer Japan than if you were at Pearl Harbor.

Rivers like the Mackenzie and Yukon are highways of one sort or another nine to ten months a year. From May to October they are navigable by steamer and scow, then idle for some weeks. Late in November or early in December the ice is strong enough for tractor and sledge, remaining so until some time in April, when for several weeks the river is neither hard enough for tractors nor liquid enough for boats.

The value of Alaska in the military situation is that it points like an accusing finger toward Japan—a finger that does not quite touch Japan's midriff but is at least our nearest threat. But if we are to strike at Japan from Alaska, if we are to collaborate effectively with the forces of the Soviet Union based in eastern Siberia, then we need in Alaska above everything else—petroleum.

But Alaska cannot at present produce petroleum in large quantities. Canada therefore must supply it with oil through the back door—the navigable Mackenzie River system coordinated with the navigable Yukon. At McMurray, the end of the rail and the head of Mackenzie navigation, is the Athabaska oil sand, which has a potential yield estimated by the Geological Survey of Canada at a hundred billion barrels. There is already a small refinery. Experts agree that the quantity of oil produced depends wholly on sufficient investment.

Richard Finnie, in *Canada Moves North,*[1] describes the pioneering of Imperial Oil, Ltd., and the development of its northernmost refinery at Norman Wells, about 100 miles south of the Arctic Circle, and thus abreast of Fairbanks. The refinery there was producing aviation gas even before World War II. Again all that is needed is to expand the operation to produce a substantial yield.

But for the military and industrial needs of Alaska, Yukon Territory, and the North Pacific it would be better, instead of expanding the Norman refinery, to pipe the crude oil either 400 miles to deep-channel Yukon steamboating at Eagle or 600 miles to Alaska's gold-mining and aviation metropolis, Fairbanks. With a refinery in either of these towns the oil would then be carried both up and down stream in regulation petroleum scows and dis-

[1] Macmillan, New York, 1942.

tributed elsewhere by the two available railways and the various roads. But this topic is developed more at length elsewhere in the present volume.

The full use of the navigable fringes of the Polar Sea depends on coordinating the north-flowing rivers with the Northeast and Northwest passages. In military operations we can do what the Hudson's Bay Company does with the Northwest Passage in peacetime, what the Soviet Union does with the Northeast Passage. North America has only two great river highways flowing north and northwest, the Mackenzie and the Yukon. Three north-flowing Soviet rivers, Lena, Yenisei and Ob, are comparable to the Mississippi, each navigable for more than 2,000 miles toward the heart of Asia, well into the wheat country, the regions of cities and developed mines. At least one other, the Kolyma, is nearly comparable to the Yukon. A number of smaller streams compare with the Ohio and the Missouri rivers, significant in our history when we were at the pioneer stage of development now found in parts of northern Siberia.

In conjunction with the operation of the Northern Sea Route, the Soviets are already utilizing the rivers of Asia on a considerable scale and are prepared to extend the use as needed. In this way they can secure, among other things, lumber from the Yenisei for use in the West or in the Far East, grain from the Yenisei and other rivers, coal and salt and various produce from the Lena and Kolyma. From our side, as part of Lend-Lease, we can send supplies in to them. From Seattle these would go up through Bering Strait and westward; from New York they would go by way of Iceland and eastward. The Yenisei crosses the Trans-Siberian Railroad at Krasnoyarsk, and much of the material used in converting it from a single- to a double-track railroad was shipped by that river. It would be feasible to transfer supplies from the Yenisei to the Trans-Siberian Railroad for shipment east or west, and to switch at Novosibirsk to the Turk-Sib, unloading at Alma-Ata or Sergiopol, where the road to China begins.

That flying within the Arctic Circle is dangerous is a popular misapprehension. Sub-zero weather is not nearly so dangerous as intermediate temperatures, such as those around the freezing point. Around 32° above zero fog, half-melted snow, and slush will turn to ice on wing and strut. But within the Arctic Circle during winter it is usually much colder so the moisture is frozen dry and brushes off; in summer it is liquid and drips off. Flying conditions are not good up the Pacific Coast to Alaska. Thus the route to Asia is bound to be, for these reasons, down the Mackenzie and Yukon rivers either across the sixty-mile-wide Bering Strait, or across the northern gulf of the Bering Sea, 100 to 300 miles wide. Reaching Siberia, the pilot will take a route such as from Markovo on the Anadyr River either southward overland to Peiping or more to westward to Irkutsk. The Aleutian Islands are so dangerous precisely because of weather around the freezing point. Flying conditions are considerably better in the Arctic than along many of the commercial routes within the United States.

Not only the continents but also the islands mass themselves toward the North; jumps between islands are short in the North, long in the South. As steppingstones they are not necessary to bombers or transport planes crossing the oceans; but they are useful to fighting planes.

In flying to the Soviet Union by way of Fairbanks and Irkutsk, Lend-Lease fighter planes do not need to be stripped or provided with built-in tankage. For ferrying in winter prepared airports are unnecessary, because every lake is by nature a reasonably good landing field, good enough for experienced Alaskan, Canadian, and Siberian flyers. Pilots will increase the distance from Chicago to Fairbanks by only about 100 miles if they avoid the more difficult Edmonton-Whitehorse-Fairbanks route and fly from Edmonton by way of Peace River and Simpson, down the Mackenzie, approximately along the route used already for many years by Canadian Airways and Mackenzie Air Service. That route makes needless the uneconomical truck haulage through a mountain country required by the Edmonton-Whitehorse route, for it can be stocked every summer by railway and by river steamboat with all the gasoline and other supplies needed in the next winter's ferrying of fighting planes—even if they come over in hundreds or thousands. Nature has provided the wintertime Arctic with natural landing fields, seaplane bases, and river ice highways thousands of miles long.

In the Arctic, then, as in tropics or temperate zone, we are free now to use the roundness of the earth in the solution of our transportation problems; and we gain more by this in the Arctic than farther south because the proportion of mileage saving is greater and the seas which have to be crossed are smaller.

20

The Northward Course of Aviation

By GRAHAM B. GROSVENOR

Because the record shows that, outside the Union of Soviet Socialist Republics, the only long-range attempts to explore the possibilities of transarctic airways have been made by an American company, Pan American Airways, the editors asked an official of this company to review early flying in the North, the problems encountered, and outline some of the potentialities of this region for air routes of the future. As a regional study, this paper supplements the articles by Charles Hurd, "World Airways," by the editors of *Fortune,* "The Logic of the Air," and William A. M. Burden, "American Air Transport Faces North" (pp. 109, 121, 137).

The author of this essay was a pioneer, with the late Carl Ben Eielson, in air transport in Alaska in the 1920's. He was a director of Pan American Airways and special assistant to the President of Pan American. He died October 28, 1943.

Ever since they realized that they were living on a global earth men have been obsessed with the search for short, northerly trade routes to their neighbors on the other side of the world. Today, after some four hundred years of earthbound exploration and painstaking scientific spadework, they are looking to the airplane to solve the problem of the northward passage in the postwar world, and provide short, safe, easily accessible trade routes across the Polar Sea.

Columbus and the sixteenth century explorers who followed him in the search for a short route to the riches of Cathay—the Cabots, Cartier, and Hudson—had nothing to guide them but one scientific fact. They knew that the world was round, and that by sailing north they were heading in the right direction. For back in the days of Columbus men of science were quick to draw all the proper inferences from the discovery that the earth was spherical, not flat. They reasoned rightly that one could go east by sailing west, that the shortest route from Europe to China, say, was by way of the north.

But when the explorers sought to make the earth's sphericity serve such a useful purpose, they were stymied by the ice of the Arctic. The ice was too much for the ships of those early days, however intrepid the ships' masters. Knowledge of the tides and the winds and the world itself was too rudimentary to admit of more than partial success.

Thanks to certain venturesome souls, however, the search for a short northerly route was continued. Minor success and major failure alike not only added to man's knowledge of the earth; they helped the trend of civilization northward. One of the most colossal failures in the north, for example, was the expedition of Sir John Franklin in 1845. Sir John and his entire party of 129 officers and men perished in a search for the Northwest Passage. Yet the series of expeditions seeking some trace of them proved eventually that the Northwest Passage was possible, if not commercially practical in point of time and expense, for nineteenth century surface craft.

In the 1870's the Swedish Finn, Adolf Nordenskjöld, made the first one-way voyage through the Northeast Passage; and in the early 1900's Roald Amundsen, the Norwegian, negotiated both the Northwest and the Northeast Passage. But paradoxically it was the airplane, which Amundsen condemned for Arctic work, that made the two passages practical for water-borne commerce. Over the entire expanse of the Arctic coasts of the Soviet Union today, and to a lesser extent off northern Canada, airplanes are serving as the eyes of the icebreakers which keep the passages open. Soaring far out over the pack ice, scouting aircraft guide icebreakers, with freight ships in convoy, to the leads of open water and thus make the northern routes serviceable in summer long enough to permit round-trip voyages between the Atlantic and the Pacific.

To aircraft the ice is no barrier, for planes can fly above it. Moreover, it has been proved conclusively in the past few years that, when necessary, aircraft can use the ice as if it were land for descents and take-offs. Use of planes for ice-scouting is consequently at best a half-measure. For not until the great transport planes carry passengers and cargo on schedule, winter and

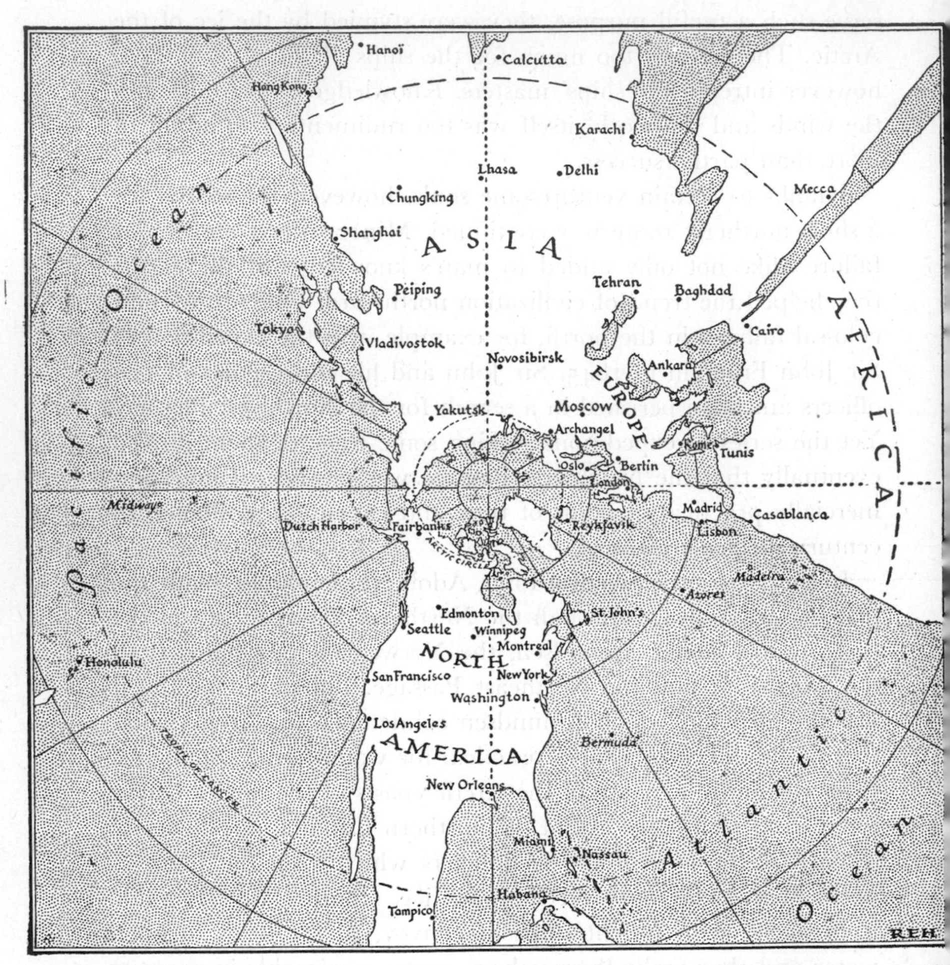

FIG. 29. This pole-centered map, containing all of the North Temperate and Arctic Zones, is on the gnomonic projection (called by navigators a great-circle chart). A straight line on it in any direction is a true great circle, and therefore indicates the shortest route between any two points on it. Although a very misleading map for comparative distances it serves to demonstrate clearly the northward course of routes connecting the power centers of the world.

summer, over the shortest Arctic air routes between the Old World and the New, will aircraft reach full stature in the Arctic and will men solve the problem of the short northward passage.

There are six principal factors to be considered in the pioneering of such a transpolar airway: (1) knowledge of the land, sea, and air within the Arctic Circle; (2) accessibility of principal population centers over a northern route; (3) the economic development of those lands of Eurasia and North America on the fringes of the Polar Sea; (4) establishment of airports, weather and radio stations throughout the polar region; (5) improvement of aircraft and perfection of the technique of operating planes over long ocean distances; (6) an international situation favorable to friendly cooperation among the nations whose sovereignty extends to the North Pole.

Since most of these factors had fallen into place in the late 1930's, it seems strange, on looking back, that some transarctic airways were not well established in the last five years of fitful peace. Civilization over the centuries had trended steadily northward, and by then all the greatest power countries of the world were in the north temperate zone; most of them indeed in the northern half of the north temperate zone. The shortest routes between the great population centers that were far from one another, therefore, lay over the Polar Sea. Nor was the Arctic still an unknown quantity. On foot and behind dog teams, in dirigibles and airplanes, men had reached the North Pole itself. In skin boats, wooden sailing ships, steel steamers, drift balloons, and modern aircraft they had charted the islands in the Polar Basin, the archipelagoes and the tortuous straits separating lumps of land from one another and the continents to which they once were attached.

Deliberately imbedding their ships in the pack ice or pitching camp upon the floes, men had drifted hundreds of miles to add to the fund of knowledge of the currents and depths of the sea, the temperature ranges, the fogs, rains, snows, winds, and storms over nearly all of the Arctic region. As a result the Arctic was known to be the world's smallest ocean, to possess the best island bridges across it as well as weather that was at least as good as that which prevails over the larger bodies of water.

Meantime aircraft had been developed by the middle 1930's to the point at which planes could cruise at relatively high altitudes and travel in excess of two thousand miles with practical pay loads of passengers and cargo without stopping to refuel. By the time World War II began, the technique of operating such aircraft had been perfected in regular scheduled service over the Atlantic and the Pacific, the world's mightiest oceans, and the loftiest mountain ranges.

Belatedly, after the First World War ended and as the Second was shaping up, nations which bordered on the Arctic Ocean had begun to look to their northlands for development rather than exploitation. Stark economic necessity, as well as the threat of war, drove them to it. Even so, with the exception of the Soviet Union, these nations were slow to accept the fact that the far north was a friendly, habitable area with no greater terrors for men than the other zones.

The international situation throughout the 1930's, therefore, was the one big factor which simply would not fall into place. Some nations were more concerned with the development of aircraft as adjuncts of military might than as essential aids to peaceful passenger and cargo transport. Air lines as private enterprises were hampered by this atmosphere of international mistrust to a much greater extent than by climatic or geographic hazards.

Among the intangibles which also held back the logical expansion of air transport northward over the shortest routes during that period were two popular misconceptions. Both proved to be big stumbling blocks. One was the belief that the Arctic was a region of such climatic and geographic extremes that the airplane was useless even for exploration except perhaps on land. This belief died hard in the public mind even when confronted with unassailable scientific proof to the contrary. The other misconception was simply this: Conditioned by centuries of sea-borne commercial expansion eastward and westward around the world, the general public accepted without question the fact that the earth was round, but persisted in flat-earth thinking, or rather in thinking of the earth as cylindrical in shape.

Not all the Arctic explorers were unaware of the advantages of the airplane even in the early stages of its development, however. The First World War had not yet reached its indecisive conclusion when Vilhjalmur Stefansson began to stress the advantages of the Arctic as an air route of the future.

Stefansson first publicly disclosed his views in detail in an article, "The Arctic As an Air Route of the Future," which appeared in the *National Geographic Magazine* in August, 1922. He pointed out that the Arctic Ocean was in fact merely a mediterranean sea separating Eurasia and North America. The shortest routes between the world's great population centers, he averred, were Great Circle sailings northward by air.

Nevertheless, for years, while all the circumpolar governments except that of the Soviet Union failed in the active support of aviation in their Arctic regions, aircraft in the hands of private flyers were rapidly supplanting the dog teams as means of transport for the trappers, prospectors, missionaries, police, and Eskimos of the Far North. Moreover, largely as a result of pioneering flights, most authorities were agreed by 1930 that Arctic flying conditions generally were good. Three air expeditions—two by dirigible and one by airplane—had reached the North Pole by then, and planes had been used extensively in both rescue and exploration operations. Still in all during the next ten years, up to the time the Second World War engaged the major Powers, the only long-range efforts to explore the possibility of trans-Arctic commercial air routes were those of the U.S.S.R. as a nation and Pan American Airways as an American private enterprise.

In 1937 Soviet flyers completed two nonstop flights over the Polar Sea from Moscow to North America in connection with the proposed development of commercial airways. To perfect transocean and Arctic air transport technique, meanwhile, Pan American long had been engaged in scientific studies and surveys covering projected Northeast and Northwest air passages. The first organized air transport service which Pan American brought to Alaska in the early 1930's was of major importance also in the economic development of the nation's northernmost outpost. Over the North Atlantic, Pan American made extensive surveys which included Iceland and the Arctic reaches of Greenland, finally establishing transatlantic service over the true New York-London Great Circle route with aircraft which would permit direct flight from North America to Europe. Although the surveys and the development of the first American ocean-passenger aircraft, the Martin-built Clipper, gave Pan American the physical means of establishing such an airway as early as 1935, the international situation delayed inauguration of service until a few months before Hitler marched on Poland and Europe was at war again.

When the Second World War broke out the United States, more than ever, needed new routes, the shortest possible; and new means, the speediest, to get war materials to her beleaguered allies holding eastern and western battle fronts, continents apart. Shortest routes meant northward Great Circle sailings. Speediest means meant air transport. War material for the most part soon came to mean aircraft, as the prodigious feats of bomber, fighter, and transport planes finally convinced even the most confirmed skeptic that Wright's Folly was here to stay.

Today it appears that the final factor and all the intangibles essential to the successful establishment of the Northwest Passage by air are but waiting for the peace to come. The war certainly has tended to create a situation favorable to friendly cooperation among the chief nations sharing political sovereignty in the Arctic—the cooperation which is essential for transit rights and the exchange of weather data and terminal facilities. Three of these nations—the United States, Canada, and the Soviet Union—are fighting side by side as allies. And on their eventual victory two others—Norway and Denmark—have pinned all hopes for the restoration of their national integrity. Iceland, though neutral, is sympathetic to the Allies. Only Finland, which on the sector principle has the smallest Arctic sphere, is opposed to us.

A glance at the globe shows clearly how the spherical shape of the earth and the distribution of its land masses and population centers favor the United Nations in war and international transarctic airway connections in a peaceful postwar world.

Viewed from above, the Arctic is like a huge pie within its bounding circle, with the United States, Canada, and the U.S.S.R. claiming wedge-shaped slabs which narrow down to a point at dead center, the pole. Norway and Denmark have slices in the pie, too. The base of United States sovereignty extends from the Canadian-Alaskan border to midway in Bering Strait. Canada's slice takes in the territory from the Alaska boundary eastward, including Ellesmere Island and the triangular archipelago north of Hudson Bay. The Soviet Union's claim of sovereignty covers nearly half of the Arctic Circle—49 per cent, to be exact—from midway in Bering Strait to its European boundary with Finland on the Kola peninsula, encompassing the islands of Novaya Zemlya, Wrangel, Franz Josef Land, and the New Siberian group.

All the islands in the north are of great value as sites for air bases, radio and weather stations, or refueling stops on some transarctic airway. Greenland, the area of Denmark's sovereignty, is of particular importance. Iceland, an independent nation since 1918, which touches yet lies entirely south of the Arctic Circle, and Greenland together provide excellent steppingstones for local routes between the United States and Northern Europe.

Another important island, strategically located as a steppingstone to Asia, is Wrangel, which lies off the Siberian coast north of Bering Strait. For several years now, Wrangel has been a well developed Soviet Arctic outpost. The status of Norway's sole Arctic holding, other than the part of her home territory which juts up into the Circle, is at present obscure. This is the island of Spitsbergen, which was favored as a base for Arctic exploration in the early days. Norway's neighbor on the Scandinavian peninsula and Germany's ally in the war—Finland—also lies in part within the Arctic Circle; but the area is important neither in strategy nor in extent.

Just as the disposition of the land masses in the Arctic is excellent for flying purposes, so are the climatic conditions peculiarly adapted to aviation. The Polar Basin has virtually no severe storms and few high winds; precipitation is light, and fogs are numerous only in transition belts.

Since 1897, when the Swedish aeronaut Andrée made the first attempt to fly over the Arctic in a drift balloon, there have been many flights in airplanes and lighter-than-air ships which demonstrated the practicability of polar aviation. Admiral Richard E. Byrd was the first to reach the pole by plane in 1926. Amundsen and Ellsworth crossed the pole in an airship, the *Norge*, three days later, on May 12, from Spitsbergen, and continued on to Alaska to make the first flight across the Polar Sea. Sir Hubert Wilkins and Carl Ben Eielson made the first airplane landings on the pack ice far from shore in 1927, and a year later completed the first airplane flight across the Polar Sea, from Point Barrow, Alaska, to Spitsbergen.

In June and July of 1937 the Soviets completed two nonstop flights from Moscow to the United States in connection with the proposed establishment of a transpolar airway. In August of that year, the worst time of year for Arctic flying, a third Soviet flight in a passenger-type plane, in charge of Sigismund Levanevsky, failed to make the Arctic crossing.

As soon as the plane was so long overdue that it was presumed lost, an extensive airplane search was organized; and the governments of the United States, Canada, Norway, Sweden, and Denmark cooperated with the Soviet Union in furnishing vital weather reports.

The last garbled radio message from the Soviet flyers indicated only that they were coming down. Within an hour after that message was picked up, three planes of Pan American's subsidiary in Alaska took off from Fairbanks for a comprehensive search of the Territory, combing the winding river valleys, the flat tundra country and the rugged mountain range of the Endicotts between mid-Alaska and the Arctic Ocean. Pan American pilots flew over a total of nearly 100,000 square miles of northern Alaska in the hope that Levanevsky might have been able to reach the Territory before he was forced to land.

Sir Hubert Wilkins was in charge of flying operations for the Soviets on the American side of the pole. Although his search ended without discovering the slightest trace of the missing plane or its occupants, Sir Hubert accomplished the greatest single piece of airplane exploration in the far north. From bases along the Canadian coast, he covered 170,000 square miles of the Arctic Ocean, including at least 150,000 square miles which had never before been seen. In the seven-month search he flew a total of 44,000 miles, using a Consolidated flying boat in the late summer and in the winter a Lockheed Electra equipped with specially designed skis.

Sir Hubert's search for Levanevsky proved that Arctic flying is easier in winter than in midsummer and demonstrated the value of moonlight in Arctic aerial navigation. During one-third of each lunar month he found moonlight nearly as useful as daylight. The value of international cooperation in supplying weather reports was attested to by the fact that Sir Hubert found belts of cloud and of clear never more than fifty miles from where they had been placed by the forecasters.

Soviet planes joined in the search for Levanevsky from Point Barrow and from the icebreaker *Krassin*; but the Soviet rescue operations were directed mainly from Rudolf Island in the Franz Josef group, on the old-world side of the pole, where the Soviets had constructed the world's most northerly air base.

The transpolar flights of the Soviets to North America in 1937 were merely the culmination of long-range Arctic research which began very early in the new regime after the First World War. While the importance of a line of communication which could not be seriously threatened by an Asiatic or a European enemy in time of war may have been one of the factors in the Arctic development project, much credit must go to the Soviet leaders for their appreciation of the potentialities of the north in the national economy. After all, the U.S.S.R.'s northern region, from the Kola peninsula to Bering Strait, comprises more than two-fifths of its entire territory. The Russians of course, did not have to be sold on the livability of the north. From prerevolutionary experiences as political exiles in Siberia, Stalin and other Soviet leaders had first-hand knowledge of the Arctic. That they profited by their experience is evident from the way they began, as soon as they came into power, to devote a large share of the national effort to the development of the north.

As early as January, 1919, a group of Soviet scientists was formed into a Commission on the Study of the Arctic. In 1930 the organization was named the Arctic Institute and attached to the Chief Administration of the Northern Sea Route. Development of the sea route, the famous Northeast Passage, into a dependable trade artery was the keystone of the entire Arctic project. With it naturally went the development of communication and transport facilities by land, rivers, and airways, the fostering of trade and industry, mining and agriculture throughout the area north of the Arctic Circle.

Aerial surveys and scientific expeditions were the high lights of the first Soviet five-year plan in the Arctic. During the second, the Soviets staged the Papanin expedition to the North Pole and the transpolar flights to the United States, founded polar stations in the Arctic basin, and greatly expanded steamer traffic on the Siberian rivers which flow north into the Arctic Sea. In the third five-year plan the Northern Sea Route really became productive, and along with it Arctic industry and agriculture began to flourish. More than sixty polar stations are well established in the area now, and key ports have been established along the sea route at Dickson Island, Kozkevikov and Tiksi bays, Ambarchik and Provideniye (Providence) Bay.

To a great extent it was aviation that made all these accomplishments possible. From the outset planes did most of the surveying, carried scientific parties to various stations, kept them supplied, and maintained contact with them. Ice scouting aircraft guided the ships through the pack ice in the passage itself and supplied the reports of meteorological conditions which were used in forecasts for the directing of the surface vessels.

The network of Arctic air routes, first grouped under the Chief Administration of the Northern Sea Route, became an important segment of Soviet civil aviation. Between 1933 and 1937 ice scouting planes alone averaged about five hundred flying hours a summer. Although a good proportion of the Arctic airways were returned to civil air administration in 1938, the total mileage of Arctic scouting planes now is estimated at more than a million miles a summer.

While the Soviet Union was quick to begin development of its Arctic resources and northern air routes with an eye to eventual transpolar commerce by air, Canada, the next largest circumpolar nation, was slow to realize the advantages of its geographical position in this regard. To most Canadians in the southern provinces, the great Northwest Territories of the Dominion were mere no man's lands of impenetrable bush and bitter cold populated by a handful of Indians, Eskimos, white trappers, prospectors, and the personnel of remote trading stations and police outposts.

As elsewhere, however, air transport found ready acceptance in Canada's northwest because the climate and topography made surface travel difficult and slow, notwithstanding the fact that by the same token successful aircraft operation there required a special technique. Skilled bush flyers perfected their own Arctic technique and soon were doing a land-office business in the subarctic regions, carrying prospectors and trappers first into the bush and then out again with their pokes or pelts.

In fact, shortly after the First World War, the airplane began to prove itself the most important factor in the exploration and development of the Canadian Northwest. Two pilots penetrated to Fort Simpson in 1921, but the first important government step was taken in eastern Canada a year later, when Robert A. Logan was sent to the islands in the archipelago east and north of Hudson Bay. An enthusiastic exponent of transarctic airways even at that early date, Major Logan[1] actually surveyed sites for airports in northern Baffin Island and Ellesmere Island. The general trend of his report was optimistic, but his recommendations for further aerial surveys and development got nowhere.

Canadian Air Force planes made important aerial surveys on a Hudson Strait Expedition in 1927 and in the western Arctic in 1930. Bases were set up at Port Burwell, Nottingham Island, and Wakeham Bay, and two Fokkers at each base made triangular flights to cover the entire strait at practically the same time. Another expedition in which aerial photography played a part was the flight of Major L. T. Burwash from Coppermine, on the Arctic coast, to the magnetic pole area on Boothia Peninsula in 1930.[2]

The pioneer commercial air transport concern in Canada, curiously enough, was an American company. In 1922 Sherman Fairchild, an associate of Juan T. Trippe, formed Fairchild Aerial Surveys. Headed by Elwood Wilson and based at Grand Mère, Quebec, this concern conducted extensive aerial surveys and was the first air transport company to carry passengers and freight in Canada and throughout the subarctic areas.

Another pioneer in Canada's Arctic and subarctic aviation development was C. H. ("Punch") Dickins, now vice president and general manager of Canadian Pacific Air Lines, who made the first flight from Edmonton to Aklavik on July 1, 1929. Other leaders were James Richardson of Winnipeg, pioneer of Mackenzie River aviation, who established Canadian Airways; W. Leigh Brintnell, who started Mackenzie Air Service, Ltd., and Grant McConachie, who founded Yukon Southern Air Transport, Ltd.

Economic factors which spurred commercial air transport development were discoveries of pitchblende and silver at Great Bear Lake, gold at Yellowknife, and oil at Norman Wells. Then

[1] This was his title as a Canadian flyer in the first World War; now a United States citizen, he is a colonel in the Air Transport Command.

[2] This flight included young Richard Finnie who since has published many articles and two books which deal with northern development, featuring aviation. The books are *The Lure of the North* (Philadelphia, 1940) and *Canada Moves North* (New York, 1942).

too, as the Second World War threatened, Canada and the United States began collaboration on a broad defense program. Significant features of this are the chain of five airfields between Edmonton and the Alaska Boundary linking the United States with the Territory, and the highway which supports the air bases.

The most significant of northward-trending commercial aviation developments, however, was the absorption by the Canadian Pacific Railway of ten north-and-south air lines in 1942, including Mackenzie Air Service, Yukon Southern and Canadian Airways. Under the name of Canadian Pacific Air Lines, Ltd., this concern flies some 18,000 miles daily and includes services to Aklavik and Coppermine on the Arctic coast of Canada.

By comparison with Canada and the U.S.S.R., the United States has relatively small holdings in the Arctic. The only land she owns there is that part of Alaska which extends beyond the Arctic Circle. As a nation the United States has lagged far behind the Soviet Union in the development of her Arctic resources. And geographically, of course, she has fewer advantages than Canada for the pioneering of transarctic airways. Still the American contributions to the potential development of transpolar commerce by air have been of major importance, and they have been made, in the main, by a private enterprise.

Pan American became the nation's first international overseas air line when it established the ninety-mile route from Key West to Havana in 1927. Using each phase of its development as a laboratory for further study of air transport, the company made major contributions to the advancement of aircraft design and construction. The Sikorsky S-40 flying boats, built to Pan American's specifications, which could carry forty passengers on the Miami to Havana run in 1932, convinced designers and manufacturers of the potentialities of increased size and horsepower in aircraft for over-ocean operation; and by their great size the S-40's did much to break down the prevailing public resistance to over-water flying. The Boeing type B-314 Clippers, used to institute and maintain the first transatlantic passenger and air-mail service, remain the largest transport aircraft in commercial service today.

In the pioneering of transpacific and transatlantic airways Pan American developed also specialized aids which became the standard technique for the operation of aircraft over long ocean distances. These aids are the multiple flight crew, the accessibility of power plants to permit repairs and adjustment in flight, the system of scientific flight control through an individual ocean flight plan.

Because of its extensive operations southward between the Americas, Pan American has been generally thought to have a tropical outlook. As a matter of fact, however, the concern was the first to recognize the geographical advantages of transarctic routes and to take definite steps towards the development of the Northwest Passage to Asia, as well as the Northeast Passage to Europe, by air transport.

From 1931 on, Pan American has engaged in survey flights in both directions, and negotiations with the various other countries concerned. At the outset the company retained authorities on all phases of northern operation. It developed scheduled air transport in Alaska, the sole Arctic possession of the United States, and in China as well, with a view to carrying the Northwest Passage to its logical conclusion as the shortest trade route to China and the Indies.

The first major survey of this nature was Colonel Lindbergh's flight north to the Orient in 1931, from Washington to Tokyo by way of North Haven, Ottawa, Moose Factory, Churchill, Baker Lake, Aklavik, Point Barrow, Nome, Karaginski Island, Petropavlovsk and Nemuro. At that time Colonel Lindbergh was chief technical adviser of Pan American. In 1932 Pan American entered the Alaska field and in 1933, in partnership with the Chinese National Government, it formed the national airline, China National Aviation Corporation.

In 1934 Pan American began negotiations with Amtorg, the Soviet commercial organization, concerning the establishment of an air service via Alaska and northeastern Siberia to China and the interior of Asia generally. Also in 1934 Pan American planes made a survey flight across Bering Strait from Nome to Cape Wellen. The negotiations subsequently were taken over by the Soviet Embassy and were carried forward, off and on, until 1939.

Alaska was the logical jumping-off place for westerly trans-arctic routes, but air transport in the Territory in 1932 was largely a hit-and-miss proposition. Four United States Army planes made the first flights from the United States to Alaska in 1920. Not long after that Juan T. Trippe, who had not yet organized Pan American Airways, saw the possibilities of the Territory and with Carl Ben Eielson, who later made aviation history with Sir Hubert Wilkins in the Arctic and Antarctic, surveyed conditions in Alaska.

Eielson carried the first United States mail in Alaska—164 pounds of it, from Fairbanks to McGrath, on February 21, 1924—and started the so-called Star Mail system by which airplanes toted the mail for the same price the Post Office Department paid for dog-team delivery. While Trippe was engaged in forming Pan American Airways and establishing the first United States international overseas air line, Eielson founded Alaskan Airways, a pioneer air transport company in Alaska. The latter perished, in 1930, on a flight to Siberia.

Air transport difficulties in Alaska were many, and in 1932 the two large companies still functioning, Eielson's original concern, Alaskan Airways, and Pacific International Airways of Alaska, had reached a point at which they felt that, because of substantial and consistent losses, they could no longer continue. Pan American took over the equipment, facilities, contracts, and operations of the two concerns in 1932.

Pan American entered the field impressed by the importance to the national interest of the maintenance of organized air transport in an area that occupied a strategic military position in the North Pacific; the vital link the Territory would be in the trans-arctic operations of the future since it lay directly on the Great Circle route between the northern United States and the Orient; Alaska's value as a laboratory in which to work out the most knotty problems of commercial air transport operations in the Arctic.

In the eleven years that followed, the company developed landing fields, communication facilities, radio and weather stations, introduced multi-engine planes, evolved a technique for subarctic air transport, and added two connecting links with the United States at Seattle, first by way of a sea route and then over the chain of defense bases in western Canada. Its service in the Territory now connects the principal population centers, Nome, Bethel, Fairbanks, and Juneau, with trunk lines to the United States.

While on the one hand Pan American put its mail routes and passenger service between the principal population centers on an organized, scheduled basis, it did not neglect the barnstorming angle. Its planes carried mining operators, prospectors, traders, and trappers from the towns into the farthest corners of the territory. Consequently its pilots got to know the country intimately from the Panhandle to Point Barrow; a fund of meteorological information was compiled on the Arctic and subarctic regions, and methods of winterizing equipment could be proved by actual practice.

While in themselves the various Alaska services never were profitable, they did fill a vital transport need in the Territory, and the Arctic flying technique perfected in the Alaska laboratory proved invaluable to Pan American for its venture over the North Atlantic. United States Army aviators had flown the northern route in 1924, and as early as 1929 Pan American began a scientific approach to the problem of a commercial airway linking North America and Europe. Foreign governments were surveying the possibilities of North Atlantic air transport service but up to the time that Pan American entered the field American efforts in this regard had been limited to uncoordinated attempts on the part of individuals. The most persistent of the individuals was Parker Cramer, who made three attempts and perished in his final effort in 1931.

Stefansson, whom Cramer had consulted, had advised against

the flight, contending that even if successful it would establish nothing about this route which was not already known, and the Transamerican Airlines Corporation, which had backed Cramer, realized that it would have saved considerable cash if it had followed the advice. The company was interested in the establishment of air transport to Europe by way of Greenland and Iceland, and in an overland air-mail service via the Great Circle route between the United States and the Philippines over Soviet territory. So it hired Stefansson as adviser and consultant on Arctic and subarctic problems.

Pan American retained Stefansson in the same capacity when it took over Transamerican's interests in 1932. Transamerican was about ready to expire, but it had entered into negotiations with Iceland and Denmark for concessions in connection with the North Atlantic air route. Pan American considered it as a matter of national interest that these negotiations be carried on by an American concern, particularly in the light of the marked interest being shown by other nations in Greenland and Iceland, both of which are in the Western Hemisphere.

There had been two important aviation surveys in Greenland previous to Pan American's first Greenland expedition. One was under the command of H. G. Watkins and was known as the British Arctic Air Route Expedition of 1930–31. Its aim was, through meteorological surveys, to discover stable bases for air routes in the region. The Canadian government authorities and the Hudson's Bay Company cooperated with this expedition, government aircraft at that time having been engaged in surveys on the west coast of Hudson Bay.

A German expedition, headed by Professor Alfred Wegener of the University of Graz, Austria, also did survey work on the icecap in 1930. By 1932 a German flyer, Wolfgang von Gronau, had made three crossings to North America via the northern route. While von Gronau's report for public consumption was to the effect that conditions were not suitable for commercial flying, his official report, it was learned, was of an altogether different tenor.

In Iceland, meanwhile, an Icelandic company, which had attempted to start a northern service with the German Lufthansa in 1928, ran into financial difficulties, and the undertaking was dropped in 1932. But when the American company sought a concession from Iceland, Lufthansa was quick to claim preferential rights under the early agreement by which it was supposed to have established domestic flying in Iceland. The concession went to the Americans, however, when the Icelandic Government notified Germany that in view of Lufthansa's abandonment of the Icelandic aviation company at a time when it needed funds, the early agreement was considered abrogated.

Pan American's first North Atlantic expedition was one maintained jointly with the University of Michigan in West Greenland in 1932–33. During the same period the company supported an expedition, organized by Watkins, which spent a year in East Greenland near Angmagssalik. Through the latter there was collaboration with the International Polar Year expeditions and the British Air Ministry, which came into the picture through Imperial Airways.

In 1933 Colonel Lindbergh surveyed the northern transatlantic route for Pan American. He flew over Labrador, Greenland, Baffin Island, Iceland, the Faeroes, the Shetlands, the Scandinavian countries, and the Soviet Union as far as Leningrad and Moscow, returning by way of Europe, northwestern Africa and South America. Commanding the steamer *Jelling*, which supported the Lindbergh flights in the Greenland area, Major Logan gathered many valuable data. He covered the coast of Labrador, the east coast of Greenland to Angmagssalik, and the crossing of the Denmark Strait to Iceland. Scientific observations were made on the possibilities of air bases in the entire area.

In its research on all conditions as they applied to northern transatlantic flying, Pan American contributed to the Rockwell Kent expedition, which spent the winter of 1934 in West Greenland at Igdloissuit; purchased the aviation reports of Knud Rasmussen, the Danish explorer; maintained Lieutenant Kurt Rudolf Ramberg, an aviator of the Royal Danish Navy, at Godthaab in West Greenland for a year of aviation study, and Flight Lieutenant Poul Jensen of the Royal Air Force of Denmark in the Scoresby Sound district of East Greenland for the same period in 1935–36. Paul C. Oscanyan,[3] meteorologist and radio technician, was employed to erect an observatory in Iceland in 1936 to study meteorological and radio conditions and other phenomena as they applied to flying.

For connecting links with northern Europe, Pan American began negotiations in 1936 with Bernt Balchen, who was then representing the Norwegian Det Norske Luftfartselskap. The negotiations developed in scope and complexity through the entrance of Danish, Swedish, Finnish, and Icelandic companies; and, tied up in the tangled international situation of the period, they continued down to the occupation of Norway by the Nazis.

That the northern steppingstone route was never flown commercially by Pan American after this long and expensive research was due not to any unfavorable conditions discovered in the area but to the international situation. Fortunately the true Great Circle course from New York via Newfoundland to Great Britain, which had a longer over-water hop, could be flown in 1935, thanks to the development of long-range aircraft.

As a consequence, after further comprehensive surveys of the Great Circle route to Great Britain and France by way of Canada, Newfoundland, and Ireland, and of a midatlantic route from New York via Bermuda, the Azores and Lisbon, Portugal, in 1937, Pan American instituted the first scheduled air-mail service over the Atlantic Ocean in the *Yankee Clipper* on May 20, 1939. By July of that year passengers and mail were being carried in both directions on regular weekly schedules. Just two months later the war in Europe made necessary some changes in the European terminals. The United States entered the war in 1941 and further air transport pioneering as a private enterprise was out of the question for the duration of the conflict.

New air routes which have been blazed since Pearl Harbor,

[3] Now Major in the U. S. Army Air Forces.

and the world-wide construction of air bases to serve them, naturally cannot be discussed. It is safe to assume, however, that the routes are many and that the Arctic and subarctic bases are spotted on Great Circle courses in so far as the fortunes of war have permitted to date. Nor can one do more than guess, inspired by the wartime accomplishments of Allied aircraft as released to the press, as to what extent wartime improvements in aircraft design and performance will influence postwar air transport. A discussion of the future, then, is limited by these factors to the realm of conjecture.

The following schedule of flights by the shortest routes from Washington, D.C.—which the Office of War Information said, in its recent report on Air Transport, would be possible after the war—gives one something to conjure with: 10 or 11 hours to Paris or London; 16 hours to Moscow or Istanbul; 18 hours to Cairo; 22 hours to Tokyo; 24 hours to Shanghai or New Delhi; 26 hours to Chungking or the Cape of Good Hope.

Under the heading of "Limiting Factors," however, the OWI had this to say: "On the air map, for example, the route from Chicago to Calcutta might ideally be across the Arctic Ocean and the North Pole. Such a route would be much shorter than the old shipping route via the Atlantic, the Mediterranean and the Indian Ocean. But the absence of navigation aids and refueling facilities along the way forms a serious deterrent. From time to time, round-the-world commercial air routes will probably bear some relation to populated areas. Certainly if a worldwide air transport system is to develop, gasoline tanks will have to be more thickly scattered around the world than at present. Gasoline is heavy. On long range flights the weight of a plane's fuel supply may well surpass the weight of its engines. And if a plane flies to an area which is without fuel reserves, fuel for its return flight has to be got there somehow."

This is a generalization by the OWI. Considered in the light of the airplane's accomplishments in the Arctic and what we can reasonably expect from war-inspired aviation developments, it only bears out the original premise that all the factors essential to the successful establishment of the Northwest and Northeast passages by air are falling into place.

To begin with, take the factors that can be expected to remain constant in spite of war or anything else men may do with the world. The earth, in the postwar world, will still be spherical. The shortest distances between the world's great population centers (New York, Detroit, Chicago, Minneapolis, Seattle, and San Francisco in the United States; Vancouver, Winnipeg, Montreal, Ottawa, Toronto, and Quebec in Canada; Vladivostok, Yakutsk, Irkutsk, Tokyo, Peiping, Chungking, Hong Kong, Singapore, Mandalay, and Calcutta in eastern and southern Asia; Teheran, Ankara, and Cairo in the Middle East; Moscow, Berlin, Warsaw, Paris, London, and Lisbon in Europe) will still be via Great Circle sailings northward by air.[4] The Arctic will still be the world's smallest ocean, with better steppingstones and better weather for flying than either the North Atlantic or the North Pacific, which already have been mastered.

As for the fuel problem, consider the prewar state of development in the Arctic holdings of the U.S.S.R., where fuel resources on the spot had already been tapped to supply local services. Spurred on by war necessity, Canada is developing its northern oil fields, and in conjunction with the United States is now engaged in the construction of a subarctic pipe line to bring oil from the Mackenzie River valley to Whitehorse in the Yukon; and Alaska has vast untapped oil reserves. The Mackenzie River oil can be floated down that stream to the Arctic mediterranean and distributed along the north coast of Canada and to the Canadian Arctic islands by the Hudson's Bay Company steamers, or other ships, that now ply the route.

Construction of new roads and railroads in Alaska, primarily as war measures, and fuller use of the north-flowing rivers of both the New and the Old World are simplifying the problem of supply. The OWI report itself stressed the fact that a vastly

[4] It is appreciated that the advantage of great-circle over true-direction flying (of spherical over flat-earth flying) is negligible for very short distances or very long ones. The saving becomes considerable when the distance rises above 2000 miles and ceases to be very material above 8000 to 9000 miles.

improved and extended system of air transport in Alaska was "the most striking development of American air transportation due to the war." Noting that operating certificates were granted in December, 1942, to twenty-one Alaska air carriers, authorizing charter trips to any point in Alaska, the report added that "Alaska has as fine a system of airways and airports as any section of the United States." Further government interest in the development of Alaska and northern Canada as a result of the war seems to be clearly indicated since events have proved that, in wartime in an age of flight, both attack and defense will involve the north.

As for navigational aids over the Arctic, Sir Hubert Wilkins and the Soviet flyers proved long ago that navigation was no insuperable problem without them. Nevertheless navigational aids now have been extended to Canada and to Alaska's northern borders. The OWI report notes that present-day aids in transoceanic flying, including the improved use of compasses and direction finders capable of picking up radio signals over a long distance, are extensive indeed as compared with facilities existing even as recently as the outbreak of the war. Our Federal Airways Service operates six intercontinental super-radio stations —at New York, New Orleans, San Francisco, Seattle, Honolulu, and Anchorage, Alaska—capable of communicating with aircraft at any point on the globe.

It is known that the Arctic region as a whole is well suited for flight. The stratosphere lies low over the roof of the world, and planes do not have to go so high to be out of reach of the weather over the transition areas of icing fogs. Technological improvements already are solving the problems of landing under adverse weather conditions. And it is safe to assume that commercial aircraft in the postwar world will be able to fly higher, faster, farther, with greater pay loads. Precisely how much higher, faster, and farther, we have no idea as yet. But even before the war Pan American had on its drawing board aircraft designed to cruise at 25,000 feet and carry a commercial pay load 5,000 miles without a stop.

Thus the improvement in aircraft eliminates to a great extent the need of island steppingstones in the transarctic airways of the future. The prime factor will be the traffic potential of the various routes that can be pioneered. Very likely the first transarctic connections will be between Moscow and Fairbanks, Alaska (a distance of only 4,050 miles), or between the Soviet Union and the continental United States with stops in the Dominion of Canada.

Of course the whole subject of international air transport in the postwar world is "up in the air" now, with parliaments, peoples, and private enterprises offering a varicty of views. The one point on which there is tacit agreement is that those aggressor nations which started this war will never again be given the opportunity to divert the airplane from its truly great task as a constructive force in world civilization.

Each of the major circumpolar nations has an important contribution to make to the transarctic airways of the future: the Soviet Union, its highly developed Arctic area; Canada, its position as a middle ground of world flight; the United States, its splendid aircraft, Alaskan air network and international transocean airways, and the air transport "know how" acquired through the kind of pioneering private enterprise that made the nation great.

Millions of people on all sides of the pole will be waiting for the aid air transport can give them in speeding the reconstruction of a war-torn world. If the democratic nations—and the individuals—cooperate in peacetime as they are now cooperating in war, the Northwest and Northeast passages will soon become accepted lines of air travel between the Old World and the New, and, at long last, men will take full advantage of the global earth on which they live.

21

Petroleum in the North

By Wallace E. Pratt

Wallace E. Pratt, born in Phillipsburg, Kansas; B.A., University of Kansas, 1907, B.Sc., 1908, M.A., 1909, Engr. of Mines in Geology, 1914; Member Executive Committee Standard Oil Co. (New Jersey) since 1937, Vice President of Standard Oil Co. since 1942.

Author: *Oil in the Earth* (1942), "Sermons in Stones," and numerous papers on petroleum geology, areal and applied geology, economic geology, and vulcanology.

Readers may be ill prepared to encounter a chapter on petroleum resources in a study on the Arctic. We have come generally to associate the origin of petroleum with abundant sunlight and teeming life. We think of the humid, equable climates of past geologic ages; of an incredibly prolific vegetation which flourished throughout eons of time over the great, swamplike lowlands of the earth's surface; and of myriad microscopic creatures which thronged the warm waters of the adjacent seas. This luxuriant former life on earth bequeathed to us our great stores of fossil fuels. The old forests left us their carbon; through countless cycles of life and death it accumulated beneath the waters of the swamps, there to be buried and gradually transformed into coal. Similarly, the organic parts of marine life, buried in the muds and sands of the sea floor, were preserved for us in the form of petroleum.

Our conception of the origin of petroleum then requires a tropical environment, quite irreconcilable with our present-day Arctic wastes, and it becomes difficult for us to realize that the great North may contain important natural reservoirs of petroleum. The difficulty is resolved immediately, however, when we remind ourselves that the earth's polar icecaps, the permanence

Note: The author gratefully acknowledges his indebtedness to his associates, Eugene Stebinger and Winthrop P. Haynes, for assistance in compiling the data brought together in this chapter, and to Vilhjalmur Stefansson for many references to manuscript and published notes by himself and others bearing on the occurrence of petroleum in the Far North.

of which we unconsciously take for granted, are in reality evanescent phenomena that have endured only for a relatively short period. In the two thousand million years through which we can peer dimly back in earth history, our present polar icecaps are discernible only over the last million years or so. For the greater part of geologic time plant and animal life alike have abounded in the polar regions. Fossil plants in the rocks of the island of Spitsbergen prove that in comparatively recent times, geologically speaking, tropical palms and ferns grew in profusion in latitude 80 degrees north. There are still plants in Spitsbergen, but where tropical forests grew twenty million years ago only a few stunted trees persist today and the hardiest of these (the Arctic willow) rarely exceeds a height of two inches.

To be sure, life still abounds in the polar regions. Birds, fish, and marine mammals thrive in both the Arctic and the Antarctic. Stefansson says that greater tonnages of animal life per cubic mile of ocean are to be found in the waters along the Arctic Circle than along the Equator. He points out that the great fisheries of Newfoundland are in the icy Labrador Current, not in the Gulf Stream, and that the richest ocean life known is among the drift ice that fringes the Antarctic Continent.

The fossil evidence in oil-bearing rocks, however, testifies to a source of oil in the remains of warm-water forms of plants and animals; and the fossils that characterize the rocks of the Northland were clearly buried in the muds of former seas, the waters of which were distinctly warm.

In the past, then, geological conditions were favorable to the generation of petroleum in the rocks of the Arctic region. And even a cursory search for petroleum in the North, such as we have already carried out, reveals widespread and unmistakable evidences of its presence there.

It is fortunate that the Far North is provided with potential stores of petroleum, because this resource will be indispensable to the development which appears to be in store for the region. The progress of civilization has been described as the slow march of humanity northward from all sides of an ever shrinking circle,

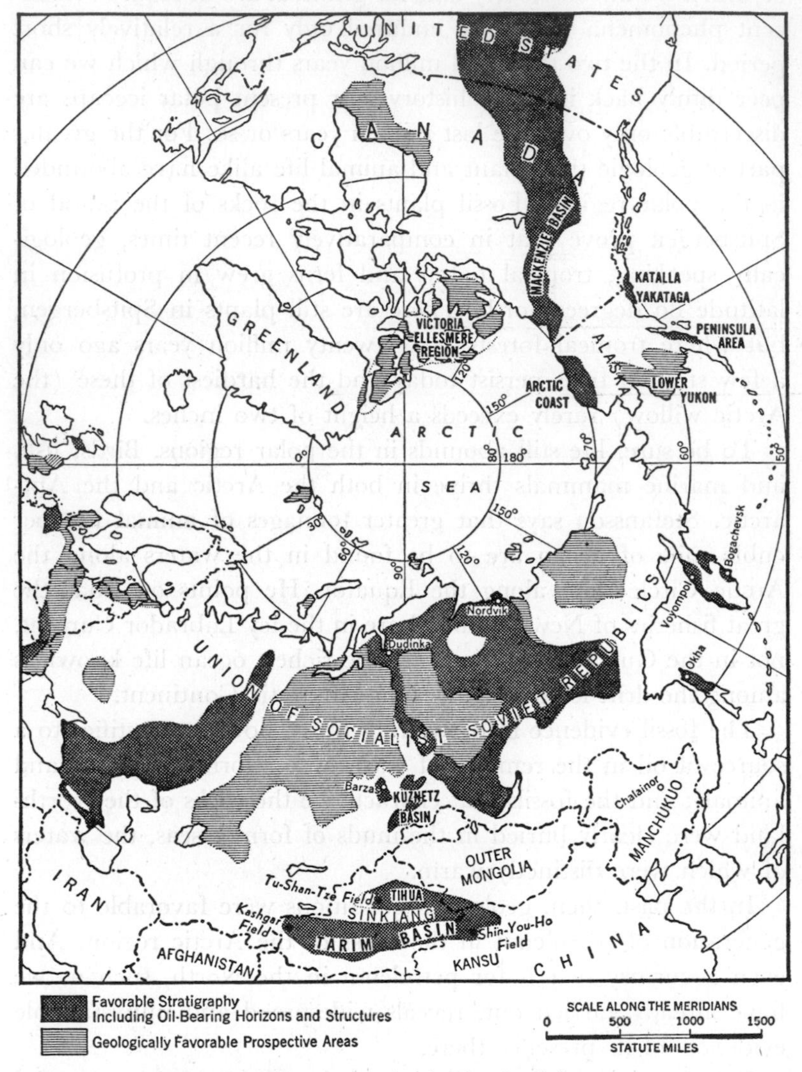

Favorable Stratigraphy Including Oil-Bearing Horizons and Structures

Geologically Favorable Prospective Areas

SCALE ALONG THE MERIDIANS
0 500 1000 1500
STATUTE MILES

FIG. 30. Oil prospects in the Arctic, July, 1943.

at the center of which is the North Pole. It is a curious circumstance, overlooked by most of us, that whereas no human being, no land mammal, and no flowering plant makes a permanent home in the south polar region (south of the sixtieth parallel of south latitude), yet in the corresponding area around the North Pole more than a million people, countless other land animals, and tremendous forests live and thrive. The pioneer explorers of the sixteenth century, persistent in their search for a "northwest passage," already realized that northward lay the shortest route from Europe to the Orient. The international commerce of the future promises so to depend on direct transport between the peoples of China, the Union of Socialist Soviet Republics, the British Commonwealth, and the United States as to make the north polar region the "crossroads of the world." For the fueling of the airplanes to be engaged in this essential traffic, indigenous sources of oil products throughout the area traversed by them should prove to be of great value.

From an area of 1,400,000 square miles in which petroleum may reasonably be expected, the United States has produced more than 60 per cent of the world's petroleum up to date. The Far North, by comparison, includes a land area (north of the sixtieth parallel) of 1,500,000 square miles which may also be described as favorable for petroleum.

Most of the land area of the north polar region in the Eastern Hemisphere lies within the borders of the Union of Socialist Soviet Republics; the most extensive exploration for petroleum in the north has been carried out by the Soviet Government. It is understandable, therefore, that the evidence accumulated so far indicates larger resources of petroleum in the Soviet domain than in the rest of the Far North. Soviet geologists have examined areas in Siberia north of the sixtieth parallel aggregating one million square miles, which they consider favorable for the occurrence of petroleum. In the Western Hemisphere our own geologists estimate at about one-half million square miles the land area north of the sixtieth parallel favorable for petroleum. Notwithstanding this disparity in area, some of the most important known prospects, including one of the oldest active oil fields in the Far North, are to be found in the Western Hemisphere.

The waters that surround the North Pole occupy a depression in the earth's surface which, although it may never have been of great depth, must have persisted throughout most of geologic time. These waters are properly to be thought of as a sea, rather than as an ocean. They are landlocked like the Mediterranean Sea and the region of the Gulf of Mexico and Caribbean Sea. It is of interest to reflect in this connection that the environs of these two mediterranean regions, the Caspian, Black, and Mediterranean seas in the Old World, and the Gulf of Mexico and Caribbean Sea in the New World, are the sources of by far the larger part of all the petroleum so far found on earth. It is in large part to their character as long-enduring mediterranean seas that these regions owe the great accumulations of petroleum we find in them. By its general character, therefore, the environs of the Arctic Sea become a likely prospect for the oil seeker. Almost continuously since a very early period in earth's history, muds and sands and rock debris have been washed into this sea by streams flowing over the weathered surface of the encircling land areas to the south of it; the great continental shields of primitive crystalline rocks that constitute all of eastern Canada in the Western Hemisphere, and all of Mongolia and Tibet in the Eastern Hemisphere. These old lands are the sources of the great accumulations of sediment that were laid down on the floor of the Arctic Sea.

The world's petroleum is found in rocks formed of the sediments deposited in former seas; the sediments of Cenozoic, of Mesozoic and of Paleozoic seas, named in the order of magnitude of their total yields of petroleum up to date. The Arctic Sea was loaded with sediments during each of these great cycles of earth history. The modern Arctic Sea, however, is only a shrunken remnant of its ancestral seas and much of the periphery of the former sea floor is now elevated above sea level.

The successive layers of sediment have hardened into the rocks which make up the encircling land areas. These rocks cover great areas, and the aggregate thickness of the series is very great. They are altogether promising source rocks for commercial accumulations of petroleum. But their promise is emphasized and made more tangible by the actual presence of petroleum and natural gas, which explorers have noted escaping from these rocks at many places in the Far North.

Alaska. One of the most impressive surface manifestations of petroleum in the Western Hemisphere is near Cape Simpson, east of Point Barrow, on the Arctic coast of northernmost Alaska. Surrounding this locality is a coastal plain and foothills region more than 60,000 square miles in area. It consists of gently folded Upper Cretaceous marine shales and sandstones exceeding 10,000 feet in aggregate thickness. Beneath this series of rocks lies the Lower Cretaceous, an equally promising series of shales and sandstones of similar thickness. Geologically, these conditions are ideal for important accumulations of petroleum. The striking character of the petroleum seepages near Cape Simpson is revealed in the following simple description:

Seepage No. 1 occurs near the inland base of this ridge. . . . Here in an irregular area several hundred feet in diameter the moss is soaked with petroleum which also slowly seeps from the gentle slope.

Seepage No. 2 is . . . 3 miles almost due south of Seepage No. 1. . . . Here the residue covers several acres.

The main petroleum flow moves southward down the slope for 600 or 700 feet to a lake. This active channel is 6 to 10 feet wide, though the area covered by residue is several hundred square feet and indicates that a considerable flow is coming from this seepage.[1]

The Point Barrow region has been reserved to the United States Navy over an area of 30,000 square miles, but no attempt at exploration has been made. This part of Alaska is open to ocean transportation only two or three months in the normal year. No good harbor is available. The country is icebound and

[1] U.S. Geological Survey, *Bull.* 772 (1925), "A Reconnaissance of the Point Barrow Region, Alaska," by Sidney Paige, W. T. Foran, and J. Gilluly, p. 23.

barren of timber. The unfavorable climate, the lack of marine transportation facilities, the isolation, and the bleak environment have discouraged development. For a navy that has been interested in petroleum principally as fuel for battleships, a reserve so icebound as to be inaccessible to the fleet for three-quarters of the time has had little appeal. With the impetus given aviation in Alaska by the present war, this attitude may change. Five hundred miles south of Point Barrow is Fairbanks, the inland metropolis of Alaska, which has become a great center of flying activity and a main base, both civil and military, for airplane maintenance and supplies including aviation fuel and lubricants.

The Point Barrow oil contains a valuable lubricating fraction and is low in sulphur, a common deleterious impurity in crude oil. Weathered samples show a gravity of 18.6 degrees, A.P.I., but the fresh oil might well be of lighter gravity. The operation of oil wells and a modern cracking plant at Point Barrow could be made largely independent of weather. Products such as aviation fuels could be moved southward by pipe line across the Endicott Range to Fairbanks despite ice and low temperature. The icebound Arctic coast is not an insuperable obstacle to the development of this promising prospect.

There are other areas in Alaska which merit exploration for petroleum. Extending north and northeastward from the deltas of the Yukon and Kuskokwim rivers over an area of 140,000 square miles are Cretaceous and Tertiary rocks of great thickness, gently folded and of a character favorable for the occurrence of petroleum. The sea at the mouth of the Kuskokwim River is free of ice throughout the year. No exploration for petroleum has been attempted in this promising region.

Another promising region is the Alaska Peninsula. Its accessible southern coast exhibits seepages of petroleum at Cold Bay and again 120 miles northeastward. The rocks of Alaska Peninsula are of Jurassic age. The oil from the seepages varies from 20 degrees to 30 degrees A.P.I. gravity. The possibly productive area is about 350 miles in length. Three successful test wells have been drilled on the peninsula ranging in depth between 5,000 and 8,775 feet. Obviously further exploration is justified in this region.

Still farther east along the southern coast of Alaska is the Katalla-Yakataga region. Extending eastward from the town of Cordova it has a length of 250 miles. Here the oil-bearing rocks are of Tertiary age with an aggregate thickness exceeding 10,000 feet. There are prominent seepages of petroleum along the entire length of their outcrop. Shallow wells at Katalla have a record of past production of about 300,000 barrels. This oil came from depths of 1,800 feet or less. Formerly, a local refinery operated at Katalla. The oil is about 40 degrees A.P.I. gravity, free from sulphur, and yields 35 per cent of naphtha.

Summarizing, it may be said of Alaska that whenever the development of its petroleum resources becomes worth while the enterprise may be undertaken with every anticipation of adding significantly to the volume of the proved oil reserves of the Western Hemisphere.

Canada. Near Fort Norman on the Mackenzie River, in latitude 65 degrees north, a small refinery has been producing gasoline and fuel oil for river boats, airplanes, and near-by mining operations for twenty years. The petroleum is obtained from an adjacent shallow oil field. Since the local demand for products is small, two or three wells have sufficed to supply all needs. Recently, however, a number of additional wells have been drilled under the stimulus of wartime planning, and these wells have proved the existence of a major oil field at Fort Norman, of first rank as a petroleum reserve. In connection with this development, pipe lines are planned to make the Fort Norman oil available at other strategic centers in the Far North.

The Fort Norman oil comes from a limestone of Devonian age through wells as deep as 2,000 feet; it is about 40 degrees A.P.I. gravity and yields a high proportion of gasoline on distillation. The first wells were drilled because of the pressure of oil and gas in the surface rocks near Fort Norman. Seepage Lake, only a few miles from the oil field, and Windy Point on the north shore of Great Slave Lake, are both celebrated for copious seepages of oil, long known to the Indians and early trappers in that region. The oil field lies in the heart of a sedimentary basin 160,000 square miles in area (north of the sixtieth parallel). Other important oil fields will almost certainly be found in this region whenever systematic search is undertaken.

The remainder of the mainland of Canada north of the sixtieth parallel, consisting of the old continental shield of crystalline rocks, is devoid of petroleum prospects. But the islands in the Arctic Ocean north of western Canada from Banks Island and Victoria Island on the southwest to Ellesmere Land and the Greenland coast on the northeast are geologically favorable for petroleum. These islands are scattered over a distance as great as that which separates the Gulf of Mexico from Lake Superior. They are composed of gently folded sedimentary rocks, rich in organic remains, ranging in age from Ordovician to Tertiary. In southern Ellesmere Land the Silurian and Devonian rocks alone attain a thickness of 8,000 feet. Coal is present in the Carboniferous, the Cretaceous, and again in the Tertiary. Stefansson reports seepages of petroleum along with outcrops of lignite on northern Melville Island, 500 miles north of the Arctic Circle. On the south coast of the same island he found bituminous shale which he burned for fuel. Though but little known, geologically this region is certainly suitable for petroleum accumulations; and the actual seepages of petroleum already observed by pioneer explorers confirm the geological evidence.

Greenland. Immediately to the eastward of Ellesmere Land lies the northern portion of Greenland. An icecap three-quarters of a million square miles in area and thousands of feet in thickness conceals the surface of this great island and denies us intimate knowledge of its geologic character. Presumably most of Greenland is unfavorable for petroleum; but its extreme northern end is not without promise. Here the rocks noted in Ellesmere Land can be identified and observed to maintain their same favorable character. Horizontal beds of Cambrian sandstones, free from deformation, present the same favorable aspect here that they do directly across the North Pole in Siberia where Soviet technologists are already recovering oil from them. Overlying the Cambrian is an extensive succession of rocks, Silurian, Carboniferous, Triassic, Jurassic, Cretaceous, and Tertiary. Coal at several horizons and abundant fossil plants in these rocks indicate warm climates which persisted until Tertiary times.

Siberia. The million square miles of territory in Siberia designated as favorable for petroleum by Soviet scientists stretches from the Ural Mountains eastward nearly 3,000 miles to the Sea of Okhotsk. Over this region many seepages of petroleum have been discovered and investigated; a large number of test wells have been drilled. Guided by exhaustive geological and geophysical surveys, this exploration has been under way since 1934. The results of the work are not generally available, but it is stated that some half-dozen regions have been outlined in which the presence of petroleum has been demonstrated in rocks of various ages: Cambrian, Devonian, Jurassic, Cretaceous, and Tertiary. This energetic search by the Soviets for petroleum in the Far North serves to emphasize the significance they accord to the Northland. Already in possession outside the Arctic regions of the largest potential resources of petroleum on earth, these people show more awareness than the rest of us of the future that beckons from the North and prepare to take advantage of it.

In looking at the petroleum resources of the Soviets in the Far North we cannot limit our view to Siberia. West of the Ural Mountains lies other favorable territory which in its extension to the south of the sixtieth parallel is already producing petroleum. And across the Urals in Siberia proper the areas favorable for petroleum also extend far to the south of the sixtieth parallel. From our discussion of the Far North, however, these extensions to the south are excluded, as are also the promising indications on Kamchatka Peninsula and the producing fields on Sakhalin Island. Excluded also are the Kuznetsk District and the Lake

Baikal area in southern Siberia, in both of which successful exploration for petroleum is reported.

Returning to the Far North in Siberia, we find petroleum coming to the surface along the estuary of the Yenisei River in latitude 70 degrees north. As a result of these showings, which persist from Dudinsk southward to Turukhansk, a distance of some 300 miles, a number of wells have been drilled.

Six hundred miles farther east along the Arctic coast near Nordvik on Khatanga Bay, there are numerous seepages of petroleum. A test well has been drilled here which encountered petroleum at successive depths in Cretaceous, Jurassic, and Devonian rocks. This is a region characterized by the presence beneath the surface of "salt domes"—remarkable intrusions of plastic salt which force themselves upward through the earth's crust from great depth and form ideal reservoirs for the accumulation of petroleum. Salt domes also distinguish our own most prolific source of petroleum, the coastal plain fringing the Gulf of Mexico.

A thousand miles still farther east along the Arctic coast, in the Yukahirs district, Soviet geologists have outlined an area of some 300,000 square miles which they consider promising for petroleum. We know little of the basis for this opinion, but it is readily acceptable in view of the extensive evidence of petroleum throughout the Lena River drainage system to the south and southeast. It is said that "oil has been found for a thousand miles along the Tolba," a headwaters tributary of the Lena River. Here the oil is found in Lower Cambrian rocks, only slightly deformed. Wells have been drilled along the Maya River in the eastern part of the district within 200 miles of the Sea of Okhotsk, and again in the Olekminsk district 600 miles to the west of the Sea of Okhotsk. The wells flow copiously, and the whole region, which includes an area of more than 3,000 square miles, is believed to have great potentialities.

Petroleum products from this region could be readily transported by pipe line to a Pacific Ocean outlet on the Sea of Okhtosk to the east as well as to the northern branch of the

Trans-Siberian Railway 450 miles to the south. Eastern Siberia, therefore, like much of the rest of the Far North, appears to be provided with resources of liquid fuel and lubricants adequate to support a greatly expanded future industrial economy.

Oil in the Arctic awaits the advance of civilization upon this, the last of our geographical frontiers. Conspicuous evidences of petroleum confront us throughout this region: prolific seepages in the rocks of Alaska; other seepages and a major oil field on the mainland of Canada; seepages on various Canadian Arctic islands; seepages and oil wells at frequent intervals along the entire Arctic Coast of Siberia. But only the forward-looking Soviet Union has so far made use of these potential sources of fuel and energy. Perhaps the rest of us have yet to grasp the fact that the Great Ice Age is already behind us. We escaped its extreme advance at the end of the Pleistocene only by "The Skin of Our Teeth," according to Thornton Wilder's colorful drama, but now at length we should have pulled ourselves together sufficiently to begin to follow up its retreat and to reclaim for mankind the vast empire released to us by the return of the sun to the "friendly Arctic."

22

The Soviet Arctic and the Future

By Ernest C. Ropes

Ernest C. Ropes, born in Brooklyn, N. Y. Educated in St. Petersburg, Russia, and Brooklyn. B.A., Columbia, 1899. Y.M.C.A. secretary in northern Russia and Estonia, 1919–1922. Since 1925, Russia specialist, Bureau of Foreign and Domestic Commerce.

Author of numerous articles on the U.S.S.R.; editor, *Russian Economic Notes,* 1929–1940.

In any discussion of American future policies in relation to other countries of the world, considerable importance must be given to the development of the newer, less known regions, both of the United States and of countries in Europe and Asia. Among these so far comparatively uncharted and unexplored sections, none is so conspicuous as the shore of the Polar Sea from the North Cape east to the Bering Strait, and from Alaska to Baffin Bay.

Aside from its geographical preeminence as the shortest airline route possible from the United States to Europe, either westward or eastward, the Arctic littoral seems, at first glance, to have few attractions, because of the short summers, the long, dark, cold winters, and the generally inhospitable aspects of the narrow strip above the Arctic Circle from the standpoint of human habitation. But in the past ten or twelve years the Soviet government has proved conclusively that this barren strip is well supplied with mineral and other natural riches, waiting development, and that the Arctic Ocean can be regarded as a safe highway for ships, connecting the northern parts of European U.S.S.R. with the mouths of the mighty Siberian rivers, and these in turn with the Pacific ports of the Soviet Union.

The following short study of the Great Northern Sea Route and of the development of the Asiatic and European Arctic littoral may well contain lessons from which both Americans and

Canadians can profit in the next great steps in the growth of the two countries—the investigation and exploitation of their own Arctic shores.

Arctic Exploration Before the Revolution. Perhaps the first event that foreshadowed the possible use of the Arctic Ocean as a water highway between Russia and other parts of the world was the trip of Captain Richard Chancellor in 1553 around the North Cape and the Kola peninsula into the White Sea. While this pioneer voyage resulted in the establishment of Archangel as one of the world's largest export lumber and timber ports, nothing was done in the way of systematic exploration of the Arctic Ocean east of the White Sea until 1915. In that year a joint English and Russian effort was made to sail freight steamers to the mouth of the Yenisei River in Siberia, and to build up a regular exchange of Siberian timber, grain, and furs for manufactured products from European Russia and England. A few trial trips established a feasible route, the Kara Sea route, running between the Novaya Zemlya and Vaigach islands, and then to the mouths of the Ob and Yenisei rivers. Farther trips to the mouths of the Khatanga, Lena, and other rivers of eastern Siberia proved too dangerous, because of fog and floating ice even in the middle of summer, and no serious attempt was made to approach these rivers from the east, the dangers to shipping increasing as one approached the Bering Strait.

During World War I, repeated attempts were made to utilize the Kara Sea route, to supplement goods traffic between the United States and England, and the Russian port of Archangel and later Murmansk. But these attempts remained spasmodic and ineffectual, although they further demonstrated the feasibility of the new highway, if only facilities could be provided for safeguarding the vessels that hazarded the trip.

First Soviet Exploration. One of the first major undertakings of the Soviet government, after the reconstruction period was over, was scientific exploration of the possibilities of converting the Kara Sea route and the stretch of Arctic littoral east to Bering Strait from a dangerous, undependable route for ocean traffic, into a safe, protected, and reliable highway along which, for two months or more a year, freight could be shipped in either direction, from end to end of the 3,000-mile haul, or from intermediate ports east or west. In about ten years this huge problem has been practically solved; a permanent government agency, the Chief Administration of the Northern Sea Route (Glavsevmorput, or G.S.M.P.) has been set up, amply financed, clothed with all necessary authority, manned by devoted scientists and technicians, and supplied with icebreakers and auxiliary craft, and planes, as required. The details of the work of this agency, and its prospects for development, form the subject of the following sections of this article.

The Glavsevmorput. When the development of the Arctic regions, and of the Great Northern Sea route, was adopted as a permanent policy, it became obvious that a specific Soviet organization must be set up, with ample authority, funds, and man power to solve the many problems sure to arise. The agency created was the Glavsevmorput, in the form of a typical Chief Administration, covering not only an enormous stretch of territory, but also all the varied activities involved. The basic purpose was, of course, to transform the dangerous water route into a safe path for ships. Previous attempts had demonstrated that the chief obstacle limiting ship movement was ignorance—ignorance of geography, winds, tides, fogs, ice conditions, and shore topography. For this reason the first ten years were devoted to clearing up this "white spot" hitherto uncharted, and providing facilities by means of which ship convoys could plan their movement ahead and always be sure in advance of what weather and ice conditions they would have to meet.

A first condition of systematic sea travel was the provision of icebreakers, to lead the way through pack ice or ice fields, likely to occur even in summer. A second was the provision of adequate weather stations on either the mainland or some large island, equipped with permanent crews, technicians, instruments, and radio apparatus, to gather and send out data on ice and storm conditions, for the guidance of convoys. And a third, the most difficult but in some respects the most important factor for safe shipping, was the provision of airplane service, for study of actual weather conditions, the transport of personnel and freight, and numerous other purposes.

The period from 1928 to 1938 was marked by slow but steady progress in all the above fields of activity, and increase in the facilities available. The only serious failure, from the maritime standpoint, was in 1937, when through faulty forecasting, twenty-five ships, including icebreakers, were caught in the ice and forced to winter. One earlier loss of a large icebreaker, the *Cheliuskin*, in 1933 was also reported; but all on board were rescued by airplane.

It was after the second mishap that the Soviet government took stock of the whole Arctic enterprise, and reorganized the Glavsevmorput from the ground up. While recognizing its success in many fields, an auditing commission pointed out many defects in its operation, mainly due to overextension, to attempting too much too quickly, to failure to integrate and balance efforts in the multifarious fields of work into which enthusiasts had diverted their energies. A redefinition of the primary goal of the G.S.M.P., the conversion of the Northern Sea Route into a safe transport route, made other phases of its work subsidiary, and concentrated attention on things of greatest importance, leaving strictly industrial, cultural, or scientific work to other agencies. These other fields, however, are also of great importance, and were not left undeveloped.

The reorganization of the G.S.M.P. stretched over two years, but did not halt the upward movement in the Arctic. From a record published in July, 1938, which summarizes ten years' achievement in convincing terms I quote a few figures illustrative of Arctic development:

Freighter convoy trips east to west or vice versa: 1935, 4; 1936, 14.

Number of ships participating in trips: 1933, 42; 1934, 59; 1935, 60; 1936, 64.

Tonnage of freight carried (metric tons): 1933, 136,000; 1934, 156,300; 1935, 230,600; 1936, 275,300; 1939, 500,000.

Number of permanent polar stations: 1937, 56.

Airplane flights to study and report weather conditions: 1932, 512 hours; 1937, 16,000 hours.

Main ports established: Dickson Island, Tiksi Bay, Provideniye (Providence) Bay.

It was in the last years before the German-Russian war began that the G.S.M.P. reached maturity as a successful pioneering agency, and the results of its work and of the huge government expenditures (100,000,000 rubles in five years on geological exploration alone) really became evident. As a result of the reorganization mentioned, attention was concentrated on problems directly affecting the safety, operation, and supply of the ships using the Northern route. In the first category was the adequate provision of meteorological information, collected and distributed in 1937 by fifty-six polar stations, covering almost the entire distance from Murmansk to Bering Strait; since then, ten are said to have been added. One of these stations, on Dickson Island, has a permanent personnel of two hundred, and conditions have been provided to make life comfortable in any weather, including an ample supply of electric current, produced by windmills, for heat, light, and power. Domestic animals have even been raised and kept at some of these stations. Supplementing radio is the systematic airplane service, already referred to. Weather and ice forecasts can now be made in general terms several months ahead, and local conditions near a station can be accurately forecast for shorter periods.

The problem of operating vessels in the Arctic involved the choice and development of ports, and the provision of bunkering and repair facilities. While much has been accomplished in all three fields, there is still, as can readily be imagined, work for years to come before all the elaborate plans are realized. In

1938, for example, the port at Dickson could accommodate but one ship at a time; Tiksi Bay had no wharf, and lighters were necessary to transship cargo; and at Provideniye, while boats could lie close to shore to unload, storehouses were nonexistent. Repair facilities for ships using the route were inadequate in 1938 also, although plans had been made for a chain of yards.

The prospects for establishing a series of coal bunkering stations along the Arctic littoral were excellent in 1938, but here too performance had been slower than was hoped. Spitsbergen coal of high quality, from Soviet-owned mines on that island, was the only reliable fuel supply, and had to be delivered to Dickson and Tiksi during the short navigation season of two and one-half months. But coal, of varying quality, had been discovered at various points on the Arctic shore, near Dickson, and at Ugolnaya Bay in the Anadyr Gulf, that promised well for the future; while coal and oil from the Pechora field could be delivered to Naryan Mar by river barge, until a railroad along the Pechora River was built. The fuel problem was evidently, in 1938, one that could be solved in due course.

In fact, in 1939 the navigation season was so successful in moving freight and passengers along the Great Northern Sea Route that ambitious plans were made, and published in July, 1940, for the 1940 season. All the shortcomings referred to were considered, and measures provided to improve port conditions. The first eastward cargoes were to include conveyors, cranes, and other port machinery for immediate installation. The mining and shipping of coal from the Norilsk (Yenisei River) and Sangara (Lena River) mines had already started, and the maintaining of bunker stocks at Dickson and Tiksi. While no report has been published of the operations of the Glavsevmorput in 1940, it is evident that progress was made in all fields of activity, giving encouragement to even greater hopes for the future. Further expansion of plans was indicated by an announcement in January, 1940, of the intention of maintaining winter connections by air between Igarka and Dickson, and Yakutsk and Tiksi Bay. In February a new air service was to be opened from Moscow to Archangel, thence to Igarka, Tiksi, and Anadyr; four-motor planes were scheduled to carry passengers, mail, and freight at regular intervals.

The Rivers of Arctic U.S.S.R. It was curiosity about the possibility of charting a short route by sea from the ports of the White Sea to the mouths of the great Siberian rivers that led to the discovery of the Kara Sea route; and one of the most important duties of the Glavsevmorput has always been to survey these rivers, construct ports in their deltas or at favorable points along their shores, and develop river steamer and barge traffic inland to a junction with the railroads. The westernmost of these rivers is the Ob, which with its tributary the Irtysh, is navigable for boats of considerable size for 3,286 miles. The Yenisei, including the Angara and Selenga, totals 3,224 miles. Farther east is the Lena—6,250 miles of navigable water, counting the Aldan, Vilui, and other tributaries. These were well known and much traveled before the Revolution; but Soviet energy has added to their facilities, and has built ports where Arctic ships can call. There have also been added to the useful list a number of smaller rivers, from 900 to 1,250 miles long, such as the Piassina, Olenek, Yana, Indigirka, Khatanga, Anabar, Anadyr, and Kolyma—the last one valuable as a route to and from the new placer gold fields. With specially built boats and barges, the traffic on these waterways has been between the districts where timber is cut and rafted, and coal mined, and the Arctic ports where these and other products of the territory bisected are shipped, for either foreign or domestic use. Even in winter, the frozen surface of the rivers is traversed by aero sleds, driven by an air propeller, delivering mail, freight, and important passengers to the isolated Arctic towns and settlements. In addition to these newer developments, the Northern Dvina, Onega, and Mezen, emptying into the White Sea, are important, while the Pechora, east of these, carries coal north to bunker the Arctic ships. In time a railroad will deliver Pechora coal and oil to the new town of Kara, on the Baidaratsk Bay, starting from Kotlas, already connected with the Soviet rail network.

Arctic Ports. As suggested above, Soviet plans for the utilization of the rivers flowing into the Arctic included the construction of numerous ports along the Arctic littoral or on the rivers. While many of these plans are still far from completion, in some places considerable progress has been made. For instance, the port of Murmansk, dating from the First World War, has been greatly expanded, and the wharves along the Murman shore can accommodate six average-size ships simultaneously, while the bay has anchorage for any number of vessels. It is also a trawler base for the extensive fishing industry developed during the Second Five Year Plan, later referred to. Recently two other smaller ports were established, one on Kola Bay, called Polyarnoye, and another above Murmansk, named Kola. No details concerning these are available.

The old port of Archangel in the Dvina delta, for two hundred years the chief shipping point of Russian export timber and lumber, has also been modernized, and is now kept open by icebreakers in all but a few months of the year. It has docks accommodating seven average ships, and some up-to-date lumber-handling equipment. West of Archangel on the southern shore of the White Sea, a new port, called Molotovsk, has been built. It has room for three ships at its wharves, but as yet no railroad connection with the line to Archangel.

Mezen and Naryan-Mar, at the mouths of the Mezen and Pechora rivers, are marked as "ports of call" although, as previously stated, coal from the Pechora field is shipped from the latter, which will probably be a bunkering station, supplying both coal and oil, in due time. Similarly, Amderma, at the eastern end of the Yugorski Shar (Strait) is hardly yet developed, though it will be the shipping point for fluorspar and other minerals found in the vicinity. The same may be said of Novy Port, at the mouth of the Ob River, and Salekhard, up that river:

their growth awaits the rail connection with Kotlas mentioned.

Dickson Island, however, has already taken its place as the chief coal-bunkering port on the Kara Sea route. Facilities for storing and handling coal are already provided, and a deposit on the near-by mainland will later supplement Spitsbergen and Pechora as sources of fuel.

Dickson lies off the mouth of the Yenisei River, which forms a wide gulf. Going upstream there are first Ust-Port and Dudinka, the latter a shipping point for minerals and ores from deposits at Norilsk. The chief Yenisei port, however, is Igarka, 420 miles from the mouth, where over fifteen years ago a small fishing village was transformed into an extensive lumber port, to which Siberian timber is rafted for working up and shipping. A permanent rock-filled quay for seven vessels was completed in 1936. Besides lumber mills Igarka has an experimental farm, fur farms, and other factories. The population has passed the 20,000 mark; it is the most active town in the new Soviet Arctic.

Another port of great promise is Nordvik, at the mouth of the Khatanga River. This point is notable for a huge deposit of rock salt, recently discovered, with inexhaustible reserves, which are counted upon to supply the Far Eastern fisheries indefinitely with cheap salt. Here also are deposits of coal, and possibly oil and metals, awaiting investigation and exploitation. Meanwhile cargoes of salt are loaded and sent eastward.

Farther east, on one of the many arms of the delta of the Lena River, is Tiksi, the most important of all Arctic ports because of its enormous "hinterland," the republic of Yakutia, for which the Lena and a few smaller rivers provide the only means of transport between north and south. For generations these rivers proved adequate because the only important industry, gold mining, was centered in the south, not too far from the Trans-Siberian Railroad, and the sparse population did little traveling. But the discovery of new gold fields as far north as the Arctic shore, and of coal along the Lena River, has stimulated the growth of the republic, and has brought about the construction of highways throughout the area. This movement resulted also in the port of Ambarchik, at the mouth of the Kolyma River, where a particularly rich placer gold deposit was found; an all-weather highway runs from Nagayevo, on the Okhotsk Sea, at least as far as Verkhne Kolymsk, and perhaps farther, connecting the whole Kolyma area with Okhotsk.

A small port named Pevek is the only one remaining on the Arctic proper. But around Capes Wellen and Chaplin is the port of Provideniye Bay, one of the three most important points on the Arctic route, serving the whole Chukotsk peninsula as a center of distribution by road. It now has modern freight and coal handling facilities, with twelve conveyors, and oil storage tanks, as well as a sawmill and brickyard. South of Provideniye is the port of Anadyr, at the mouth of the river of the same name. It is also a distributing center for a large area.

Little information is available on the port, road, and airfield developments on the shores of the Okhotsk Sea and on Kamchatka peninsula. These areas are hardly a part of the Great Northern Route; but they key into the work of the Glavsevmorput, and form a valuable extension of the activities of that organization.

Natural Resources of the Soviet Arctic. A very important and rewarding part of the Soviet effort to develop the Arctic regions has been prospecting for deposits of minerals and metals along or near the shores of the Arctic Ocean. Systematic work of this description began in 1934 under the All-Union Institute, set up under the Academy of Sciences to investigate, by land, sea, or from the air, deposits that might be worked for the benefit of the Arctic industry of the future, or consumers thousands of miles away. This work has been continued each year since, and in 1941, thirteen expeditions, including 2,000 members, were engaged.

Even before 1934, the apatite resources of the Kola peninsula had been mapped, and large-scale exploitation of the inexhaustible reserves of apatite and nephelite, both rich in phosphates, and used in huge quantities as fertilizers and in industry, had begun. Since then other minerals and metals have been unearthed in this vicinity, the only spot in the Arctic where hydroelectric power is as yet available (Niva and Tuloma rivers). The town of Kirovsk has arisen, to process apatite ores; Monchegorsk has been created near the new nickel and copper "combine"; and other cities will probably grow up along the Murmansk railroad as the deposits of iron, titanium, mica, molybdenum, etc., are developed.

Development of the coal and oil fields of the Pechora River district, known before 1917, took place only under the Soviet regime. No estimate can be made of production; but the fields are believed to be rich.

As has been pointed out, Archangel has for many years exported huge quantities of timber and lumber. Igarka is now a close second in the cutting and shipment of the inexhaustible forest products of the Soviet North. The forests stretch from the Finnish frontier to the Pacific Ocean, varying only in species and height, according to the contour of the district and the climate. In the European districts conifers predominate; in the Asiatic, larch occupies a prominent place, though cedar, pine, and spruce are also important. The U.S.S.R. is estimated to have a forested area of 1,407,000,000 acres, over one-fifth of the wooded area of the world. Under controlled lumbering, there will always be an abundant supply of wood, both for domestic needs and for export; and the larger part will be provided by the Asiatic forests, hardly yet surveyed, except from the air. The arduous and expensive work of opening the Kara Sea and Arctic Ocean to regular, safe commercial sea traffic is perhaps justified by the single result already accomplished, the making accessible of the timber resources of the Far North, probably the only virgin forest area in the world.

But Soviet planners have not been satisfied with access to the known inland resources, such as apatite and timber: they have also, as suggested, searched inland and along the coast for deposits of metals and minerals of industrial importance. By 1935 they had located fifteen hundred of these, though only two to three hundred were proved. Two of the most important are the reserves of magnetic iron quartzite at Kovdozero near Kola Bay, and the iron-ore deposits near Vorkuta, on the new railroad from Kotlas. Development of these depends on the provision of transport.

The program for 1941 included work on coal deposits opposite Dickson Island and at Ugolnaya Bay, of the Chukotsk peninsula, and drilling for oil and gas at the mouth of the Yenisei River. The presence of extensive coal fields always suggests the possibility of oil strata at greater depths, and Soviet geologists count on tapping the pools of petroleum more than suspected to exist at certain points on the Arctic shore, and even on Novaya Zemlya.

Space does not permit more than a catalogue of the metals and minerals [1] discovered by the Arctic Institute, and the places listed for immediate or early development. The anthracite coal deposits at Nordvik, and the bituminous at Sakhalin, Ugolnaya, the Yenisei, Dudinka, Bulun on the Lena, and Zyrianka and Nizhne-Kolymsk on the Kolyma, all fall into the category of "first things" for prompt exploitation. The huge salt mines at Nordvik and the fluorspar mines at Amderma, though the ore from the latter is more expensive delivered than that found in the Pamir mountains, because of present lack of concentrating plant, are both producing, at a constantly rising rate. Tin has been discovered on the Yana River near Verkhoyansk in Yakutia, and on the Chukotsk peninsula near Anadyr. Nickel deposits have been discovered at Norilsk and on Chukotsk, while the new copper-nickel "combine" at Monchegorsk has been producing for several years. Zinc reserves have been located at four places in the Arctic; lead, in one. The old graphite mines at Kureika, south of Igarka, are being intensively worked, and copper is being mined at Norilsk. Tungsten and molybdenum deposits have been found, but no record of their development has ap-

[1] Cf. the article following, "Siberia's Role in Soviet Strategy," by George B. Cressey.

peared; nor of new silver finds on the Lena, nor of the gold fields of the Kolyma River; though the last are known to be very rich, and are being worked.

Agriculture in the Arctic. While agriculture and the Arctic appear to be antitheses, Soviet scientists and agronomists have scored surprising success in adapting truck gardening and even grain growing to the adverse conditions presented by long winters with low temperatures, short, hot summers, and ground that never thaws more than a few feet down. Beginning with hothouse vegetables under glass, they have progressed to vegetable and root crops in cold frames and the open ground, and finally, in selected spots on the Yamal and Chukotsk peninsulas, and in Yakutia, to grain ripened in the open. The Igarka experiment station is now most active in selection and acclimatization of crops, as is also the station at Naryan-Mar, at the mouth of the Pechora. Drainage and use of heavy agricultural machinery have converted bogs into fertile land. Even apple and pear orchards, of dwarf type, are growing north of the Arctic Circle.

The raising of pure-bred cattle at Kholmogory, near Archangel, which started before the Revolution, has expanded since. Gradually, it is hoped, all northern settlements will have their own herds of cows and pigs.

Reindeer raising, long practiced by the Saami and Chukchi peoples, has become a federal industry, with collectivized herds financed by the government, and breeders and veterinaries trained at a station at Igarka. Herds had increased to 2,000,000 head by 1940, and breeding was being extended all along the Arctic littoral.

Reindeer skins supplement the large output of fur skins, for which the Russian north has always been famous. The numbers of native fur-bearing animals are supplemented by those raised on farms: a sable farm at Pechora, polar fox, and ermine farms on islands in the Arctic Ocean, and beaver farms in Lapland, are examples of this growing new industry.

Fishing in the Arctic Waters. Fishing in the Arctic—not counting Kamchatka—was limited to the catches in the White Sea, which supplied the northwest provinces. Soviet development of the northern fisheries since the thirties has been very active, and Murmansk has become the home port for a large steam-trawler fleet, while shore stations, mechanized, motor-boat fleets, and canneries are in operation, and multiplied rapidly until the outbreak of war. Between 1929 and 1934 the catch in northern waters rose from 44,700 metric tons to 267,400 (or six times), while the total Union catch increased only from 956,400 tons to 1,303,000 tons. Until the war threw the responsibility for supplying the country with fish on the fisheries in the Pacific and the Caspian Sea, the proportion supplied by the Arctic continued to rise; in the future peace its share may again be large.

Education of the Peoples of the Far North. Space does not permit an enumeration and description of the small nationalities that have inhabited the Arctic shores for many generations, many of them shrinking steadily in numbers under pressure of cold, underfeeding, and disease. For these peoples the nationality policy of the Soviet government has been described as a lifesaver: they have been rescued from poverty, taught, and given an opportunity to work; industries have been built up in their native areas, and they have been given facilities to educate themselves up to a level with the other inhabitants of the U.S.S.R.

The Institute of the Peoples of the North, founded in 1926, has followed the ingenious system of bringing promising young men and women from their far-off homes, and supporting and training them in practical ways of living and working, under their home conditions. These selected young people were then sent back, to become leaders in their own communities. As industrial development spreads, the natives will be further trained to become miners, chemists, and other kinds of workers in the new plants that are growing up, and will also learn the latest scientific agricultural methods found to be suitable. Nor is the cultural side neglected: while in many cases it was necessary to create a written language, because of the absence of an alphabet for their tongues, they are being encouraged to preserve their folklore and native music, and to take part in dramatic reproduction of their life and history. There are also traveling motion-picture theaters, which show Soviet films and establish a connection between the outlying settlements and Soviet centers in the South. Radio broadcasting stations cover the Far North, and loud-speakers are placed in every village and clubhouse, through which decrees, news, and propaganda are distributed direct from Moscow.

The constitutional right to "universal, compulsory elementary education" is possessed by every citizen in the U.S.S.R., and is gradually being implemented by schools dotting the Far Northern area. Chukchi, Nenetsy, Evenki, and other tribes are fast learning their rights, and their duties, as Soviet citizens, and abandoning the rude ways and superstitions of their forefathers.

Soviet Plans for the Arctic. The Soviet government controls a planned economy, and it may be stated without qualification that, without careful planning, the developments briefly described in this article would not, probably could not, have occurred. That there is still a great discrepancy between plans and execution is understandable: the Arctic, while an area of immense possibilities, cannot be conquered quickly or by mere enthusiasm. Trial and error is often the only method of learning the successful way to attack a problem, and Soviet developers have made many of both. But enough is now known about the vagaries of the Far North to justify a few predictions, and the last two five-year plans have established a firm basis for the fourth, which will doubtless get under way as soon as the cessation of hostilities becomes predictable.

It may be said that the basic purpose of the Glavsevmorput—to make of the Kara Sea and the Eastern Arctic a reasonably safe, charted, and inexpensive sea route, from northern ports in European U.S.S.R. to the ports, old and new, along the Arctic littoral, and beyond, through the Bering Strait to Soviet Pacific ports, and even to the United States, Canada, and Mexico—has been accomplished, at least in its general outlines. With the aids to navigation already provided, ships have for several years sailed for long and short trips, with increasing safety and regularity, and decreasing freight and insurance rates. The most important ports are well equipped, and the subsidiary ones are handling constantly larger quantities of freight. New and more powerful icebreakers have been placed in service, and many new river boats have been built.

It is certain that the Soviet government will resume, after the war, its large appropriations for maritime, scientific, and exploratory work in the Arctic, and will continue the industrial development already so well started. The problem of internal transport, by river, highway, and later by railroad, will undoubtedly take many years to solve, although it is possible that with war-prisoner labor much can be accomplished in the last two categories before the war ends. There are already reports of a railroad completed south from Yakutsk to the Trans-Siberian Railroad, cutting the new Baikal-Amur trunk road, the latter believed by some to be in operation. As a beginning of the first north-south line from the interior of Asiatic U.S.S.R. to the Arctic, this road can be regarded as a forerunner of other lines, both north and south, and east and west, in the area north of the Arctic Circle, stimulating more rapid colonization, and development of the mineral resources, of this whole strip of northern Asia. The war has focused the attention of the Russian people on the Asiatic portion of their vast country. It may confidently be predicted that the pioneering spirit which has inspired the work already done in the Arctic will continue, and spread, stimulating other countries possessed of an Arctic shore line to seek within their own boundaries similar opportunities for development, and providing these countries with bases for air and water transport as important as those already discovered and utilized are to the Soviet Union.

23

Siberia's Role in Soviet Strategy

By George B. Cressey

George B. Cressey, born in Tiffin, Ohio. B.S., Denison, 1919; Ph.D. in Geology, University of Chicago, 1923, and in Geography, Clark, 1931. He has traveled widely in Asia and in the Soviet Union and has served as consultant to the governments of China (1943) and the U.S.S.R. (1937). Since 1931, he has been chairman of the Department of Geology and Geography at Syracuse University. Author, *China's Geographic Foundations* (1934), *Asia's Lands and Peoples* (1944), and of numerous other studies on Asia.

Some of the material used in this essay was originally published in the *Journal of Geography*, 1942, pp. 81–88.

When we come to look back on the strategy of the Second World War, few areas will assume the importance which belongs to Siberia. Not that fighting occurred there; rather that it did not reach the heart of Eurasia.

If Germany had been able to conquer the Soviet Union, England might have been unable to resist, and the United States would have faced the World Island alone. But the Union of Socialist Soviet Republics did not collapse. Her great size made it possible for her to sell space with which to gain time; it gave her defense in depth which is the most valuable of all strategic assets. Space alone is of little avail unless it has productive possibilities. No large army could withdraw into Mongolia and remain effective. Fortunately Siberia has both resources and industries.

As we relearn the geography of our global world, it is well to view the Union of Socialist Soviet Republics with adequate perspective. Here is a nation as big as all of North America. Since 1928 it has been in the midst of a virile economic expansion which is creating a major industrial state.

Could the Soviet Union have defeated Germany alone? Probably not, but without the U.S.S.R., Britain and the United States might have found the job insuperable. Had the Soviets collapsed, Germany and Japan would have had access to each other and to the resources of northern Eurasia. Much depended on the capacity of the Soviet Union to carry on effective production, and this in turn rested on geological and geographical considerations. What is Siberia's role in Soviet strategy?

FIG. 31. Orthographic projection centered on Kuznetsk

Within the Union of Socialist Soviet Republics are five major geographic provinces. In the center is an agricultural zone which forms a thin triangle projecting eastward to Lake Baikal. Here are most of the people and the bulk of the industry. To the north are two lands of cold, the taiga and the tundra. To the south are two lands of drought, the steppe and the desert. Russian expansion has driven the wedge of settlement eastward into Siberia between the steppe and the forest. At the same time this advance has pushed the frontier northward and southward into areas of shorter and shorter growing seasons on the one hand, and areas of marginal rainfall and famine hazard on the other.

Most of Soviet Asia lies in the unattractive realm of cold or of drought. Essential Siberia is limited to a strip along the wisely located Trans-Siberian Railway. There are important mineral deposits on either side, but the developed reserves, the major industries, the agricultural production, and the chief cities all lie

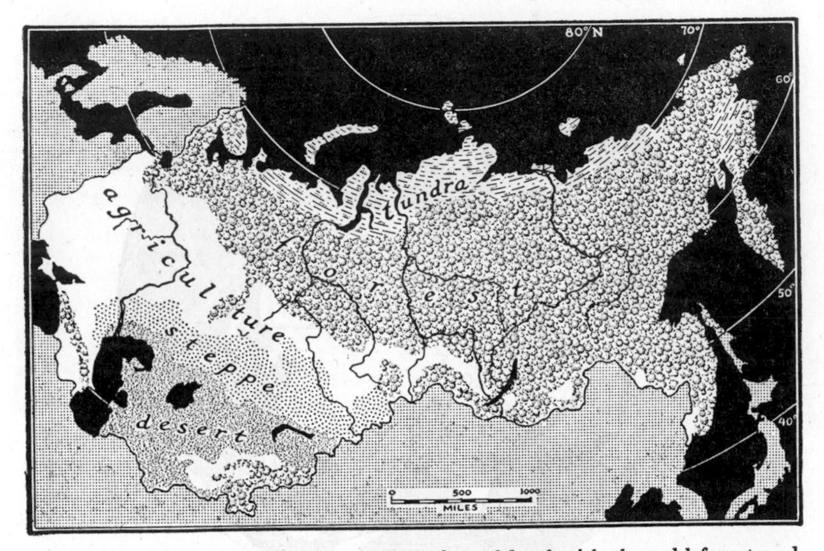

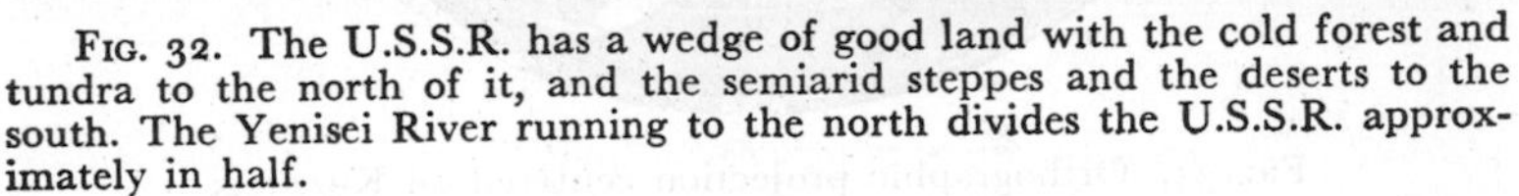
FIG. 32. The U.S.S.R. has a wedge of good land with the cold forest and tundra to the north of it, and the semiarid steppes and the deserts to the south. The Yenisei River running to the north divides the U.S.S.R. approximately in half.

near this transcontinental highway. Within this tapering end of the triangle are still large agricultural possibilities. The pioneering nature of Siberia is shown by the increase of population from 10,400,000 in 1914 to 25,636,900 in 1933, while cultivated land rose from 32,058 square miles to 97,949 square miles.

Since 1928, the five-year plans have laid great stress upon the development of heavy industry. This has enormously increased mineral production, industrial output, transportation facilities, and urbanization throughout the Union, but especially in the Ural Mountains and in Siberia. The strategic value of these developments is obvious, both in the war with Germany and in any possible conflict with Japan. Geographers have played a significant role in the various planning boards, for the Soviets conceive the function of geography to be "the development of the productive resources of the state."

In terms of transportation, the Union's weakness is still the lack of a second transcontinental line across Siberia. The existing road is double-tracked and carries an enormous volume of traffic. In 1937, I counted passing freight trains on several occasions, and found an average of one each seventeen minutes. Although there is still no continuous parallel line, an extensive mileage of auxiliary railways was completed in the interwar years. Western Siberia already has the beginnings of an orderly rail net. In the east, a new line north of Lake Baikal was started in 1936, and completed during the Second World War. In view of the ease with which the Japanese might cut the existing railway around the north of Manchuria, this alternate route is of major strategic value. Not until it was in operation could the Soviet Union have waged effective war against Japan.

The development of Siberia has stimulated the growth of cities, many of which have doubled or trebled their population in the interwar years. There are now ten centers in the Urals and eastward whose population exceeds 200,000. While they do not compare with Soviet Europe in urbanization or industry, they nevertheless represent great productive capacity. Both Sverdlovsk and Novosibirsk exceed 400,000.[1]

This is an age of competitive production, so that access to raw materials is of vital importance. Fortunately the U.S.S.R. is rich, second only to the U.S.A. in mineral wealth. There is not even a good third unless federations such as the British Commonwealth are included.

It must be admitted that Soviet mineral estimates are optimistic and often incapable of verification; but the general outline is now clear. Those unfamiliar with Soviet geological work in the interwar period should remember that the five-year plans laid great

[1] For a detailed study of recent population trends in the Soviet Far North, cf. p. 443, "Population Movements in Imperial Russia and in the Soviet Union," by Frank Lorimer.

stress upon heavy industry and the underlying mineral production. Few sciences received such consideration as geology, and as a result the known reserves have been enlarged several fold.

To sum up the military prospects, it appears probable that even if Germany had been able to hold all Soviet Europe, and even if Japan had seized Vladivostok, the Ural Mountains and central Siberia would still have had enough mineral wealth in

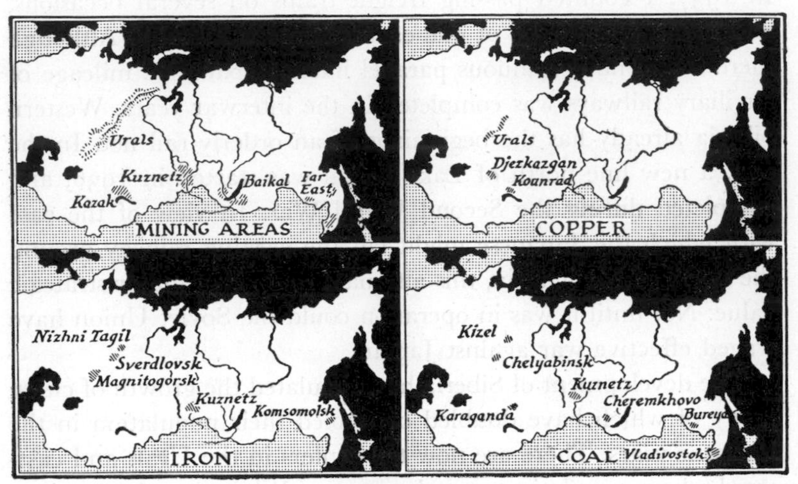

Fig. 33.

production to maintain significant military output as long as the Second World War might last. Hitler's troops failed to overrun Soviet Europe, but even had they done so the Union would still have had the minerals, and the industrial capacity, to carry on. This applies not only to undeveloped reserves but to actual mines and smelters in operation.

The various resources will be reviewed in a moment, but the situation is well in hand with respect to coal, iron, copper, lead, zinc, and gold. Problems may arise concerning oil, aluminum, and manganese, but there is a limited output of each within Siberia. Large resources of oil, manganese, lead, and zinc are available in the Caucasus, and Turkestan is also well supplied with minerals, but this paper is limited to Siberia.

The Soviet Union now credits itself with 1,654,361,000,000

metric tons of coal, second to the United States. Of this reserve, 90 per cent lies in Siberia. So far as current production is concerned, three-fifths comes from the Donets field in the Ukraine, still largely in Russian hands, but there has been great expansion in newer areas in Asia. This is notably true in the Kuznetsk Basin of central Siberia, where the current production exceeds 20,000,000 tons, the equivalent of the output in Ohio. In this Kuznetsk

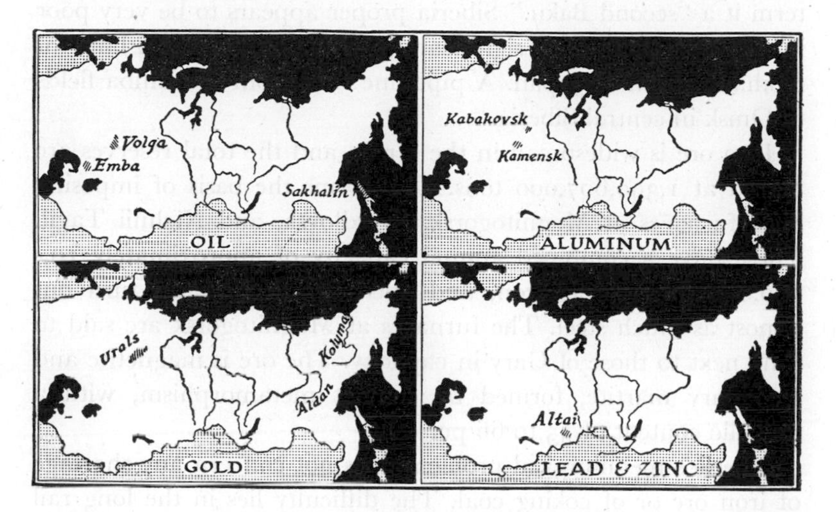

field the bituminous reserves are more than 450,000,000,000 tons, equal to our entire Appalachian field.

Within the Ural Mountains, coal is mined to the extent of 8,000,000 tons, chiefly at Kizel and Chelyabinsk, but none of it is of coking quality. Elsewhere in Siberia is the new Karaganda field, north of Lake Balkhash, with an output of over 4,000,000 tons; near Lake Baikal are the Cheremkhovo mines yielding 3,000,000 tons; other mines near Vladivostok produce nearly 3,000,000 tons; and a new field is developing at Bureya near the Amur River.

The annual yield of coal in Soviet Asia is 40,000,000 tons out of a national total of 146,800,000 (1940). While the total is but a third of American production, it is quadruple the tsarist output. Since the Kuznetsk area is more than 2,000 miles from both

German and Japanese frontiers, its operation appears reasonably dependable.

Petroleum [2] production is no longer concentrated in Baku or even along the slopes of the Caucasus, although these still dominate. Northeast of the Caspian Sea is the important Emba district with salt-dome structures. From the Urals westward to the Volga River is another new oil field, so promising that the Soviets term it a "second Baku." Siberia proper appears to be very poor in oil, but there is a significant production on the island of Sakhalin north of Japan. A pipe line runs from the Emba fields to Omsk in central Siberia.

Iron ore is widespread in the Urals, and the total reserves are placed at 1,390,607,000 tons. This forms the basis of imposing blast furnaces at Magnitogorsk, Sverdlovsk, and Nizhnii Tagil. These have a combined annual capacity of approximately 10,000,000 tons of pig iron, and open hearth furnaces turn out almost as much steel. The furnaces at Magnitogorsk are said to rank next to those of Gary in capacity. The ore is magnetite and secondary martite, formed by contact metamorphism, with a metallic content of 55 to 66 per cent.

Siberia's metallurgical problem does not concern any shortage of iron ore or of coking coal. The difficulty lies in the long rail haul required to bring them together. To the Ural plants, coal is brought 1,417 miles from Kuznetsk in central Siberia; and on the return trip the trains carry ore to blast furnaces near the coal. Steel plants thus operate at both ends of the combine. I have spent five days in the Kuznetsk Basin, going through mines and blast furnaces, and found them up to the best American standards. Since the development of Kuznetsk, near-by ore has been found which nearly meets the need of the local furnaces, while coal for the Urals has been developed at Karaganda, much closer to Magnitogorsk ore. There is a small iron output east of Lake Baikal, and a blast furnace has recently been built in the Far East at Komsomolsk on the lower Amur River.

In the Soviet Union as a whole, the principal steel production

[2] Cf. p. 336, "Petroleum in the North," by Wallace E. Pratt.

has been in the Ukraine, north of the Black Sea, based on Krivoi Rog ore and Donets coal; but the Ural-Kuznetsk combine has grown to the point where it now supplies one-third of the nation's iron.

Manganese has been obtained from two major sources; the larger of the deposits is in the Ukraine, but the highest grade ore is in the Caucasus. Within Siberia itself, there is a limited production of low-grade manganese in the Urals, in the Kazak Republic and near Kuznetsk. While inadequate, these Asiatic manganese deposits provide an emergency supply.

Reserves of copper have been greatly expanded under the five-year plans, but the quality of the ore is poor. There is a small production from pyrite-bearing ores and other types in the Ural Mountains, but the largest mines are north and west of Lake Balkhash. These are porphyritic deposits with about 1.1 per cent copper. A new smelter at Kounrad has an annual capacity of 100,000 tons of metal, and even larger works are under way at Djezkazgan to the west.

Lead and zinc reserves are estimated at 11 and 19 per cent of the world totals, respectively. Soviet production is from the northern Caucasus, from the important Ridder mines in the Altai Mountains and from scattered Siberian deposits. Lead production in 1936 amounted to 55,000 tons, while in the same year zinc totaled 63,000 tons.

Aluminum was regarded as a deficit metal in tsarist Russia because the known bauxite deposits were limited and poor. Within recent years, the U.S.S.R. has built up a significant output, amounting to 60,000 tons in 1939, which lifted the nation to fourth place. Two deposits in the Urals supply a considerable part of the bauxite: Kabakovsk in the north and Kamensk in the south. Unfortunately the chief reduction plants are in those parts of Soviet Europe currently occupied by Germany.

Siberia also produces enough gold to give the Union second place, next to South Africa. This is secured partly from lode mines in the Urals but chiefly from placer works along the tributaries of the Lena River, notably the Aldan. Other Siberian localities are along the Kolyma and Yenisei rivers. Modest amounts of nickel are mined in the Urals and the Arctic. Within the Urals are large amounts of platinum, chromium, asbestos, potash, and magnesite; while small amounts of tin and tungsten are produced east of Lake Baikal.

To turn from specific resources to mining areas, two major districts stand out, along with three lesser areas. By far the most valuable is the Urals, for there are few mountain ranges on earth which produce the variety or quantity of minerals secured here. Iron has been mined since the days of Peter the Great, and there are now thirty-nine localities which produce iron or steel. Great metallurgical plants provide the base for scores of industries, notably railway equipment, automobiles, tractors, heavy machinery, and chemicals. Coal is mined in the Urals but is not of metallurgical quality. Oil is available on the western flanks and also to the south. Nonferrous minerals include copper, gold, platinum, silver, nickel, aluminum, manganese, lead, zinc, chromium, asbestos, magnesite, potash, and salt. All these place the Urals next to the Ukraine as the Union's number two metallurgical base. There are eight industrial cities of over 100,000 people, led by Sverdlovsk.

The Altai-Sayan Mountains of south-central Siberia are a region whose mineral significance has scarcely been appreciated by non-Russians. Here is a third of the country's coal, lead, and zinc, plus significant occurrences of iron ore, silver, gold, copper, tin, and manganese. The coal basin of Kuznetsk, southeast of Novosibirsk, dominates this second industrial base of Soviet Asia. The development of the Kuznetsk steel works is one of the triumphs of the First Five Year Plan.

Third in significance is the Kazak area, north of Lake Balkhash, where coal and copper were developed in the interwar years.

The fourth of Siberia's minerally productive districts lies east and west of Lake Baikal, while the fifth is along the Amur River in the Far East. Reserves are considerable, but production is only partly developed. Coal and iron are secured in a number of localities, and there is the beginning of a steel industry at Komsomalsk. Petroleum is obtained on the island of Sakhalin.

While Far Eastern developments are somewhat vulnerable to Japanese attack, production in the Urals and at Kuznetsk seems secure from any feasible invasion, whether from east or from west. If mineral production will win wars, the Union of Socialist Soviet Republics has what it takes.

During the decades between the First and Second World wars, the American public was very reluctant to recognize the industrial potentialities of the Soviet Union. From the military record since the German invasion, however, it should be clear that any nation which can afford to lose tens of thousands of planes and tanks, and millions of soldiers, and still take the initiative, has far greater productive capacities than is commonly appreciated. In the post-war world, it seems inescapable that the Soviet Union's mineral foundations will place it in the first rank among industrial nations. Siberian resources have a significant role in Soviet planning.

CHAPTER V

Reflections on Asia

24

The Inland Crossroads of Asia

By OWEN LATTIMORE

OWEN LATTIMORE, born Washington, D.C. Graduate School, Harvard, 1929. Director, Walter Hines Page School of International Relations, Johns Hopkins University. At present, Director of Pacific Operations, Office of War Information.

In China, engaged in business and newspaper work, 1920–1942, and in research and field work after 1929; political adviser to Generalissimo Chiang Kai-shek, 1940–1942.

Author: *The Desert Road to Turkeston*, 1929; *High Tartary*, 1930; *Manchuria, Cradle of Conflict*, 1932; *The Mongols of Manchuria*, 1934; *Inner Asian Frontiers of China*, 1940; and numerous articles on Asiatic affairs.

Polar projection maps have recently become fashionable, showing the importance of direct routes by air from America to other parts of the world. The principles of these routes are simple. Routes over land are better than routes over water, because there are more places where a plane can come down safely. They are also faster, because refueling points can be laid out in straight lines. Long flights over oceans must tack from island to island, because Nature did not lay the islands out in straight lines from continent to continent. Even if we had a plane that could fly nonstop from San Francisco to Shanghai, it could not operate competitively, because it would have to carry such an immense weight of fuel instead of pay load.[1]

In time of war, aircraft working from continental bases are on the whole of more strategic importance than aircraft working from island bases or carriers. Over the land, planes can be

[1] Cf. pp. 137–147, "American Air Transport Faces North," by William A. M. Burden.

coordinated with artillery, tanks, man power, sources of supply, and continuous lines of supply. Planes operated over the sea from carriers are ultimately forced, like the carriers themselves, to return to land bases for fueling and repair. Even island bases are dependent for supply on control of the sea. Sea-air operations therefore can never escape from certain intermittent, back-and-forth limitations as compared with the more continuous and dependable character of land-air operations.

When these conclusions are checked against the geography of the world's continents and oceans, the first thing to be noted is that the major land masses lie north of the Equator. The greatest northern land masses—North America, Europe and Asia—approach each other most closely in the Arctic. The great-circle route from any point in North America to any point in Asia which combines

(1) shortest flying time
(2) maximum flight over land
(3) minimum flight over water

is a great-circle route through the Arctic.

South America and Africa are partly independent of this formula. Their vast bulk reaches far to the south of the Equator. The ocean crossing between South America and Africa is shorter than that between North America and Europe (south of the Arctic). Yet it is also possible to fly from South America to North America and from Africa to Europe or Asia with only short over-water hops. In the future there will accordingly be excellent flying routes from South America to Europe and Asia both through Africa and through North America and the Arctic; but not across the Pacific.

The next conclusion is that the United States, because of the vast scope for land-air flying within its own territory, is like Brazil, Canada, the Soviet Union, and China a primary natural habitat of the plane. In international flying the United States ought, because of its situation north of the Equator, to be even more interested in long-range land-air flying to Europe and Asia through the Arctic than in long-range sea-air flying across the Atlantic and Pacific. The sector of the Arctic held by the United States—drawn from the easternmost and westernmost points on the northern coast of Alaska to the North Pole—is not so large as either the Soviet or the Canadian sector, but it holds a key position between them.

Fig. 34. Orthographic projection centered on China

Here it should be noted that the ideal American-Alaskan route to Asia is not by way of the Aleutian "steppingstones," in spite of the close approach from the Aleutians to Kamchatka, the Kuriles, Japan, and the coast of China. The Aleutians lie in the dangerous fog band and temperature band in which ice forms on planes. At lower temperatures moisture has already condensed and been precipitated, so that ice cannot form on planes.

The rule of the Arctic is: *Go north for safety.* For this reason, as well as for the sake of shorter flying time, the American trunk lines of the future ought to be flown right through the heart of the Arctic. The rational line to Asia strikes directly into Arctic Siberia, and from there down through the Northeastern Provinces (Manchuria) to the coast of China, or across Mongolia to inland China, or through Chinese or Russian Central Asia to India, Afghanistan, or Iran.

The safety factor is to be found in the development of sound techniques of Arctic flying, the construction of Arctic flying fields, and the development of a network of Arctic weather stations. There are already Arctic or subarctic sources of oil. In all of these requirements the Canadians are ahead of us, and the Russians are ahead of the Canadians; but in all of them there is nothing that American technical skill and resources cannot quickly master. The main point to be grasped is that flying the Arctic in June is no more dangerous than flying the Great Lakes in June, while flying the Arctic in December is no more dangerous than flying across North Dakota in December.

It is an interesting thing that although these ideas are elementary they have scarcely begun to affect the thinking of Americans in politics, economics, or strategy. We have in Vilhjalmur Stefansson one of the early pioneer theorists of Arctic flight and over-all technological development of the Arctic; [2] but his ideas have been carried into much wider operational practice in the Soviet Union than they have in Alaska. It is not only in Arctic flying that the Russians excel; they have worked on the whole development of the Arctic as a complex.

Yet the recent "one world" flight by Mr. Willkie gave great publicity to every essential fact that we need to understand. Before Pearl Harbor, it took six days to fly from San Francisco to Hong Kong, zigzagging from San Francisco to Honolulu, Midway, Wake Island, Guam, Manila, and finally Hong Kong. From Hong Kong there was a final flight of a few hours to Chungking. Mr. Willkie, flying by the land-air, great-circle route, left Chungking in the deep hinterland of China and flew north over Mongolia. Not all the stopping points of his journey have

[2] See especially Stefansson's *The Northward Course of Empire* (New York, 1922), and the first few chapters of his *The Adventure of Wrangel Island* (New York, 1925).

been published; but he touched at Yakutsk, which is deep in the subarctic mainland of Siberia. Flying on into Alaska and down across Canada, he reached Minneapolis—a more direct port of entry, when flying from Asia, than any port on the Pacific coast—on the fourth day from Chungking.

With the fuller development of suitably placed and spaced air fields, to make night flying practical, this time could of course be smoothly averaged out over regular schedules. It is in fact already a common saying that after the war we shall be able to fly from anywhere to anywhere in not more than sixty hours—two and a half days—of actual flying time.

In terms of competitive flying this means something important and as yet novel to our accepted thinking: it means that Hong Kong and Shanghai are not the only front doors of China. In the near future, there will be front doors for both land and air traffic on the frontiers of the Northeastern Provinces (Manchuria), on the Mongolian frontier, and on the frontier between Chinese Turkestan (Sinkiang Province) and Russian Turkestan (the Soviet Central Asian Republics).

How little the significance of this is yet realized could be shown by any number of quotations from books and articles written since Pearl Harbor, urging acquisition of new American island bases in the Western Pacific, to improve America's position strategically and give access to the mainland of Asia. To these must be added the proposals for international air and naval bases on Formosa or in Korea or even in the Northeastern Provinces of China, and the proposals that Japan, after being defeated, should be built up once more in order to maintain the balance of power between Russia and China.

There is a brief comment to be made on all this which is not perhaps in itself a complete answer, but is certainly something to make every responsible person stop and think. It is this: A combination of air and naval power, geared to zigzag routes between islands in the Pacific and to the Mediterranean-Suez approach to Asia can assure control over the mainland of Asia only so long as the Asiatic countries remain colonial or quasi-colonial politically, industrially, and technologically. A developed Asia will completely alter the value of such bases and maritime approaches and put an end to the imperialism which, even under the disguise of an "international security system," they unmistakably express.

We need imagine only one example. Air and naval bases on Formosa would menace the coast of China even if they did not control it; but even the most strongly fortified bases on Formosa would in fact rest on the control of the sea necessary to bring across the Pacific the fuel necessary for planes and warships. A self-contained aviation industry could never be developed on Formosa because control of the sea would still be necessary to bring to the factories most of the metal and other necessary war materials. In the long run—and here it does not matter whether we speak in terms of one decade or several decades—China's own aviation industry will develop deep in the western hinterland, where all or most of the resources for a complete aviation industry are available, including oil. In the long run, it would be impossible for sea-supported air power, based on Formosa and projected toward China, to challenge the land-supported air power of China, based on secure industries and communications in the deep hinterland and projected toward the coast and Formosa.

The Northeastern Provinces of China, together with Korea, do not provide an example to the contrary. This region is the hub between the sea and air power of Japan, the present land and air power of the Soviet Union, and the potential land and air power of China. The idea that Japan could be "revived" and with the distant support of British and American sea power made to function as the stabilizer of relations between China and Russia is fantastic. It could only be done if China were permanently held down to an approximately colonial level of industrial development. Even so, such a system would not assure permanent peace. On the contrary, it would ensure the renewal of the whole imperialistic process by which Japan conquered Korea, invaded the Northeastern Provinces, defied the League of Nations, and wrecked the international security system which was beginning to grow up around the League. It was this which facilitated the rise of Hitler, Mussolini's defiance of the League in Ethiopia, the forcing of fascism on Spain, the destruction of the Czechoslovakian bastion of democracy in Eastern Europe, and so made the present war inevitable.

As for the relations between Japan and the Soviet Union, the basic fact is that Russia is already dominant. Even without a war between Russians and Japanese, as many Japanese troops are tied up in watching the Siberian frontier as are engaged in active operations either in China or in the South and Southwest Pacific. These idle troops, moreover, are the flower of the Japanese army, the best trained and the most fully equipped. We do not know the figures, but it is safe to assume that a heavy proportion of Japan's air power is also immobilized by the cat-and-mouse uncertainties of not being at war with the Russians. For the future, it would be pure folly to think of basing air power in Japan, supporting it with British and American sea power, and projecting it toward Siberia. It is not a question of the exposed position of Vladivostok. It is a question of the deep Siberian bases from which Soviet air power could defy any such challenge, and project a far more formidable counter challenge.

In short, there is danger in the kind of thinking about air communications and air power that is in fact only a hasty modernization of old ideas about sea power. Communications by sea and sea power are only a part of the whole complex of our technology, our ability to use the resources of the earth. Use of the air is a recent and still rapidly growing part of man's power over his environment. We need to apply this new resource in balanced adjustment to and modification of the total complex of previously accumulated resources, not as merely an extension of any one part of the complex.

A fresh view of the potentialities of our time can be won by getting away from hackneyed approaches. Great-circle air routes cutting through the Arctic emphasize immediately the importance of the vast Soviet and Canadian sectors of the Arctic, separated by the smaller United States and Norwegian sectors. Every Arctic air route that leads into Soviet territory, either in Europe or in Asia, also emphasizes the importance of the land frontiers between the Soviet Union and Western Europe, the Near and Middle East, and the Far East. The short, safe Arctic route to rapidly developing Siberia is also the short, safe route to China, India, Afghanistan, or Iran; and by striking down from the north through Norway and European Russia the Mediterranean and Africa can be reached with a minimum of over-water flight.

This leads on to a realization that one of the world's most important phenomena in the next few decades will be the growth in importance of the land frontier between the Soviet Union and China. It is a longer frontier than that between the United States and Canada. Across it, in the first century after Christ, trade filtered between the Han Empire in China and the Roman Empire in the Mediterranean and Near East. In the year 800, when Charlemagne was crowned, the power of the T'ang Dynasty in China reached far into Central Asia. The vast Mongol conquests of the thirteenth century were bred between Siberia and the Great Wall of China. Only with the rise of the maritime empires was the importance of this frontier eclipsed. From the time of Columbus to the time when steam navigation became general in the nineteenth century, the Spanish, Portuguese, Dutch, British, and French adventurers, conquerors, and traders founded their colonial empires and completely changed the balance of the world.

These colonial empires are now approaching the end of their historical span. Some of the colonial territories, like the Philippines and Korea, will be free of the colonial status immediately after the war is won. Others will rise from subjection within a very few years. For still others a decade or even several decades will be needed, and therefore the colonial era, like other historical eras, will not end sharply but will taper off. Nevertheless, the important fact is that it is tapering off. Nor will it be replaced by an era that can be adequately described by some one new factor, like air power. Perhaps the real significance of air power is that it is a transition factor, playing a part both in the end of the colonial era and in the emergence of the new era. The new era itself, however, will be a complex of new geographical, technological, and political forms, none of which can be studied in function except as it interacts with the others.

In the meantime, all attempts to control Asia from its coasts and islands and ports, by the combination of sea power and air power, will tend to prolong the colonial era and will prove to be politically retrogressive. Conversely, a world order that is both stable and progressive must include the concept of large Asiatic states, each of which is politically free and each of which has its political and economic system centered in the heart of its own territory, reaching out from the center to defend and control the land frontiers and the coasts and ports. This is true today of China, and of the Soviet Union to the extent that it is an Asiatic power; it will be true tomorrow of India and Burma; and only to the extent that it becomes true of India and Burma will freedom become secure for countries like Korea and Thailand and archipelagoes like the Philippines and Indonesia, which lie most exposed to the combination of sea power and air power.

If the equation be stated in this way, the importance of the land frontier between China and the Soviet Union at once becomes compellingly obvious. The eastern end of this frontier pivots around the junction of the frontiers of the Soviet Union, the Northeastern Provinces of China, and Korea. The western end pivots around the junction of the frontiers of China, India, Afghanistan, and the Soviet Union. (Actually, it is the frontiers of China and Afghanistan which touch each other, thereby forming a narrow insulating strip between Soviet and Indian territory.)

At the end of the war the Northeastern Provinces of China will step into an importance which ought by no means to be underestimated; but neither should it be exaggerated. There may well be a period of great tension and danger in this region until the uncertainties of United Nations policy are clarified; but in time it will become evident that there are only two dominant factors to be considered; that these two factors are China and the Soviet Union; and that the relation between the two cannot be determined at the eastern end of the frontier alone, but must depend on the frontier as a whole.

The Northeastern Provinces are a mighty outthrust of China proper. In a wide but vague western fringe of this territory there is the Mongol population which, though itself sparse, outnumbers the Chinese population. We cannot overlook the possibility that parts of this fringe may eventually adhere to Mongolia, whether or not the present Outer Mongolia also acquires additional territory from Inner Mongolia on its southern frontier, and whether Mongolia as a whole enters into a federative relation with China, or with the Soviet Union, or establishes a clearer and more generally recognized independence than at present. Apart from this, the Northeastern Provinces are not only indisputably Chinese, with a population more than 95 per cent Chinese; they comprise a territory which is very probably vital to the survival of China as a state. The Chinese of the Northeast not only consider themselves Chinese; they are inclined to consider themselves as in some ways the pick of the Chinese people. Their territory contains coal, iron, timber, grain, and soybeans that make it comparable in wealth of resources to any equivalent area of China; and in actual development, in terms of railway mileage to square miles of territory and factory horsepower to hundred thousands of population, it is more advanced than any Chinese area of equal size.

Westward from the Northeastern Provinces are two territories, Mongolia and the province of Sinkiang or Chinese Turkestan, where factors of a very special kind must be considered.

Mongolia is one of the vast territories of the world. That part of it which is called Outer Mongolia and organized politically as the Mongol People's Republic has an area well over 600,000 square miles and a population between 800,000 and a million. So few people in such a wide land must necessarily be a weak nation; yet the Mongols are also potentially a strong nation. For one thing, they are a very solid people; their language, culture, and traditions are uniform; there are few minorities among them, and they are a people as sharply distinct from the Russians to the north of them as from the Chinese to the south.

For about twenty years the Mongols of Outer Mongolia have been under a Mongol People's Republic, controlled by a Mongol People's Party, similar in general to the one-party governments of both China and the Soviet Union. The Mongol People's Republic claims complete independence and sovereignty. Although there has been no war between Mongolia and China, the Chinese deny the Mongol claim to independence, and advance the counterclaim that all Mongolia is Chinese territory, under Chinese sovereignty. The Soviet Union follows a double policy; in dealing with Mongolia it recognizes the Mongol People's Republic; in dealing with China, it recognizes China's claim to sovereignty over Mongolia.

The Soviet policy has been attacked as equivocal, obscure, and a disguise for "Red imperialism"; but it can also be argued that the Russians have simply followed a policy which does not either tie their hands or commit their prestige. That is to say, the Russians have not attempted to force either the Mongols to recognize the Chinese claim, or the Chinese to recognize the Mongol claim. If, as the result of negotiation, Mongols and Chinese were to come to terms with each other—agreeing, for instance, on some sort of federation—the Soviet Union would be in a position to withdraw from its present close association with Mongolia without loss of prestige.

West and southwest of Outer Mongolia stretches another vast territory, the province of Sinkiang, with an area of more than 600,000 square miles and a population of about four million. This province is in a way a Chinese India. The Chinese number only about 10 per cent of the population, and even so are internally divided by the fact that some are Moslems while others are not. Like the British in India, they control the largest trade interests and the top positions in the civil service and the armed forces, of which the most reliable nucleus is Chinese. As in India, again, the subject people are a medley of cultures, languages, and religions. For the largest group, described in most Western books of travel as Turki, the medieval name of Uigur has recently been revived. The language of these Uigurs is a very pure form of Turkish, owing to Turkish conquests in the Middle Ages; but before that they spoke Indo-European languages. They are in fact one of the purest "white" races in the world, of the group which anthropologists call "Alpine."

The Uigurs are farmers and town dwellers living in irrigated oases separated by deserts. On the wide grazing lands and in the mountain pastures of the province live other Turkish-speaking groups, the Kazaks and Kirghiz, who, like the Uigurs, are Moslems, but live as herdsmen, not as farmers. Other herdsmen are Mongols, akin both to the Mongols of western Outer Mongolia and to the Kalmuk Mongols of the lower Volga, far away in Russia. There are also a number of smaller groups; for instance, a curious by-product of the Manchu conquest of the seventeenth and eighteenth centuries is the fact that there are more people who speak the Manchu language in Sinkiang, far away in the heart of Central Asia, than there are in Manchuria (the Northeastern Provinces), where the Manchu language is so nearly extinct that those who speak it can be called museum survivals with no museum to protect them.

Both Outer Mongolia and Sinkiang have important peripheries, which are tidemarks of the age-old Central Asian migrations and the Mongol conquests of the thirteenth century.

North of Mongolia are the Buriat Mongols of Siberia, who have an Autonomous Republic of their own within the Soviet Union. East of Outer Mongolia, forming the western fringe of the Northeastern Provinces, is what the Japanese call Eastern Inner Mongolia. South of Outer Mongolia is Inner Mongolia, where the Mongols are now greatly outnumbered by the Chinese, but where most of them live separately from the Chinese and adjacent to the Outer Mongolian frontier, so that it is quite conceivable that they might in the future adhere to Outer Mongolia rather than to the Chinese provinces among which they are at present divided.

Similarly in Sinkiang the sedentary Uigurs are akin to the oasis dwellers of the Soviet Central Asian Republics; the Kazaks and Kirghiz are akin to Kazaks and Kirghiz who are organized into political entities of their own in Soviet territory; the Mongols are akin to Mongols in Outer Mongolia and in Soviet territory, and so forth. Even on the southeastern or Chinese side of Sinkiang, small minorities of Turkish-speaking people live as separate communities within the larger Chinese community; and it must not be forgotten that in the northwestern Chinese provinces of Kansu and Ningsia even the Chinese-speaking Moslems are not only a religious minority but a political minority, and in many ways an important political minority.

Legally minded commentators on international relations have focused their attention on such matters as the Chinese sovereignty over Outer Mongolia; the question whether Outer Mongolia is a "puppet state" of the Soviet Union; or the supposition that the Russians may have ambitions in Sinkiang amounting to a "Red imperialism." Obviously such questions are important; but I submit that for those who are historically minded, or politically minded in any deeper sense, this legalistic approach does not even touch the two primary factors, which are geographical and ethnic. Geographically, the frontier between China and Russia in Mongolia and Sinkiang is not a line but a zone. Ethnically, this frontier zone is neither Chinese nor Russian, but Mongol, Uigur, Turkish, Kazak, Kirghiz, etc. Realization of these primary facts casts a new light on the land frontier between "China" and "Russia." Except for the Amur and Ussuri frontiers between the Northeastern Provinces and Siberia, the entire land frontier could be arbitrarily shifted either several hundred miles to the north or several hundred miles to the south and still affect practically no Russians and practically no Chinese. The main body of Russia and the main body of China would still be intact.

To think in this way is to concede an entirely new importance to the "minority" peoples of Mongolia and Sinkiang. These peoples are "minorities" only in respect to the Russians and the Chinese. In their own habitats they are majorities. Yet they are also weak peoples of small numbers living in vast territories with very valuable natural resources. All the precedents of history indicate that in the long run one of two things must happen to them: they will be forcibly subjected to either Russia or China, or they will voluntarily gravitate toward either Russia or China.

Weak though they are, the non-Russian and non-Chinese peoples of the frontier zone have a degree of choice between these alternatives. If both of their great neighbors move forward into the dividing zone with policies of control by force, the weak peoples of the zone have little choice; but if one powerful neighbor follows a policy of subjecting the border peoples by force, while the other works by attracting them, giving them the feeling of participation in a larger federalized political structure, then the peoples of the border zone will have reason to exercise their own choice to the best of their ability.

The political problem, and challenge, inherent in this situation is even more urgent for China than for Russia. The handling of minority peoples has been one of the outstanding successes of the Soviet Union; and since the policy was worked out in theory by Stalin himself, even before the Revolution, its successful results are associated both with his prestige and with the reputation of the Soviet Government. Nowhere is this more important than in Central Asia and Siberia. Here the non-Russian peoples have been granted autonomy of education in their own languages and in the preservation of everything in their own cultures that does not conflict with the basic political and economic standards imposed on all, minorities and Russians alike, by the Soviet regime. Those who lost privileges associated with the tsarist regime were Russians rather than minority peoples. Thus the minority peoples were among those who clearly gained more than they lost by the Revolution, because they were given free access to technological opportunities and to government and military service which they had not had before. For the first time they began to adhere to the government of their country, rather than merely submit themselves to it, because they had both a feeling of participation and a feeling of promotion to wider opportunities, without that fear of obliteration which goes with the suppression of minority languages and traditional customs.

China has been overcoming domestic difficulties which have thus far delayed the application of an equally enlightened minority policy. President Chiang Kai-shek and other important Chinese spokesmen have made declarations reassuring to weaker nations or people over whom China claims no jurisdiction; but the Chinese as a people and the Chinese Government as a government have not yet won the confidence of such peoples as the Tibetans, the Mongols, or the Central Asian minorities over whom China does claim jurisdiction. There are a number of historical reasons for this, and one very massive reason: For decades Chinese Nationalism itself, in spite of the size of China and the numbers of the Chinese people, has been equivalent to a minority nationalism in the sense that China has been fighting for a minimum status of equality in the world. Japan's claims to special rights and privileges in China, especially in the Northeastern Provinces, also had a great deal to do with retardation of the development of a generous Chinese minority policy in such regions as Mongolia. With Japan constantly pressing its claims, and with a world security system which never adequately checked Japan, the Chinese could not afford to abate their own claims to sovereignty over such territories as Mongolia. Any gesture of the kind would have run the danger of encouraging the Japanese to increase their demands, on the ground that Chinese generosity was really weakness, and that the Japanese were entitled to take up where the Chinese left off. Similarly in Tibet the Chinese had a long-standing diplomatic dispute with the British, who maintained that the Tibetans must be allowed to take part in negotiations between Britain and China concerning Tibet.

For such reasons as these the Chinese have as yet developed little ability to attract toward themselves the minority peoples in their own outer territories. On the southern frontier the prestige of China, as a symbol of freedom, stands higher in the eyes of the Burmese and Indo-Chinese, to whom the British and the French denied independence, than on the northern and western frontiers where the Chinese themselves encroach on the freedom and self-government of Mongols, Central Asians, and Tibetans. This is a serious flaw in the prestige of the kind of Asiatic revolution and liberation for which China stands, as compared with the kind for which the Soviets stand, because the Russians can already exhibit an impressive record of what they have done for minority peoples, while the Chinese as yet have little to show but declarations of good intentions for the future. Since the people of the Soviet-Chinese frontier, living in a border zone, have their own ways of knowing what is going on both on the Chinese side of them and on the Russian side of them, they also have reasons for making their own decisions. It is quite true that these decisions would not be unanimous. The aristocracy of Inner Mongolia, with special privileges to preserve, might well feel that they could preserve more of them under Chinese protection than under Russian protection; and the same is probably true of privileged groups in Sinkiang. The majority, however, would be much more likely to sympathize with the majority of their kinsmen who have prospered under Russian association.

In order to understand the way in which people think and feel in these remote parts of the world, which to us are very obscure, we must be prepared to appreciate their standards of comparison between the Chinese and Russians as representatives of civilization and progress. These standards are by no means the same as our own; and it is of the greatest importance that we should realize that it is we, not the peoples of Asia, who must make allowances for these differences. It will be many decades before we can expect them to understand the Massachusetts or Iowa or California standard of democracy or progress. On the great inland frontier the only standards on which we can expect them to make a political choice are those of comparison between the Chinese and the Russians. Where do the Chinese stand as representatives of progress and democratic aspirations? The civilization of China has never been blemished by racial discrimination. Throughout their history, the Chinese have distinguished between nations and peoples on grounds of culture, not race.

Confucius made a maxim of this. From his time onward, anyone who was not a Chinese was "barbarian"; but at the same time any barbarian who wished to cultivate the land like the Chinese, eat the same food as the Chinese, dress like the Chinese, speak their language, and study their books, was readily accepted as a Chinese with no discrimination against him on grounds of his national or tribal or racial origin.

Since the culture of the Chinese was by far the highest in that part of the world, the Chinese attitude meant that anyone dwelling on the periphery of China, whether he were Mongol, Turkish, Tibetan, or tribesman from the far Southwest, on the border of Burma or Thailand, could become a Chinese and enter the Chinese society. This was more than tolerance on the part of the Chinese: it may be described as a standing offer of the opportunity to become civilized, to any individual or group interested in progress.

This ancient liberality of the Chinese does not of itself entitle them to claim that their contemporary policy toward frontier minorities is liberal. There are many things in the inherited culture and society of China that are civilized and urbane by any historical standard; as elements of a culture-complex, they deserve to be preserved in the present and cultivated for the future. Nevertheless, to look only at the past of China is to look backward and to be reactionary. The traditional culture of China, taken as a whole, as a complex, has insufficient survival value in the modern world.

For this reason, the traditional Chinese attitude toward the border peoples, which was once a strength, has now become a weakness. The Chinese can no longer say to these peoples that the whole sum and meaning of progress and civilization is to become Chinese; and if they say to these peoples that they *must* become Chinese, then they will certainly be feared and resisted as oppressors. For the truth is that these peoples can no longer be convinced that it is a sufficient promotion to become merely what the Chinese were yesterday, or are today. If the only changes are to be made by them, while the Chinese remain as they are, the border peoples will not be attracted but repelled. They can be interested and attracted only if they are convinced that they are offered an opportunity to go forward rapidly in conjunction with a Chinese economy, society, and political structure which is changing as rapidly as their own. Put in its baldest terms, this means that they can be attracted toward a revolutionary China, but not toward a conservative China. The importance of this question of the joint progress of the Chinese and the peoples dwelling in the zone between them and the Russians goes far beyond the apparent weight in the world today of a handful of Mongols and Central Asians.

Where do the Russians stand—not as *we* compare them with the Chinese, but as the border peoples compare them? The success of the Russian policy toward minority peoples has made the Soviet Union as a whole not only a standard but *the* standard of progress from the Ussuri and Amur rivers to the Pamirs. The fact that progress is not merely conferred or bestowed on minority peoples, but offered to them in such a way that they participate in it and feel that they have made it their own sets up the Soviet standard, in the eyes of those who take part in it, as one not only of technological progress but of democratic progress. Most Western writers have demurred against admitting this, because neither Soviet principles nor Soviet policies are democratic according to the accepted standards of America or Britain. To argue this is quite pointless. The peoples of Mongolia and Central Asia are not in the least interested in whether the Soviet Union is democratic or not by Anglo-American standards. They are only interested in whether the Soviet present and future, or the Chinese present and future, are more attractive than their own present and their own past; and their sole standard of "democracy" is the degree to which they are allowed to participate in and make their own whatever is offered to them.

For the Chinese, the problem comes down to this: More border peoples are attracted to the Soviet Union than are repelled by it. The Chinese cannot stabilize their own land frontier unless they set up an attraction toward China equal to the attraction toward Russia. They cannot set up such an attraction unless they actively encourage a general participation of the majority in social and economic changes tending to create a system much more democratic than anything the border peoples had in the past or the Chinese people have today. Finally, they cannot advocate rapid changes and democratic policies among the border peoples and at the same time oppose these among the Chinese people, because to do so would stimulate irresistible demands on the Chinese Government by the Chinese people. The situation may be summed up by saying that the border peoples, so weak and few, are destined to be a critical factor in the political future of Asia, because the Russians are setting the pace for them, and consequently they will have an appreciable effect in setting the pace for the Chinese.

There is already an important example of this pace-setting, in Sinkiang, isolated in recent years from the main body of China but powerfully affected by the development of communications, industry, and education in Soviet Central Asia, across the border. In order to create an attraction offsetting the attraction of progress in Soviet territory, the ruling Chinese minority in this province began to encourage "native" as well as Chinese education, and to accept "natives" as administrative officials. Still more recently—in 1943—communications between Sinkiang and the rest of China have greatly improved, and the authority of the national government has become dominant over the local administrative body. There will be as a result an important test of Chinese policy toward minority peoples. If officials from the national capital begin to supersede local and "native" officials, and to stand between them and further promotion, there will be a loss of faith in the Chinese government spreading from Sinkiang into Tibet and Mongolia. If on the other hand the progressive policy toward national minorities is continued and developed, the younger and more progressive groups among the Turkish-speaking minorities and the Tibetans and Mongols will tend to gravitate toward China.

This brings us back to the inland crossroads of Asia. The question cannot be narrowed down to terms of political systems and political ambitions any more than it can be restricted to terms of the new importance of air power in the world. We must enlarge our frame of reference until it takes in the total complex of the significant factors of our time. We may for the moment disregard political frontiers. We cannot foretell the future of the inland heart of Asia either by an exclusive analysis of the political factors, or by redrawing frontier lines on a map, or by stressing the importance of some one new technological development like air transport. We must deal with groups of interacting factors.

If, for his first crossing of the Atlantic, Columbus had somehow miraculously been supplied with a steamer, made outside the Europe of his time and having nothing to do with the established European structure of economy and society, that one steamer could not have converted Europe from navigation by sail to navigation by steam. The age of steam had to wait until Europe had evolved the whole industrial and financial structure of which steamers are only one manifestation. In exactly the same way, a few airplanes more or less flying in from distant industrial lands cannot of themselves change the structure of Central Asia. The real question is whether air traffic in that region—and throughout Asia—is to be merely a kind of air-borne colonial enterprise, or whether the full fabric of a modern industrialism can be created to "naturalize" the use of the air and make it part of an inclusive social command over the environment.

All depends therefore on whether the other factors of a twentieth century economic system exist in Central Asia and can be developed. They do exist and they can be developed. The region where the frontiers of China, India, Afghanistan, Iran, and the Soviet Union touch or approach one another is not only a crossroads of air traffic. It is also a crossroads of future long-haul railways and motor roads. All the essential requirements of a high industrial development also lie to hand: oil, coal, iron, copper; water for both irrigation and electric power; water, climate, and soil conditions for growing cotton of the highest quality on the largest scale; and the capacity to provide food for a population many times larger than at present. Finally, political methods enabling Asiatic societies to evolve rapidly the capacity for a fully developed technology and industry have already been demonstrated in the Soviet Union. Other methods are being discussed and experimented with in China. Discussion, experiment, and achievement are equally within the grasp of the peoples of India, Afghanistan, and Iran.

There can be only one conclusion. The inland crossroads of Asia will not be a crossroads in a desert. The age in which Asia was penetrated and developed from its fringes toward the center is drawing to an end. A new age is opening out in which the focus or development will lie at or near the center, and the effect of this development will radiate outward to the fringes. This in turn means that for countries like America and Britain the age of control is vanishing. For us the problem is no longer whether to impose or how to impose our ideas and our methods. Asia can now make its own way forward—with us if we are wise, or in spite of us if we are stupid. Our problem is not how to control this development, but how to adapt ourselves to it.

25

Asia Through Haushofer's Glasses

By HANS W. WEIGERT

HANS W. WEIGERT, born in Berlin, Germany. Dr. juris utriusque, University of Freiburg, 1926, Professor of Area Studies and Political Science at the University of Pittsburgh and Professor of International Relations at Trinity College (on leave of absence).

Author: *German Geopolitics*, 1941; *Generals and Geographers: The Twilight of Geopolitics*, 1942; and articles on political geography and international relations.

"Asia Through Haushofer's Glasses" was published, in a slightly different version, in *Foreign Affairs*, July, 1942, pp. 732–743 ("Haushofer and the Pacific").

We but teach
Bloody instructions, which, being taught, return
To plague the inventor.
—*Macbeth*, Act I, Sc. 7.

What we call a "global view" in this country is a new kind of geographical thinking and imagination which we have acquired only recently. Our difficulties in seeing our own way clearly, in perceiving the fateful importance of new highways and skyways in a shrinking world, make it almost impossible for us to understand the "world view" of other peoples, and particularly that of our enemies. Yet such understanding is of vital importance in the battles to win the war and a durable peace.

Nowhere in the world have the attempts to apply geographical factors to strategy and world conquest been more audacious than in Germany. I refer, of course, to its geopolitical school under the leadership of General Haushofer. This group of men has had a significant influence on the strategy of the Germany army. For this reason, and in order to reexamine our own vision, it is of more than academic interest to review some of Haushofer's geopolitical axioms in world politics.

One of the methods by which Karl Haushofer, the hero of

geopolitikers all over the world, hammers his ideas into the minds of his readers is the constant repetition of simple truths. He likes, for instance, to quote a remark by the English geographer and statesman, Sir Thomas Holdich, about "the absolutely immeasurable cost of geographical ignorance," and he never tires of citing Ovid's "Fas est ab hoste doceri" (It is right to learn from the enemy), and Disraeli's "At last the best informed one wins."

These three simple maxims help also to explain the American public's sudden and amazing interest in German geopolitics and its master. Not so long ago our geographical education was insufficient and uninspired. Then all at once the man in the street and the political leader alike became aware that we might have to pay a high price for our ignorance. In the hour of danger we were ready at last "to learn from the enemy." The magic word "geopolitics" and the mysterious personality of its prophet kindled the interest of a broad public, and the interest was intensified by the manner in which this "secret weapon" of Hitler's was first presented. German geopolitics invaded the United States as some sort of superscience. We were given an exciting lesson on "the thousand scientists behind Hitler"; we were told that Haushofer and his followers dominated the thinking of Hitler, and that it was Haushofer who directed the German General Staff's plans for world dominion.

Even if one turned from such journalistic approaches to recognized authorities in the field of international politics, one came upon remarks like the one by Colonel Beukema of West Point that history will rate Karl Haushofer as more important than Adolf Hitler because Haushofer's studies made possible Hitler's victories both in power politics and in war. No wonder, then, that everywhere "geopolitics" became the political catchword of the day, that the highest eulogy a political writer could earn was to be called "the American Haushofer," and that colleges all over the country hurried to organize "Institutes of Geopolitics."

But German geopolitics is not a thing we can adopt outright for American use, for it has all the characteristics of a typical German *Weltanschauung*. This is an important point for us to keep in mind when we deal with geopolitics in theory or practice. Some of the proponents of geopolitics in this country have, coolly and cynically, surrendered to this *Weltanschauung*. They do not see that geographical materialism is nothing but a dynamic nihilism which flourishes only in a nation which has buried its gods and is worshiping Mars instead. Freedom and justice for all and not only for the mighty ones, the simple tenets of Christianity—such "impractical" concepts as these do not figure in modern German geopolitics. Nor do we find them in the theses of some American "realists." They forget that there are imponderables which can defeat the most precise schemes of power politicians.

It is also necessary to call attention to the wall which separates German geopolitical thought and ideology from the geopolitics of other nations. There is no such thing as a general science of geopolitics. It does not have a single form. There are as many geopolitics as there are conflicting states struggling under geographic conditions which are—in the case of sea powers and land powers, for example—as different as day is from night. As it has been said that every nation has the government it deserves, so it can be said that it has the geopolitics it deserves. The German definition limits its use to Germany—a warning which should be heeded by those who try to adapt the sinuous ways of Haushofer's geopolitics to American use.

We shall discuss certain ways of "seeing" on a global scale which German geopolitics has developed in regard to the Pacific and to Asia. Daring and farsighted as they are in many respects, we must warn, however, against the widely accepted myth that Haushofer and his men possessed truly a "global view" of our new world. Haushofer saw the world as his great master, Sir Halford Mackinder, had seen it. That made him understand the pivotal importance of the land masses connecting the territories of Germany, the Soviet Union, and China in one immense transcontinental block. But both Mackinder and Haushofer remained captives of Mercator's map. And the fateful mistake made them see the *North American* continent as a satellite sphere beyond the sphere of Eurasia. Thus in appraising Haushofer's view and vision of the Pacific and of Asia, we must keep in mind that it neglected the power and the geopolitics of the United States in this area.[1] A fateful blunder!

Of more than thirty studies which Karl Haushofer wrote (in addition to his regular monthly reviews) on what he called the Indo-Pacific space, his *Geopolitik des Pazifischen Ozeans* (Geopolitics of the Pacific Ocean), first published in 1924, has held its position as his most significant work—as the Bible of German geopolitics. Its subtitle, "Studies on the Relationship Between Geography and History," clearly indicates that it was intended to contain more than an analysis of the geopolitical importance of the Pacific area. The book is, therefore, the ideal introduction to German geopolitics.

As early as 1908, when he first went to Japan, Haushofer had grasped what the rise of new forces in the East meant to the destinies of Europe. He had been deeply impressed by Friedrich Ratzel's fascinating concept of the "law of the growing spaces." It had led him naturally to the shores of the Pacific, which he describes as the largest "physiographic region on earth." He saw it as a power sphere, slowly awakening, for the first time in history, to the consciousness of being one of the largest land and sea spaces. "A giant space is expanding before our eyes," he wrote, "with forces pouring into it which, in cool matter-of-factness, await the dawn of the Pacific age, the successor to the aging Atlantic, the overage Mediterranean, and the European era." [2] Theodore Roosevelt had said the same thing when he spoke of the declining resources of the Atlantic area and predicted the dawn of the Pacific age. But Haushofer was more specific. He drew the outlines of an actual, if long-term, politics, following the elementary lesson taught by Leopold von Ranke that "politics is the attempt to safeguard and further national interests in the midst of a conflict of the Great Powers, both in the realm of ideas and in that of realities."

When the General Haushofer of the First World War had led

[1] Cf. R. E. Harrison and H. W. Weigert, "World View and Strategy," p. 74.

[2] *Zeitschrift für Geopolitik*, 1925, p. 63.

his division, unbeaten in battle, back to his suffering fatherland, he had begun immediately to draw new blueprints of gigantic dimensions. He knew that the war had ruined not Germany alone but all of Europe. He repeats many times what Lord Kitchener said to him in 1909: that he was opposed to the coming war between England and Germany because it would ruin Europe's future in the Pacific forever. America and Japan would be the only ones to profit from such a war, he added.

Deeply offended pride and hatred against the Powers which had humiliated his beloved fatherland caused Haushofer to welcome the rise of the colored world. He foresaw the coming doom of the white race with fatalism and even with malicious joy. This attitude is characteristic of Haushofer's thinking: he constantly points to the fatal mistake which the white winners of the war made when they permitted the Japanese to take over Germany's Pacific islands. The loss of Germany's foothold in the Pacific gave Haushofer a basis for the claim that German and Japanese vital aims no longer overlapped anywhere. Germany, he said, could therefore subscribe to the cry of "Asia for the Asiatics" and prepare to co-operate with Japan on the ground of a "symbiosis of cultural politics." [3]

The following quotation from *Geopolitics of the Pacific Ocean* contains the whole of Haushofer's Pacific philosophy and indicates its roots of resentment and fatalism:

"By a dreadful decision, with consequences of utmost gravity for those who made it, the ocean-embracing cultural and economic powers of our own race have expelled us from their midst. They have left us in no doubt about the fact that only their destruction and decomposition will create another life for us who are now mutilated and enslaved. Thus they have forced us to search for comrades of destiny who are in a similar situation. We see such companions of disaster in the nine hundred million southeast Asiatics. They struggle, as we do, for their right of self-determination, against the same oppressors as ourselves; but they

[3] *Geopolitik des Pazifischen Ozeans,* 1924, p. 162. Unless otherwise indicated, subsequent citations will refer to this edition.

fight to some extent with more efficient weapons created by the living conditions of the Indian and Pacific oceans, the arsenal of a Pacific geopolitics. We see that in these spaces the results of a punishing justice are partly in preparation and partly already consummated, to be felt by our merciless economic and political enemies and oppressors."

The right of self-determination plays a large part in this concept. But how different it is from Woodrow Wilson's ideal! The right of self-determination of small nations does not enter a mind which is preoccupied with the idea, first clearly defined by Ratzel, that every people must be educated up from smaller to larger space conceptions. Haushofer is dominated by his conviction that a declining space conception brings decay of the state.

Thus he looks to the awakened people of the Pacific:

"Thrown back upon the minimum of existence, driven from the sun into the shadow, cut off from the free sea, and even deprived, until 1936, of free traffic on our own rivers, the Germans find two-thirds of mankind as fellow sufferers on the beaches of the Indo-Pacific spaces. They long to break the same chains, they long for the same liberation and for the achievement of the highest goal of nations and individuals alike, the free personality governed by its own laws. That is the ultimate reason why the Germans must not lose contact with the Pacific." [4]

By studying the Pacific the Germans must learn again to think and feel in large space terms. Germany must play her part, if possible with Haushofer as director, in the great tragedy of world history in which the people of the largest continent will shake off the guardianship imposed on them by the sea Powers.

"The struggle of India and China for liberation from foreign domination and capitalistic pressure," Haushofer writes, "agrees with the secret dreams of Central Europe." [5] He compares his own views with Canning's, after the Napoleonic Wars: "While Europe was paralyzed by small-space conditions, Canning laid the foundations for an almost riskless growth in the early Vic-

[4] *Zeitschrift für Geopolitik*, 1938, p. 820.
[5] *Geopolitik*, p. 132.

torian period by the recognition of the independence movements in the Near East and South America. Now the Indo-Pacific forces, moving in the same direction, look out with increasing confidence for help from the outside. . . . They look to Germany for help, and it is there that they should find a greater understanding of their geopolitical fundamentals." He continues:

"The instinct of these things to come has become a living force, and the battlecry of the self-determination of small nations, which was used as a temporary tactical means to deceive the world, is now turned against its inventors. It has awakened the self-consciousness of the big neighbors of the small nations, of the great cultural spaces which are bound together by the eternal manifestations of their soil. Suddenly the cultural sphere of Central Europe, tormented for thousands of years like the others, becomes aware of a world-embracing community and destiny. It feels that it is liberated from artificial isolation; it sees itself accepted into the community of the struggling large spaces of the earth. It is for this reason that the geopolitical giant of the monsoon-lands and the struggle of its nine hundred millions for self-determination mean destiny for the people of Central Europe, too."

Nothing is left in Haushofer of the instinct of the unity of the white race as it was expressed by William II. He deliberately and sometimes even cynically denounces such feelings: "It is not up to the Germans to create a white bloc. This bloc was smashed by those who used colored troops in the Rhineland to keep down a white race. The opposite postulate, 'Oppressed peoples of the world, unite!' can be much better justified on ethical grounds." [6] The following quotation is even more outspoken: "We must counteract the oppression which we suffer from the uncultured colored peoples of a half-African power [France] by helping to liberate the cultured races which will rise against our oppressors. Thus we shall hold the strategic lines of a future geopolitics of the Pacific: there lies our chance to share actively in world politics in the spaces from which we have been displaced." [7]

[6] *Zeitschrift für Geopolitik,* 1928, p. 1040.
[7] *Geopolitik,* p. 242.

Such are the factors and the emotional background which explain the destiny-laden connection between German geopolitics and the Pacific. But since German geopolitics and Haushofer are identical, we must also take into account the strong ties which bind the man Haushofer to the Far East, particularly to Japan. German geopolitics would not have turned to the Far East and centered so definitely in the Pacific if Haushofer had not decided to make this part of the world the center of all his planning. It was not only in his *Geopolitics of the Pacific Ocean* that he tried to bring the East close to the German people. As far back as 1911 his doctoral thesis dealt with the geographic bases of Japan's military power; in 1913 he published *Dai Nihon*, reflections on Japan's military power, her position in the world and her future; and other books and articles on Japan followed.

He would not have followed this course had it not been that in Japan and China he had received the deepest impressions of his life. Thus the September day in 1908 when as a thirty-nine-year-old captain on the Bavarian General Staff he received the unexpected order to leave immediately on a two-year mission as Bavarian military attaché in Japan, was not only the decisive date in Haushofer's life; it was also an important date in history. For Haushofer then started to forge the weapons of a new German Far Eastern policy. In addition, he became "the geopolitical adviser of Japan itself," as one of his closest friends declared in 1929.

It is impossible to describe briefly the contents of Haushofer's *Geopolitics of the Pacific Ocean*, which, as already indicated, is not only a political book but an attempt to educate the German people for a global view of world politics. Only such a view would make them "see" the coming clash between "the pirates of the steppes and the pirates of the sea," to use a favorite formulation which Haushofer borrowed from Mackinder.

Always in the background of *Geopolitics of the Pacific Ocean* stand Germany and Japan. It is this attempt to link the great spaces of the Pacific to the small spaces of Germany that makes the book and its author so powerful a current factor in foreign politics. Japan is the nucleus of the revolution in the East.

Haushofer sees Japan as a nation with two faces: one gazes toward the Pacific, the other toward Asia. In the past, because of her insular location, Japan has always turned to the ocean. Only in this century has she started her expansion in Asia.

As the years passed, Haushofer could not help becoming more and more doubtful about the chances of Japan in her continental adventure. "Will power and purpose remain in balance?" he asks in 1938. "Or will the Pan Asiatic drive for world dominion drag the insular empire beyond the limitations of her strength? Are her leaders prepared to think in terms of continents instead of oceans, as they would have to think in order to accomplish so far-reaching a task?"

The following sentences written at the same time did not differ basically from what he had been writing since 1924:

"Vladivostok, from which bomber squadrons and submarines can be sent against Japan's most vulnerable arteries and communication centers, is the only place which 'the proud, oceanic face' of the Japanese Navy is not able to control. Furthermore, the possibility of cooperation between Soviet Russia and the United States on the northern shores of the Pacific takes shape from month to month [1938]. It would be a great mistake for the Berlin-Rome-Tokyo triangle to delude itself about the role of the United States. Its antagonism against the Axis makes it possible to throw a bridge across the deep gulf between Wall Street's supercapitalism and Moscow's Bolshevism." [8]

Fully aware of the tragic possibilities of Japan's adventure, Haushofer worked for years on the task of persuading Japan to come to terms with China and the U.S.S.R. and, on the other side of the world, of convincing Hitler that he should live in peace with the Soviet Union. The persuasion of Hitler was, of course, the chief problem. The editors of the *Zeitschrift für Geopolitik* had stubbornly advocated reconciliation and friendship with the Soviets from the beginning, and Hitler's noisy crusade

[8] *Zeitschrift für Geopolitik*, 1938, pp. 937–942.

against the archenemy, Bolshevism, made no impression on them. Since 1924 they had written in favor of an Asiatic alliance including the U.S.S.R., Japan, India, and China, with Germany as partner. "Germany will have to decide," wrote one of the editors in 1925, "where she stands: does she want to be a satellite of the Anglo-Saxon powers and their supercapitalism, which are united with the other European nations against Russia, or will she be an ally of the Pan Asiatic union against Europe and America?" The answer is that "no nation is closer to Russia than is Germany; only Germany can understand the Russian soul; Germany and Russia have been friends for centuries; their economic structures are complementary; they must hang together." The German-Soviet nonaggression pact of August 23, 1939, was Haushofer's greatest triumph; it brought him close to the fulfillment of his most audacious dreams. "Never again," he prayed, "shall Germany and Russia endanger, by ideological conflicts, the geopolitical foundations of their adjustable spaces." [9]

The following sentences, written by Haushofer in February, 1932, throw a dazzling light on the manner in which he viewed Russia's—and particularly Stalin's—foreign policy in the Far East:

"The attitude of Moscow and of the Eurasiatics towards developments in India, East Asia, and the Near East deserves increased attention. Will Moscow be ready to jump into action at the right moment? And will such action be dictated by conceptions of Russian international policy or by a world revolutionary ideology? The policy towards Japan will be the test. Stalin's extremely cautious policy has been explained . . . by the claim that the Russian leader is not master of his own decisions. This, I believe, is wrong. Stalin's policy seems to me to originate from a much better understanding of the situation than the West is capable of perceiving. . . . In Moscow it is realized much better than elsewhere that the victor, in great-Asiatic dynamics, is the one who succeeds in letting the others discern his

[9] *Zeitschrift für Geopolitik*, 1939, p. 773.

plans *last*, and who takes the initiative in the power-center *last*. Also, the limits of the dangers threatening from Japan are known there precisely, as well as the areas where one is secure from Japanese aggressive infiltration. Moscow, with great skill, has passed the option to the North Americans, whose nerves are considered inferior; and indeed certain symptoms can be found to support this assumption." [10]

With the same patient farsightedness, Haushofer labored to guide Japan toward friendship with Soviet Russia and China.

In May, 1940, he wrote: "If it were possible for the nations of the Rising Sun and of the Hammer and Sickle to end their mutual distrust . . . they would be invincible in their domestic seas." [11] It was destiny, alike for Japan and for Germany, to come to terms with the U.S.S.R., "the geographical pivot of history." Sir Halford Mackinder had first given Haushofer this grandiose view of Russia in 1904. He never forgot it, and made it the basis of all his grand strategy. Japan and Germany were two stations on the "inner line" which, in the age of the railroad and the airplane, gave continental Powers such decisive advantages over the aging sea Powers; but between those stations was Russia. "The geopolitical future will belong to the Russian-Chinese bloc." Therefore, he concluded, Japan must reconcile her aims with Russia's.

"The less friction there is in the relations between Japan and Russia, the less chance there will be for the Anglo-Saxons and the Chinese to impose a policy of divide and rule. Japan and Russia, if united, are invincible in East Asia. . . . A Mongolia led by Russia, a South Manchuria led by Japan, and between them a buffer region . . . that could be a more durable combination than all the constructions of Versailles. . . . Japan could become the continent-minded partner of a continental politics of the old world. . . . This would give Japan complete protection and freedom for action in the Pacific, a geopolitical

[10] *Zeitschrift für Geopolitik*, 1932, p. 132.
[11] *Ibid.*, 1940, p. 292.

possibility of immense importance not only for Japan and Russia but also for Central Europe and its enemies." [12]

Haushofer's concept of the grand strategy of the future, as set forth in the *Zeitschrift für Geopolitik* in 1930 (page 961), is more candid than he is accustomed to being in the pages of his journal:

"The ultimate solution of Japan's problem of overpopulation is expansion into the spheres of least resistance. . . . At this time, Japan's strategy still cautions her against a direct attack on Australia. But it should not be forgotten that the tropical north and northeast of Australia today give shelter to only a few thousand white men although they could offer homesteads for thirty million people. Heat and humidity make these spaces unfit for large-scale colonization by the white races; the climate is more suitable for the Japanese."

In this connection it is interesting to note Haushofer's criticism of the United States which, because of its "extensive colonial space structure," is unable to understand the dilemma caused in Eastern Asia and Central Europe by population pressure. "It is an exceptional case," writes Haushofer, "when an American, Isaiah Bowman, becomes impressed by the population density of Japan and admits that 'it must overflow its boundaries.' " [13] Haushofer forgets to say, however, that Bowman added, "if not by people then by exports." This instance of Haushofer's utter disregard of all attempts to solve such problems by international economic cooperation is characteristic.[14]

But Japan did not listen to Haushofer's admonitions to strike first against the British Empire (and France and the Netherlands). Instead of turning to the south, Japan started her drive on the continent. Haushofer warned that this would draw the Chinese and the Indians together and would result in the formation of an unconquerable human bloc of eight hundred millions.

[12] Haushofer calls it the "Eurasian continental organization from the Rhine to the Amur and Yangtze" (*Geopolitik*, pp. 142–143).

[13] *Geopolitik*, 3rd ed. (1938), p. 212.

[14] Cf. I. Bowman's comments in his article "Geography vs. Geopolitics," p. 49.

He reminded the Japanese generals who won the upper hand over the admirals that they would have to win the peace, too.

Haushofer himself has no real illusions: "Japan has underestimated the immense spaces of China, and she will never understand the spirit of modern China. She has not understood the greatness of Chiang Kai-shek, symbol of the new China, the first leader in history to represent the whole Chinese nation." [15] Again: "China is a sea which makes all rivers flowing into it salty; if Japan penetrates too far into China she will be drowned." If an empire could arise with "Japan's soul in China's body," it would be a power that would put even the empires of the U.S.S.R. and the United States in the shade. But this, Haushofer knew, was an old man's empty dream.

In the world of realities there was but one solution: the inner line would have to be held in peaceful collaboration with the powers of the "geographical pivot of history." Germany as well as Japan would have to seek peace and friendship with the Soviet Union and China. Then Japan, with her back secure against continental attack, could start her crusade for an empire in the Pacific. But neither Germany nor Japan listened to their would-be mentor. On June 22, 1941, Haushofer's plans were smashed by another dreamer in the Bavarian mountains. Eastward the course of German self-destruction took its way.

Fas est ab hoste doceri; we *must* learn from the enemy. The "transcontinental bloc" which Mackinder's disciple Haushofer had seen on the horizon, has become a reality in the power-center of the U.S.S.R. Its influence is felt throughout Asia and will deeply affect the future destinies of China and India. We cannot, in fact no nation or combination of nations can, destroy the fundamentals of a transcontinental bloc based on centralized land power and land-based air power. We have no option but to adapt ourselves to a geopolitics which ties the vital interests of the United States to those of the great land Powers.

[15] *Zeitschrift für Geopolitik*, 1939, p. 30.

CHAPTER VI

The Shifting Balance of Man Power

26

Population Trends and International Relations

By QUINCY WRIGHT

QUINCY WRIGHT, born in Medford, Mass. A.M., University of Illinois, 1913; Ph.D., 1915. Chairman, Committee on International Relations and Professor of International Law, University of Chicago.

Author: *Control of American Foreign Relations*, 1922; *Mandates Under the League of Nations*, 1930; *The Causes of War and the Conditions of Peace*, 1935; *A Study of War*, 1942, and numerous other studies on international law and relations.

"Population Trends and International Relations" is a slightly different version of Chapter XXXI in the author's *A Study of War*.

Population changes are measurable, and are being measured to an increasing extent in all countries. They are also, given time, controllable by restrictive, expansive, or eugenic population policies. If the effect on international relations of such changes proved to be determinate, statesmen would have at their disposal a means which might be useful both for predicting and for controlling war.

Unfortunately, it appears that no such determinate relation exists. A general increase in the world's population may lead to closer cooperation among peoples. On the other hand, a general increase of population may lead to more friction and war. Extreme differentials in the density of population in different areas may lead to mutually advantageous exchanges and to the development of peaceful interdependence, as is customarily found in the relations of the city and the rural areas within a state or in the relations of motherland and young migration colony. Population differentials may, however, lead to tensions, mass migrations, aggressions, wars, and conquests, as did the relation of Europe to the American Indians in the sixteenth and seventeenth centuries. A country whose population is growing more rapidly than its neighbor's may start a war of conquest; and a country whose population is growing less rapidly than its neighbor's may start a preventive war. On the other hand, neighboring countries with very different rates of growth in population may live at peace.

Population changes, like climatic changes, geographical and geological discoveries, technological and social inventions, greatly influence political behavior; but the more "civilized" peoples become, the less determinate is this relationship. Among primitive peoples, the possible alternatives, when confronted by such changes, are limited, definite, and predictable. Such peoples may be said to behave under "necessity," although ethnological investigation proves that the behavior is dictated not by physical or physiological laws but by tribal custom. These patterns have sometimes prescribed war or migration in case of population pressure. When desert Arabs increased in population beyond their pasturage, they raided their neighbors.[1] When desiccation reduced the pasturage of nomads of the steppes, great hordes moved into the agricultural areas of Russia or China.[2] When a Pacific island became overcrowded, certain of the Polynesian inhabitants took to their boats to find new islands.

The essence of civilization is increased realization that there are alternative solutions to problems and increased opportunity to explore different alternatives. Civilized man is able to substitute "rational" for "necessary" solutions. What Great Britain, France, Germany, Italy, Japan, the Netherlands, Russia, or the United States will do in the presence of population changes is not predetermined.

In all these countries the mass of the population is normally so much above the starvation line that population pressure influ-

[1] Ellsworth Huntington, *The Character of Races* (New York, 1924).
[2] Arnold J. Toynbee, *A Study of History* (New York, 1934), III, 420 ff.

ences not the the means of subsistence but rather the "standard of living." Remedies for incipient population pressure are explored before starvation or even a serious diminution of the standard of living is threatened.

Among the many circumstances which affect both the ends and the means of foreign policy are racial and cultural characteristics, the state of public opinion, historic traditions, national laws and treaties, the conditions of international communication and organization, the balance of military forces in the world, the state of credit, trade, and production, the theories and temperaments of individuals who happen to be in power; all these may differ from country to country and from time to time, and the policy will be influenced by the particular combination operative at a given time and place.

Japan, Italy, and Germany with growing populations embarked upon plans of conquest. Java and China, with even more serious population problems, attempted to intensify their agricultural methods and to develop rural industries. Russia, confronted by a similar situation in 1917, had a revolution, abandoned territory which it had possessed, suspended projects for further expansion, and changed the emphasis of its economy from agriculture to mining and industry. Belgium and Switzerland have met their population problems by continually expanding their industrial exports and their imports of foodstuffs and raw materials.

Few writers contend that international disturbances of a definite type will flow from the numerical population situation alone. Warren Thompson, who attempted to draw rather precise prescriptions for international policy from his study of population, realized that the tendency of certain states toward conquest does not flow from population pressure alone. It also depends upon whether the nation is at the "swarming stage of development," whether its people are literate and aware of superior conditions elsewhere, whether racially and culturally they are better adapted than the present possessors to develop available areas.[3] In other words, he recognizes that the international disturbance to be

[3] *Danger Spots in World Population* (New York, 1929), pp. 14, 17, 45

anticipated is a function of a number of variables, of which population pressure is only one.

The indeterminateness of the situation is emphasized by the opposing influences upon population policy of population pressure and the balance of power: "As soon as a population grows big, its leaders say: 'Our people are so numerous we must fight for more space.' As soon as war has taken place, the leaders invert this appeal, and say: 'We must breed more people in preparation for the next war.' "[4]

It is obviously difficult for the state to adopt a policy which both restricts population to the food supply and expands it to supply cannon fodder at the rate set by a growing neighbor. "The political doctrine exhorts man to propagate and prevail; the economic to be cautious and comfortable."[5] War may result from the inability of statesmen to choose either horn of this dilemma. On the other hand, it may result, whichever horn is chosen. The international consequences, however, will usually differ according to whether policy is directed toward economic welfare or toward military power.

It may then be concluded that population pressure in the world as a whole, or differential population pressures in neighboring nations, or the differential growth of populations considered as war potential are none of them necessary causes of war among civilized nations; nor are they rational causes of war, although theories about population changes and conditions have at times provided both reasons and rationalizations for war.

Even though no determinate international consequence can be predicted from given population conditions, an analysis may suggest certain tendencies to be anticipated from population changes on the assumption that other conditions remain constant. The subject will be examined by the (1) philosophical, (2) historical, (3) psychological, and (4) sociological methods.

(1) *The Philosophical Method*. The philosophical method relies upon the logical deduction of consequences from a general

[4] Harold Cox, *The Problem of Population* (New York, 1923), p. 97.

[5] Ezra Bowen, *A Hypothesis of Population Growth* (New York, 1931), p. 12.

proposition assumed to be true. Most writers on population accept the Malthusian theory that population tends to increase more rapidly than the supply of food, and that population is kept down to the subsistence level by preventive and positive checks. They differ, however, as indeed did Malthus himself in succeeding editions of his work, as to whether the subsistence level means the maintenance merely of life or of the customary standards of living; as to whether rapid local or general technological advances may not, for considerable periods, augment the food supply more rapidly than the population increases, permitting a higher standard of living to become established; and as to whether the preventive checks such as postponed marriage, moral restraint, and birth control may not render unnecessary the positive checks such as vice, famine, pestilence, migration, and war. Malthus himself always doubted the latter and thus felt to the last that the perfectibility of mankind by social reform would be thwarted by the operation of the positive checks.

Recent writers tend to insist that the desire to maintain a customary standard of living, not starvation, stimulates utilization of population checks, that the kind of checks utilized is determined by custom, and that even among primitive peoples these have been "preventive" (if infanticide and abortion are included in that category) as often as positive.

Quotations can, however, be cited suggesting that war is a necessary consequence of the Malthusian doctrine. The Prussian General Bernhardi writes:

> The strong, healthy, and flourishing nations increase in numbers. From a given moment they require continual expansion of their frontiers, they require new territory for the accommodation of their surplus population. Since almost every part of the globe is inhabited, new territory must, as a rule, be obtained at the cost of its possessors —that is to say, by conquest, which thus becomes a law of necessity.[6]

[6] F. Bernhardi, *Germany and the Next War* (London, 1911), p. 50. The *Lebensraum* theory of writers on geopolitics (F. Ratzel, R. Kjellén, K. Haushofer) is similar (Derwent Whittlesey, "The Role of Geography in Twentieth-Century War," in J. D. Clarkson and T. C. Cochran [eds.], *War As a Social Institution* [New York, 1941], p. 84).

Even this quotation refers only to "strong, healthy, and flourishing nations," implying that there may be nations which need not engage in aggression, although they may be in danger of becoming victims of aggression.[7]

In the contingency suggested it is hard to see how even war might prove a satisfactory alternative. If one considers all the qualifications added to the original Malthusian doctrine, the idea of "necessity" to fight evaporates in all situations of the contemporary world. Even if the entire world should become overpopulated under the most efficient economic system so that migration could not provide a remedy, the other positive checks—vice, famine, and pestilence—might operate within each state, and thus the overpopulation might have no effect on international relations.

However, in such a state of civilization, it is more likely that the preventive checks would eliminate the "necessity" for war. The birth controllers have emphasized this, although they view the alternative too narrowly when they write: "The different races of the world either must agree to restrain their powers of increase or must prepare to fight one another."

There are still other alternatives. If the entire world is not filled up, cooperation to utilize the remaining land might be feasible as indeed Sir Thomas More suggested, though the Utopians accounted it a most just cause of war if the inhabitants of such inadequately used land refused to cooperate. Furthermore, the limits of agricultural and technological advance have as yet not been reached, although doubtless the law of diminishing returns imposes such limits, given the limited resources and surface of the earth.[8]

[7] *Op. cit.*, p. 108. "In one way or another it is economic pressure, resulting from population pressure, that has caused most major conflicts in the world. If all the world had the same standard of living, if no nation were under serious economic pressure, if all populations were stationary at the same high standard of living, there would be nothing to gain by war, by conquest or by exploitation. Only if and when we reach this state does there seem to be much chance for universal peace" (Carl Alsberg, in Institute of Pacific Relations, *Problems of the Pacific* [Chicago, 1929], p. 317). See also E. M. East, *Mankind at the Crossroads* (New York, 1923), pp. 343–44.

[8] The limits of population seem now to be set by the supply of mechanical energy-producers—coal, oil, natural gas—rather than by that of food.

Leaving aside consideration of alternative positive or preventive checks to ameliorate present or anticipated overpopulation, under what conditions is overpopulation most likely to suggest such internationally disturbing policies as migration or war?

In the first place, there must be another area which to the overpopulated area appears to be underpopulated. This does not mean that the area is underpopulated judged by the state of the arts or the standard of living of its population. California may, for example, have an optimum population for the Californian standard of living, and Massachusetts may, in 1620, have had an optimum population for the Indians' technology. But for the Japanese standard of living today, California is underpopulated, and for the Pilgrims of England, Massachusetts was underpopulated in 1620.

Second, there must be knowledge of this area within the overpopulated area. Before Columbus, overpopulation in Europe caused no migration to America. Even today, knowledge of areas where people might better their conditions may be very limited among the people who are most depressed.

In the third place, there must be means of mobility. Horsemen and seamen tended to migrate and fight more than agriculturalists until the advent of the railroads and steamboats and organized armies with artificial means of mobility.

Energy is also necessary. People who have long suffered from overpopulation, as in the famine areas of China and India, are usually so depressed and feeble that they lack the initiative either to migrate or to fight.

But with knowledge, mobility, and energy the physical obstacles to be overcome must not be too difficult. Geographical barriers

Food supply is limited by the supply of mineral fertilizers rather than by land (Alsberg in *Op. cit.*, pp. 121 and 317; but see O. E. Baker, in *Ibid.*, p. 322). Estimates of the maximum population the world could feed run from five billion (East) and eight billion (Penck) to ten billion (Kuczynski, in Corrado Gini *et al.*, *Population* [Chicago, 1930], p. 285). Kuczynski, considering the trend in the balance of births and deaths, sees "no real danger of a general overpopulation (*Ibid.*, p. 302)—an opinion shared by Pearl (*The Biology of Population Growth* [New York, 1925]).

to travel—seas, mountains, deserts—may be less deterrent than the difficulty of reducing the pioneer area to productivity.

If the coveted area is inhabited, social and moral barriers may be even more formidable. Immigration laws and discriminations against aliens may augment the psychological desirability of the area; but in the presence of such obstacles war may have to be resorted to, and consequently the prospective migrants must have military instruments and habits which give promise of adequacy. Even with prospects of military success the practical problem of assimilating, governing, driving out, or exterminating the inhabitants may be a deterrent, to say nothing of ideas of humanity and respect for international law.

Finally, there are a host of subjective conditions to be considered. Overpopulated and depressed as they may be, are the people prepared to sacrifice an accustomed way of life in order to endure vaguely perceived hardships in an unfamiliar environment?

Experience suggests that only rarely do all these conditions conspire actually to bring about large-scale migration, war, and conquest as a result of overpopulation. Apart from the gradual pushing-out from the center by primitive peoples, the adjective "necessary" hardly seems appropriate to apply to the behavior of those who migrate or fight for a new home.

Thus it appears that the Malthusian doctrine, properly qualified, leads only to the proposition that population pressures may or may not lead to international difficulties, depending upon a multitude of geographic, cultural, technological, physiological, political, military, psychological, and other factors in the particular situation.

(2) *The Historical Method.* The conclusion reached by application of the philosophical method seems to be supported by application of the historical method. By the latter is meant the establishment of the consequences of actual changes which have occurred in the past.

The most superficial historical consideration amply supports the proposition that "a reduction of the world's population will not in fact necessarily prevent all wars." Certainly, historic instances abound of falling population without peace, as in Europe from A.D. 252 to 700 and from A.D. 1346 to 1500. In both these periods political structures were disintegrating and smaller political units were engaging in wars. In the first instance the imperial wars of the Roman Empire gave way to smaller wars of barbarian groups, and in the latter instance the Crusades gave way to feudal wars and wars between the rising princes. While in both cases depopulation was begun by epidemics, it was promoted by the political and economic disorganization which followed these disasters. Depopulation did not prevent but promoted war and international disorder.

On the other hand, the periods of most rapidly increasing population in Western history have been the first two centuries of the Roman Empire and the nineteenth century, the periods of the *pax Romana* and the *pax Britannica,* when international relations were on the whole most tranquil.

It is, of course, recognized that periods of declining population may be periods of increasing population pressure (in the sense of decreasing standards of living), because the production of food and other goods may be diminishing even more rapidly. Conversely, periods of rising population may be periods of decreasing population pressure, because, as was true in nineteenth century Europe, the technology of production is increasing even more rapidly. However, consideration of the diverse foreign policies of neutralized Belgium, expansionist Japan, and commercial England in the latter nineteenth century, during which they were all rapidly increasing in population and standards of living as a result of industrialization, suggests that many factors besides population changes contribute to foreign policy. The same suggestion would flow from a comparison of policies of dominantly agricultural countries with a rising population but a probably declining or stationary standard of living during the same period, such as disintegrating China, expansionist Russia, and colonial India.

It is very difficult to compare the degree of population pressure (or rate of change of standards of living) in different countries. It seems clear, however, that historic tradition, geographic position, stage of technological development, state of literacy and communication, and relative military power influence the consequences upon foreign policy of variations in such pressure.

In fact, it would appear that population changes have more often influenced international relations because of their effect upon military potential than because of their effect on standards of living. A country growing in population more rapidly than its neighbor may be less belligerent than the latter because, with respect to relative military potential, time is with it and it feels increasingly secure. While, on the other hand, a country increasing in population less rapidly than its neighbor may view with increasing alarm the shift of the balance of power against it. These conditions, which were obvious in the relations of France and Germany from 1870 to 1890, may, of course, be altered by the establishment of alliances, as when France, with a stationary population, allied herself in 1891 with Russia, whose population was growing more rapidly than that of Germany. Germany, which previously had viewed her relations with France with comparative equanimity, now became alarmed.

These two types of population influence have worked in opposite directions. In the period after 1871 it might have been supposed that France, with a declining population pressure, would be satisfied and nonexpansionist; but actually, with its declining military potential relative to Germany, it rapidly expanded in Africa to supplement its armies by black troops. Russia, on the other hand, with a rising military potential with relation to Germany—at least in respect to the supply of cannon fodder—was also continuously expansionist because of the need to find new lands for the extensive farming of a teeming, low-standard population. Germany, with a population growth between France and Russia, viewed its military position vis-à-vis France with equanimity, and vis-à-vis Russia with alarm, while industrialization made it possible to provide a growing population with a rising standard of living if an expanding international trade could be maintained. The supposition that colonies and a navy would mutually help each other and both would help trade led Germany also to expansionism. The roles of population change in these three cases were different, though the expansionist results had a resemblance.

(3) *The Psychological Method.* The psychological method refers to the use of facts or theories to influence opinion and policy. Population changes have frequently provided legislators, statesmen, and journalists with arguments in discussions of immigration, tariff, colonial, and military policy.

In the United States the assumption has been commonly made that population tends to flow from low- to high-standard-of-living countries and ultimately reduces the standard of the latter. Thus American immigration legislation has been based on the theory that higher bars should be provided for Orientals than for Europeans because the economic level of the former averages lower. In such discussions, however, cultural difference and the possibility of assimilation have also been stressed. It is difficult to tell whether the dominant motivation has been economic or cultural.

On the other hand, Italian publicists have asserted (as did American politicians of an earlier period) that their low-paid industrious labor will cheerfully do work which American workers eschew. The Italians add that the virile blood of the Italians will provide a desirable race mixture and prevent the biologic decline of the more effete Americans. They have sometimes added that Italy wishes to lose neither the labor nor the blood of its sons, and thus it welcomes immigration bars, unwise as these may be from the American standpoint.

In the tariff issue American protectionists commonly assume that the products of countries with low-wage populations would flood American markets and reduce the pay envelope of the American worker, while free traders stress the mutual advantage if each population produces what it is adapted to make most efficiently and then trades.

Imperialist orators have suggested the need of colonies as an outlet for population as well as a source of raw materials and markets, while anti-imperialists have emphasized the insignificant migration from the motherland to most overseas colonies, the slight relief to home population pressure from such migration because workers left behind rapidly fill the gap, the relative unimportance of colonial markets and raw materials, as compared with foreign markets and raw materials for most industrial states, and the generally unfavorable balance of the colonial account when the total advantages and costs are counted.

Most of the talk by politicians and publicists about the general economic value to a country of colonies is "rationalization." The "reason" for supporting such policies is to be found rather in the military advantage of having certain key raw materials, a source of cannon fodder, and perhaps a naval base or a strategic frontier under military control; in the hope for colonial jobs and concessions from which a very small minority of the home population can profit at the expense of the general taxpayer; in the realization that colonial jobs for younger sons and college graduates may be a preventive of revolution in a country where centralization of political and industrial responsibility steadily diminishes the number of leadership jobs while higher education increases the number of those who think themselves qualified to lead; in the expansiveness which the average citizen with a rather limited and humdrum experience feels in identifying himself with a growing area on the map, even if he has to pay for it by a diminished standard of living; in the need which the political and economic élite feel, in times of depression, for diverting the public mind to distant adventure as a protection against criticism or revolutionary impulse; and in the anxiety which both leaders and average citizens feel lest the national brand of culture die out or diminish in relative importance unless it is growing in an ever larger section of the earth's surface.

The latter point does indeed frequently appear in political oratory on the subject. Thus Treitschke, one of Hitler's torchbearers, writes:

All great nations in the fullness of their strength have desired to set their mark upon barbarian lands. All over the globe today we see the peoples of Europe creating a mighty aristocracy of the white races. Those who take no share in this great rivalry will play a pitiable part in time to come. The colonizing impulse has become a vital question for a great nation. . . . The consequences of the last half century have been appalling, for in them England has conquered the world. . . . It is the short-sightedness of the opponents of our colonial policy which prevents them from understanding that the whole position of Germany depends upon the number of German-speaking millions in the future.[9]

Mussolini presented the same arguments in 1927 to the Chamber of Deputies:

I affirm that the fundamental, if not the absolutely essential datum for the political, and therefore the economic and moral power of nations is their ability to increase their population. Let us speak quite clearly. What are 40,000,000 Italians compared to 90,000,000 Germans and 200,000,000 Slavs? Let us turn toward the west. What are 40,000,000 Italians compared to 46,000,000 Englishmen plus 450,000,000 who live in England's colonies? Gentlemen, if Italy is to amount to anything, it must enter into the second half of this century with a population of at least 60,000,000 inhabitants. . . . If we decrease in numbers, gentlemen, we will never create an empire but become a colony.[10]

This ambition for a growing place in the sun for a national culture explains the usual union of demands for a growing population and colonies—a union which would be, to say the least, anomalous if the economic argument provided the sole motive.

German publicists tended to stress the need of a virile people to expand by conquest and the constant requirement of an army adequate to the task. Hitler was but following in the footsteps of Bernhardi and Treitschke when he said:

The right to soil and territory can become a duty if decline seems to be in store for a great nation unless it extends its territory. . . . Never forget that the most sacred right in this world is the right to

[9] *Politics* (2 vols., New York, 1916).
[10] Quoted in Warren G. Thompson, *Danger Spots in World Population*, p. 228.

that earth which a man desires to till himself, and the most sacred sacrifice that blood which a man spills for this earth.

A study of these discussions of immigration, tariff, colonial, and military policy creates the impression that population arguments, especially of an economic type, do not always express the real motives of the speaker. The economics is often so patently bad that one concludes that expansionist policies flow from the sentiment that national expansion and military power are ends in themselves. Economic arguments are advanced only because in an economic age it sounds more reasonable to act for greed than for glory. This is not to say that economic self-seeking by financial and commercial magnates, retention of political position by leaders and politicians, and military self-sufficiency for the army may not also be an undisclosed motivation behind some of this oratory; nor does it deny that many of the rank and file are persuaded that the nation and perhaps they, individually, will reap economic gains from the proposed policy.

Political proposals and discussions of the 1930's indicated wide acceptance of the theory that territorial redistribution was required by justice or expediency to relieve the population pressure of certain "unsatisfied states." Thompson suggests that, to avoid serious trouble, "the haves" must

> voluntarily undertake to equalize to some extent the gross injustices of the present distribution. We all know that justice had nothing to do with the establishment of the *status quo* in the distribution of resources. Force and force alone determined it. It can be maintained, if it can be maintained at all, only by force.[11]

This proposition requires some examination. Justice, in any objective sense, inheres not in any situation of possession but in the process by which that situation developed and is maintained or changed. To examine the justice of any claim to territory, one

[11] *Danger Spots in World Population*, pp. 14–15. To the same effect see Hitler, p. 949. See also the discussion of territorial transfers by Lord Lugard ("The Basis of the Claim for Colonies"), Arnold J. Toynbee ("Peaceful Change or War?"), and others, *International Affairs*, Vol. XV, No. 1 (Jan.-Feb., 1936).

would have to examine the procedures by which that particular territory was obtained and is retained and to ascertain the status of these procedures in international law and in the general public opinion upon which that law rests. If it is assumed without such examination that "force and force alone" determined and maintained a given state of possession, it is to be anticipated that the same assumption will exist after "voluntary transfers" have been made and that there will still be "dissatisfied powers" to whom further voluntary transfers must be made. Perhaps the fact that they had already received some territory would augment their anxiety to receive more as well as their ability to demand it.

Justice, therefore, requires detailed examination of any particular proposal for transfer by an acceptable procedure. The conditions under which it is expedient to make such transfers will be considered in the next section.

(4) *The Sociological Method.* The sociological method of relating population to international relations implies the analysis of a given population problem in its concrete setting with a view to prediction or control through application of the best learning on the subject.

Analysis and comparison of the composition of different populations discloses differences in respect to the proportion of each grouping (sex, age, race, occupation, income, health, education, social status, etc.) into which the population may be classified. The rates of change of these proportions usually vary in the history of a population and among different populations. As a result the character of every population and its relation to others is continuously modified in time.

Applications of this method have suggested that the age composition of a population may have a significant effect upon the psychology of the nation. A rapidly growing population is a young population. According to Gini:

> A population in which young age-groups abound bears the imprint of their spirit of daring in all its social organization and in the trend of its collective policies; whereas cold, calculating prudence is

the characteristic of populations in which the older age-groups prevail.[12]

The study of the population situation in particular areas of international tension may often assist in the practical solution of that problem. International commissions, such as those sent by the League of Nations to Mosul (1925), Manchuria (1932), and the Gran Chaco (1933) have usually paid attention to the population situation in the area; but, of these three, only the first contributed immediately to a settlement.

The number of factors which must be considered to estimate the international trends in such an area was well illustrated by the discussion regarding Manchuria in the Institute of Pacific Relations in 1929. The different character of the population movements from China, Korea, Russia, and Japan into this area, the differences in the stage of economic organization of the sources of these migrations, the political and economic interests in the area of states other than the three most interested, the problem of military defense, the nature of historic rivalries, and the character of international institutions for adjusting difficulties were discussed, with the conclusion:

> The problems of Manchuria are, therefore, complex. They present in a new area of striking and even dramatic development, all the problems of international intercourse which a modern world is groping to control. If economic necessities can be reconciled with national sovereignty, international co-operation with national security, population pressure with peaceful intercourse, a large part of the common problem confronting all nations will have been solved in one area at least.[13]

Difficult as it is to predict trends in a concrete population situation, it is even more difficult to decide upon the wisest policy to meet such a situation.

Japan in 1933, with a population under twenty years of age 10,000,000 greater than the population between twenty and forty years old, was confronted by the very real problem of find-

[12] *Population*, p. 29.
[13] Institute of Pacific Relations, *Problems of the Pacific*, p. 160.

ing 10,000,000 additional jobs in twenty years. Birth control could do nothing to relieve this situation. The possibilities of further intensification of agriculture in Japan were very limited. Emigration, conquest, industrialization, and trade expansion were suggested. If the general welfare of its people had been the object of Japanese policy, as most of the abstract economists assumed, the possibilities of various alternatives might have been explored.

With migration to Australia, New Zealand, Canada, and America barred by law or administrative practice under the law, and to the Philippines, Indonesia, China, and Korea barred by lower-grade and frequently denser indigenous population, migration seemed to offer little relief without successful war against the overseas countries. This undoubtedly would be extremely expensive, even if the war were successful and if the problem of providing sufficient tonnage to transport Japanese away more rapidly than new ones were born could be solved. With an annual increase of nearly a million, provision would have to be made for exporting about 3,000 Japanese a day, or, assuming that birth control would at once prevent further increments, the problem of the potentially unemployed 10,000,000 in the next twenty years would require an export of 1,500 a day.

Conquest of territory seemed hardly practicable except in Asia, where it was undertaken. The prospects of large-scale migration, however, have remained slight, the raw materials have been more expensive to exploit than those which were available to Japan by trade in other places, and the indigenous population, while large, has not provided a market for high-grade manufactured goods.

A third alternative, further industrialization and expansion of trade throughout the whole world, importing more and more foodstuffs and raw materials and exporting an increasing proportion of manufactured goods, seemed to offer the best economic solution—one which had the economically desirable feature that industrialization tends to urbanization and reduction of the birth rate, so that the problem might be permanently ended if the

10,000,000 additional workers already born could be cared for during the next twenty years.[14]

Perhaps the policy embarked upon by Japan in 1922, which seems to have been along this line, would have been persisted in if the United States and others had not seen fit to slap Japan in the face with discriminatory immigration policies interpreted as implying racial inferiority, and to hamper the enlargement of Japan's industrial exports by ever higher tariffs. It is not surprising that the military faction in Japan, which had always scoffed at the liberal policy, gained more and more popular support until it was able to embark upon a policy which had little to offer economically but might induce the Japanese to lower their standards of living in exchange for glory and might even slaughter some of the 10,000,000 in war. In spite of the anti-industrial tone of the military party which came into control, Japan inflated its currency and expanded its export trade to a large extent. Industrialization and international trade may in the long run be the means by which Japan will meet its problem, but the problem will be rendered somewhat more difficult by the tremendous burden of military expansion and colonial adventure which the country has undertaken.

A rational study of the alternatives in any population situation of the modern interdependent world from a purely economic point of view seldom suggests a military or colonial policy—a fact which confirms the conclusion that the objectives of foreign policy are generally only in small degree economic among the leaders who understand, and who make the policy. The rank and file who do not understand may frequently be influenced by bad economic arguments.

If, instead of general welfare, some other end is assumed as

[14] *Ibid.*, pp. 136–53; above, nn. 60 and 69. After discussing four policies open to Germany to meet the problem of "an annual increase in population of almost 900,000 souls" (birth control, domestic colonization, territorial conquest, and further industrialization), Adolf Hitler concluded that "taking with the fist" of new soil "at Russia's expense" was a "healthier" course than the policy of industrialization and trade followed by the German Republic, because it would preserve a healthy peasant class, promote economic self-sufficiency, destroy "pacifistic nonsense," and enlarge the homeland (*Mein Kampf*, pp. 168, 178, 180, 182).

the end of policy—for example, national self-sufficiency, augmentation of relative military power, or retention of the present relative position of rulers and classes within the state—similar exploration of the best alternatives for attaining this end in a given population situation could be made. The actual policy by which most states meet their population problems is likely to be a compromise between the results of these different analyses. In other words, policies are the result of compromises among a number of objectives, not rigorous coordination of means to a single end. Doubtless, however, in a given state at a given time, prosperity, security, power, stability, prestige, or some other end tends to dominate and so for a time to coordinate the concrete policies of the state and to tend toward particular forms for meeting the population problems.

(5) *Influence of Population on War.* The conclusions to be drawn with respect to the relation of population changes to international relations in the contemporary world are in the main negative, but six points may be noted.

(i) The rapid growth of world population during the past century has augmented international communication, interpenetrated cultures, increased international cooperation, and tended to bring the entire human race together into a single community. But it has also, in augmenting contacts between people of different culture and political allegiance, increased opportunities for friction between nations, each of which often places retention of its cultural individuality, its political unity, and its relative power position above its economic prosperity. Thus, while becoming more united, the world has become less stable and tensions have increased. This situation gives the human race more capacity, if its various divisions can agree, to control its future through orderly processes. On the other hand, its eggs all being in one basket, if it cannot agree to exercise these now possible controls, its capacity to annihilate itself is also augmented.

(ii) Policies of war and expansion have been less influenced by population changes than by the willingness of people to accept unsound economic theories on the subject. A more general knowledge of the economic value of the various alternatives for meeting particular population problems would under present conditions make for international peace and cooperation rather than for war, provided people really wished to make general welfare the object of policy.

(iii) Differentials of population pressure in neighboring areas, if generally known to the inhabitants of the overpopulated area and if maintained by artificial barriers to trade and migration, tend to international violence, provided the people of the overpopulated area have energy and mobility, are accustomed to the use of violence as an instrument of policy, and are dominated, as people in the mass usually are, by political rather than by economic objectives.

(iv) Population is one factor in military potential, and differential rates of population growth in neighboring states tend to disturb the balance of power if such neighbors are in positions of traditional rivalry and depend for their defense upon their own resources rather than upon the mutual jealousies of others. Such disturbances in the balance of power between the great Powers have tended to the development of all the states into a system of two rival alliances. This is likely to lead to the conviction that war is inevitable and to general war initiated by the group against whose military potential time is running.

(v) The two preceding propositions suggest that imperial wars tend to be initiated by countries with the most rapidly rising populations, while balance-of-power wars tend to be initiated by the alliances with the less rapidly rising populations, provided other factors of the military potential are equally affected by time.

(vi) While population conditions in the broad sense are a major factor in international politics and establish limits to the possibilities of international relations during any historical epoch, the possible variations of policy within these limits steadily increase as civilization develops, and today such variations are very great. Consequently, today the character of the influence of a particular population change is so dependent on other factors that it is impossible to predict from a study of population phenomena alone what international policies or occurrences to expect.

Studies relating aspects of population composition to warlikeness and studies indicating the optimum population composition under given conditions may yield theoretical and practical insight into the problem of war. Such studies cannot, however, in themselves, exhaust the subject. While wars are fought between populations, no statistical analysis of the populations can disclose all their causes. Changes in individual and group opinions; establishment of new national and international institutions; the evolution of treaties, legislation, and juristic analyses; technological discoveries and inventions, especially in the arts of war and of economic production—all affect international relations rather directly. All these changes are affected by one another and also by population changes. The influence of the latter must be taken into account, but in its proper relations and proportions. The temptation to state overprecisely and without adequate qualification the international consequences of, or the remedies for, population conditions may thus be avoided. Alarming statements regarding the relations of population conditions to international affairs have often been made as propaganda for policies of value to the few rather than to the many; consequently, it is in the general interest that the indeterminateness of the actual relationship should be understood.

Fundamentals of Population Change in Europe and the Soviet Union

By FRANK W. NOTESTEIN

FRANK W. NOTESTEIN, born in Alma, Michigan. Ph.D., Cornell, 1927. Since 1936, Director of the Office of Population Research of the School of Public and International Affairs, Princeton University, and Co-editor of *Population Index*, the official publication of the Population Association of America.

Author: *The Future Population of Europe and the Soviet Union* (with others), 1944; *Controlled Fertility* (with R. K. Stix), 1940; and numerous articles in the field of demography.

The relation between size of population and national power is neither simple nor direct. The military potential of a nation depends on many interrelated factors including man power, resources, technical development, political solidarity, and morale, some of which are only indirectly related to population trends. Even the obvious relation of population to power is not necessarily direct. Large populations can be a source of national weakness as well as of strength. For example, in its present backward stage of industrial development India's vast population is too large to yield maximum military effectiveness. On the other hand, as between nations of roughly equal industrial development, the size of working and fighting populations may be decisive. Moreover, differences in man power may become more important in the future, for modern technical skills are spreading rapidly. The U.S.S.R. is a conspicuous demonstration of the fact that a nation can be changed rather quickly from an agrarian state, unable to make its numbers effective, into a relatively modern industrial

NOTE: This paper draws on materials developed by the Office of Population Research, Princeton University, in cooperation with the Economic, Financial, and Transit Department of the League of Nations. The project was made possible by funds granted by the Carnegie Corporation of New York and the Milbank Memorial Fund. Neither foundation, however, is the author, owner, publisher, or proprietor of the publication, nor is to be understood as approving, by virtue of its grants, any of the statements made or views expressed therein.

nation capable of bringing its man power to bear on an enemy. It must always be borne in mind that man power not now in a position to be effective may become so in a relatively short span of years.

Differences in the rate of population growth between nations are at once a source of political friction and a rationalization for the moves of aggressive leaders. For better or worse, the boundaries of nations are much more rigidly fixed than the human contents of those boundaries. Congested and rapidly growing nations cast envious eyes on the empty spaces of neighboring countries. Nations being outstripped in population growth contemplate defensive measures "before it becomes too late." Whether competing claims are soundly based or not is of small consequence so long as they are believed by the national constituencies. The fact is that differences in rates of growth of nations have powerful effects on economic life, political climate, and military potential. Any analysis of the future military potential requires as careful an evaluation as possible of prospective changes in population. The following note illustrates briefly some of the possibilities in this direction by discussing first the pattern of recent population change in Europe and the U.S.S.R., and secondly a series of population projections for the period 1940 to 1970.

Recent Trends and Their Meaning for Future Growth. It is important to realize that we have been living in a unique period of the world's demographic history—a period of unparalleled population growth. Since 1800 the world's population has more than doubled and the number of people of European culture has increased perhaps threefold. For Europe the end of this unusual period is now in sight; and it will not return in a future that matters.

The source of this rapid, almost explosive, increase of population lies in revolutionary changes of birth and death rates. Before the vital revolution, high death rates nearly canceled high birth rates to yield little natural increase. In the modern industrial West, where the revolution has most nearly run its course, both death and birth rates are now low, yielding again small increase. It was in the period of transition from high to low vital rates that the growth occurred. It came because death rates declined first, and faster than birth rates. Birth rates remained virtually unchanged long after the initial decline in mortality, and they have only approached death rates again within recent years. This is not the place to discuss in detail the reasons for the difference in the timing of the transition. To oversimplify, death rates began to fall almost as soon as technical developments permitted because there is universal agreement that it is better to live than to die. There is no such agreement that a small family is better than a large one. The transition from the ideal of the large family to that of the small one came only gradually under the stress of modern urban living with its high cost of child rearing and its sloughing of family functions. Eventually a sharp drop in birth rates began to reduce natural increase and check rapid growth. This whole pattern of lagging transition in vital rates and the resulting wave of growth did not begin simultaneously all over Europe. Instead, it spread slowly from West to East with the technical and industrial revolution. The result is that the various regions are in widely different phases of the wave of population growth.

This oversimplified description of the course of population change gives the key to understanding present differences in the growth of populations and some insight into the broad prospects for population change. At present China has scarcely begun its vital revolution, and the U.S.S.R., Southern, and Eastern Europe are in different phases of the growth stage. In Northwestern and Central Europe the transition is most nearly complete, and the prospect for future growth is small.

Lest the assertion that the period of growth is drawing to a close in Europe appear to be mere crystal gazing, it will be well to consider the interwar position. The rate of population increase was consistently much smaller in the thirties than in the twenties throughout Europe. In both decades it was lowest in the Northwestern and Central region, higher in the South, higher still in the East, and probably highest of all in the U.S.S.R. Still, in the thirties births exceeded deaths in all countries except France and Austria. At first glance therefore, predictions of widespread incipient population decline do not seem warranted.

However, the excess of births over deaths, i.e., the natural increase, does not accurately portray the underlying situation. Past vital trends have left the nations of the modern West with abnormal and transitory concentrations of population in the young adult ages. Populations thus overloaded with young adults have high birth rates and low death rates, even if families are small and hazards to life great. As time goes on, these large groups will pass out of the childbearing period and be replaced by smaller contingents, which are already born. Then, barring changes in size of families, in the hazards to life, or heavy immigration, deaths will rise, births fall, and natural decrease replace natural increase. France had already reached that position in the early thirties because her vital revolution began earlier, and her period of favorable age distribution passed sooner. She had more deaths than births despite the fact that her fertility was higher than that of England, Germany, Sweden, and a number of other countries. In the absence of a rise in fertility or of immigration, other nations will quickly join her with a natural decrease just as surely as time passes.

The meaning of the vital balance of the early thirties for future growth is best shown by the net reproduction rate. This rate is the ratio of the child to the parent generation that would result from a continuance of existing age schedules of fertility and mortality. Rates of 1.25, 1.00, and 0.75 mean that at existing age schedules of fertility and mortality, 100 live-born children would produce in the course of their lifetime 125, 100, and 75 live-born children, respectively. To put it another way, they mean that if there were no change in the family size or in the hazards to life and no migration, the population would ultimately increase by 25 per cent every generation (about thirty years), remain stationary, or decline by 25 per cent every generation. In 1933 the net reproduction rate was below 0.75 in Austria, Germany, and

England and Wales. In the early thirties it was from 15 to 24 per cent below the permanent replacement level in Estonia, Sweden, Norway, Belgium, and Switzerland. It was 5 to 14 per cent below that level in France, Latvia, Scotland, Denmark, and Czechoslovakia; and less than 5 per cent below it in Finland and Hungary. Ireland (1.16) and the Netherlands (1.28) were the only Western nations above the permanent replacement level. Although the statistics in many cases are inadequate, it is clear that the remaining European countries had net reproduction rates which, if maintained, would yield population increases ranging from 10 per cent to, in the case of the U.S.S.R., more than 50 per cent per generation.

Toward the end of the interwar period, the elements necessary for the maintenance of population growth were still present in the South and East. They had already disappeared in the Northwestern and Central region. Changes in mortality and fertility would alter the situation. If mortality rises, it will check growth in the South and East and hasten the decline in the West. If it falls, it will stimulate growth and delay the decline, but in many countries not prevent it. In such countries as Austria, Germany, England, Estonia, Sweden, Norway, Belgium, and Switzerland fertility by the early thirties had reached such a low level that it would not permanently maintain a stationary population even if there were no deaths at all from birth to the end of the childbearing period. In such countries, barring migration, only a substantial increase in fertility above the level of the early thirties can forestall the onset of a progressive decline in numbers.

Fertility may rise in the future. It has already done so in Nazi Germany, where drastic pro-natalist policies and reemployment carried the net reproduction rate from 0.70 in 1933 to about 0.98 in 1940. However, in the absence of a strong pro-natalist policy, there is every prospect that fertility will continue to decline rather than rise. Even in countries where the average fertility is low, there are substantial sections of the population in which it remains high but is falling rapidly. There is every indication that the small-family ideal is spreading into these still divergent groups.

On the other hand, probably there is no substantial population group having its fertility now under effective control that is reproducing at more than three-fourths of the replacement level. In these low-fertility groups there is no evidence of a real upward trend. In the absence of drastic social-economic changes, it is reasonable to expect the general trend of fertility to continue downward for some years, even in the low-fertility countries. Such a trend would hasten the onset of population decline already set in motion by the aging process previously discussed.

Summarizing the position at the end of the interwar period, we may say that the eastward wave of population growth probably was near the crest in the U.S.S.R., high but receding in Southern and Eastern Europe, and at a developing trough in Northwestern and Central Europe. Superimposed on this wave, in some places reinforcing and in others canceling it, will be the consequences of the present war and its aftermath on birth, death, and migration. No one can foretell the magnitude of the war's impact. That fact, however, does not prevent useful evaluation of the prospects for population change. The direction of the impact is all too clear.

Population Projections, 1940–1970. It is, of course, impossible to predict population changes of the future except in the broadest terms. However, it is useful for analytical purposes to show the kinds of population structures that would develop under certain definite, even if highly artificial, assumptions. With such models, we can consider ways in which alternative assumptions would modify the results. Those presented here embody the kind of changes that have already been discussed, and are believed to be broadly predictive. However, it cannot be asserted too emphatically that they are projections and are not to be considered as predictions in detail. Rather, they are working models, useful for analysis.

The projections relate to the populations within the national boundaries of 1937 in the period 1940–1970. They are based on three assumptions: (1) that the future course of mortality and fertility will represent an orderly development of the trends of the interwar period, (2) that there will be no international migration, and (3) that there is no war. The first assumption is reasonable only in the event of a United Nations' victory and in the absence of strong pro-natalist policies or other sweeping social-economic changes. The assumption of no migration is false, but has the virtue of permitting us to examine the internal potentialities for growth. It was believed desirable to leave the war out of the account since its consequences cannot be estimated at present. The projections, therefore, may be thought of as showing the results to be expected from undisturbed underlying demographic trends.

The construction of such projections is simple in principle. One has only to continue adding estimated births to, and subtracting estimated deaths from, the population appropriately aged. The chief problem is that of obtaining future fertility and mortality rates appropriate to the underlying assumptions. The methods used in deriving age schedules of fertility and mortality cannot be described here. For present purposes only a few points need to be made about them. All operations were carried out separately for each quinquennial age group. The procedures were uniformly applicable to all countries with the result that identical projected schedules would be obtained for any two countries having identical observed rates at the same initial date. Perhaps the most important facts to bear in mind about the projections of both fertility and mortality are that they provide for: (1) the most rapid declines where the last observed rates were highest and the least rapid declines where they were lowest, and (2) *decreasing rates of decline as time goes on.* The general course of the projected schedules of vital rates seems reasonable in the light of past experience and of the assumption that the future will yield an orderly unfolding of trends developing in the interwar period. It should be noted that the actual experience certainly will not follow the projections in detail. Economic fluctuations, political disorders, indeed, changes in the weather, will introduce at least minor year-to-year fluctuations. In the case of a United Nations'

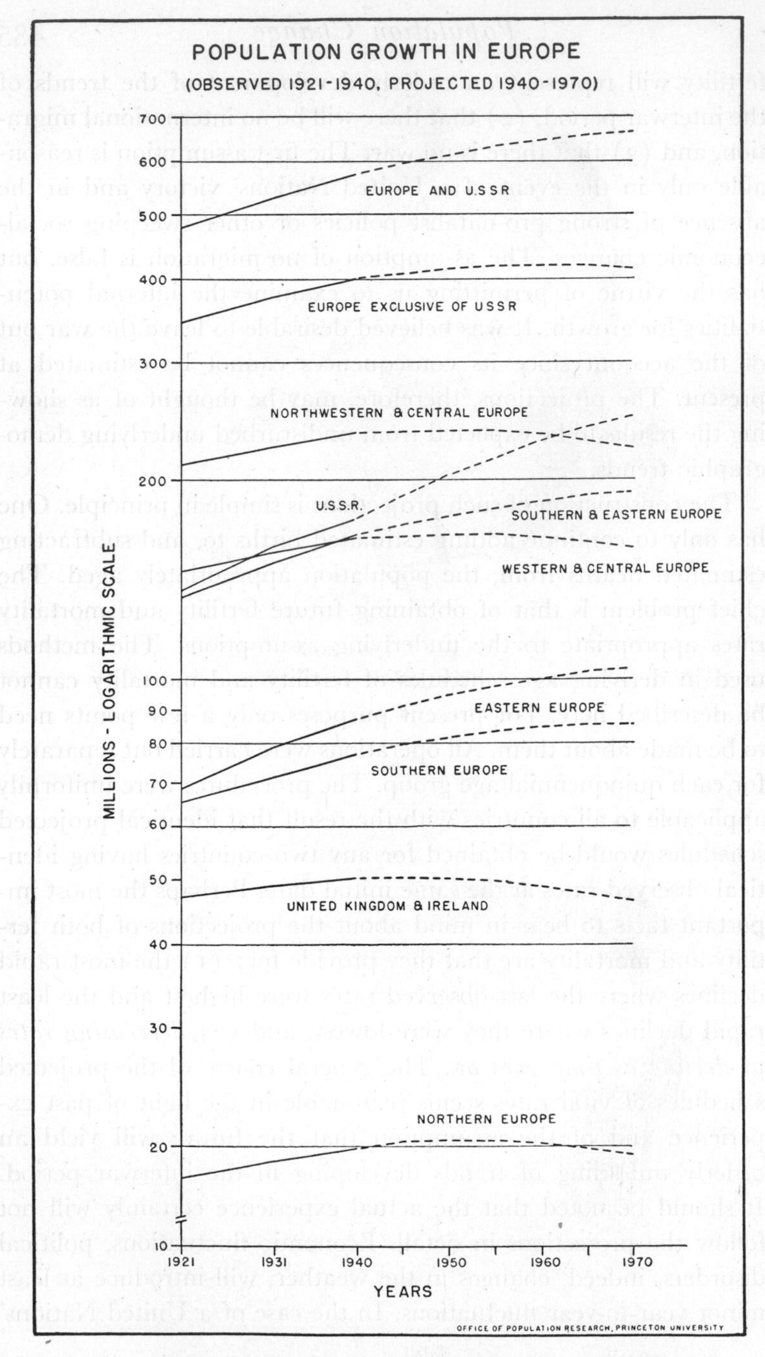

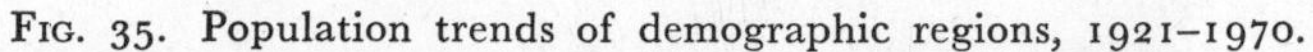
FIG. 35. Population trends of demographic regions, 1921–1970.

defeat or, as seems quite likely, the introduction of strong pronatalist policy, even the general course of the projected fertility schedules might become inapplicable.[1]

Given fertility and mortality rates for each age group at five-year intervals to 1970, the derivation of population projections is mechanical. The appropriate rates are applied to the census population, giving expected births classified by sex and expected deaths by age and sex for the subsequent five years. The process of aging the population five years, adding expected births, and subtracting expected deaths yields the population five years after the census. This process repeated at successive five-year intervals brings the population up to 1970.

Figure 35 summarizes the results, as far as total numbers are concerned, for the U.S.S.R. and regions of Europe.[2] The solid lines show the actual populations between 1921 and 1940; and the dotted lines, the projections. The scale is semi-logarithmic; hence equal rises indicate equal percentage increases, not equal absolute increases. The figure speaks for itself. Under the assumption of no war, no migration, and an orderly development of past trends, the U.S.S.R. can be expected to have much the most rapid growth, moving from 174,000,000 in 1940 to 251,000,000 in 1970. Changes to be expected in Europe outside the U.S.S.R. are relatively small, with the beginning of the decrease appearing between 1960 and 1965. This relatively stationary population for non-Soviet Europe, however, is the resultant of widely divergent trends between regions. Without war, Southern and Eastern Europe could be expected to grow, the former more rapidly than

[1] The development of these projections is primarily the work of Lieut. (j.g.) Ansley J. Coale, formerly a member of the technical staff of the Office of Population Research.

[2] The following classification of countries into regions is used:

Northwestern and Central Europe: United Kingdom and Ireland—England and Wales, Ireland, Northern Ireland, Scotland; West-Central Europe—Austria, Belgium, Czechoslovakia, France, Germany, Hungary, Netherlands, Switzerland; Northern Europe—Denmark, Estonia, Finland, Latvia, Norway, Sweden.

Southern and Eastern Europe: Southern Europe—Italy, Portugal, Spain; Eastern Europe—Albania, Bulgaria, Greece, Lithuania, Poland, Roumania, Yugoslavia.

U.S.S.R.

the latter. Northwestern and Central Europe would reach a maximum of about 237,000,000 by 1950 and then decline to 225,000,000 by 1970.

More important than changes in total numbers, which occur

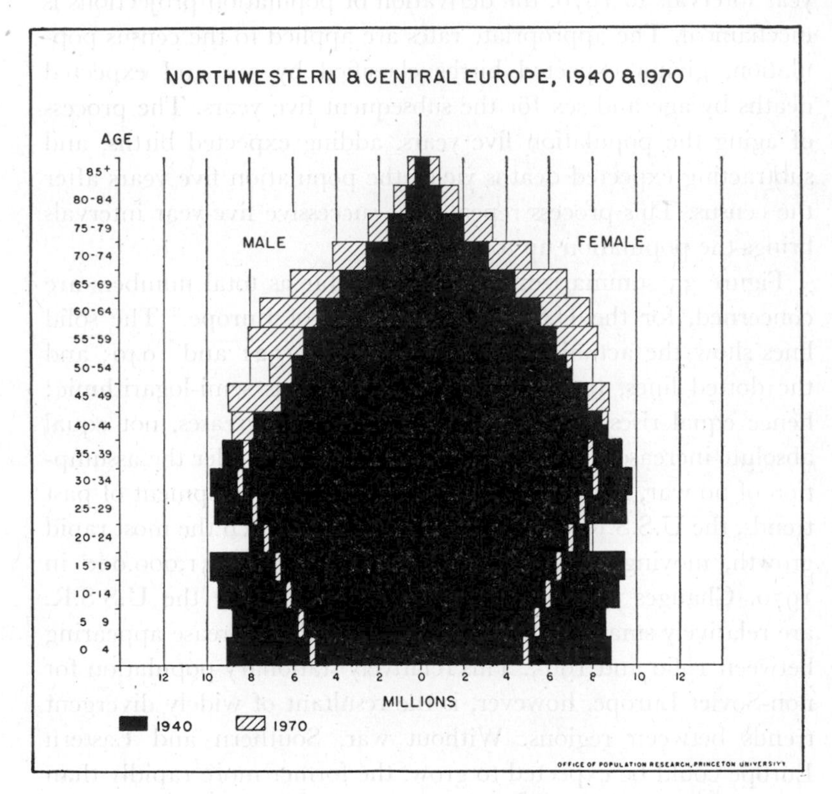

Fig. 36. Age pyramids of projected population for Northwestern and Central Europe, 1940 and 1970.

only gradually, are those in the size of constituent age groups. How drastic such changes can be is shown in Figures 36, 37, and 38, which contrast the age-sex distribution of 1940 and 1970 for Northwestern and Central Europe, Southern and Eastern Europe, and the U.S.S.R., respectively. The pyramids in solid black represent the age-sex distributions of the 1940 population. The shaded pyramids represent the projected distributions for 1970. Much of the history of past events may be read from the pyramids ıor 1940. For example, in that for Northwestern and Central Europe (Figure 36) persons 30–34 years of age are more numerous than those 0–4 years of age because the birth rate had been dropping.

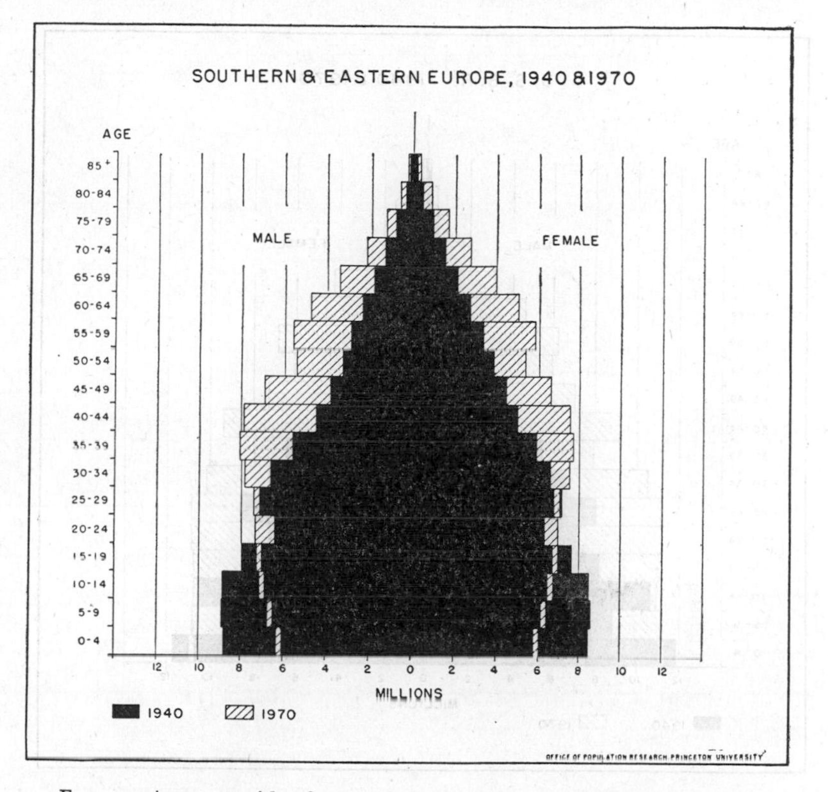

FIG. 37. Age pyramids of projected population for Southern and Eastern Europe, 1940 and 1970.

The bar for persons 5–9 years of age is relatively short because of the depression dip in the birth rate. The gash in the population 20–24 years of age is the result of the short crop of babies during the last war. There are relatively few males 40 to 55 years of age in the 1940 pyramid because that group was 15 to 30 years old in 1915 and bore the brunt of the first war's casualties.

In the pyramid of 1970 the age groups are all advanced thirty years (6 bars), after appropriate reduction by mortality. The result is a rapid increase in the size of the older age groups. In the pyramid for 1970 all cohorts under 30 come, of course, from projected births. The rapid narrowing of the base of the pyramid

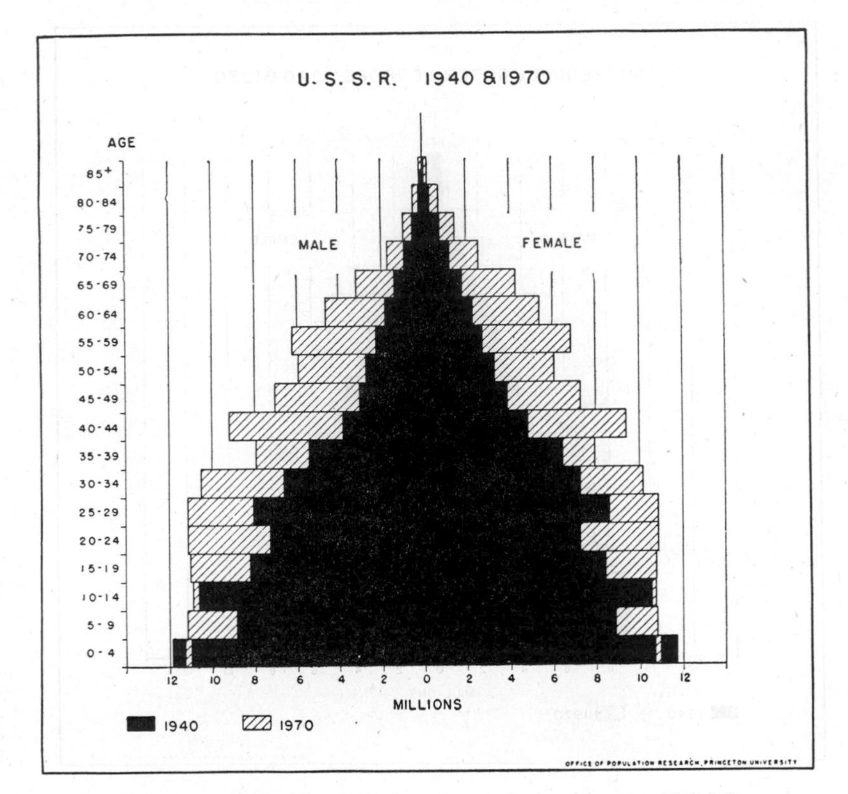

FIG. 38. Age pyramids of projected population for the U.S.S.R., 1940 and 1970.

suggests that the projected birth rates drop very rapidly. In fact, however, since birth rates in this region are already low, they were reduced much less rapidly than those either in Southern and Eastern Europe or in the U.S.S.R. The heavy erosion of the base of the pyramid is due less to the projected decline of fertility than to the fact that after 1940 large contingents move out of the childbearing period and are replaced by smaller ones. The narrowly based pyramid of 1970 is, therefore, not so much the result of what we assume will happen between 1940 and 1970 as the result of what has already happened to the contingent of potential parents of that period.

The pyramid for the U.S.S.R. stands at the other extreme, with that for Southern and Eastern Europe in the middle. Both pyramids show in 1940 the characteristic narrow top and broad base of regions with high mortality and high fertility. Both, but particularly that for the U.S.S.R., show the characteristic notching of populations that have had a history of catastrophes; both show the rapid increase of the population of all adult ages resulting from the assumption that death rates will fall most rapidly where they are now worst. Neither gives the immediate impression that sharp declines in fertility were projected between 1940 and 1970. In fact, however, projected schedules of fertility decline very substantially in Southern and Eastern Europe and most rapidly of all in the U.S.S.R. In the latter case it was assumed that gross reproduction rates would fall by more than 37 per cent between 1940 and 1970. The base of the pyramid for Southern and Eastern Europe is only slightly eroded, and that for the U.S.S.R. is scarcely undercut at all because in both regions the number of potential parents increases rapidly between 1940 and 1970. This increase in potential parents offsets the assumed shrinkage in the size of their families. Because of this situation the U.S.S.R. can coast into a huge population, even if its fertility undergoes a spectacular decline.

It is clear that, under the assumptions stated, the center of population growth will shift eastward, the U.S.S.R. will face very rapid growth, substantial growth will go on for a generation in Southern and Eastern Europe, and Northwestern and Central Europe face an imminent cessation of growth with a rapid increase in the older age groups. The war will modify these trends. The U.S.S.R. has already suffered heavy losses, particularly in the reproductive age group. Its growth between 1940 and 1970 will in all likelihood be substantially less than the projected 77,-000,000. Perhaps it will be only 50,000,000, but even so its increase alone would exceed the total present population of the United Kingdom and Ireland. In Eastern Europe large regions have already been devastated, and mortality is appalling. These events will hasten the onset of decline projected for 1965–1970. However, it must be borne in mind that populations such as those of Eastern Europe and the U.S.S.R., in which both mortality and fertility remain high, have great resiliency in recovering from catastrophes. The energetic application of modern techniques to reduce high civilian death rates can do much to compensate for catastrophic losses, and it requires only a slight check in the assumed downward trend of fertility to yield large numbers of children. The nations of Northwestern and Central Europe have no such resiliency. Peacetime death rates are already low, and future gains, especially at ages under 40, will be obtained with growing difficulty. The war's casualties are falling most heavily on the small cohort of children born during the last war. It is these groups that would normally be expected to be the most fruitful source of children in the next five or ten years. Without a war, the nations of this region face an imminent decline in numbers and rapid aging of their peoples. The current destruction of life can only hasten those processes. Barring heavy immigration or strong measures to increase family size, Northwestern and Central Europe's period of youth is over, and its period of growth is past.

28

Population Movements in Imperial Russia and in the Soviet Union*

By FRANK LORIMER

FRANK LORIMER, born in Bradley, Maine. Ph.D., Columbia, 1929. Professor of Population Studies, the American University, and Research Associate, Princeton University. Dr. Lorimer's activities during the last five years have included service as consultant to the Virginia State Planning Board and several Federal agencies. He has been engaged in the study of population trends in the U.S.S.R. in connection with a program undertaken by Princeton University in cooperation with the League of Nations.

Author, in association with F. Osborn, of *Dynamics of Population* (1934); also, under National Resources Committee, of *The Problems of a Changing Population* (1937).

The Russian population has been characterized by a constant expansion into virgin territory since the middle of the sixteenth century, when the forces of Ivan the Dread broke the power of the Tatar Khans on the middle and lower Volga. Turkic nomads from time immemorial had dominated the steppe regions of southern Russia and central Asia. By recurrent raids into exposed border regions they prevented the effective settlement of the rich black-soil prairies between the semi-desert zone and the forest zone across northern Russia and Siberia. The Tatars, in alliance with the Porte, remained in control of the Black Sea region until the end of the eighteenth century; but the growing power of the Moskva realm made possible the gradual extension of agriculture into the black-soil zone—slowly at first, and then more rapidly after the time of Peter the Great, who died in 1725. This movement to the south was the principal line along which the Russian

* This article is based on statistical investigations and materials from Russian and non-Russian sources presented in *The Population of the Soviet Union: History and Prospects* (1944). The preparation of this book was sponsored by the Office of Population Research, Princeton University, in cooperation with the Economic, Financial, and Transit Section of the League of Nations. Financial aid, involving no other obligations, was granted to Princeton University for these studies by the Carnegie Corporation of New York and the Milbank Memorial Fund. The author is solely responsible for the present statement.

population broadened its base through the seventeenth, eighteenth, and most of the nineteenth century. There was also a small movement northward in the direction of Archangel. Meanwhile, Siberia was defended against Russian settlement, not by the strength of the indigenous tribes, whose resistance from the Urals

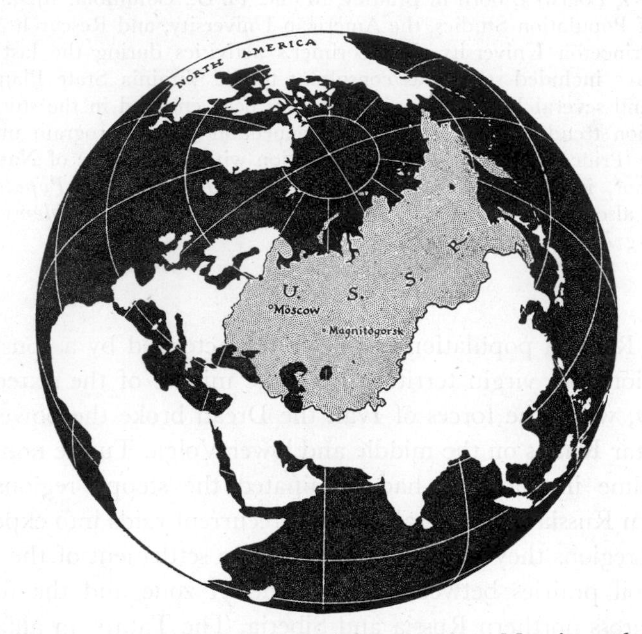

FIG. 39. Orthographic projection centered on Magnitogorsk

to the Pacific was broken by Cossack pioneer bands in the course of a half-century (1581–1636), but by the power of distance and the force of the wilderness. Far to the south, beyond the vast, arid Asiatic steppes, the ancient civilization in the oases and irrigated fields, mountain coves, and cities of Central Asia remained culturally and economically isolated, even after its conquest by Imperial Russia in the third quarter of the nineteenth century. Although the Kazakh hordes in the Asiatic steppes had submitted to the authority of the Tsar two centuries earlier, the nomad culture persisted in this region until it was broken by the program and power of the Soviets in the early 1930's. Russian colonization in Asia was limited to a narrow corridor of fertile land with sufficient rainfall to support agriculture—along the southern margin of the forest zone and the northern and eastern borders of the steppe region. Thus the Russian population was long confined to a restricted base (1) by the interior "land ocean" which cradled sparse but swift and powerful tribes who raided its "shores"—until the forest dwellers became sufficiently numerous, organized, and fortified with European arts of destruction to establish their supremacy—and (2) by the formidable character of the Siberian terrain. For this reason, Russia remains demographically a young country, like the republics of the western hemisphere, with a relatively low ratio of population to natural resources.

In 1724, there were about 17,500,000 persons in the European part of the later Russian Empire, exclusive of the Duchy of Finland, Congress Poland, and the provinces of Esthonia, Lifland, Kurland, and Bessarabia, and exclusive of the non-Slavic peoples in southern Russia and the Caucasus. If we divide this European area into two parts—(1) a northern part extending roughly to the edge of the black-soil zone, and (2) a southern part, including the black-soil and steppe regions—we find that there were about 11,000,000 persons in the northern part (including adjacent districts to the west outside Peter's realm); but there were only about 6,000,000 Russians, Ukrainians, and Belorussians in the southern part (along with some 2,000,000 non-Slavic people). Two-thirds of the Russians in the southern part lived in districts that had been settled during the late sixteenth, seventeenth, and early eighteen centuries. There were only about 400,000 Russians east of the Urals at this time. All the estimates cited above are subject to a large margin of error, but they represent the approximate situation at that time. From 1724 to 1859, about 9,000,000 persons were added to the northern area (through excess of births over deaths, minus net out-migration). During the same period, about 29,000,000 persons were added to the Slavic population in the southern area, which now contained the most densely populated districts outside the immediate vicinity of Moskva. The number of Russians (plus Ukrainians and Belorussians) in the

Asiatic parts of the Russian Empire increased by about 5,400,000 during the same interval. As late as 1897, there were, on the average, fewer than 2 persons of all ethnic groups per square mile in Asiatic Russia, outside Russian Turkestan (in Central Asia) and the Transcaucasus. The total population in trans-Ural Perm and Siberia in 1897 was 7,200,000, including 6,000,000 Russians. There were 2,500,000 people in the Asiatic steppe region, of whom about one-fifth were Russian. There were slightly over 12,000,000 persons in Russian Turkestan (including Khiva and Bukhara) and the Transcaucasus, combined, including about 450,000 Russians. The tide of migration to Siberia, the eastern portions of the steppe region, and Central Asia, however, was rising at this time, after the occupation of all readily available farm lands in European Russia and the opening of the Trans-Siberian and Tashkent railroads.

European Russia around 1900, though obsessed with a sense of population pressure, had a relatively low actual density of population per unit of land (50 persons per square mile). The density was lower in every province of European Russia, considered separately, than in Congress Poland (192 persons per square mile), although many of the Russian provinces had superior natural resources. The low productivity of the Russian population under the Imperial regime was not due chiefly to limitation in natural resources, but to retarded technology and to lack of effective economic organization.

The expansion of population within the Russian Empire remained essentially *superficial*—the mere occupation of soils, or movements in search of surface wealth, such as gold and furs. The agrarian structure of Russian society made its population "land-hungry"; but it lacked both the motivation and the capacity to make effective use of the resources that were potentially most important in the newly organized territories—once the expansion had passed the black-soil prairies, which were primarily adapted to agricultural exploitation. Even the coal and iron resources of the Ukraine remained untouched until their development, largely with foreign capital, during the last four decades before the First World War. The superficial character of the demographic and economic development of the Russian Empire is most apparent in its eastward expansion. Asiatic Russia is, for the most part, severely limited in agricultural resources by climate, heavy forest cover, poor drainage, or low rainfall—though possessing some narrow or isolated tracts of excellent farm lands; but it is one of the richest areas in the world in fuel and mineral resources.[1] Nevertheless, when Siberia finally attracted the serious attention of European Russians in the late nineteenth century, their interest was centered almost exclusively on its potentialities as an area for agricultural colonization—to relieve the sense of population pressure. Such pressure is, of course, inevitable in any society that remains predominantly agrarian (i.e., agricultural at a low technical level) after it has progressed sufficiently to establish a stable political order and to control the ravages of famine and epidemics. The attempt to solve the problem by mere extension of land area or emigration always proves illusory; but this illusion has had wide vogue in many countries.

The distribution of persons within the Soviet Union by residence in 1926 and by place of birth gives a composite picture of the residual effects of migration over the previous half-century. Among all Soviet citizens born within the territory of the U.S.S.R., 7.4 per cent reported that they were born in one of twenty-nine regions other than that in which they were enumerated. This indicates fairly high mobility, but relatively less than that in the United States. In 1930, 15.4 per cent of all native persons in the United States were living in another of the nine geographical divisions (23.5 per cent in another of the forty-eight states) than that in which they were born. The net gains and losses of various areas through exchange of population accounted for similar proportions of the gross number of persons involved in these transfers in the two countries—61 per cent in the U.S.S.R., 59 per cent in the U.S.A. (using data on birth and residence by geographical divisions).

[1] Cf. the articles by E. C. Ropes and G. B. Cressey on Siberia, pp. 348, 364.

The movement of persons from European districts eastward through the Urals, Siberia, and the Soviet Far East had effected a net relocation of 2,696,000 persons living in 1926. A similar movement, drawing more heavily from southern Russia, accounted for the relocation of 910,000 persons in Kazakhstan and Central Asia. Also, through net movements between various areas, 662,000 persons had been added to the Central Industrial and Leningrad areas (including net movements from the Central Industrial region to Leningrad); 1,226,000 persons to the Mining-Industrial section of the Ukraine and to the new farm lands in the North Caucasus. The movement, mostly in the early part of the period reflected in these figures, to the Ukraine (exclusive of the Mining-Industrial section) and the Crimea, and that to the middle and lower Volga and Bashkiria, accounted for net transfers of 540,000 and 268,000 persons living in 1926, respectively. These were the only large streams of net redistribution revealed by the 1926 census data. These streams plus three smaller movements involving all together the net transfer of fewer than 100,000 persons account for 98 per cent of all net exchanges between each region and each other region among persons living in 1926.

The relatively slow growth of cities in European Russia had already become the most magnetic force in migration west of the Urals. Among persons living in European Russia outside the region of birth in 1926, 61 per cent were enumerated in cities. The small movement to the Transcaucasus had also been almost wholly to cities, chiefly to the petroleum center around Baku, where foreign capital had stimulated an important industrial enterprise which reached its peak about five years before the First World War. By contrast, the eastward expansion into the Urals, Siberia, and the Asiatic steppe region had remained chiefly a movement of agrarian colonization, although in comparison with the native population, a large part of the in-migrants were engaged in trade, transportation, administration, or industry. Among the 4,446,000 persons in the Asiatic part of the U.S.S.R., exclusive of the Transcaucasus, plus the Ural and Bashkir regions, who were enumerated in 1926 outside the region in which they were born, only 1,203,000 lived in urban communities (27 per cent).

According to the census of 1897, there were only 12,969,000 persons in places then classified as urban within the U.S.S.R. area. The urban population was really somewhat larger because many communities avoided incorporation in order to escape increased taxation. Places in the U.S.S.R. that were classified in 1926 as urban had 15,955,000 inhabitants in 1897—representing 15.0 per cent of the total population (106,070,000 persons). This proportion is slightly less than the corresponding figure for the United States in 1850 (on the basis of criteria that are somewhat less inclusive). There was an appreciable increase of urban population within the territory later organized as the Soviet Union during the next seventeen years. The number of persons living in urban places (1926 list) rose to 24,888,000 by January 1, 1914—representing 17.9 per cent of the estimated total population (139,313,000). The urban population was then 4,000,000 greater than it would have been if the cities had merely increased at the same rate as the whole population. The proportion of the Soviet population living in cities on December 17, 1926, was exactly the same as the estimated proportion in 1914 (17.9 per cent)—after the influx to cities during the World War, the later exodus during the revolutionary period, and a return movement after the civil wars. The absolute number of persons living in urban places according to the 1926 census was 26,314,114 (total population, 147,027,915).

About twelve years later, January 17, 1939, the urban population of the U.S.S.R. was more than twice as great as it had been in 1926. In 1939, 55,909,908 persons were enumerated as living in towns and cities, forming about one-third of the total population (170,467,186)—a proportion roughly equal to that of the United States in 1890. The urban population in 1939 was 25,000,000 greater than it would have been if the growth of cities during the intercensus period had merely paralleled that of the whole population. The increase of urban population includes 5,800,000 persons in places not classified as urban in 1926; but the criteria of classification were not radically different in 1939, and the increase of population in places added to the list of cities represents, in large part, a true increase of urban population.

The growth of population within the territory of the U.S.S.R. was less rapid during the Soviet intercensus period (average increase, 1926 to 1939, 1.23 per cent per year) than it had been during the late prewar period (average increase, 1897 to 1914, 1.7 per cent per year). This is somewhat surprising in view of the fact that the annual rate of natural increase at the beginning and near the end of the latter period was about 2 per cent per year, i.e. considerably higher than in the prewar years. The departure from expectation in the growth of the Soviet population, 1926–1939, can be attributed in part to the rapid decline in births during the years when the services of the abortion clinics were freely available—a trend which was reversed after 1935. In part, it must be attributed to the effects of rapid industrialization, the collectivization of agriculture, and the settlement of nomads (especially the Kazakhs in the Asiatic steppe region) on the populations immediately affected by these programs.

World War I and its aftermaths of civil strife, foreign intervention, famine, and epidemics caused a total loss (including deficit in births) of at least 25,000,000 persons within the territory of the U.S.S.R. In effect, it wiped out the natural increase of the years 1914–1922. However, from 1897 through 1926 there was an increase of 38.6 per cent in the population of the U.S.S.R. area. During the twelve years of the Soviet intercensus period, December 17, 1926, to January 17, 1939, there was an increase of 15.9 per cent in the same territory.

Using arbitrary divisions of Soviet territory, referred to here as "Population Study areas" which correspond very roughly to the Gosplan regions of 1926, we can compare population changes in different parts of the U.S.S.R. from 1897 to 1926, or from 1926 to 1939. Obviously, if each area held a constant proportion of the total, its population would have increased 38.6 per cent in the early period and 15.9 per cent in the later period. By applying these proportions, we find the "expected increase" in each area 1897–1926 and 1926–1939. The "observed increase" in each area (with any absolute loss treated as a negative increase) *minus* the "expected increase" shows the *relative increment* (or decrement) during the period in question (i.e., its gain or loss above or below the amount of increase expected on the assumption of uniform growth in all areas). This operation is carried out separately for the urban and rural parts of each area, 1926–1939.

Most of the European areas showing relative decrements during the earlier period—i.e., Belorussia, Ukraine, the Black Soil Center, Western, Old Industrial, Kirov, and Tatar and Central Volga areas—also appear as areas with relative decrements in the later period. One notable exception is the northern part of European Russia, including the Leningrad area and the Northeastern districts. This had a relative decrement from 1897 to 1926, but shows a relative increment during the Soviet period, 1926–1939. The same is true of the Crimea.

One of the most striking contrasts between the two periods is the relative increase of population in the Transcaucasus and Central Asia from 1926 to 1939, whereas these regions failed to hold their share of the total during the earlier period. During the Soviet period, these regions were characterized by relatively high natural increase; there was also fairly heavy migration into Central Asia. Population growth in these regions was formerly checked by high mortality, especially in Central Asia, and by violent disturbances during the era of war and revolution. High mortality among the Yakuts and Buryats probably also accounts for the failure of East Siberia to show more than an average percentage of increase from 1897 to 1926, in spite of an appreciable net in-migration. There were also movements across the border into Sinkiang and Mongolia from Kirghizia in Central Asia and from Buryat-Mongolia in East Siberia during the World War and the early revolutionary period. High mortality among the Finnic and Turkic nationalities in the Volga-Kama region and the effects of the famine in the Volga regions in 1921–1923, combined with heavy emigration from the eastern districts of European Russia across the Urals, account for the large relative decrement in the Kirov and Tatar area and in the Central Volga area, 1897–1926. High mortality, as well as eastward migration, may also account for the apparent failure of the Ural-Bashkir area to increase more rapidly than the whole population within the U.S.S.R. from 1897 to 1926. In general, it appears that most of the areas largely occupied by non-Slavic elements increased less rapidly than the Slavic population during the period from 1897 to 1926. This relation was reversed in most cases, with the conspicuous exception of Kazakhstan, during the Soviet period, 1926–1939.

The relative increment of Siberia plus the Ural and Bashkir areas and the Soviet Far East (i.e., the eastern part of the R.S.F.S.R.) was larger during the earlier period, 1897–1926, than during the Soviet period. The relative increment during the earlier period was 4,400,000 persons, in contrast to 3,300,000 during the later period. The former figure is roughly 25 per cent above the net in-migration to this area during the years 1897–1914, and there was little net migration to Siberia, 1914–1926. One must bear in mind that the migrants to Siberia before 1914 who remained in this area contributed their natural increase over two decades to the growth of the Siberian population. Also, the population of Siberia suffered less severely than that of European Russia during the World War and its sequelae. The relative increment of the eastern part of the R.S.F.S.R., 1926–1939, can be attributed, at least for the most part, to migration.

All together, the cities in the European part of the U.S.S.R. exclusive of the Ural area received about two-thirds of the total population redistributed to urban places, as measured by the relative increments of population increase, 1926–1939. However, the percentage increase of the urban population in the eastern part of the R.S.F.S.R. was nearly twice as high as in the European part. The increase of urban population in the Transcaucasus and in Central Asia was smaller, both absolutely and relatively, than in the other divisions.

The Population Study areas which show very rapid growth, 1926–1939, and where the relative increments can be directly attributed to migration are: the Ural area (increase, 31 per cent—relative increment, 1,000,000), Central Siberia (increase, 38 per cent—relative increment, 500,000), Eastern Siberia (increase, 59 per cent—relative increment, 600,000), the Soviet Far East (increase, 88 per cent—relative increment, 900,000), and the Karelian-Murmansk area (increase, 159 per cent—relative increment, 400,000). These are all relatively sparsely settled areas, rich in industrial resources. The Soviet Far East, the adjacent Eastern Siberian area, and the Karelian-Murmansk area are also border regions of great strategic importance.

West Siberia does not appear as one of the areas of unusually rapid population growth from 1926 to 1939. This area includes the important Kuznetsk coal region, and the urban population of the whole area increased rapidly during these years (187 per cent). But the percentage of urban population in West Siberia was small in 1926 (12 per cent), and its rural population decreased during the intercensus period by the same percentage as the rural population of the whole U.S.S.R.—being 5 per cent less in 1939 than in 1926. West Siberia, as a whole, therefore, had no appreciable increment of population growth, 1926–1939, over the average increase of the U.S.S.R. West Siberia includes important and expanding wheat areas. But as agriculture was collectivized and mechanized and labor demands reduced, the surplus farm population was, in net effect, absorbed by industries in the same area.

The rapid industrial expansion in the Urals during the era of Soviet planned economy has been widely heralded. Sverdlovsk, the largest city in this area, increased threefold to a total of 426,000 persons in 1939. Chelyabinsk grew even more rapidly to a total of 273,000 persons. Magnitogorsk rose on the vacant southern Ural steppes on the site of the "magnetic mountain" to a city of 146,000 in 1939. There were many other boom towns in this region—including those built around the new petroleum operations. Iron, steel, and other metal industries, paper mills, and chemical plants were built or expanded. Central Siberia, as here defined, includes the cities of Irkutsk, Krasnoyarsk, and Cheremkhovo in the center of a new coal-mining area—all near the Trans-Siberian Railway. It also includes, around the lower (i.e., northern) Yenisei River, an important share of the scattered, small, but rapidly growing settlements in the Arctic zone. The East Siberian area comprises Buryat-Mongolia, Yakutsk, and the Chita districts. Ulan Ude, the capital of Buryat-Mongolia, with its important railroad shops and other industries, is one of the most rapidly growing cities—showing a 450 per cent increase to 129,000 persons in 1939. Yakutia, at the time of the census, had no city of 50,000 population or over; but its capital, Yakutsk, in the Lena valley, halfway between the Trans-Siberian Railway and the Arctic Ocean, is reported to have passed this point shortly thereafter. The new gold-mining towns in the Aldan River region, southeast of Yakutsk, are also reported to have, all together, some 50,000 inhabitants.

The development of East Siberia is closely linked with that of the Soviet Far East (i.e., the Khabarovsk and Maritime districts). This whole region has both peculiar strategic importance and rich natural resources in the areas that already have been explored. The population here is highly concentrated near the upper Amur and the Ussuri River and the vicinity of Vladivostok (the line of the Trans-Siberian Railway), but there has been expansion away from this line. The city of Komsomolsk on the Amur has had the most phenomenal growth of any city in the U.S.S.R. It was founded in the wilderness by 4,000 members of the Communist Youth Organization, for which it is named, in 1932. It was equipped to launch its first ocean-going steel vessel in 1939. It had 71,000 persons at that time, and a fourfold increase in this number in the next four years was anticipated. The Jewish Autonomous District (formery Biro-Bidzhan), south of the Trans-Siberian Railway, near the junction of the Sungari River from Manchuria with the Amur River, is predominantly a rural settlement with agriculture and various small industries. The progress of this region, which has been handicapped by swampy soil, has been the subject of much controversy. Settlers were located here in large numbers during the thirties. In 1939 it had a population of 108,000 persons, of whom about one-fourth, or possibly slightly more, were Jews. No exact figure is available on the population of the Soviet portion of Sakhalin Island. Its population was 12,000 in December, 1926, which was supposedly about 20 per cent above the figure when the Soviets acquired title in 1925. It is reported to have had a tenfold increase in population from 1925 to 1936.

Soviet policy during the Third Five Year Plan (1938–1942) has been directed toward making the Far East "an economically balanced region, strengthening the economic and military power of the U.S.S.R. in the East." One-tenth of the total budget in the Third Five Year Plan was devoted to the development of this region. Much energy has, therefore, been spent on the development of complementary industries: cement and lumber for industrial and residential construction, fuel for regional industries (using the older coal fields near Vladivostok, and new mines on the Bureya River, as well as petroleum resources); an adequate transportation system; increase in livestock to a per capita level above the average for the U.S.S.R. and a projected increase in sown land.

The growth of the initially small urban population in Kazakhstan was stimulated by new railway lines within and through this region, the development of the Karaganda coal fields and other mining and industrial enterprises. The coal output of Kazakhstan jumped from 73,000 tons in 1928 to 4,400,000 tons in 1938. The population of the towns and cities of this republic rose from slightly over 500,000 persons in 1926 to 1,700,000 in 1939. However, the rural population of Kazakhstan decreased sharply, from 5,555,000 persons in 1926 to 4,440,000 persons in 1939—i.e., 20 per cent. The total population of this area, therefore, remained practically stationary during the intercensus interval. If the population of Kazakhstan had increased at the same rate as the total population of the U.S.S.R., this absence of growth would imply a net out-migration of 896,000 persons. Moreover, since industrial enterprises and the new farming areas in northern and eastern Kazakhstan drew migrants from other republics, a much larger out-movement of the original population of this republic to other regions would be indicated. There is other evidence, however, to suggest a serious depletion of the indigenous population of the Asiatic steppe region during these years. Whereas 3,968,000 persons were reported as Kazakhs by ethnic affiliation in 1926, only 3,099,000 persons were reported as belonging to this nationality in 1939—an absolute decrease of 869,000 persons, and 1,500,000 fewer persons than would have been expected on the hypothesis of natural increase equal to that of the whole Soviet population. On the other hand, the construction of the Turkestan-Siberian Railway through eastern Kazakhstan stimulated agricultural as well as commercial development in this region. Irrigation projects in southern Kazakhstan have led to a great expansion of cotton production there. The total sown land in Kazakhstan was 44 per cent greater in 1938 than in 1928.

Among the twenty-nine Population Study areas, eleven show relative increments of population increase in rural communities from 1926 to 1939. Three of these areas with an increase of rural population above the average proportional increase of the whole Soviet population have already been noted as rapidly developed frontier regions: the Soviet Far East, East Siberia, and the Karelia-Murmansk area. The remaining eight areas with a rapidly growing rural population form a belt across "the deep south" of the U.S.S.R. These areas with percentage increases of rural population are: the Crimea (41), Georgia (19), Armenia (28), Azerbaidzhan (23), Daghestan (20), Uzbekistan (36), Tadzhikistan (33) and Kirghizia (35). The only area within this belt which shows a different trend is Turkmenia, which is intermediate, in this as in other respects, between Kazakhstan and the old agricultural communities of Central Asia; there was a decrease of 3 per cent in the rural population of the Turkmen S.S.R. The increase of rural population in the southern republics favored the expansion and intensification of semitropical agriculture, which was promoted in the interest of greater all-Union economic self-sufficiency. The population increase, however, was not necessarily a direct result of the emphasis on this phase of Soviet economy. In some of these areas, rapid population increase was largely the result of rapid natural increase. It should also be noted that special types of agriculture developed in the deep south required intensive cultivation and were least adapted to mechanization—so that the demand for farm labor in these areas was more rigid.

The situation of the Crimea is unique among the regions in the deep south, listed above, in that the productivity of agriculture per capita of farm population was far above the average for the U.S.S.R., 1925–1928, whereas in the Transcaucasus and Central Asia agricultural productivity per capita of farm population was definitely below the general average at this time. The Crimea had also been characterized by fairly heavy net in-migration prior to 1926. Continued in-migration and rapid growth of rural population in this area is, therefore, not surprising—although the increase of urban population in this area from 1926 to 1939 was somewhat below the average for the U.S.S.R.

The total population growth from 1926 to 1939 in Georgia (32 per cent), Armenia (46 per cent), Azerbaidzhan (39 per cent) and Daghestan (35 per cent)—in contrast to the average for the U.S.S.R. (16 per cent)—can be properly attributed, in the main, to the high natural increase characteristic of these areas. This is evidenced by the fragmentary data on vital statistics. The comparison of persons classified by "ethnic group" in 1926 and persons classified by "nationality" in 1939 probably reflects natural increase fairly accurately for the principal groups in this region, except for the assimilation of small numbers of Kurds, Abkhazians, and other minor groups. The percentage increases, 1926–1939, for all groups of the Caucasus Mountain and Transcaucasus regions are, in general, much higher than that of the whole Soviet population during the same period. When all evidence is taken into account, it appears that the accumulation of population through rapid natural increase and the relative immobility of the population in this region were chiefly responsible for the large relative increment (1,358,000 persons) in the population growth of the Transcaucasus republics and Daghestan.

The population movements in Central Asia, during the intercensus period, were more complicated. The relative increments of the four republics in this region (the Kirghiz, Uzbek, Tadzhik, and Turkmen S.S.R.) total 1,671,000—the absolute increase being 2,883,000. To take at face value the data on persons classified by ethnic groups or nationality, the principal indigenous groups in this region except the Turkmen show increases that are as high as or higher than that of the whole Soviet population (15.9 per cent): Uzbek, 23 per cent; Tadzhik, 25 per cent; Kirghiz, 15.9 per cent; Turkmen, 6 per cent; Kara-Kalpak, 27 per cent. If we suppose that these proportional excesses in the increase, 1926–1939, in number of persons classified by ethnic group or nationality represent unusually high rates of natural increase, they will account for a net gain of 300,000 persons to these republics above the expected increase at the average rate of the whole Soviet population—leaving an additional net gain of 1,400,000 persons attributable to net inmigration. These results, though quite hypothetical, seem reasonable. The opening of the Turkestan-Siberian Railway connecting Central Asia with western Siberia, the large irrigation projects and other public works in Central Asia, the development of industry and agriculture (especially the rapid expansion of cotton production), and the expansion of health and educational services would account for an appreciable influx into this region. It is also likely that many of the former nomads of the steppe region eventually settled as agricultural or industrial laborers in the Central Asian republics.

In most parts of the U.S.S.R. there was an appreciable increase in the ratio of sown land to the number of persons in rural communities from 1928 to 1938. This change was most spectacular in the Lower Volga-Don area (the ratio here being doubled), where there was a drop in rural population, and agriculture was highly adapted to rapid mechanization. The ratio rose by 40 to 80 per cent—partly because of increase in sown land and partly because of decrease of rural population—in the Western, Central Volga, Ural, West Siberia, and Kazakh areas, and by 23 per cent in the Ukraine. In the Transcaucasus as a whole, there was practically no change in the ratio between 1928 and 1938; and the proportional increase in Central Asia was only half as great as in the whole U.S.S.R.—because of high natural increase, low mobility in these regions, and the emphasis on the use of all available personnel in the production of semitropical and tropical raw materials, such as cotton, citrus fruits, essences, and rubber substitutes. The Soviet Union achieved a remarkable degree of economic self-sufficiency before the outbreak of the present war, but apparently at the cost of devoting a considerable proportion of its total productive energies to the cultivation of restricted and naturally limited areas adapted to producing raw materials that were previously imported from other countries. However, in so far as this shift was effected by an extension of irrigation, it represents a substantial increase in the productive resources of the nation.

In general, it is apparent that the redistribution of population within the Soviet Union during the three successive five-year plans has been directed toward the effective utilization of the potential resources of different regions. The principal population movements have been complementary to the transition of Russian economy from a diffuse, largely agrarian order to an integrated national economy with an effective balance between agriculture, industry, commerce, and the social services. As industrial activities increase, and as agriculture becomes technically more advanced, the latter, which in 1939 supported about 55 per cent of the Soviet population, will eventually require a much smaller proportion of the total labor force. The transition to a balanced, industrial economy in the U.S.S.R. is still in its initial stages. Its progress has, in large part, been violently interrupted by war—though in some respects, including the forced movements of population eastward—wartime changes fit with the pattern of prewar trends. After the war, when the reconstruction of devastated areas passes beyond its first most urgent phase, the basic trends of the previous years will presumably be resumed, though probably at a somewhat less feverish tempo.

We shall not discuss the problem of postwar population projections here, except to state that, in contrast to Western Europe, the population of the Soviet Union is destined to increase rapidly for many years. It is equally clear and more important that the resources of the Soviet Union, properly utilized, can support this growing population on a rising plane of living. The possible rise in the plane of living was checked during the last decade by concentration on creation of a basic industrial structure and preparation for defense. But tremendous advances were made in provisions for education, health and social services. This progress was most impressive in the outlying regions, such as the Central Asian republics, where literacy and provisions for health and social welfare had been at a pitifully low level at the beginning of the Soviet era.

The technological and cultural progress of the population in the Soviet republics of northern and central Eurasia is bound to exert a profound influence on the development of other Eastern European and Asiatic nations. Among other changes, there is certain to be a large increase in the volume of trade between a technically more advanced Soviet Union and Asiatic nations where the progress of the mechanical arts is more retarded. The basis on which these relations will be worked out and the basis of cooperation between the Soviet Union and the Western European and American nations in the development of Asia are crucial issues in the future course of world affairs.

Index